THE GREAT MIGRATOR

THE GREAT MIGRATOR

ROBERT RAUSCHENBERG AND THE GLOBAL RISE OF AMERICAN ART

HIROKO IKEGAMI

THE MIT PRESS
CAMBRIDGE, MASSACHUSETTS
LONDON, ENGLAND

Publication of this book has been aided by a Wyeth Foundation for American Art Publication Grant of the College Art Association.

MIT Press books may be purchased at special quantity discounts for business or sales promotional use. For information, please email special_sales@mitpress.mit.edu or write to Special Sales Department, The MIT Press, 55 Hayward Street, Cambridge, MA 02142.

This book was set in Minion Pro by Graphic Composition, Inc. Printed and bound in Spain.

Library of Congress Cataloging-in-Publication Data
Ikegami, Hiroko, 1973–
The great migrator : Robert Rauschenberg and the global rise of American art / Hiroko Ikegami.
p. cm.
Includes bibliographical references and index.
ISBN 978-0-262-01425-0 (hardcover : alk. paper)
1. Rauschenberg, Robert, 1925–2008—Criticism and interpretation. 2. Rauschenberg, Robert, 1925–2008—Travel. 3. Art, American—20th century. 4. Modernism (Art)—Influence. I. Rauschenberg, Robert, 1925–2008. II. Title. III. Title: Robert Rauschenberg and the global rise of American art.
N6537.R27I38 2010
709.2—dc22
2009044340

10 9 8 7 6 5 4 3 2 1

FOR TSUKASA

CONTENTS

Acknowledgments ix

Notes to the Reader xiii

INTRODUCTION 1
DISCOVERING "THE GREAT MIGRATOR"

1 **A TRIUMPH IN PARIS** 17
ENGINEERING RAUSCHENBERG'S GLOBAL MARKET

2 **A SPECTACLE IN VENICE** 57
INSIDE AND OUTSIDE RAUSCHENBERG'S VICTORY

3 **A CONFLICT IN STOCKHOLM** 103
THE RISE AND FALL OF *MONOGRAM*

4 **A DIALOGUE IN TOKYO** 153
RAUSCHENBERG MEETS THE JAPANESE AVANT-GARDE

CONCLUSION 205
BECOMING "THE" AMERICAN ARTIST

Appendix: Robert Rauschenberg's Exhibition History outside the United States, 1953–1968 213

Notes 217

Bibliography 247

Index 265

ACKNOWLEDGMENTS

This book has become a reality with the support of a great number of people and institutions. I have been fortunate to have a community of scholars support my project throughout the course of its different iterations. At Yale University, where it began as my Ph.D. dissertation, I owe my deep gratitude to my advisor Alexander Nemerov for his committed mentorship. Without his encouragement and faith in my work, I would not have undertaken or completed this ambitious project. I owe an equally large debt to my dissertation readers, Thomas E. Crow, David Joselit, and Christine Mehring, for their helpful and insightful comments. I am also grateful to Marcia Brennan, Robert Jensen, and Branden W. Joseph, whose constructive suggestions on this book's manuscript have substantially improved its quality and content. My special thanks are due to Reiko Tomii, who was first my guardian angel during my years of graduate studies, and later a personal editor of this volume's content. The transformation from a dissertation to a book manuscript would never have happened without her assiduous help and encouragement.

This book examines the impact of post-1945 American art in four different cities, while keeping in its scope the implications for global art studies. Whereas I benefited from the expertise of James Elkins on the issue of world art history, the study of each city required advice from specialists in each area. For chapter 1, on Paris, I received kind advice from Joachim Pissarro concerning research in the city, and useful comments from Kaira Cabañas on the chapter's draft. Chapter 2, on Venice, developed out of a term paper for Thomas Crow's seminar at Yale, which eventually became the kernel of this volume. With his profound insight and keen eyes as a historian of art and his generosity as a teacher, Thomas Crow has been a role model for me ever since I took his class at the University of Sussex as an undergraduate exchange student. I consider myself very fortunate to have him as a mentor. Regarding chapter 3, on Stockholm, I would like to thank Patrik Andersson, who kindly sent me a file of his dissertation on the Moderna Museet, and Marianne Hultman for her advice on research in Stockholm. Chapter 4, on Tokyo, developed out of a paper I presented at the 31st International Congress of the History of Art (Comité international d'histoire de l'art, CIHA), held in Montreal in 2004. I received valuable advice on this topic from Reiko Tomii, Ryan Holmberg, Shin'ichirō Osaki, Mizuho Katō, and Michio Hayashi.

Of equal importance to the scholarly assistance I received were the inspiration and encouragement of my graduate colleagues at Yale and elsewhere over the years leading to the completion of this book. In addition to the comradeship and intellectual exchange we shared, Bingyi Huang, Joan Kee, and Ming Tiampo offered much-needed help when

I started envisioning this book project. I would also like to thank Ryan Holmberg, Kaira Cabañas, Irene Small, Prajna Desai, Kenji Kajiya, Mari Takamatsu, Miki Sogi, Miwako Tezuka, Midori Yamamura, and Yoshiko Naiki.

If this book makes any contributions to the field of post-1945 art, they are not only to my credit but also to that of all the individuals listed above.

As for my research on the artist who is the subject of this volume, I am hugely indebted to David White, Thomas Buehler, Gina Guy, and Matthew Magee at Robert Rauschenberg Archives in New York. Their invaluable help significantly advanced my research and manuscript preparation. They accommodated my numerous visits, fulfilled my needs, and answered my particular questions when they had many other tasks to attend to. I am especially thankful to Gina for her patient and generous assistance. Although I never had the fortune of greeting Rauschenberg in person, I believe his reputed generosity and openness are reflected in the staff at the Archives.

Research and writing for this book were facilitated by the assistance of many people and institutions. I am particularly thankful to the following: all the individuals who granted me interviews (listed in the bibliography); Nader Vossoughian, Michele Alberto Matteini, and Eva Pankenier for their language assistance respectively in German, Italian, and Swedish; Harutaka Oribe, John Weinstock, and Deanna Lee, who proofread different stages of dissertation manuscripts; Kathleen Friello, a copy editor of the book manuscript and indexer of the book; the late Kazutada Tsubouchi, who shared his archival materials with me; Julie Martin for her advice on EAT projects; Michelle Elligott and Michelle Harvey at the Museum of Modern Art Archives, New York; Masako Isobe at the Sōgetsu Foundation Archives, Tokyo; and, last but not least, Stefan Ståhle at the Moderna Museet, my "catcher in the rye" in Stockholm who spared no effort to make my wishes possible.

This project benefited from financial support from a number of institutions. My graduate studies would not have been possible without a generous fellowship and numerous research grants from Yale University. I also received the following grants for the research and writing of this study, including its dissertation stage: Yale Council on East Asian Studies Summer Travel and Research Grant; Robert M. Leylan Dissertation Fellowship; Henry Luce Foundation Dissertation Award; Getty Research Institute Travel Grant; and Grants-in-Aid for Scientific Research from the Japan Society for the Promotion of Sciences.

No portion of this study has been published in English before, but earlier versions of parts of several chapters have appeared in Japanese journals such as *Bijutsushi* (Art History, 2005 and 2007) and *Seiyō bijutu kenkyū* (Studies in Western Art, 2008). I would also like to acknowledge the intellectual community in Japan that helped me to refine the ideas and arguments in this volume.

Writing of the manuscript took place at Osaka University, where I was an assistant professor in its Global COE Program, "A Research Base for Conflict Studies in the Humanities." I would like to thank my colleagues for their interest in and comments on my work. At Osaka University, where I started my graduate studies, I am also grateful to the professors and graduate students in its lively community of art history. Shigebumi Tsuji, Eiko Wakayama, and Shunroku Okudaira always encouraged my study; Hiroshige Okada offered helpful comments on the ideas of this project; Yōko Ōno shared the challenge of book writing with me; and Yūsuke Isotani and Yoshiko Suzuki always helped me more than I helped them. By far, I am most grateful to Tsukasa Kōdera, my advisor for my master's degree, for his unflagging support and faith in my work, which have been my safeguard for many years of graduate study and beyond.

At the MIT Press, I would like to thank Marc Lowenthal and Anar Badalov for their invaluable assistance, Paula Woolley and Matthew Abbate for their painstaking work as manuscript editor and production editor, and Margarita Encomienda for her fabulous design, all of which have significantly contributed to the quality of this volume. My special thanks are due to Roger Conover, who took a risk with an inexperienced first-time author and supported me all the way. His expert advice and belief in this project were always a source of encouragement.

Finally, I would like to thank my family for their continuing support. I must first acknowledge the precedent set by my late father, Chūji Ikegami, who specialized in French modern art and Japonisme. He would have enjoyed reading this book. After his untimely death, my mother, Chieko Ikegami, encouraged my decision to pursue an academic career and always supported me in times of difficulty. My thanks are due to the rest of my family as well, especially Yūko Watanabe, my mother-in-law, for her firm belief in me.

In gratitude and love, I dedicate this study to my husband, Tsukasa Ikegami, who was simply there for me whenever I needed him. Without his moral, intellectual, and technical support—which he gave me not only when we were together but also when we were apart during my years at Yale—I would never have been able to complete this book. Although writing is a solitary act, I consider this study to be ours.

NOTES TO THE READER

1. Because this study references materials in six different languages including English, a language protocol for citations is necessary. All quotations from non-English sources have been translated into English, as noted below. In notes, titles of French, German, and Italian sources are cited in the original language, while titles of Swedish and Japanese sources are cited in English translation and indicated respectively by [S] and [J]. Non-English materials are grouped separately in the bibliography, with the Swedish and Japanese original data also to be found there.
2. Translations from French and Japanese to English are mine unless otherwise noted. For German, I have benefited from the assistance of Nader Vossoughian; I also used translations by the United States Information Service and the Press Department of the Museum of Modern Art, New York. Translations from Italian and Swedish to English are made respectively by Michele Alberto Matteini and Eva Pankenier, unless otherwise noted.
3. All Japanese names are given in the Western order, with given names first, followed by family names. Macrons are used to indicate long vowels, e.g., Yūsuke Nakahara and Yoshiaki Tōno.
4. Every effort has been made to find the original copyright holders for permission to illustrate images in this book. Where this effort was unsuccessful, I will be happy to add or revise credits in a subsequent printing, if appropriate information is provided.
5. The titles and captions for Rauschenberg's artworks follow the precedent set in Walter Hopps and Susan Davidson, eds., *Robert Rauschenberg: A Retrospective* (New York: Solomon R. Guggenheim Museum, 1997), as well as information provided by the Robert Rauschenberg Archives, New York.

INTRODUCTION
DISCOVERING "THE GREAT MIGRATOR"

An image struck Robert Rauschenberg while he was leafing through recent issues of *Sports Illustrated* in the spring of 1958. It was a color photograph of a Canada goose in flight, a double-page spread in an article on the migratory bird (figure 0.1). "The great migrator," as the photogenic bird was called in the title, was captured en route to some destination.[1] The artist in turn captured this arresting impression by cutting out the picture and transferring it onto a sheet of paper. With a few more transfers and touches of paint and pencil, he created *Course* (1958) (figure 0.2), a work little known among his transfer drawings, in which the reversed image of the bird creates a dynamic flow from right to left. The significance of the image of the migratory bird goes beyond this particular piece. Migration—or movement in general—forms a central theme and structure in Rauschenberg's artistic production.[2] Among the images in *Course*, there is another striking picture related to movement: a runner with an agonized expression, which Rauschenberg found in the following issue of *Sports Illustrated* (figure 0.3). In stark contrast to the uplifting image of the flying bird, this gloomy picture speaks of physical hardship, of pushing one's body to its limits.

The theme of migration, including its difficulty, emerged as particularly important for the artist at the time; in the late spring of 1958, he embarked on a series of thirty-four drawings for Dante's *Inferno* (hereafter the Dante Drawings), a project that took him more than two years to complete, in which Dante's angst-ridden journey through hell is depicted with imagery from American mass culture. As if to reinforce the point, Rauschenberg used pictures of both the bird and the runner in the Dante Drawings, which proves their significance for him (see figures 2.12, 2.14). Indeed, the two pictures seem to epitomize a dynamic that lies at the heart of Rauschenberg's artistic practice. On the one hand, the "great migrator," described in the *Sports Illustrated* article as having "an air of restlessness,"[3] speaks for the artist's own migratory nature, an impulse to move beyond existing boundaries in both artistic and geographic senses. On the other hand, the runner in agony—featured in an article titled "Triumphs and Tribulations"[4]—indicates gravity or any other force that restrains such movement.

Migration was more than an aesthetic metaphor in Rauschenberg's art: soon after completing the Dante Drawings and exhibiting them at the Leo Castelli Gallery from December 1960 to January 1961, Rauschenberg himself began a period of frequent travel. Starting with a trip to Paris in April 1961 for his first solo show in the city at Galerie Daniel Cordier, the artist repeatedly crossed the Atlantic during the 1960s, participating in numerous exhibitions and artistic collaborations. The year 1964 was his most migratory, as he

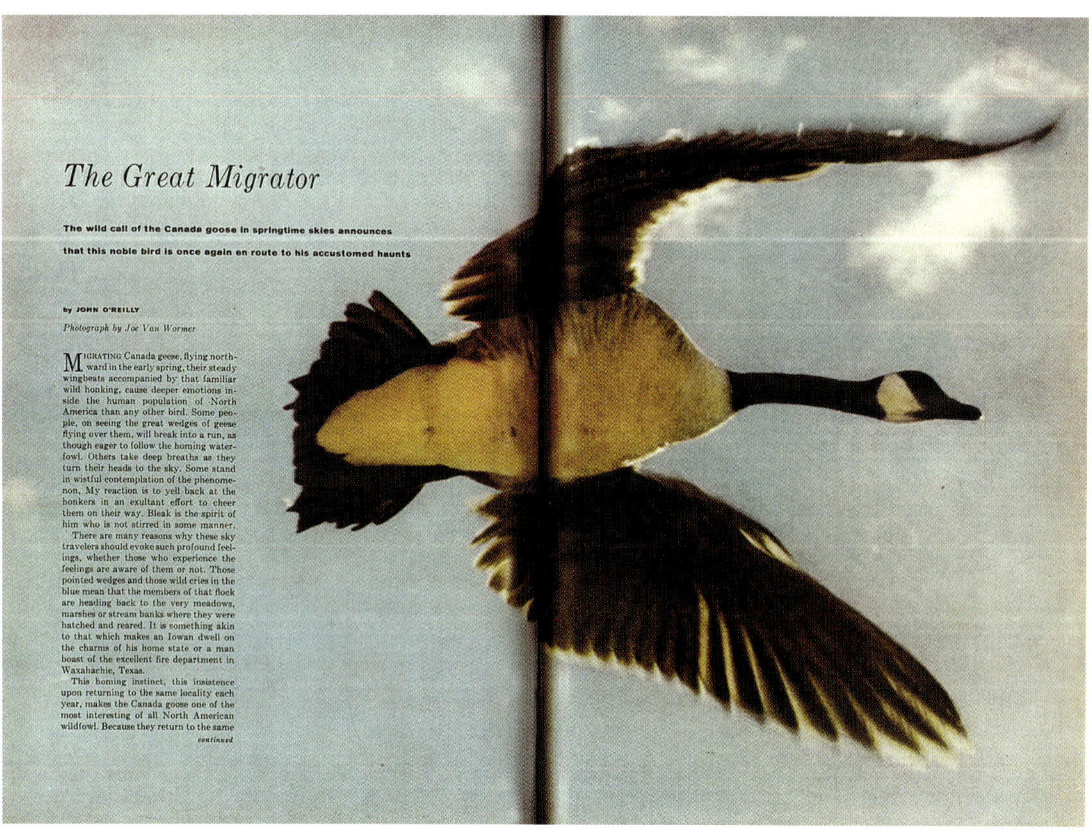

The Great Migrator

The wild call of the Canada goose in springtime skies announces that this noble bird is once again en route to his accustomed haunts

by JOHN O'REILLY

Photograph by Joe Van Wormer

MIGRATING Canada geese, flying northward in the early spring, their steady wingbeats accompanied by that familiar wild honking, cause deeper emotions inside the human population of North America than any other bird. Some people, on seeing the great wedges of geese flying over them, will break into a run, as though eager to follow the homing waterfowl. Others take deep breaths as they turn their heads to the sky. Some stand in wistful contemplation of the phenomenon. My reaction is to yell back at the honkers in an exultant effort to cheer them on their way. Bleak is the spirit of him who is not stirred in some manner.

There are many reasons why these sky travelers should evoke such profound feelings, whether those who experience the feelings are aware of them or not. Those pointed wedges and those wild cries in the blue mean that the members of that flock are heading back to the very meadows, marshes or stream banks where they were hatched and reared. It is something akin to that which makes an Iowan dwell on the charms of his home state or a man boast of the excellent fire department in Waxahachie, Texas.

This homing instinct, this insistence upon returning to the same locality each year, makes the Canada goose one of the most interesting of all North American wildfowl. Because they return to the same

continued

Figure 0.1
John O'Reilly, "The Great Migrator," *Sports Illustrated* 8, no. 18 (April 21, 1958): 60–61. Photograph by Joe Van Wormer; Van Wormer Collection, Denver Museum of Nature and Science; reprinted courtesy of *Sports Illustrated*.

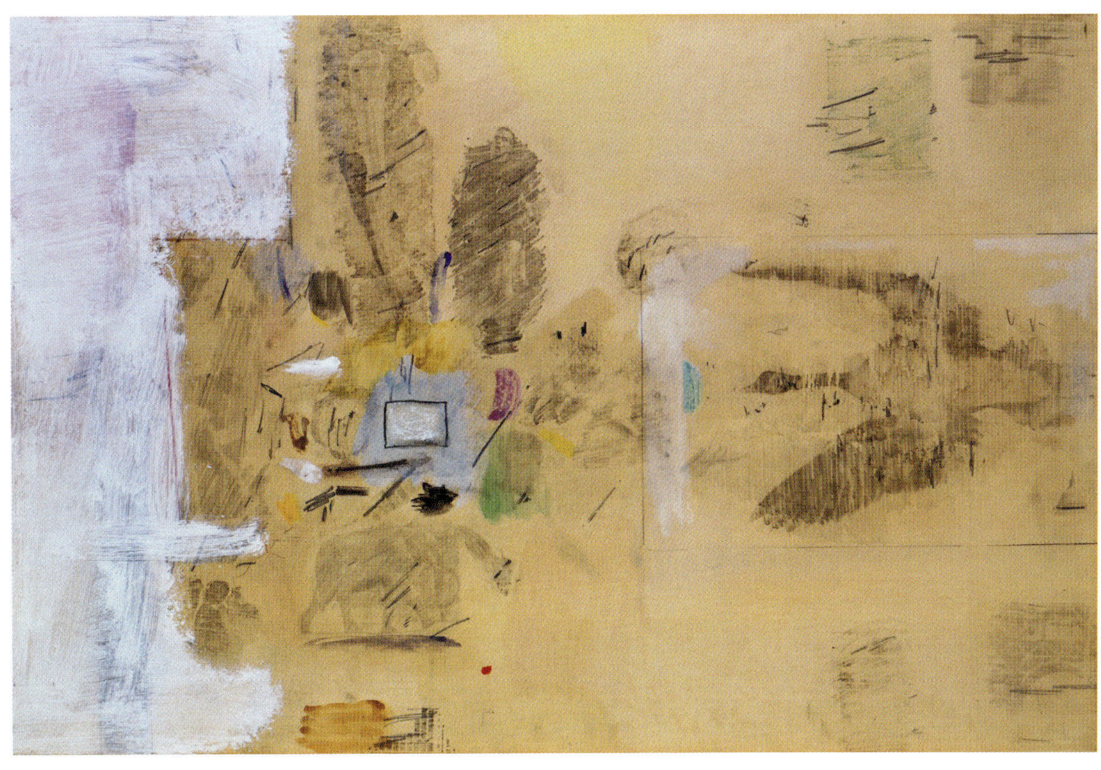

Figure 0.2
Robert Rauschenberg, *Course,* 1958. Solvent transfer on paper, with pencil, gouache, watercolor, paint, and grease pencil, 23¾ × 35½ inches (60.3 × 90.2 cm). Aichi Prefectural Museum of Art, Nagoya.

WONDERFUL WORLD OF SPORT

TRIUMPHS AND TRIBULATIONS

Far from the madding stadiums and congestions of the big spectator sports, participants on quieter fronts of sport were pursuing goals of their own. The schoolboy miler strained for the tape, and set a record. An amateur tennis player, pursuing a principle, disguised himself in a black mask to play with the pros—and lost in the first round. A rider and his horse went swimming. Herewith, a representative selection of triumphs and tribulations.

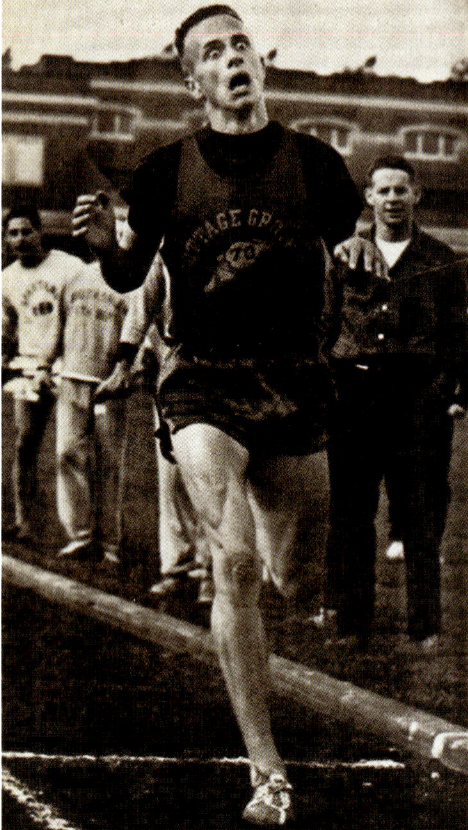
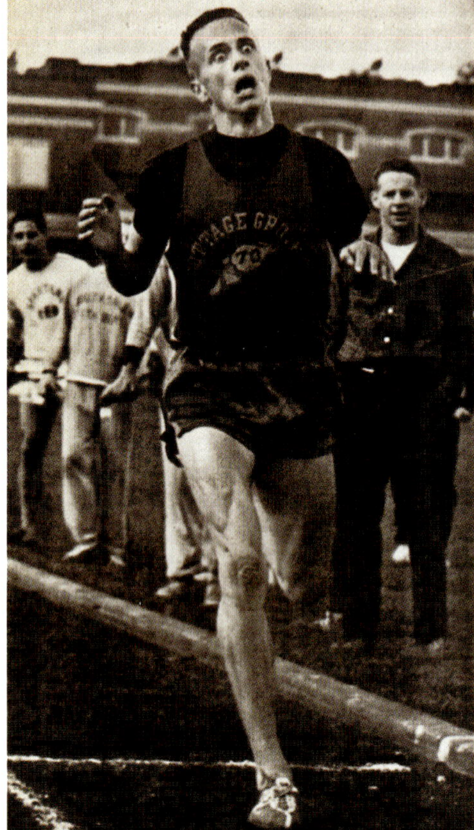

FEATURES CONTORTED. Dyrol Burleson, 17-year-old Cottage Grove, Ore. miler, seems to have spent the last drop of his energy, but he snaps tape to set new schoolboy mark of 4:13.2.

DRAMATIZING HIS FIRM BELIEF in open tennis, Mr. Nemesis challenges Lew Hoad to guess his identity before Cleveland tournament. Best guess: Florida's Eddie Alloo, 39.

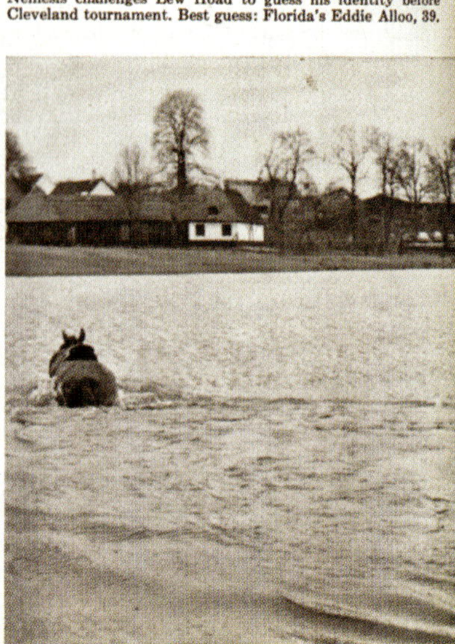

WET, LUGUBRIOUS PURSUIT occupies Dr. Gerhard Roenne, who was leading annual chase of Copenhagen Hunt Club when his mount dumped him into a pond, then lit out for a swim.

20 SPORTS ILLUSTRATED *May 12, 1958*

Figure 0.3
"Triumphs and Tribulations," *Sports Illustrated* 8, no. 19 (May 12, 1958): 20. Reprinted courtesy of *Sports Illustrated*.

TABLE 1

MERCE CUNNINGHAM DANCE COMPANY, 1964 WORLD TOUR ITINERARY

Date	Country	City (Venue)
June 6 June 8 June 12, 13, 14 June 16	**France**	Strasbourg (Théâtre de la Comédie) Paris (Ballets Modernes Studio) Paris (Théâtre de l'Est Parisien) Bourges (Comédie de Bourges)
June 18	**Italy**	Venice (Teatro La Fenice)
June 24	**Austria**	Vienna (Museum des 20. Jahrhunderts)
June 27 July 5 July 12	**Germany**	Mannheim (Nationaltheater) Essen (Folkwang Hochschule) Cologne (Opernhaus)
July 16	**France**	Les Baux-de-Provence (Festival de Danse des Baux-de-Provence)
July 23, 24 July 27–31, August 1 August 5–8, 10–13, 14–18, 19–22	**England**	Devon (Dartington Hall) London (Sadler's Wells Theatre) London (Phoenix Theatre)
September 8, 14 September 9	**Sweden**	Stockholm (Moderna Museet) Stockholm (Kungliga Operan)
September 16 September 18	**Finland**	Turku (Åbo Svenska Teater) Helsinki (Ruotsalaeisessa Teatterissa)
September 22 September 24	**Czechoslovakia**	Prague (Park of Culture) Ostrava (Opera House)
September 27 September 29	**Poland**	Warsaw (Teatr Dramatyczny) Poznań (Państowa Opera)
October 3	**Germany**	Krefeld (Theater der Stadt Krefeld)
October 6 October 7	**Belgium**	Brussels (Palais des Beaux-Arts) Antwerp (Koninklijke Nederlandse Schouwburg)
October 8	**Netherlands**	Scheveningen (De Kurzaal te Scheveningen)
October 15, 16 October 21, 22 October 25, 26 October 29, 30	**India**	Bombay (Bhulabhai Desai Auditorium) Ahmedabad, Gujarat (Mangaldas Town Hall) Chandigarh, Punjab (Tagore Theatre) New Delhi (AIFACS)
November 3	**Thailand**	Bangkok (high school auditorium)
November 6, 10, 11 November 12 November 16 November 24, 25	**Japan**	Tokyo (Sankei Hall) Kobe (Kobe Kokusai Hall) Osaka (Festival Hall) Tokyo (Sankei Hall)

traveled worldwide as the costume and set designer for the Merce Cunningham Dance Company on its first world tour, visiting no fewer than thirty cities in fourteen countries (see table 1). The company arrived in Paris on June 4, 1964, starting its tour in Strasbourg two days later. When they moved to Venice, Rauschenberg was crowned as winner of the International Grand Prize in Painting at the XXXII Esposizione Biennale Internazionale d'Arte Venezia (hereafter the 1964 Venice Biennale). The company had great success in London in July and August, followed by a little summer vacation and a few performances in Stockholm. In September, the company became the first avant-garde dance company to perform in Eastern Europe. The Asian leg of the tour began with performances in Bombay in mid-October. In Bangkok, they even danced before the Queen and the King of Thailand. Finally, the company completed its tour in late November with a trip to Tokyo.[5]

With this intense period of travel during the first half of the sixties—especially 1964—one could call Rauschenberg himself "the great migrator." During the 1964 tour, Rauschenberg not only devised sets and costumes from materials collected in each locale but also enacted his own performances and created works of art, which often involved collaboration with local art communities. In fact, *Story*, a central part of the repertoire for the Cunningham world tour, had a site-specific nature that required such interchange (figures 0.4, 0.5): Cunningham directed that the costumes would "be picked up or found in the particular playing situation [they] were in, and that the set, or the way the stage looked, would also be devised from the existing circumstances and environment at the time of the performance."[6] Accordingly, Rauschenberg, as the company's costume and set designer, played a pivotal role in incorporating specific local qualities into the program of the world tour. Moreover, he worked in the same way for his own activities during the trip, as he always made works of art from local materials and collaborated with artists and critics he newly met in each place. Rauschenberg's overseas interchanges thus functioned as a nexus in the transnational network of avant-garde art in the 1960s.

What makes this particular aspect of his career worth investigating is not just the sheer appeal of his travels and interchanges with various local art scenes, but also their exact synchronicity with the increasing international dominance of American art. Whereas Abstract Expressionism announced to the world the existence of a lively avant-garde art in the United States in the 1950s, the emergence of Neo-Dada and Pop Art officially changed the power balance in the topography of the global art scene of the 1960s. Not coincidentally, indeed, it was during Rauschenberg's world trip that Alan Solomon, commissioner for the American Pavilion at the 1964 Venice Biennale, announced that the world's art center had shifted from Paris to New York. Thus, the goal of this study is to map the global rise of American art by examining Rauschenberg's international activities in relation to the context of the places where he traveled. Tracing the itinerary of his 1964 world trip, this book presents a close analysis of the ways in which the art communities of four cities—Paris (chapter 1), Venice (chapter 2), Stockholm (chapter 3), and Tokyo (chapter 4)—responded to Rauschenberg's presence and the increasing dominance of American art.

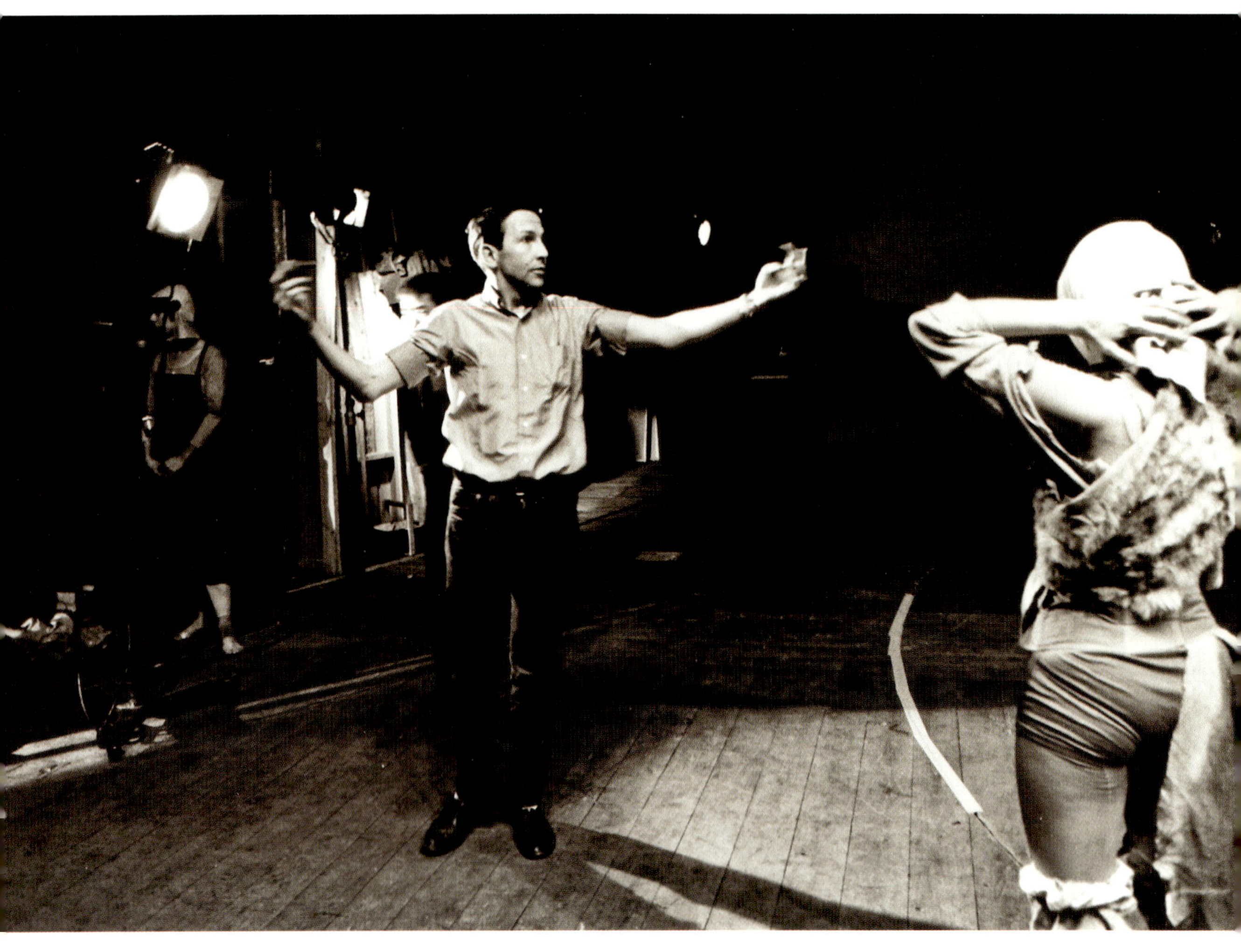

Figure 0.4
Rauschenberg (center) working on a costume and set design for *Story*, Tokyo, November 1964. Photograph by Masaaki Sekiya; courtesy Sōgetsu Foundation Archives, Tokyo.

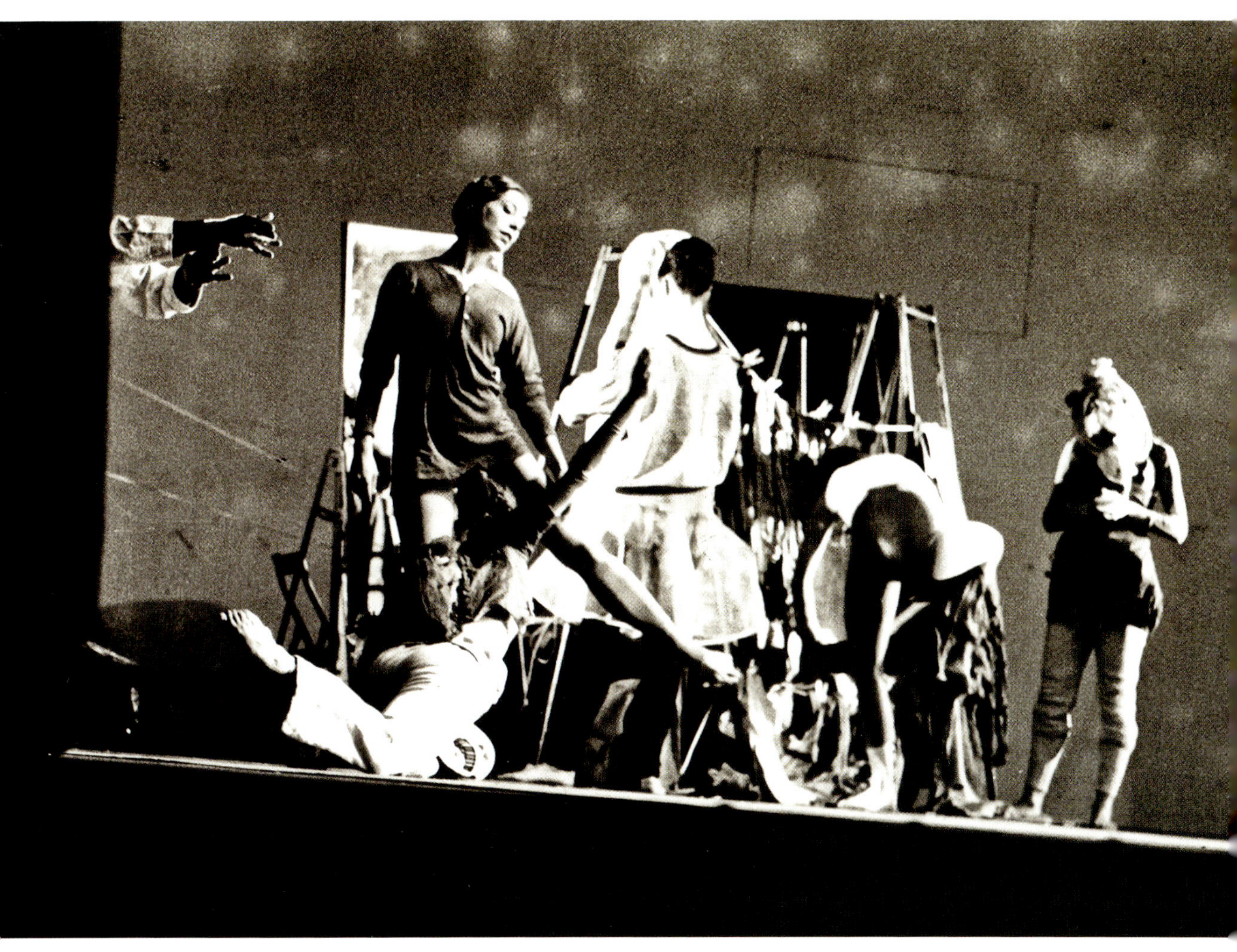

Figure 0.5
Merce Cunningham Dance Company performing *Story*, Tokyo, November 1964. Photograph by Masaaki Sekiya; courtesy Sōgetsu Foundation Archives, Tokyo.

As is clear in the selection of these four cities, the "global" rise of American art was in fact restricted: all four of the cities—and most of the venues of Cunningham's tour—belonged at the time to the so-called "Free World," which did not have much cultural interaction with the countries behind the Iron Curtain. The phenomenon was thus at work only in the Western Bloc[7] of the Cold War era, and would not tell us much about what was going on in the art of the Eastern Bloc or in any other regions that did not fit a simple East-West division—such as Latin America, Africa, and South Asia. In other words, the geography of postwar avant-garde art more or less overlapped with the geography of international politics of the time. In fact, the art scenes of the four cities were connected with one another, as their major players often shared mutual interests and worked together in promoting postwar American art—and sometimes specifically Rauschenberg's art. This intercity network created an important transnational avant-garde art community, which played a significant role in the global rise of American art.[8]

In each city, Rauschenberg had an enthusiastic promoter of his art. In Paris, the art dealer Ileana Sonnabend focused her energies on him, her favorite artist, and helped to engineer a global market for American art in the early 1960s. In Venice, Alan Solomon's curatorial and organizational strategies for the 1964 American Pavilion were clearly intended to bring the Grand Prize to Rauschenberg, whose winning would then declare the preeminence of American art. In Stockholm, Pontus Hultén, director of the Moderna Museet, enthusiastically imported the art of Rauschenberg—particularly *Monogram*, arguably his best-known work—and of the New York avant-garde in his attempt to transform the city into a new art center. Finally, in Tokyo, the art critic Yoshiaki Tōno acted as a mediator between the American artist and the Japanese avant-garde, organizing "Twenty Questions to Bob Rauschenberg" upon his visit to Tokyo in 1964. Although these individuals have hitherto been little studied, each of them in a different way played a crucial role in establishing the international dominance of American art.

Still, the global rise of American art was far from being a smooth process, as the art scene of the "Free World" had its own internal politics. The exported American art, including Rauschenberg's activities during his travels, evoked as much resistance as enthusiasm in the places where it landed. In Paris, Rauschenberg's otherwise esteemed reputation suffered from the perception of American manipulation of the 1964 Venice Biennale award. In Venice, his winning of the Grand Prize became a huge international scandal, which compromised his reputation in his home country as well. In Stockholm, *Monogram* became a scapegoat as a symbol of American invasion in the era of the war in Vietnam. And in Tokyo, Japanese artists employed the strategy of imitation to destabilize Rauschenberg's authority as a cutting-edge avant-garde artist. Finally, the world tour itself had an unfortunate ending, as Rauschenberg's status of global celebrity created tension within the dance company, leading to the end of his collaboration with Cunningham and John Cage.

Perhaps all this conflict resulted from a fundamental ambivalence in Rauschenberg's international activities. On the one hand, his physical presence in many different cities opened up a new kind of transnational network for the post–World War II art scene and was welcomed as such, as it fostered exchanges and collaboration among artists from different backgrounds. On the other hand, such a utopian conception of the cosmopolitan avant-garde soon resulted in the centralization of American art, with Rauschenberg emerging as the "winner"—epitomized by his victory in Venice. In other words, Rauschenberg became a symbol of both utopian universalism and the gross asymmetry of power in the world art scene of the 1960s. This study will thus examine the global rise of American art as a reciprocal, cross-cultural, and yet necessarily conflicted process rather than as a result of unilateral cultural imperialism.

By doing so, this book sets itself somewhat at odds with previous revisionist studies, which have criticized the export of American art during the 1950s and 1960s as U.S. propaganda for the cultural Cold War.[9] While productive in questioning the formalist narrative of modern art and expanding its discourse into a sociopolitical dimension, such ideological critique could undermine the actual complexity of a historical phenomenon. As Frédéric Martel demonstrated in *De la culture en Amérique*, the idiosyncrasy of the system of American culture lies in its high degree of independence from governmental control.[10] Certainly, the U.S. government's traditional disregard of its arts and culture started to change during the Cold War era. For instance, the United States Information Agency, established in 1953, made a series of efforts abroad to shed America's sorry image as a country without its own respectable culture, while the National Endowment for the Arts was belatedly founded in 1965 to financially assist domestic cultural activities. However, the government's role in the promotion of its arts and culture, both at home and abroad, was always a topic of heated debate in the country and tended to be kept to a minimum. Indeed, what Martel calls "action culturelle"[11] in America is a complex of spontaneous activities by individuals, public communities, nonprofit organizations, and private enterprises, all of which propel themselves without specific administrative agendas. In fact, precisely because government intervention is limited, American culture can maintain its dynamic diversity and even a self-critical element—it is a rare culture whose mainstream *and* alternative force are both internationally regarded as role models—and hence its overpowering worldwide appeal.

Let us look at the field of modern dance as an example. It is true that during the Cold War era the U.S. government sent various dance companies abroad in order to enhance American cultural prestige. However, as Naima Prevots reveals, the government was very careful in selecting which dance companies would be sent to foreign countries. As a matter of fact, Cunningham's company was never considered appropriate for U.S. public diplomacy in those days; the Dance Panel, the government's consulting committee, saw the company as "too avant-garde and controversial" to represent American dance abroad.[12] As a result, the Dance Panel turned down Cage's eager appeals to bring the company and his music to Asia in 1955 and again in 1962, instead sending Martha Graham's company for an Asia tour in 1955–1956. When Cunningham's attempts to procure funding from the State

Department for his company's 1964 world tour were also unsuccessful,[13] the company had to raise funds on its own and was left at the end with a deficit of $85,000.[14] Importantly, however, the lack of governmental or institutional support saves the company from being criticized as an example of American cultural imperialism. Since its 1964 world tour originally started with invitations from India and Japan, it can even be seen as a product of genuine mutual interest. Still, such a private and voluntary cultural exchange in the end contributed to the international recognition of the "excellence" of American arts and culture as much as the government-sponsored projects did. It is this complex, multilayered mechanism of American cultural hegemony that has escaped attention in previous revisionist criticism.

With a number of efforts to "revise" revisionism,[15] the limitations of revisionist arguments are already well recognized. Yet the myth they created dies hard, and the topic of Rauschenberg is no exception: his winning of the Grand Prize at the 1964 Venice Biennale is still largely regarded as an outcome of America's imperialistic public diplomacy, a cultural triumph that followed the country's political and economic dominance over Western Europe after 1945.[16] In order to find a way out of the cul-de-sac of ideological critique, it is helpful to look at the "global turn" that the discipline of art history took in the previous decade.[17] On the one hand, an increasing amount of scholarly attention has been paid to the issue of "world art history,"[18] or what Thomas DaCosta Kaufmann calls the "geography of art,"[19] although this emerging field has no coherent voice or agreed methodology yet. On the other hand, a number of scholars have voiced their discontent with a nation-based, Euro-America-centric narrative of modernism and have started accumulating case studies toward what Partha Mitter advocates as a "more heterogeneous definition of modern art."[20] Such attempts, which have so far been made from various locales from the so-called margins of the world art scene, emphasize the hybrid and transnational aspect of modern art, challenging the center-periphery paradigm that has shaped so much of its discourse.[21] From this viewpoint, revisionist accounts were limited not only because they often lacked positive proof of their insinuations (such as the allegation that the CIA had secretly funded the overseas promotion of Abstract Expressionism),[22] but also and more fundamentally because they were mostly written within a framework of "national" art history—even though their subject matter was the international transport of art. Aiming their critique at the supposedly monolithic efforts of American cultural imperialism, many revisionist historians remained ironically America-centric.[23]

This is not to suggest that national art history be entirely abolished. On the contrary, its framework is still useful or even required as a historical reference, since much of art in modern times—including the very system of art and the formation of art history as an academic discipline—was not only produced, exhibited, exchanged, and narrated but also suppressed and even destroyed in the name of nation-states and nationalism. Though nations exist only as "imagined communities," they bring about "real" effects that condition our lives and psyches in many ways.[24] Yet it is necessary to recognize the nation-based approach as a relative and partial one (like any others), which could blind us to what lies between and beyond national boundaries as well as to the actual agency of artists and their creations. It is thus important to search for a broader, comparative perspective based on the actual analysis of works of art in order to obtain an entire picture of a global phenomenon in art. Intellectual historians of the 1970s and 1980s focused on ideological critique so much that they rarely paid attention to how the exported American art had actually been received in different locales abroad. They seldom discussed the actual morphology of works of art, either, viewing them as objects at the mercy of cultural propaganda and art marketing. As a result, they neglected the fact that in reality the artists and works of art often had their own agency in acting on local art communities, both at home and abroad.[25] Thus, this study takes up a postrevisionist approach through a close look at interactions among artists, curators, critics, and dealers in the global art map of the 1960s. By situating American art—the very central force of post-1945 art—in relation to the art of other regions that constituted the world art scene of the day, it will attempt to decenter the canonical discourse of postwar art.

Even so, why were Rauschenberg and his work particularly suited to be such important catalysts in the world art scene of the day? It is true that no other American artist traveled or exhibited abroad as extensively as Rauschenberg did in the 1960s (see appendix). His physical presence in many cities, along with what Solomon once called the "special kind of openness" in his personality, must certainly have added to his global celebrity.[26] However, a more fundamental reason has to be found in the specific nature of his art. Rauschenberg's update of the collage method in his Combine technique, his free use of ready-made objects, and the cross-boundary nature of his art and performance—all these qualities appealed to his overseas audience, sometimes even more than to his domestic audience. Equally important is his use of American popular imagery. Numerous images and objects related to America in Rauschenberg's art have long established him as a quintessentially American artist. However, while his reference to contemporary American culture remained basically neutral, it appeared sometimes celebratory and optimistic, other times gloomy and critical. Among the works discussed in this study, for instance, the silkscreen painting *Buffalo II* (1963) (figure 2.4) shows President Kennedy in a heroic gesture, whereas the Dante Drawings convey a darker image of America. This ambivalence is crucially important in an international context, because the very perception of America often influenced the reception of his art in a foreign land. In this sense, even an apparently blithe work such as *Coca-Cola Plan* (1958) (figure 4.9) needs to be reconsidered against the background of post-1945 Euro-American history, as the work, with its title punning on the Marshall Plan, invites some reflection on the relationship between American culture and the so-called "Coca-Colonization" of European lands. Such complexity actually worked in Rauschenberg's favor abroad, because it allowed his overseas audiences to embrace his art without compromising their own mixed feelings about postwar American hegemony. In other words, the ambiguity of Rauschenberg's America allowed them to see *their* America in his work.

Thus, a close formal reading of relevant works by Rauschenberg—especially those he exhibited or created abroad—is vital in understanding his international reputation. This study necessarily incorporates the examination of their overseas reception, and a comparison with their reception at home. This approach will cast new light on Rauschenberg's art, since this aspect of his career has not received full attention beyond Calvin Tomkins's biography of the artist,[27] Thomas Crow's discussion of his trip to Italy in the 1950s,[28] and Jean-Paul Ameline's essay on European reception of his work.[29] Whether based on the so-called postmodern theorization of his art as an icon of multivalence,[30] an iconographical and/or queer interpretation of his work,[31] or a celebration of its vernacular nature,[32] Rauschenberg literature has so far remained within the realm of "American" art history. In the wider scope of global art studies, though, even the famous controversy between postmodernists and iconographers regarding the "meaning" of Rauschenberg's art can and should be recontextualized, as it is basically a domestic debate and does not necessarily translate transnationally.[33] While benefiting a great deal from these preceding studies, this project seeks to synthesize different approaches—from formal analysis to reception theory, from the study of marketing strategies to the sociopolitical context of the Cold War era—in order to assess the significance of Rauschenberg's art and career in world art history.

Such an approach will make clear why it is misleading to see Rauschenberg as an agent of American cultural imperialism. In fact, there was never a consensus within the American art community to promote Rauschenberg as it had promoted Jackson Pollock. For instance, Alfred Barr Jr. of the Museum of Modern Art, New York, remained unconvinced of the artistic virtue of Rauschenberg's work,[34] and formalist critics such as Clement Greenberg and Michael Fried never acknowledged that there was any to begin with.[35] The question to be asked is, therefore, just how Rauschenberg became a "representative" American artist, since his fame was constructed outside his native country as much as within it. If he took on this role upon winning the Grand Prize in Venice in 1964, how did his preceding overseas activities contribute to such a drastic "Americanizing" turn in the global art scene of the day? How this geopolitical change in turn affected the American art scene is another question. Although this last question lies outside the scope of this study, a few of its ramifications include the increased migration of non-American artists to New York, the accelerated centralization of the New York art market, and the decreased importance of European art to American artists—as Donald Judd somewhat chauvinistically stated in 1966, "I'm totally uninterested in European art and I think it's over with."[36]

Thus, in order to precisely situate Rauschenberg's agency in the global arena, it is necessary to go beyond the nation-based framework and look at the phenomenon in a wider, transnational, and multinational scope that enables us to talk across cultures. This approach is particularly significant in the discourse of post-1945 art, which has hitherto been notoriously America-centric. This study aims to open up the field to a global perspective by situating Rauschenberg's career—the representative canon of American art—in the context of postwar art as an international event. Although the reception of Rauschenberg's art, and of American art in general, was unique in each particular case, the art communities of the four cities I discuss were engaged with the same essential question: how to take part in the international art scene as an active and unique force vis-à-vis the most powerful agent, American art.

If this study has a "global" dimension in the true sense of the word, it is attained by articulating this struggle. The quest for cultural and artistic identity in the midst of Americanization permeated the Free World throughout the 1960s, and the pressing nature of this issue has only increased today, when accelerated globalization requires each locale to express its global and local voice simultaneously. In other words, I hope that this book will serve as a model for going beyond the binary of the global and the local, in order to understand the cross-cultural, hybrid, and conflicted nature of modernism and modernity, which is not at all unrelated to our own living conditions.

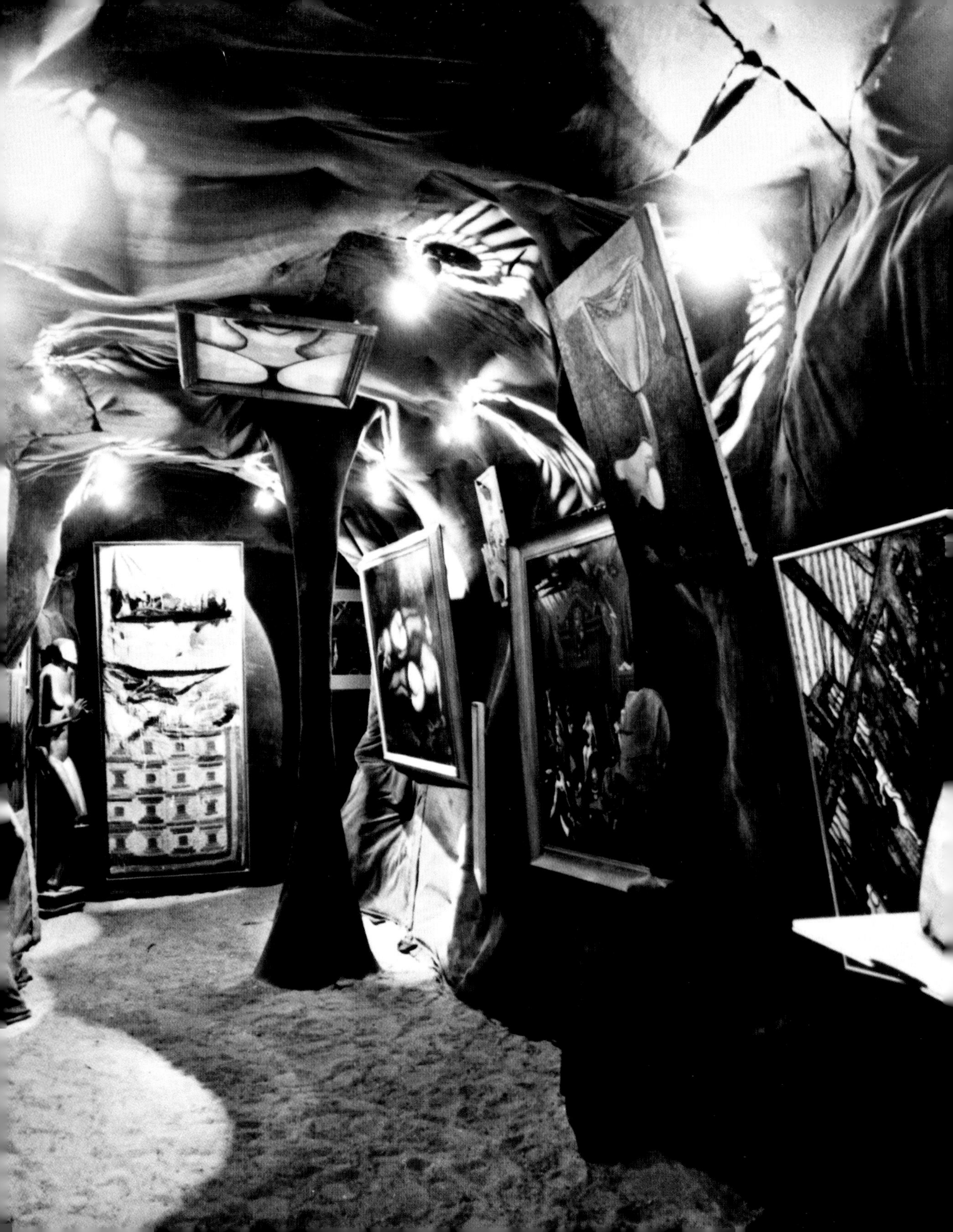

1

A TRIUMPH IN PARIS

ENGINEERING RAUSCHENBERG'S GLOBAL MARKET

Rauschenberg and the Merce Cunningham Dance Company left New York on June 3, 1964, arriving in Paris the next day. From Orly Airport, they traveled by bus to Strasbourg, where their world tour was scheduled to begin on June 6. On that night, the Théâtre de la Comédie in Strasbourg was full. Despite Cunningham's trepidation that the program might be difficult for the upper-class audience in the balcony, they applauded warmly for a curtain call. "But it was the top gallery that made the night," Cunningham recollected. "They yelled and stamped and bravoed and booed for a considerable period, the young people who had filled it, and cued me in for the rest of the trip. Everywhere we were to play for the young, they were alive and eager, pro and con, about what we gave them, and Strasbourg began it."[1] The next day, the company headed back to Paris for performances at the Théâtre de l'Est Parisien, and Rauschenberg's great migration of 1964 began.

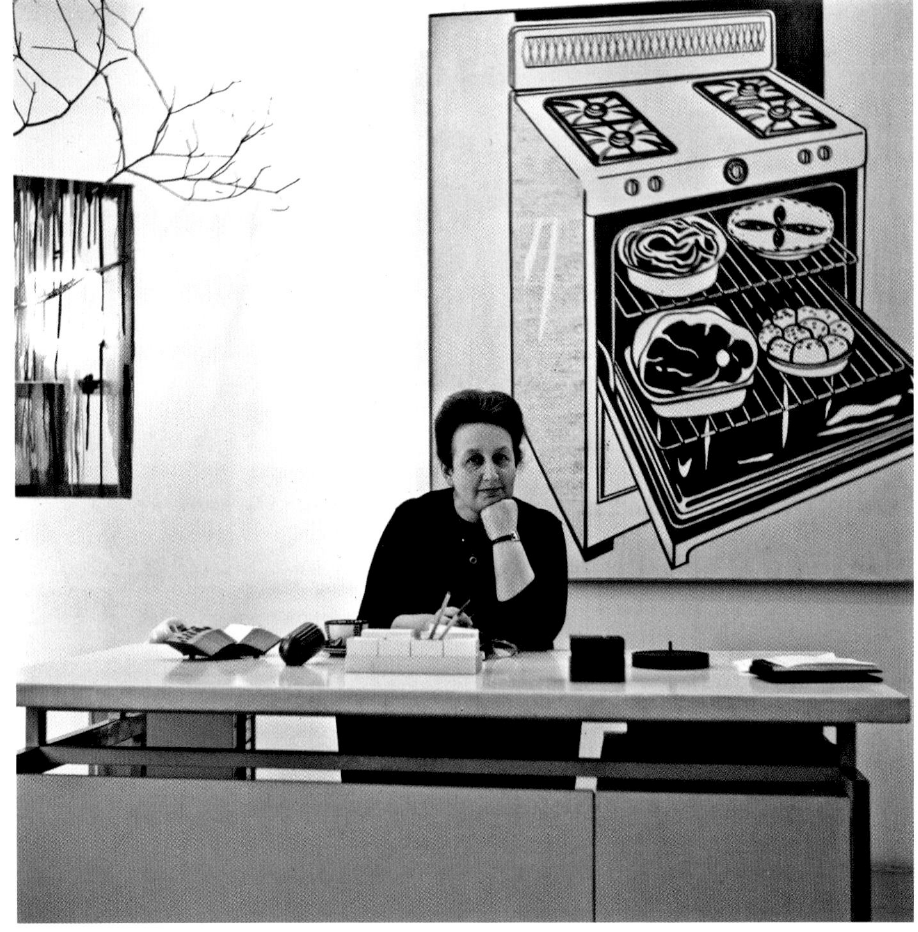

Figure 1.1
Ileana Sonnabend at her desk at Galerie Ileana Sonnabend, Paris, ca. 1965. Photograph courtesy Sonnabend Gallery.

Paris was not unfamiliar to Rauschenberg. Indeed, the city's art community had always been kind to him, receiving his art with enthusiasm ever since his first solo show there at Galerie Daniel Cordier in 1961. In fact, this exhibition had established his fame abroad well before he was awarded the Grand Prize at the 1964 Venice Biennale. Because he had eloquently showed a way out of the dead end of gestural abstraction with his Combines, Rauschenberg was considered a hero in the Parisian art scene of the time. This critical success established him as the most influential American artist after Jackson Pollock in Paris—a status confirmed two years later, when he returned to the city in 1963 with the notorious *Monogram* (1955–1959) (figure 3.2). His strong reputation in Paris did not crumble even after the scandal caused by the perceived American maneuvering behind his triumph at the 1964 Venice Biennale. Exactly a year after the Biennale, the French weekly *Arts* elected him the most important living artist.[2]

Behind Rauschenberg's success in Paris were promotional efforts by his dealer, Ileana Sonnabend, who opened her gallery in the city in 1962 (figure 1.1). A fan of Rauschenberg's work and personality ever since she met him in 1951, when she was married to Leo Castelli, Sonnabend became his guardian angel in 1957. Although Castelli was unsure at the time whether he wanted to ask Rauschenberg to join his gallery, she promised a firm date of a show to the artist, thereby forcing her husband to make the decision.[3] In Paris, where she moved after her divorce from Castelli, Sonnabend promoted American art with a particular focus on Rauschenberg, her favorite artist. The feeling was mutual, to say the least: "Let's say I've never finished a painting without wondering what Ileana would think of it," Rauschenberg once stated.[4] His strong reputation in Paris in 1965 was thus a consequence of her marketing as well as the artistic appeal of his work.

In reality, this success was merely critical. When *Arts* singled Rauschenberg out as the best contemporary artist in 1965, not one of his works was in a public collection—and very few, if any, were in private collections—in Paris. As far as Paris was concerned, commercial success never followed a critical one. The French capital proved to be a futile market for American art throughout the 1960s and 1970s. This, however, did not necessarily present an obstacle to the work's international promotion. For the city's strategic merit lay elsewhere: from Paris, American art dealers such as Sonnabend reached other European cities, including Milan, Düsseldorf, and Amsterdam, where the work they carried found other interested dealers, collectors, and museum directors. Paradoxically, it was Paris—New York's sworn archenemy—that gave birth to the global rise of American art.

TRANSATLANTIC MARKETING: PARIS VERSUS NEW YORK

How did Paris allow such a humiliating shift in cultural cartography to happen? In the years immediately following the end of World War II, the city seemed poised to regain its status as the world's art capital. European artists exiled in New York or elsewhere during the war returned to Paris, and it was still the place to be for many young Americans who wanted to become artists—including Rauschenberg, who briefly studied at the Académie

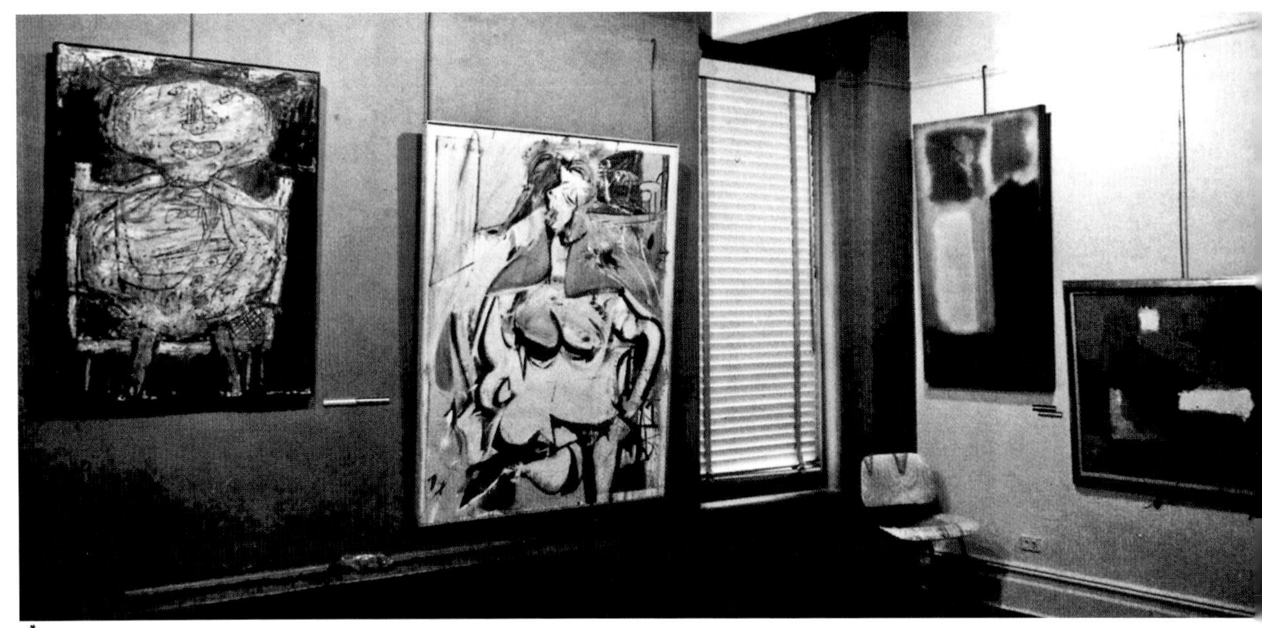

Figure 1.2
"Young Painters in the U.S. and France," installation view at the Sidney Janis Gallery, New York, 1950. Photograph by Oliver Baker; courtesy Carroll Janis Inc.

Julian in 1948 under the G.I. Bill.[5] With a sense of cultural elitism intact from the prewar era, artists based in Paris showed a general disinterest in contemporary American art. Even those who sought exile in New York during the war years showed little respect for what they saw in America, which they regarded as poor imitations of their own works.[6] Before a market for American art could even begin to be engineered, it was necessary to stoke interest among denizens of the Parisian art community, who still believed that they inhabited the capital of world art.

Leo Castelli, the most famous dealer in post–World War II American art, made a conscious effort at transatlantic marketing before he opened his gallery in New York in 1957. One example was "Young Painters in the U.S. and France," the first exhibition he curated at the Sidney Janis Gallery in 1950 (figure 1.2). In collaboration with Janis, he placed American painters (selected by Castelli) side by side with their French counterparts (selected by Janis): Willem de Kooning with Jean Dubuffet, Mark Rothko with Nicolas de Staël, and Franz Kline with Pierre Soulages—the last pair causing a dispute over which painter first started painting in the shared style.[7] Despite being "rather naïve" and "a little bit screwball," as Castelli himself admitted, the comparisons of the artists (including the dispute) nonetheless helped to create an image of the Abstract Expressionists as equals to their Parisian counterparts.[8] Castelli organized another exhibition, "American Vanguard for Paris," which took place at Janis's gallery in 1951 and traveled to the Galerie de France in Paris in 1952.[9] With his background as a Trieste-born Jew who had spent the prewar years in Paris—where he opened his first gallery with the architect René Drouin—it only made sense for Castelli to explore business opportunities in both the United States and Europe. Toward the mid-1950s, he even entertained the idea of opening a Paris branch of the Janis Gallery, which he felt "would have changed my life, my career, and perhaps also a great deal of things in the promotion of American painting."[10] The idea did not come to fruition, however, because of Janis's reluctance to invest capital in such a risky venture.

Although Castelli had to abandon this idea, the International Program of the Museum of Modern Art, New York, began to bring American art of substantial quantity and quality to Paris. Established in 1952, the program, headed by the director Porter McCray, launched its international exhibition activity with "Twelve Modern American Painters and Sculptors" at the Musée National d'Art Moderne in 1953 (figure 1.3). According to Darthea Speyer, who collaborated with the International Program as a cultural attaché at the American Embassy in Paris in those days, the United States government was initially against such a program. As she recollected: "They thought it was terrible, and they were against the Museum of Modern Art, N.Y., and kept sending telegrams, 'Don't have anything to do with them; they're communists.'"[11] She nonetheless managed to acquire a budget for the project from the United States Information Service in Paris, and in 1955 helped McCray mount "50 ans d'art aux Etats-Unis," the largest American modern art exhibition ever sent abroad to that date. Such an export of American art was by no means unilateral, as the show was organized by request of the French government.[12] Moreover, in 1956, a number of European

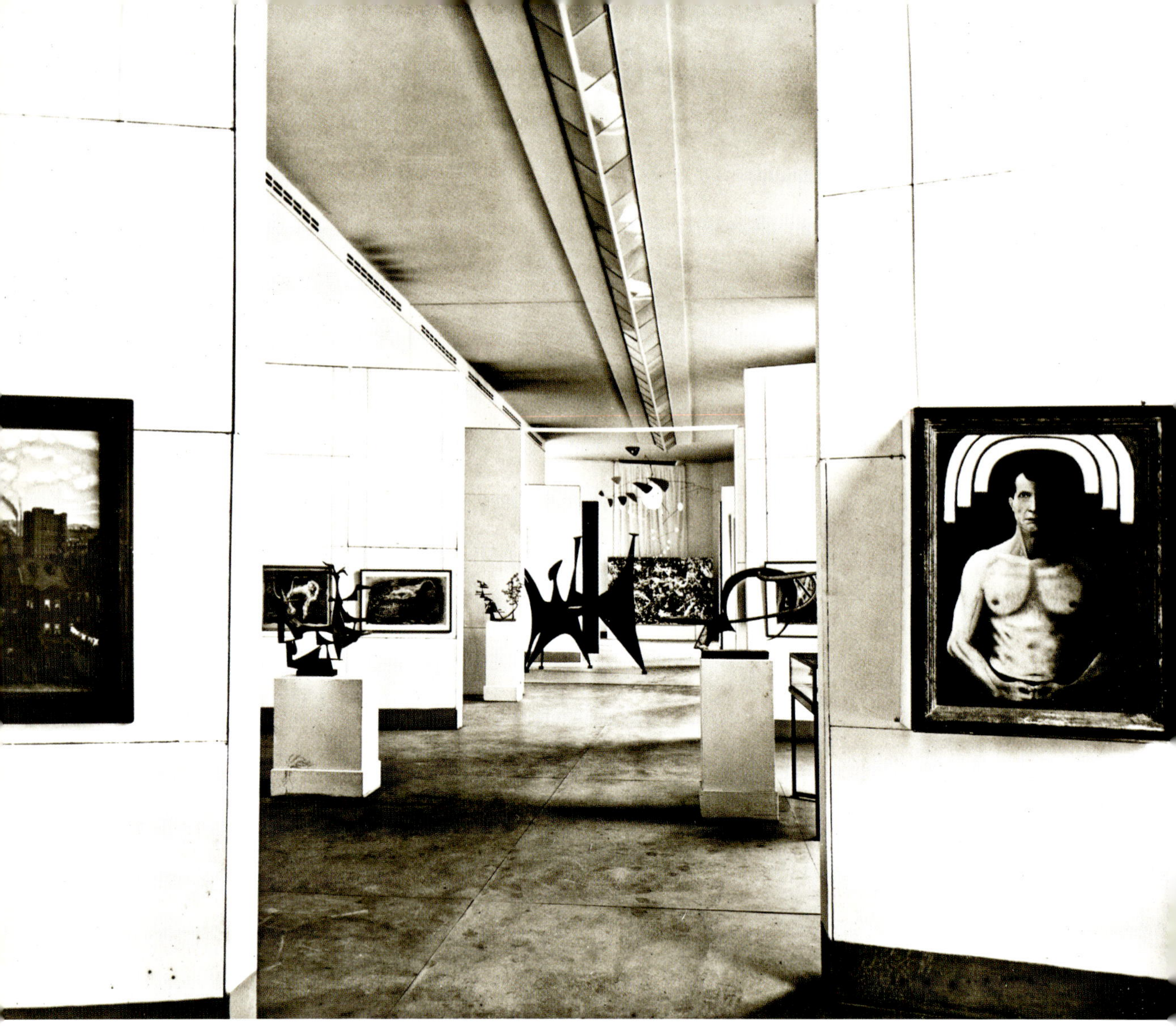

Figure 1.3
"Twelve Modern American Painters and Sculptors," installation view at the Musée National d'Art Moderne, Paris, 1953 (organized by the International Program of the Museum of Modern Art, New York). Digital image © 2009 The Museum of Modern Art, New York/SCALA, Florence.

museums asked the Museum of Modern Art for a show more specifically about the American avant-garde.[13] This prompted the presentation of two touring exhibitions, "Jackson Pollock: 1912–1956" and "The New American Paintings," which were shown in Paris together in 1959. These shows caused a considerable stir in the Parisian art scene, making it impossible for the French to continue to ignore American art. The critic Pierre Restany admitted as much, albeit in a condescending tone, when he wrote in the quadrilingual art journal *Cimaise*:

> This Yankee rendezvous was not useless. It gave proof to those who didn't know, or didn't want to know, that from now on a spiritual climate exists on the other side of the Atlantic that is capable of bringing some original solutions to the essential necessities of art. So go back home, Americans, and come back to see us when you have something new to astonish us with: for instance, a second Pollock.[14]

Indeed, Americans did come back with Rauschenberg as the "second Pollock" in 1961—an event to be examined in detail in the next section. In addition to the exhibitions prepared by the International Program, Speyer organized her own exhibitions of American art and circulated them to provincial museums. As she would eventually open her own gallery in 1968 after resigning from the embassy, Speyer was aware of the larger potential of trans-atlantic art promotion: "France was very interested. Actually, the intelligent thing was, then, to send these exhibits, which were major, somewhere else. But because USIS [*sic*] in Washington was against this, the shows were only in France."[15] Despite the limitation set on her activities, Speyer's efforts helped raise interest in American art in France in the fifties, with *Cimaise* publishing special issues on the subject in 1956 and 1959.[16]

To make things more complicated, French artists and critics—especially those involved with Art Informel, or *un art autre* (hereafter Informel), the Paris-based abstraction movement—were also engaged in transatlantic marketing in those days. Above all, they sought to open an American market for contemporary French paintings by co-opting Abstract Expressionism. Georges Mathieu, the representative painter of Informel, was actually one of the first to show American art in Paris after World War II.[17] In 1948, he organized a binational group exhibition—possibly the first of its kind in Paris or elsewhere—at the Galerie du Montparnasse, in which he showed works by Jackson Pollock, Arshile Gorky, Willem de Kooning, and Mark Tobey next to those by Camille Bryen, Hans Hartung, Francis Picabia, and himself. Michel Tapié, a critic who vigorously promoted Informel, also organized a similar international group show entitled "Véhémences confrontées" at Galerie Nina Dausset in 1951, while organizing the first Pollock show in Paris at Galerie Paul Facchetti in 1952.[18] However, as it was fairly obvious that Mathieu and Tapié were actually trying to establish Parisian control over the world art scene—Tapié once even tried to promote a few artists on the West Coast as "L'École du Pacifique" in an attempt to curb the rise of New York—their agenda was received with caution in the city's art community.[19]

Nonetheless, Mathieu was persistent in his effort to open a New York market for his work. Although American dealers were mainly interested in European modern masters, he managed to hold numerous solo shows in New York throughout the 1950s, working with Samuel Kootz, one of the few gallery owners who would show contemporary European artists. Exploring possible market opportunities around the globe, Mathieu traveled extensively during the latter half of the fifties. He embarked on a world trip in 1957, after he thought he had built a secure relationship with Kootz. Starting with Tokyo, where his spectacular performance of action painting added a great deal of momentum to the "Informel whirlwind" in the local art scene (see figure 4.4), he traveled to such cities as New York, Stockholm, Vienna, and Rio de Janeiro, forerunning Rauschenberg's world trip of 1964.

The Paris–New York rivalry, however, took a toll on the trajectory of Mathieu's international ambition. In October 1957, arriving in New York via California, he encountered trouble with Kootz, who reportedly told the artist not to create works in public in the city. As narrated by Mathieu's biographer, Kootz apparently feared that Mathieu might undermine the pioneering image of the late Pollock.[20] As a result, Mathieu created works in solitude in a hotel room, and his relationship with Kootz was permanently strained. Other gallery owners shared Kootz's cultural protectionism;[21] they saw no reason to handle Informel, which had so many stylistic similarities with Abstract Expressionism—a market that was finally maturing after so many years of domestic neglect.[22] American dealers hence no longer represented Mathieu after his solo show at Kootz Gallery in 1960, by which time Informel's international influence had been greatly diminished.

Leo Castelli, who finally opened his own gallery in 1957, eventually opted for only American artists as well, albeit for a strategic reason. Because he was originally interested in showing both European and American artists, his first group shows featured works by artists from the two continents.[23] The immediate success of Johns's first solo show in January 1958—all but two works sold—determined the direction of his gallery. The exhibition proved that post–Abstract Expressionist art with recognizable American imagery had great potential for a new market. From then on, the focus of Castelli's stable clearly shifted to American artists who were going to define the new trend of American art called Neo-Dada and Pop Art. Castelli's new direction was nonetheless a risky business at a time when Abstract Expressionist paintings were finally starting to sell in a domestic market. Johns's phenomenal success seemed an exception, rather than the rule; Rauschenberg's solo show two months later made only two sales, with one of the buyers being Castelli himself. Castelli clearly needed to devise an effective marketing strategy for this new generation of American artists. In an interview conducted in 1977, he described his idea of a "team" that functioned to create tastes for new art:

> **Castelli:** Dealers and collectors have a joint function, they do it together, it's a team—do the choosing. Well, they are allowed more mistakes than a museum is, although museums also make lots of mistakes of course, but what the museums then do acquire is filtered through this preliminary work that is done by the dealer-collector team.

Q: So you are saying the dealer-collector team is a more significant tastemaker than the museum, because they help …

Castelli: Not really necessarily. They usually are a little bit ahead of the game, that's true, but sometimes—often as a matter of fact—there are museum directors, especially the younger ones, who are part of the team. It's a part of the dealer-collector team, so that there's three people there, and then there is the fourth member of the team, and that's the really good critic. So actually there are really four elements there that work at finding and then collecting.[24]

In a nutshell, it was the collective effort of this team of dealer, collector, museum director, and critic that determined the new direction of art. Castelli, who spent no fewer than ten years observing how the New York art business operated before opening his gallery, must have had this system in mind, if vaguely, by the beginning of the 1960s.

Accordingly, he built a four-part system that one could call "Team Leo Castelli" during the first half of the 1960s. As a dealer-member, he showed the new generation of artists such as Johns and Rauschenberg, who constituted the core of the Castelli stable. He was very careful in choosing collector-members, a crucial constituent for the team. When Giuseppe Panza in Milan wrote to him to purchase a Rauschenberg work in 1959, he replied, "His work is in great demand here, and there is hardly anything of importance that I would have available for the moment."[25] Given the poor sales of his show from the previous year, this cannot have been entirely true. Although he nursed a plan to open a European market for his artists, Castelli prioritized establishing his team in the United States first. Robert and Ethel Scull and Emily and Burton Tremaine fulfilled the function of collector-members, vigorously buying works by Rauschenberg and Johns. The director-member was Alan Solomon, who in 1962 became the director of the Jewish Museum, where he organized the first retrospectives of Rauschenberg and Johns in 1963 and 1964; he later chose them as the main features for the American Pavilion at the 1964 Venice Biennale. Finally, Leo Steinberg discursively supported the two artists, filling the team's fourth slot of critic-member. He published the first critical essay on Johns in 1962, and initiated the postmodern evaluation of Rauschenberg's art with the famous term "flatbed picture plane" later in the decade.[26]

Nevertheless, it would be misleading to assume that "Team Leo Castelli" was a Machiavellian creation of the dealer alone, since each party acted on his or her own motives and interests. For instance, Steinberg's motive was to understand the art of the younger generation and construct a nonformalist critical discourse: "Castelli had his motive, but it wasn't my motive," he told this author.[27] It can therefore be said that the team functioned effectively precisely because each member focused on his or her activities as an independent agent. This kind of labor efficiency did not exist in the Paris art market. As the capital of modern art since the nineteenth century, Paris had always had an abundance of dealers and critics, although art criticism in France was traditionally practiced by literary critics or philosophers in their spare time, not as a full-time profession. What Paris lacked

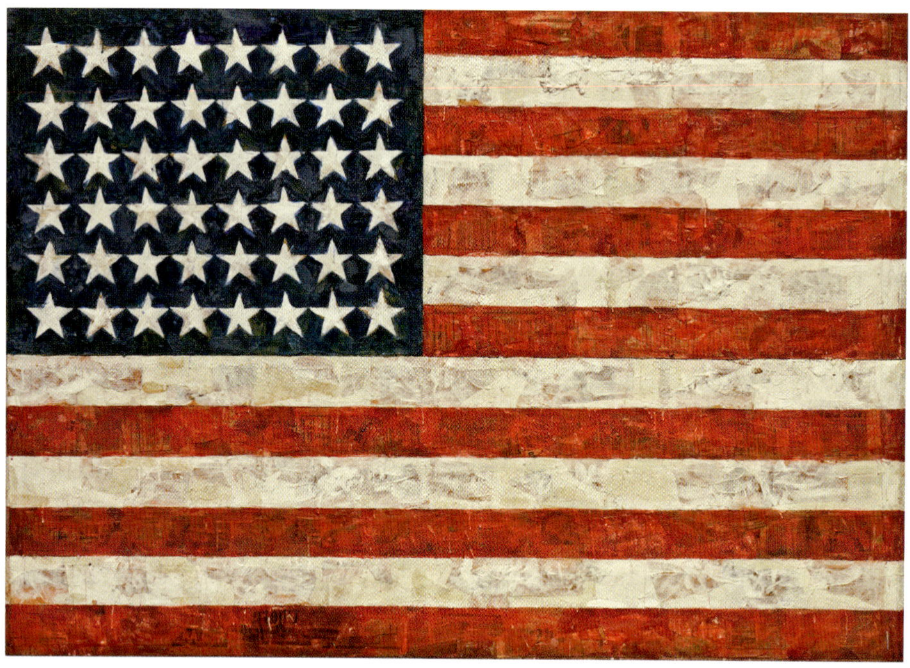

Figure 1.4
Jasper Johns, *Flag*, 1954–1955; dated on reverse, 1954. Encaustic, oil, and collage on fabric mounted on plywood, 42 ¼ × 60 ⅝ inches (107.3 × 153.8 cm). The Museum of Modern Art, New York. Gift of Philip Johnson in honor of Alfred H. Barr, Jr. (106.1973). © Jasper Johns/Licensed by VAGA, New York, NY. Digital image © 2009 The Museum of Modern Art, New York/SCALA, Florence.

were collectors and museums that would buy modern art produced in their own city. After all, there was a good reason why Paris became the first city to create an international market for modern art at the end of the nineteenth century: the legendary backwardness of French collectors and museums forced dealers to seek markets outside France.[28]

This tendency accelerated during the 1910s and 1920s, when the most important artists working in Paris were increasingly from outside France. In other words, the pre–World War II internationalization of the art world was synonymous with the denationalization of French art, and cultural xenophobia might partly explain the lack of avant-garde art collectors in France.[29] Since the situation did not change much in post–World War II years, Informel artists and critics often had to act as promoters for their movement. Mathieu, for instance, did everything by himself, from curating his and other Informel-related shows to writing a treatise on the movement, while Tapié valued sales activities over the critical support of individual artists. In fact, Mathieu and Tapié did not even constitute a "team" since they disagreed on many points, including the very term "Informel."[30] As a result, the multiple roles they played, as artist/critic on the one hand and as dealer/promoter on the other, created suspicion in their audience abroad, who detected—quite reasonably—a latent cultural nationalism and economic motives in the Informel movement.[31]

"THE MOMENT OF TRUTH": PARIS, 1961

In the meantime, Castelli set out to promote American artists in the world art scene. At first, Johns seemed destined to become the "second Pollock" in Europe. He was already included in the international section for emerging artists at the 1958 Venice Biennale—where his *Flag* (1954–1955) (figure 1.4) impressed overseas critics such as Restany and Yoshiaki Tōno—and held his first solo show in Paris in January 1959 and another one in Milan in March. Castelli's concentration on Johns was a logical choice after the artist's critical and commercial success in New York. However, Johns's debut show at the Galerie Rive Droite went "virtually unnoticed," resulting in only a few short reviews.[32] The reason for this neglect is not entirely clear. A lack of sufficient publicity probably played a role, and it is also possible that the French audience had a very different response to paintings of the Stars and Stripes than the American audience.

The difference in artistic sensibility between Europe and America loomed large for Rauschenberg as well, bringing him the exact opposite reception to that given Johns. In fact, Michel Ragon, perhaps the only French critic who saw both Johns's and Rauschenberg's shows in New York in 1958, made an observation quite different from those of American critics. Upon his return to Paris, he contributed a long New York report to the special issue on American art in *Cimaise*, in which he compared the two artists. For Johns, he reserved aesthetic judgment: "Most of his paintings are badly painted, but since the quality of his drawings is close to that of Redon's lithographs, he must be painting badly on purpose.... We should not cry out 'Fraud' too quickly." In contrast, his praise of Rauschenberg was openhanded:

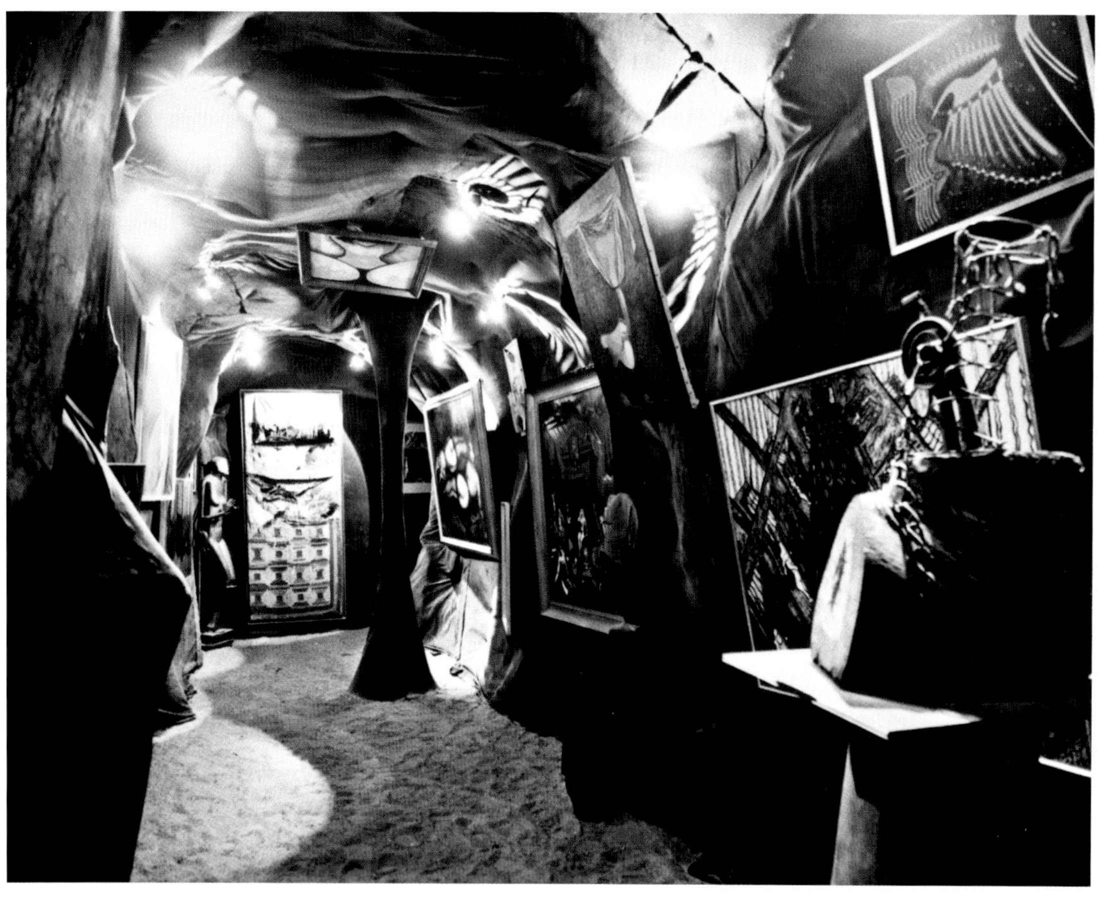

Figure 1.5
"L'Exposition inteRnatiOnale du Surréalisme" (EROS), an installation view with *Bed* (1955) by Rauschenberg, 1959. Photograph by Henri Glaeser; courtesy Centre Pompidou–MnamCci–Bibliothèque Kandinsky.

On the other hand, Robert Rauschenberg, a Texan of thirty-two years old, won me over completely.... Let me emphasize that everything he does is well done. And one of his most original qualities is to combine his grand knowledge of classical paintings with a Dada spirit.... Rauschenberg is one of those artists who can, by means of their enthusiasm, bring joy back to art, which could quickly turn into routine and standardization in New York as well as in Paris.[33]

As if to justify Ragon's praise, Rauschenberg had an immediate and decisive success in Paris with his first solo show at Galerie Daniel Cordier in April 1961. Sonnabend explained the difference in cultural climate between the two cities to the art journalist Calvin Tomkins: "To many of the older artists and critics of the fifties, Rauschenberg was 'a menace'—a menace to high art, ideals, attitudes. This made it difficult for US museums to do much about him. In Europe, on the other hand, he was understood almost immediately. Partly because of the heritage of Dada and Surrealism there is less self-righteousness about capital A art there."[34] Although Dada and Surrealism had already been accepted in America by the 1950s, the recognition of Rauschenberg was slow in New York, mainly because of formalist resistance to his art by both museum curators and art critics. It is therefore significant that Rauschenberg's overseas fame had to be imported to the United States, where it helped to establish his domestic reputation. Castelli pointed out: "As a matter of fact his international fame spread much more rapidly than Jasper Johns's. His whole approach seemed to be more easy to understand than Johns's. People were, in Europe especially, not here so much,... reminded of Schwitters, say, and they had been quite familiar with Abstract Expressionist techniques which were and still are part of Rauschenberg's paintings. So that his acceptance abroad and then by ricochet in the States ..., as soon as it started, was really quite rapid."[35]

Rauschenberg's participation in the world art scene began in earnest in 1959.[36] In that year, he had a solo show in Rome and was included in the Bienal de São Paulo, Documenta II in Kassel, and the inaugural Biennale de Paris, the last of which included works by those who would join Nouveau Réalisme the following year.[37] At the end of 1959, he and Johns were also featured in the "Exposition inteRnatiOnale du Surréalisme" (EROS) at Galerie Daniel Cordier (figure 1.5). Organized by Marcel Duchamp and André Breton, the show included Rauschenberg's *Bed* (1955) and Johns's *Target with Plaster Casts* (1955). Although their works were not the main feature of the show and thus elicited only a few responses from crititcs, the Parisian art circle had been exposed to Rauschenberg's work before his first solo show in the city.[38]

In April 1961, then, Rauschenberg did become the "second Pollock" in Paris. Unfortunately, the day that his solo show opened coincided with the seizure of Paris as part of the "Algiers putsch," a failed coup d'état to replace President Charles de Gaulle with a junta in French Algeria. The city was thus deserted and Cordier had to shutter his gallery lest the windows be broken. Moreover, Cordier—prominent in the Resistance during World War II—was involved in the crisis as a supporter of de Gaulle. As a result, the installation

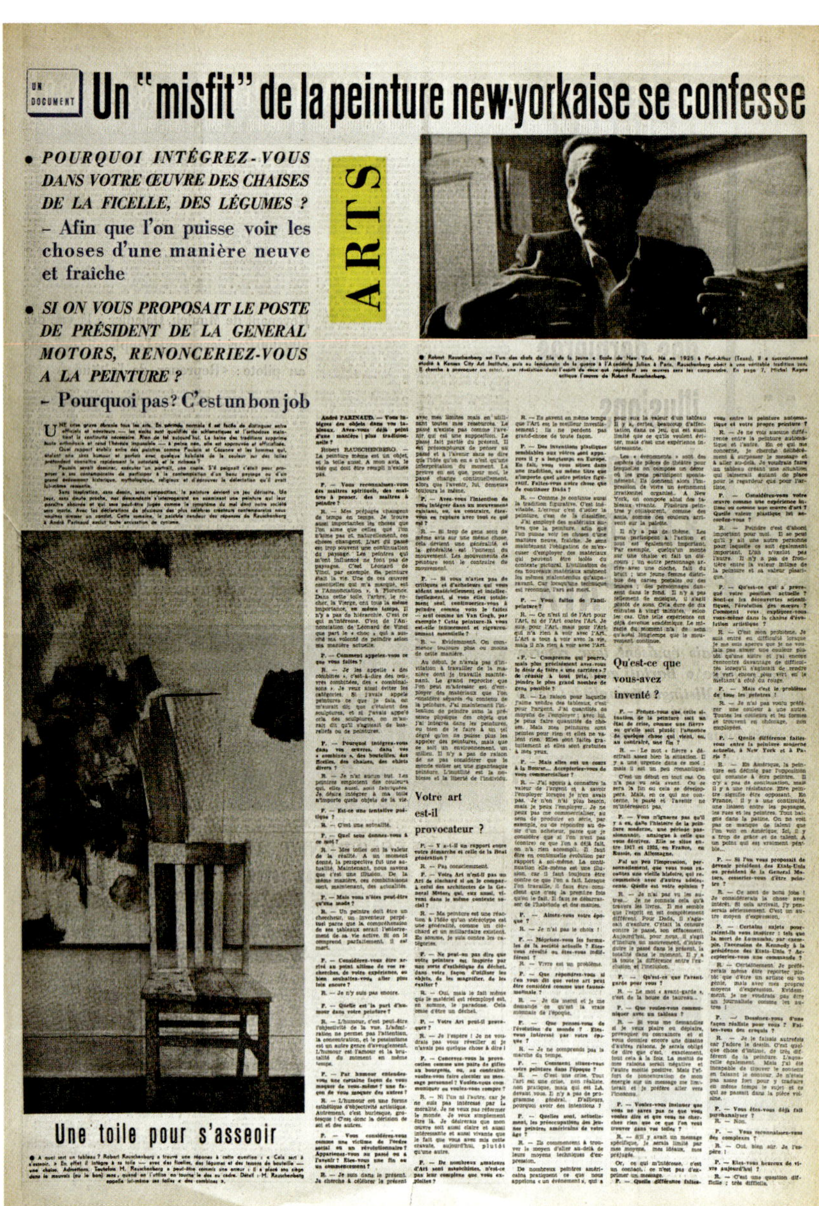

UN DOCUMENT

Un "misfit" de la peinture new-yorkaise se confesse

ARTS

- *POURQUOI INTÉGREZ-VOUS DANS VOTRE ŒUVRE DES CHAISES DE LA FICELLE, DES LÉGUMES ?*

  – Afin que l'on puisse voir les choses d'une manière neuve et fraîche

- *SI ON VOUS PROPOSAIT LE POSTE DE PRÉSIDENT DE LA GENERAL MOTORS, RENONCERIEZ-VOUS A LA PEINTURE ?*

  – Pourquoi pas? C'est un bon job

Une toile pour s'asseoir

Votre art est-il provocateur ?

Qu'est-ce que vous-avez inventé ?

Figure 1.6
Interview of Robert Rauschenberg by André Parinaud, *Arts*, no. 821 (May 10, 1961): 18. © Photos Guy Carrard–Centre Pompidou–MnamCci–Bibliothèque Kandinsky.

of the show was more than wanting, as Cordier was hardly at the gallery before the opening.[39] Yet the show made an immediate impact on young artists in Paris, despite Rauschenberg's frustration with Cordier, the half-closed opening, and perhaps also the poor sales (only one painting and one gouache were sold).[40] As Sonnabend remembered the event: "The day after that [unfortunate opening], my husband Michael and I went to see the show, and it was closed, but, through the window, one could see a little bit. So there were two young people there, discussing . . ., very very excited about the work. They turned out to be Arman, the artist, and Martial Raysse, another artist of Nouveau Réalisme. And that was sort of the sign of how young artists would react."[41]

Reflecting the impact of Rauschenberg's show, *Arts* published a full-page interview of the artist by its editor, André Parinaud (figure 1.6). Sonnabend, who served as the translator for the interview, was convinced by Parinaud's first question that "he planned to use Rauschenberg as an example of all that was sick, materialistic, and degraded in American society."[42] But Rauschenberg answered Parinaud's questions with candor and intelligence. For instance, when asked how he would respond if someone described his art as similar to fake money, he answered: "I [would] say thank you and wonder what the real money of the age is." Asked what he would do if he were offered the position of president of General Motors or of the United States, Rauschenberg replied: "I would seriously consider [it]. It's another form of expression."[43] In addition to these witty answers, he also explicated his position in the history of modern art with clarity when asked if his art might be a mere repetition of the pre–World War II European avant-garde: "It seems to me the spirit is completely different. For Dada, it was about exclusion, it was censorship against the past, its effacement. Today, for us, it's about the inclusion of a movement, introduction of the past into the present, the totality in the moment. There is a big difference between exclusion and inclusion."[44] In this way, Rauschenberg finally won over the interviewer, who said at the end, "Well, obviously we can't nail you to the cross."[45] After the publication of this interview along with Ragon's favorable review of the show,[46] "Rauschenberg did become a hero to the French artists," Sonnabend stated.[47] She further pointed to Rauschenberg's physical presence and his open, engaging personality as another crucial factor for his popularity in Paris: "Bob fulfills their idea of the American myth. Pollock would have done that too if he had gone to Europe. Bob's presence was very important."[48]

Johns also had his second solo show at the Galerie Rive Droite a few months later, but it did not create nearly as strong an impression as Rauschenberg's Combines. What appealed to both formalist and nonformalist critics of Johns's work in America—the banal subject matter combined with the quasi-modernist rendering of the picture plane—somehow did not make a mark in Paris.[49] Although the two artists were actually engaged in intimate artistic dialogue during their formative years in the fifties,[50] their works were perceived very differently in the two cultures. In New York, Rauschenberg's Combines show in 1958 was described as "very good" but "nothing like Jasper Johns."[51] In Paris, Johns's show in 1961 was positively reviewed,[52] but its impact was not even close to that of Rauschenberg's.

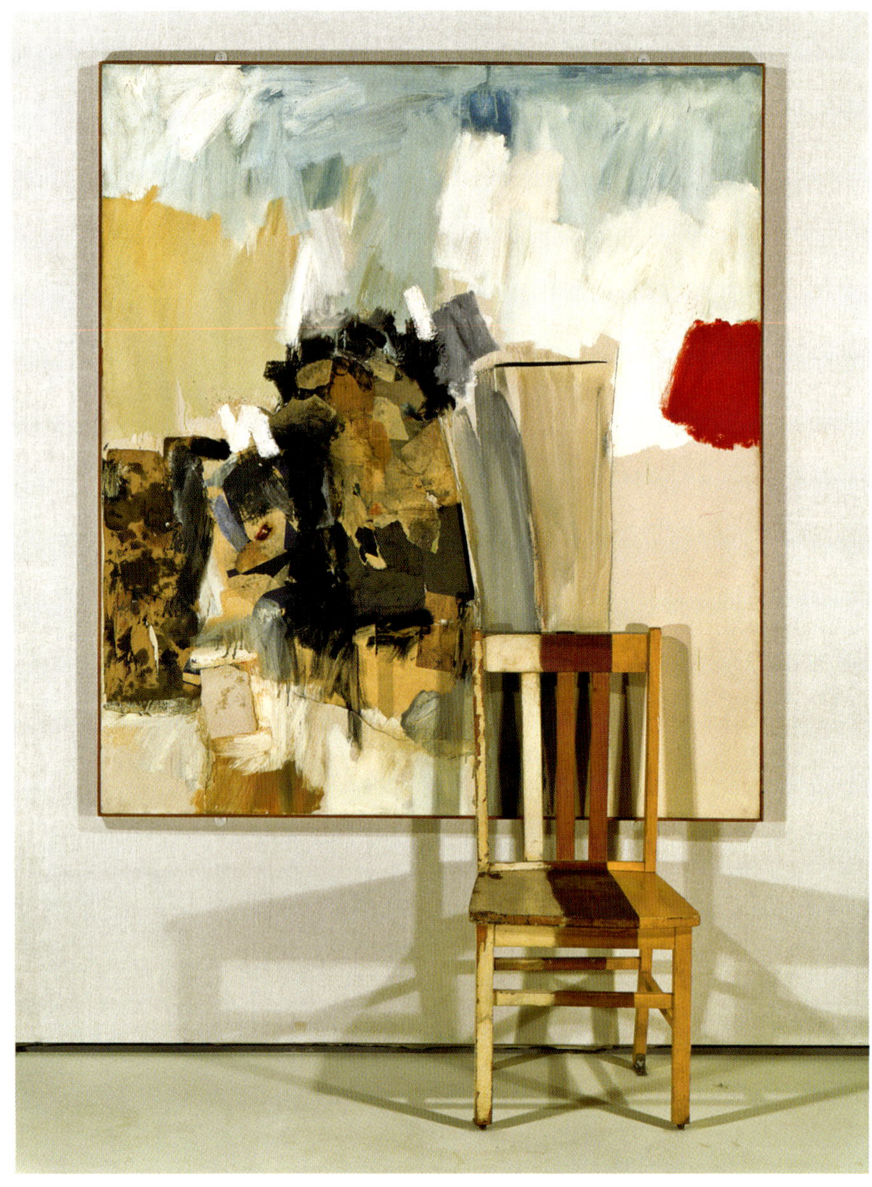

Figure 1.7
Robert Rauschenberg, *Pilgrim*, 1960. Combine painting: oil, pencil, paper, printed paper, and fabric on canvas, with painted wood chair, 79 ¼ × 53 ⅞ × 18 ⅝ inches (201.3 × 136.8 × 47.3 cm). Sammlung Onnasch, Berlin.

What was it that Parisians saw in Rauschenberg that they did not in Johns? Among the works exhibited in the show, *Pilgrim* (1960) (figure 1.7), a Combine painting with a real chair attached to the canvas, was considered the most provocative. According to the critic Robert Pincus-Witten, who lived in Paris as a graduate student at the time and worked for Sonnabend when she opened her gallery in 1962, the work represented some kind of "moment of truth" for the Parisian audiences.[53] While the writer José Pierre enthusiastically saw a revolt against action painting in this piece,[54] Parinaud also considered it the most important in the show and reproduced it in the *Arts* article.[55] Divided into three colors that were contiguous to those on the canvas, the chair appeared to emerge from the painting, literally coming "off the wall." As such, it destroyed the concept of painting as a medium of illusionistic or expressionistic representation, recreating it as an "actuality" that had "reality-value," as Rauschenberg described his art in the *Arts* interview.[56]

For European artists, especially Nouveaux Réalistes who had started using ready-made objects out of frustration with the manneristic abstraction of Informel, Rauschenberg's gesture confirmed the artistic freedom to make a work of art with anything one wanted. Pontus Hultén, then director of the Moderna Museet in Stockholm, recollected: "When Rauschenberg's works were first shown in Europe, it was a great shock for many people. I saw the first show in Paris in 1961. It was something we had waited for. It was like a revelation in one way, and a confirmation in another. Something was shown that was so strong and so powerful. For me, I can't say it was a surprise, it was more like, ah, finally somebody did it right."[57] In addition, European audiences detected something intrinsically American in his work. As Hultén described Rauschenberg's effortless, high-spirited attitude: "This is something American, I think, in the sense that in America there is enough freedom from heavy tradition, as well as the very different sense of scale in America and in American art—the essential role of space without limitations, the great freedom of space, the fact there's a lot of it, and scale is very large."[58]

Importantly, this "American" quality did not contradict the transnational appeal of the artist's method, which was based on the prewar avant-garde techniques of collage and readymade. Alain Jouffroy, the most enthusiastic critic in Paris of Rauschenberg's work, singled out this quality as especially praiseworthy:

> The art of Rauschenberg doesn't define itself within the limit of just one nation. Since his debut, he has participated in an artistic creation of international consciousness, which is shared by his generation. . . . In this regard, Rauschenberg's work is particularly representative of the globalization [*mondialisation*] of every form of expression. . . . Thus, his great and uncontestable talent lies in "actualizing" and "globalizing" aesthetic and poetic discoveries accomplished by the revolutionary European avant-garde.[59]

This critique illustrates an important reason for Rauschenberg's prominence in Paris. By updating prewar avant-garde collage methods for a contemporary purpose, his art manifested a general, "global" quality that could be applied to a variety of postwar art practices. While artists of the postwar generation—especially the French—shared the heritage of the prewar European avant-garde as a basic discipline, the debris of postwar commercial or technological culture was available virtually everywhere in the so-called Free World as inexpensive materials for art making. Rauschenberg's Combine technique thus demonstrated a universal method that allowed artists with diverse cultural backgrounds to incorporate whatever they considered had "reality-value" into their artistic practice. Sonnabend got it quite right when she stated, "He took them out of painting, you see, into something else—life, maybe."[60]

NOUVEAU RÉALISME, NEO-DADA, AND POP: AN EXHIBITION BATTLE

When Informel began to wane in Paris and elsewhere at the end of the 1950s, Pierre Restany emerged as a newly influential critic. He supported young European artists of the post-Informel generation who employed ready-made objects in their art production. For instance, Swiss sculptor Jean Tinguely used abandoned metal parts for his *Méta-Matics* (a mechanical construction that automatically produced drawings), Yves Klein painted monochrome canvases with industrial paints, Arman created reliefs of accumulated products, American-raised Niki de Saint-Phalle created *Shooting Paintings* with her 0.22 caliber rifle, and *affichistes* such as Raymond Hains and Jacques Villeglé presented torn posters from the street as artwork. Despite the diversity in media and in the presentation of their work, Restany claimed that these artists shared a method of direct appropriation of the exterior world that, unlike a Dadaist anti-art gesture, was marked by their positive attitude toward art and society.[61] Grouping them under the name Nouveau Réalisme, Restany launched the first group exhibition in Milan in April 1960, followed by the official declaration of the group in Paris in October.

Although this group formation was clearly made in emulation of Informel, Restany, a critic with international ambitions, found his role model in Michel Tapié, calling his concept of *un art autre* "a historic point of reference."[62] Small wonder, then, that Restany quickly recognized the stylistic affinity between Nouveau Réalisme and the so-called Neo-Dada, and tried to take advantage of it, just as Tapié had done with Informel and Abstract Expressionism. In late July, Restany organized a comparative group exhibition, "Nouveau Réalisme à Paris et à New York," at the Galerie Rive Droite, featuring representative Nouveaux Réalistes along with American artists such as Rauschenberg, Johns, John Chamberlain, and Richard Stankiewicz. Given that Restany's model was Tapié, it was again hardly surprising that he prioritized the French artists over the Americans. Having been a press attaché and a speechwriter for governmental functionaries, Restany had a writing style that was even more aggressive than Tapié's.[63] For instance, in the exhibition's catalog he compared American and European artists as follows: "More rigorous in logic, more simple and precise in presentation, and more directly appropriative in method, Europeans, for the most part, remain 'Nouveaux Réalistes' in the true sense of the word. Romantics at heart, Cubist in spirit, Baroque in tone, and also more susceptible to the Surrealist temptation, the so-called Neo-Dada Americans are in the middle of recreating the modern fetishism of the object."[64]

Restany's chauvinistic agenda notwithstanding, the first few years of the 1960s actually saw a peak in the transnational, if utopian, collaboration among European and American artists. Tinguely and Rauschenberg met for the first time in New York in 1960, when Tinguely presented the infamous self-destructive machine *Homage to New York* at the Museum of Modern Art. Rauschenberg contributed to the work his piece *Money Thrower for Tinguely's H.T.N.Y.* (1960), a small contraption that threw money into the air. In May 1961, a large international survey exhibition of Kinetic Art, "Rörelse i konsten" (Art in Motion), was held at the Moderna Museet in Stockholm, providing a collaborative occasion for such diverse artists as Rauschenberg, Tinguely, de Saint-Phalle, and the Swedish artist Per Olof Ultvedt (see chapter 3). In the following month, Tinguely, de Saint-Phalle, Rauschenberg, and Johns reunited in Paris for an event organized by Speyer at the Théâtre de l'Ambassade des États-Unis. During the event, entitled "Hommage à David Tudor" (figure 1.8), each artist simultaneously performed a task within a set time. Rauschenberg, for instance, created the work *First Time Painting* (1961) by turning the back of the canvas to the audience, who were not able to see the painting but only to hear the sound of its making via microphones attached to the easel; Tudor played John Cage's *Variations II* (1961) on the piano; Tinguely put a self-stripping sculpture on stage, which moved around the performance space while shedding its metal parts; de Saint-Phalle enacted the *Tir* performance by having a marksman shoot at her painting; and Johns, who refused to appear on stage, contributed a *Target* made of real flowers along with a painting shown during the intermission that said "Entr'Acte."[65] Although Speyer was forbidden by the embassy to organize an event of this kind from then on,[66] the artists enjoyed the occasion so much that Rauschenberg, Tinguely, and de Saint-Phalle enacted another performance, "The Construction of Boston," in New York in May 1962. The beginning of the sixties was thus different from the more stiffly competitive fifties, in that it involved—if briefly—a friendly transatlantic art exchange.

This did not mean, however, that the centralization of New York–based art and its discourse was slowing down. In October 1961, when "Nouveau Réalisme à Paris et à New York" closed in Paris, William Seitz opened "The Art of Assemblage" at the Museum of Modern Art in New York, a large exhibition that surveyed object-based art from Cubist collage and Duchamp's Readymades to contemporary art practice in Europe and America. In fact, during his preparatory trip to Paris in May, Seitz saw the second Nouveau Réalisme show, "À quarante degrés au-dessus de dada." According to Restany, he and Seitz had a long discussion on that occasion, which the French critic claimed influenced, at least partly, the idea of "The Art of Assemblage."[67] If Restany's sales pitch led to the inclusion of a number of Nouveaux Réalistes in Seitz's show, the American curator also made sure that the authoritative voice of modern art would remain New York's. In this exhibition, Duchamp was

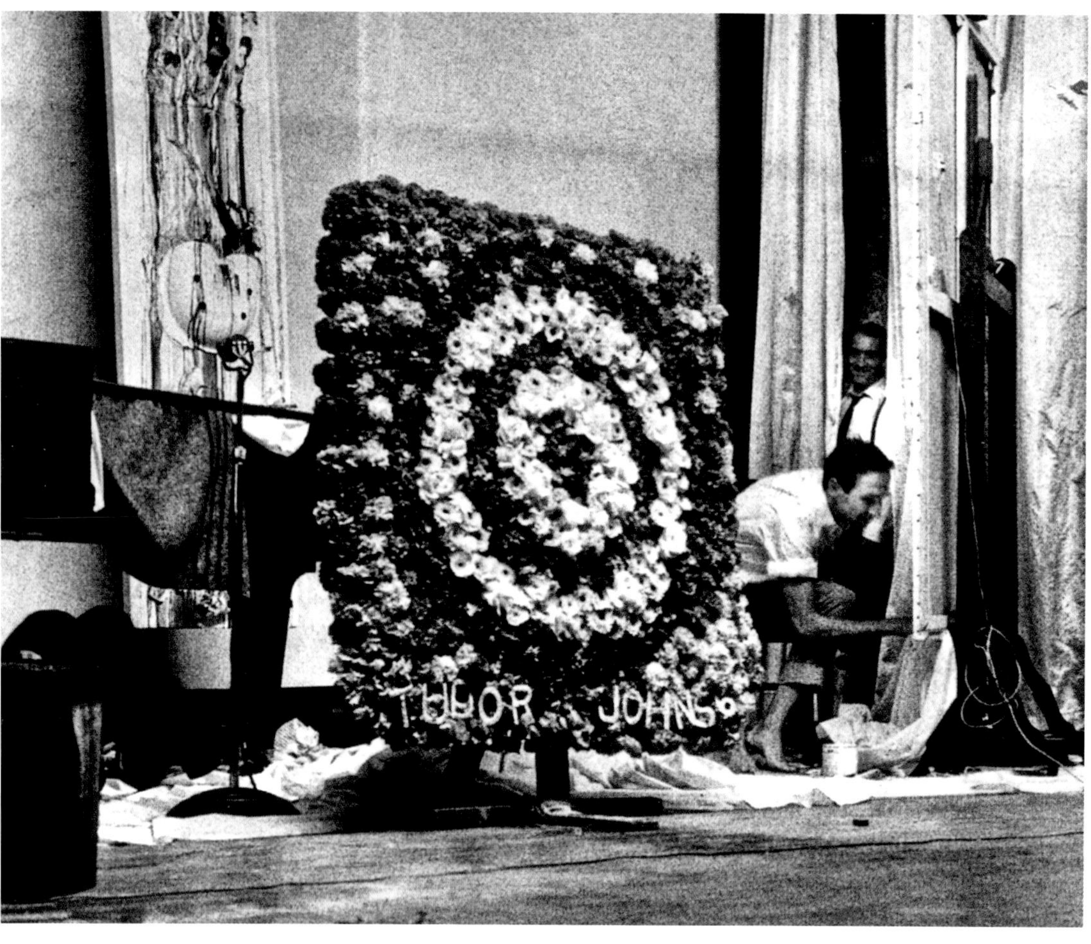

Figure 1.8
"Hommage à David Tudor," Théâtre de l'Ambassade des États-Unis, Paris, 1961. From left to right: *Tir* by Niki de Saint-Phalle, *Target* (made of real flowers) by Jasper Johns, Rauschenberg painting onstage, and Jean Tinguely looking through stage curtain. Photograph by Harry Shunk; Photo: Shunk-Kender, © Roy Lichtenstein Foundation.

presented as the father of assemblage art, just as Restany had treated him as the precursor of Nouveau Réalisme. But in Seitz's narrative, Duchamp's successor was neither Tinguely nor Klein but Rauschenberg, an artist who had invented Combines out of his dialogue with Duchamp and Abstract Expressionist artists—all of whom were based in New York at the time.

In the catalog essay, Seitz asserted that the urban environment of New York nurtured the works that incorporated ready-made or junk materials. He wrote, for instance, that "the city—New York above all others—has become a symbol of modern existence. The tempo of Manhattan, both as subject and conditioning milieu, has been instrumental in forming the art of our time." Moreover, Seitz situated Abstract Expressionism as the important precursor of assemblage art, hailing de Kooning's use of a picture of a magazine advertisement in his oil study as "[setting] the tone of the new collage"; "de Kooning recorded the impact of commercial culture on postwar art. Although he was surely not an isolated voice, he intensified the interest in 'pop culture'—in the expendable art and literature that became so important as a subject matter for Rauschenberg, Johns, [and] Conner.... For a new generation and in another spirit, de Kooning's adulterative gesture may have had an effect not unlike Picasso's in 1912."[68] In this linear, heroic trajectory that granted the authority of the avant-garde to prewar Paris and then shifted it to postwar New York, there was not much room for artists from other regions. As Rebecca Solnit argued in her study on postwar California artists, "Pop was a New York phenomenon, with precursors in England, France, and the West Coast, and it seems New York was happy to have the anointed avant-garde in its own backyard again."[69] Just as California artists such as Jay DeFeo, Edward Kienholz, and George Herms were included in the show but neglected again after 1961, European artists—Nouveaux Réalistes for the most part—were given little space in this New York-centric narrative.

Although some critical voices were raised against this rather hasty institutionalization of assemblage art,[70] Seitz completed his agenda with a public forum entitled "The Art of Assemblage: A Symposium." That Rauschenberg and Duchamp were among the panelists made sense, since Rauschenberg, the inventor of Combines, was the legitimate successor of Duchamp in Seitz's narrative. The other panelists included Lawrence Alloway, Richard Huelsenbeck, and Roger Shattuck. Although Seitz himself was the moderator, the panelists did not necessarily follow his agenda. While Shattuck considered Dada as basically a historical movement and was therefore skeptical of the validity of shock value in Neo-Dada, Rauschenberg adamantly rejected the idea of shock or negation itself as something valuable in art.[71] Nonetheless, the symposium established assemblage art—and hence the forthcoming Pop Art—as the latest trend from New York, which would subsequently be promoted overseas.

This direction was reaffirmed exactly one year later, in October 1962, when the Nouveaux Réalistes were shown again with American artists in the show "The New Realists" at the Sidney Janis Gallery (figure 1.9). Restany was, in fact, involved with the conception of this show; when Janis visited him in Paris in the spring of that year, they agreed that Janis should organize a show that would be a more precise and updated version of "The Art of Assemblage." After they agreed upon the title of the exhibition and the selection of European artists, Janis went back to New York to organize the American part of the show. However, Janis had his own agenda, as Restany would learn when he visited the city on his return from Tokyo, where he had been invited to participate in a memorial event for the late Yves Klein. He recalled the experience: "I understood everything in one glance. Farewell to Schwitters, farewell to Duchamp, farewell to the problem of object appropriation! Here was a great style of realistic presentation. The logical interlocutors of Parisian Nouveaux Réalistes (Rauschenberg, Johns, Stankiewicz, and Chamberlain) had been replaced by the most accomplished figures of the aesthetic-analytical line, whose expression reached definite clarity during that year: Oldenburg, Dine, Segal, Indiana, Lichtenstein, Warhol, and Rosenquist."[72] Next to the large American works that would soon be called Pop Art, the comparatively smaller works (both in size and number) by the Nouveaux Réalistes—including Tinguely, Klein, Arman, Christo, Hains, Raysse, Mimmo Rotella, and Daniel Spoerri—looked like "venerable ancestors."[73] A smattering of other European artists—Öyvind Fahlström and Per Olof Ultvedt from Sweden, Enrico Baj and Mario Schifano from Italy, and Peter Blake and John Lathem from England—did not alter this impression but perhaps augmented it.

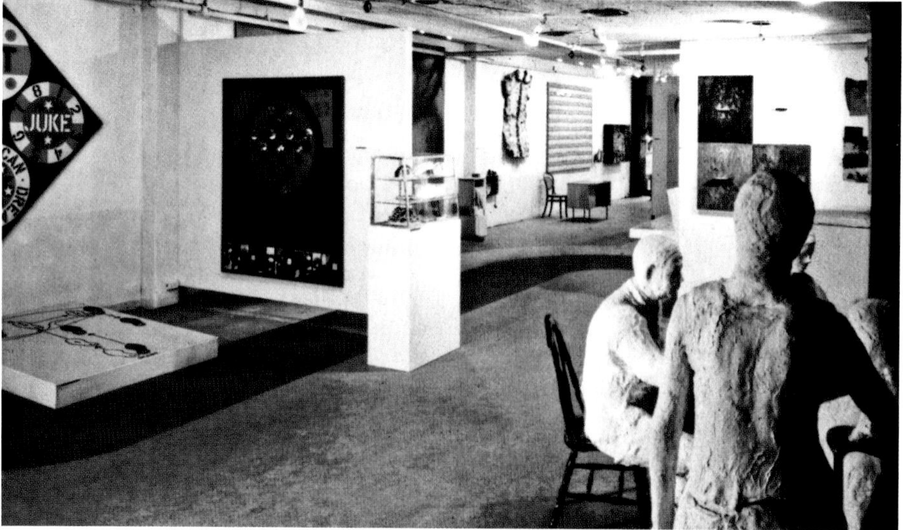

Figure 1.9
"The New Realists," installation view at the Sidney Janis Gallery, New York, 1962. Photograph by Eric Pollitzer; courtesy Carroll Janis Inc.

Moreover, Restany found that his essay for the exhibition catalog had been greatly shortened.[74] The lengthy comparison between Nouveau Réalisme and Neo-Dada, which Restany had repeated from his catalog essay for "Nouveau Réalisme à Paris et à New York," was considered irrelevant for a show that did not include any works by Johns or Rauschenberg. His favoring of European artists over Americans would have been unacceptable in New York in any case, since cultural provincialism was not only a French product; the majority of American critics, from Harold Rosenberg to Thomas Hess, judged European works to be weaker than American.[75] Restany set out for revenge, publishing "Le nouveau réalisme à la conquête de New York" in *Art International*, in which he called American Pop artists "young stylists" who had much to learn from the "more radical" Nouveaux Réalistes.[76] Despite this rhetoric of denial, Restany was well aware that "the game was won [by the Americans]: Pop Art, pop music, pop song—a veritable phenomenon of civilization. The forecasts came true at lightning speed."[77]

Similarly, the friendly relationship between Rauschenberg and the Nouveaux Réalistes came to an end with the collaborative project "Dynamisch Labyrint" (Dynamic Labyrinth; hereafter "Dylaby") at the Stedelijk Museum in Amsterdam in August and September of 1962. For this project, Willem Sandberg, the director of the museum, invited Rauschenberg, Tinguely, de Saint-Phalle, Ultvedt, Raysse, and Spoerri to work as a team to construct an environmental piece that could be walked through. To Rauschenberg's disappointment, however, each of the six artists ended up making his or her own room because of the difficulty of the collaboration. Rauschenberg felt frustrated by the others' unwillingness to work collectively on a single piece as well as by Tinguely's tendency to control and dominate the situation.[78] The conflict resulted not only from the clash of artistic egos but also from the cultural tension between the five European artists and Rauschenberg, the sole American. As Ultvedt recalled the experience, "No matter how hard we all tried to speak English, we ended up speaking French, which Bob did not understand. I guess he must have felt quite alienated."[79] After "Dylaby," Tinguely and Rauschenberg never worked together again.

MARKETING RAUSCHENBERG IN PARIS: GALERIE ILEANA SONNABEND

As the utopian conception of transatlantic art exchange was coming to an end, Ileana Sonnabend opened her gallery in Paris in November 1962. After her divorce from Castelli in 1959, she had married Michael Sonnabend, an amateur Dante scholar she had met at Columbia University. She moved to Europe with him in 1960 to seek her own life as an art dealer—or, in Robert Pincus-Witten's words, "to be someone other than 'Mrs. Castelli.'"[80] After a fruitless attempt to arouse the interest of Roman art galleries in American art, she visited the 1962 Venice Biennale, where she sought advice from Annette Michelson. In those days, Michelson lived in Paris and wrote art criticism, serving as a correspondent for *Arts Magazine* and *Art International*. A formalist critic at the time, she knew little about Sonnabend's artists and did not care much for the work that she did know. Reviewing photos of their art, though, she saw that Sonnabend had a "consistent program."[81] Michelson thus advised her to open her own gallery in Paris rather than trying to find a French art dealer who might be interested in showing them.

Had she tried, Sonnabend would have had a hard time finding such a dealer in Paris. Since the 1952 Pollock show at Galerie Paul Facchetti, few commercial art galleries in Paris had shown American artists other than those who lived in the city. It was exceptional that Johns and Rauschenberg, thanks to Castelli's connection with French art dealers, had been given solo shows in Paris at a very early stage of their careers. In 1962, in fact, there were only two galleries that specialized in contemporary American art in Paris. At Galerie Neufville, Lawrence Rubin showed Color Field painters such as Morris Louis and Kenneth Noland, while David K. Anderson, the son of Martha Jackson, opened Galerie Anderson-Mayer in 1962 to deal with Abstract Expressionism. In a market where collectors were not even buying French contemporary art, both Rubin and Anderson had great difficulty cultivating interest in American artists.[82]

In this situation, Sonnabend decided to follow Michelson's advice in a rather modest manner. According to Antonio Homem, her son-in-law, her initial plan was to rent a small place on a monthly basis, put on shows of American art, gain some recognition for her artists in Paris, and then close the gallery to go back to U.S.[83] All she wanted to do was to show works by the artists she already had on her roster. She had no grand scheme of usurping the French hegemony in the world art scene, as she would later be accused of. Nonetheless, she was clearly aware of the historical significance of what she was doing. Showing in Europe during the early stage of their careers was something Abstract Expressionists had not done in the 1940s or 1950s, both because they lacked the opportunity and because they had mixed feelings about the European art scene. Sonnabend made this point clear to Tomkins:

> I wanted Bob's and Jasper's work to be seen *then*, in Europe. The first year of my gallery in Paris was really important to art history, I feel. This was 1962. The first show was of Jasper's *Flags*. The second was Bob Rauschenberg's. Then shortly after came Lichtenstein, Warhol, and the others. It was revolutionary. People were shocked but very enthusiastic. The gallery was full every day. We thought we would just be there for a year, show these things and then leave, come back to New York. But it didn't happen.[84]

Thus, the opening of Galerie Ileana Sonnabend "marked a new era for the relationship of American art to Europe."[85]

What differentiated Sonnabend's gallery from Rubin's and Anderson's was the total support she received from Castelli in New York. Keen on expanding a market for his artists outside New York, Castelli had already lent the entire Rauschenberg show to Galerie Daniel Cordier in Paris in 1961 and to the Virginia Dwan Gallery in Los Angeles in March 1962. For these shows, he covered the shipping and insurance costs and waived his own commission on sales.[86] Castelli not only did the same for Sonnabend but also put a self-imposed restriction on his own business—to the great annoyance of Ivan Karp, then his gallery manager—so that she could monopolize the market for her artists in Europe. Although this generous gesture was meant to improve their post-divorce relationship, it was also a wise marketing move for American art in Europe. As Castelli recollected:

> I think that, in the long run, this disciplined sacrifice that I imposed upon myself not to deal with any Europeans—dealers or collectors or even Americans that went to Paris and would buy these Rauschenberg or Johns instead of buying here—were immensely useful in the end. Because that sort of monopoly she had for several years did create a market. Otherwise, it would have been all very imprecise. She gave that whole structure through post–Abstract Expressionism.[87]

It would be wrong, however, to assume that Galerie Ileana Sonnabend was essentially Castelli's satellite gallery in Paris, succeeding only thanks to his help and generosity. As the initial success of Castelli's own gallery is often attributed to the combination of his "good ear" and Sonnabend's "good eye,"[88] her artistic sensibility and keen sense for detecting an artist's talent were quite independent. In Paris, too, Sonnabend exercised her talent in her own way, making her European monopoly more solid through arrangements with Sidney Janis and directly with some other artists.

In November 1962, Sonnabend inaugurated her Paris gallery with Johns's *Flags*. She wrote to Castelli about the gallery's less than satisfactory beginning:

> Jap's opening was a great success. A lot of people came, drank champagne, admired what they could see of the show—some said it was the first time they saw Jap this way, i.e. could follow his development.... Unfortunately, very few visitors came since. It seems that collectors have stopped collecting in Europe (over $1,000, I mean).... I spent $1,500 on publicity and might do more—$600 of announcements and there you are! Not a chance in the world to come out even.[89]

Undaunted by the grim commercial prospect, Sonnabend continued to mount shows of American artists, with some Europeans. Her shows from the gallery's opening to the beginning of 1965 included:

November 1962	"Jasper Johns"
February 1963	"Robert Rauschenberg, Première exposition (oeuvres 1954–1961)"
February–March 1963	"Robert Rauschenberg, Seconde exposition (oeuvres 1962–1963)"
March 1963	"Jim Dine"
April 1963	"Mario Schifano"
May 1963	"Pop art américain" (figure 1.10)
June 1963	"Roy Lichtenstein"

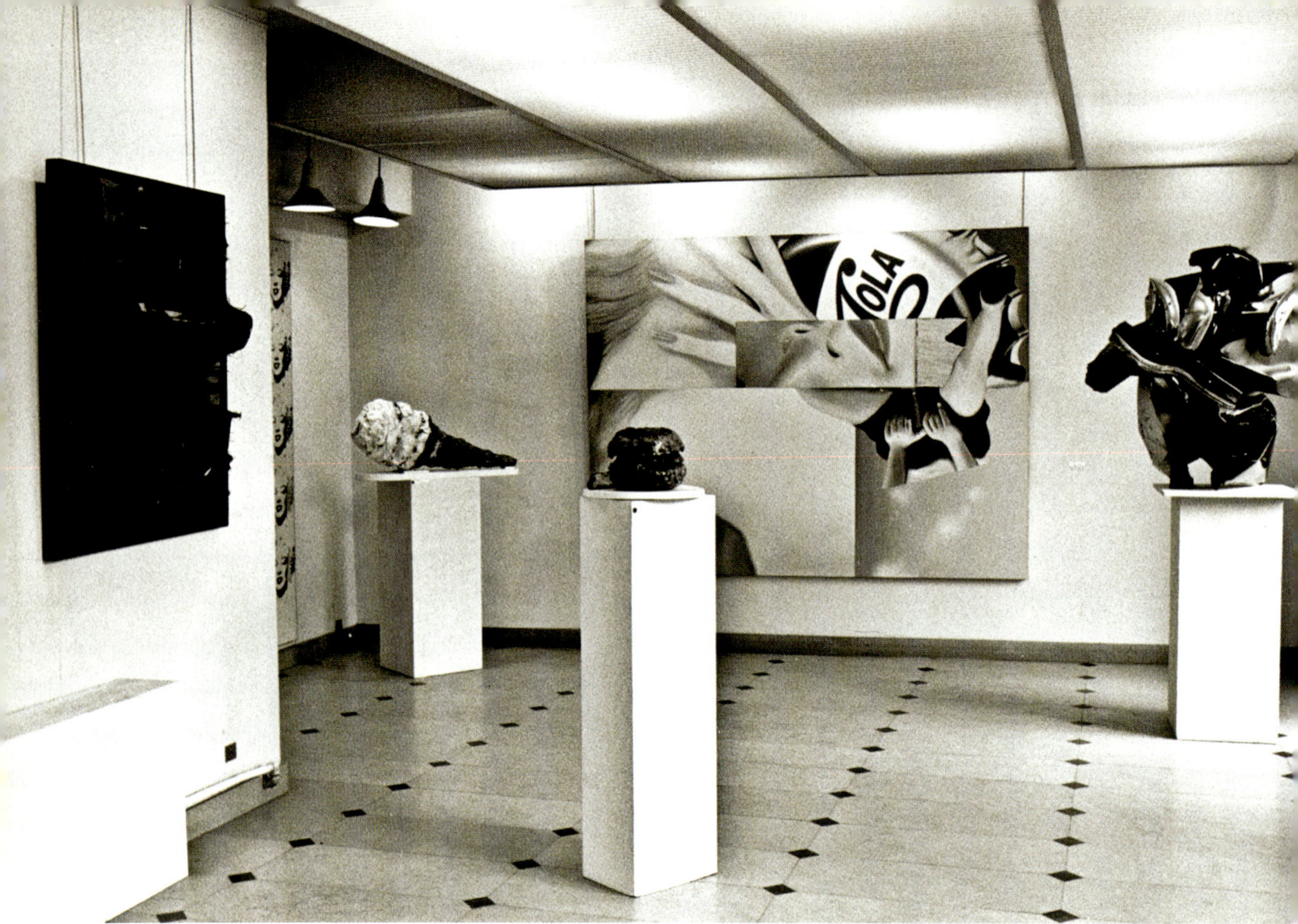

Figure 1.10
"Pop art américain," installation view at Galerie Ileana Sonnabend, Paris, 1963. From left to right: *Untitled* by Lee Bontecou; *Black and White Marilyns* by Andy Warhol; *Ice Cream Cone* and *Hamburger* by Claes Oldenburg; *Vestigial Appendage* by James Rosenquist; and *Butternut* by John Chamberlain. Photograph courtesy Sonnabend Gallery.

October–November 1963	"George Segal"
November 1963	"Dessins pop"
January–February 1964	"Andy Warhol"
March 1964	"Michelangelo Pistoletto"
April–May 1964	"John Chamberlain"
May 1964	"Robert Rauschenberg"
June 1964	"James Rosenquist"
October 1964	"Claes Oldenburg"
December 1964–January 1965	"Robert Rauschenberg: *Untitled* 1953–1954 and Thirty-four Dante Drawings"

As evident from this list, in a little more than two years since opening her gallery, Sonnabend showed the Parisian audience the grand narrative of post–Abstract Expressionist art in America, from Rauschenberg and Johns to the Pop Art craze. Even Castelli had not achieved such a feat at that time, since he did not have a unified monopoly on Pop artists; in New York, Dine was part of the Reuben Gallery, Oldenburg was with the Green Gallery, and Warhol and Rosenquist only joined the Castelli Gallery in late 1964.

Because she was originally planning to promote American artists in Paris for only a brief period, Sonnabend spared no cost for publicity to achieve her goal. The "$1,500 on publicity" and "$600 of announcements" mentioned in her letter to Castelli reveal only a fraction of her publicity efforts. She put posters for her shows not only on billboards but also on a sort of signboard called a "mast," a tall street pole that had two rectangular surfaces on opposite sides for displaying advertisements. Since the "mast" was very expensive and was usually used to advertise large museum exhibitions, it was quite unusual for a small commercial gallery to rent space for a poster there.[90] Moreover, Sonnabend published a high-quality catalog for each show, with illustrations and essays by both French and American critics. The catalogs were part of her strategy to foster the understanding of American art by providing her European audience with a chance to read about it as well as to see it.

Beyond the expenses Sonnabend lavished, her promotion of American art in Paris was highly systematic, as she created her own Castelli-like team in Europe. Here is how "Team Ileana Sonnabend" worked. As the dealer, Sonnabend showed American Neo-Dada and Pop Art in her gallery in Paris. Collectors such as Giuseppe Panza in Milan and Peter Ludwig in Cologne bought these works in large numbers. The museum directors, such as Pontus Hultén of the Moderna Museet in Stockholm and Edy de Wilde of the Stedelijk Museum in Amsterdam (who succeeded Sandberg in the beginning of 1963), included the American artists in their exhibitions and acquired such important works by Rauschenberg as *Monogram* and *Charlene* (1954) for their museum collections. Finally, sympathetic French critics such as Michel Ragon and Alain Jouffroy supported Sonnabend's project by writing for catalogs and reviewing her shows in art journals.

In addition, Sonnabend made sure that most of her shows would be seen elsewhere in Europe, at sympathetic galleries in Milan, Rome, Zurich, Munich, and Cologne.[91] As a result, Rauschenberg became an object of admiration among young artists in those cities. In this sense, it can be said that Sonnabend began where Speyer left off. Whereas Speyer was not allowed to circulate her exhibitions outside France because of the public nature of her job, Sonnabend was free to make connections with dealers and collectors in other European cities. This was crucially important for Sonnabend's business, for it was increasingly clear that while Paris was a good place to show her artists, it was not a good market for selling. Even though she failed commercially in Paris—"Only ten per cent of our clientele then and now was French,"[92] she stated in 1976—she was able to reach other European dealers and collectors interested in American art with her systematic "team" operation.

Sonnabend's success sharply contrasts with Restany's failure in their respective marketing endeavors. Above all, Restany lacked an effective mode of operations and the transatlantic network that Sonnabend had. Although he had contacts with galleries in Milan and Düsseldorf, where he arranged a Nouveau Réalisme show, the movement's importance to Italian monochrome artists such as Piero Manzoni or Gruppe Zero in Germany did not translate to the other side of the Atlantic.[93] Once again, the Paris–New York rivalry played a role in his failure to open a market for Nouveaux Réalistes, even before the show "The New Realists." When Klein had his first (and last) solo show at Castelli's gallery in 1961, he found the New York audience—including Castelli himself—unsympathetic to his theory of monochrome paintings. Arman, who had a show at the Cordier-Warren Gallery the same year, also found a change in Rauschenberg, with whom he thought he had become good friends in Paris; the American artist reportedly told him, "The automatic repetition is not a creation."[94]

Meanwhile, Rauschenberg occupied *the* central place in Sonnabend's gallery operations as her favorite artist. His two-part exhibition took place from February to March 1963. The first exhibition featured important Combines such as *Charlene* and *Monogram* from the fifties, while the second showed the artist's most recent silkscreen paintings (figures 1.11, 1.12). With twenty-six works altogether by the artist, this two-part show was in effect a retrospective, which preceded his first museum retrospective at the Jewish Museum in New York at the end of March 1963. Aware of the importance and impact of the show, Sonnabend produced a full-blown catalog, which included a number of reproductions of Rauschenberg's work, Jouffroy's introduction, and a reprint of the *Arts* interview from two years earlier, along with previous writings on the artist by Lawrence Alloway, Michel Ragon, Françoise Choay, Gillo Dorfles, and John Cage.

If his 1961 exhibition at Galerie Daniel Cordier had established Rauschenberg's reputation in Paris, the 1963 show at Sonnabend decided his fame in the wider European art scene. This show was seen by many Europeans besides the French, who all responded to Rauschenberg's work—especially *Monogram*—with great enthusiasm.[95] Sonnabend recollected its opening:

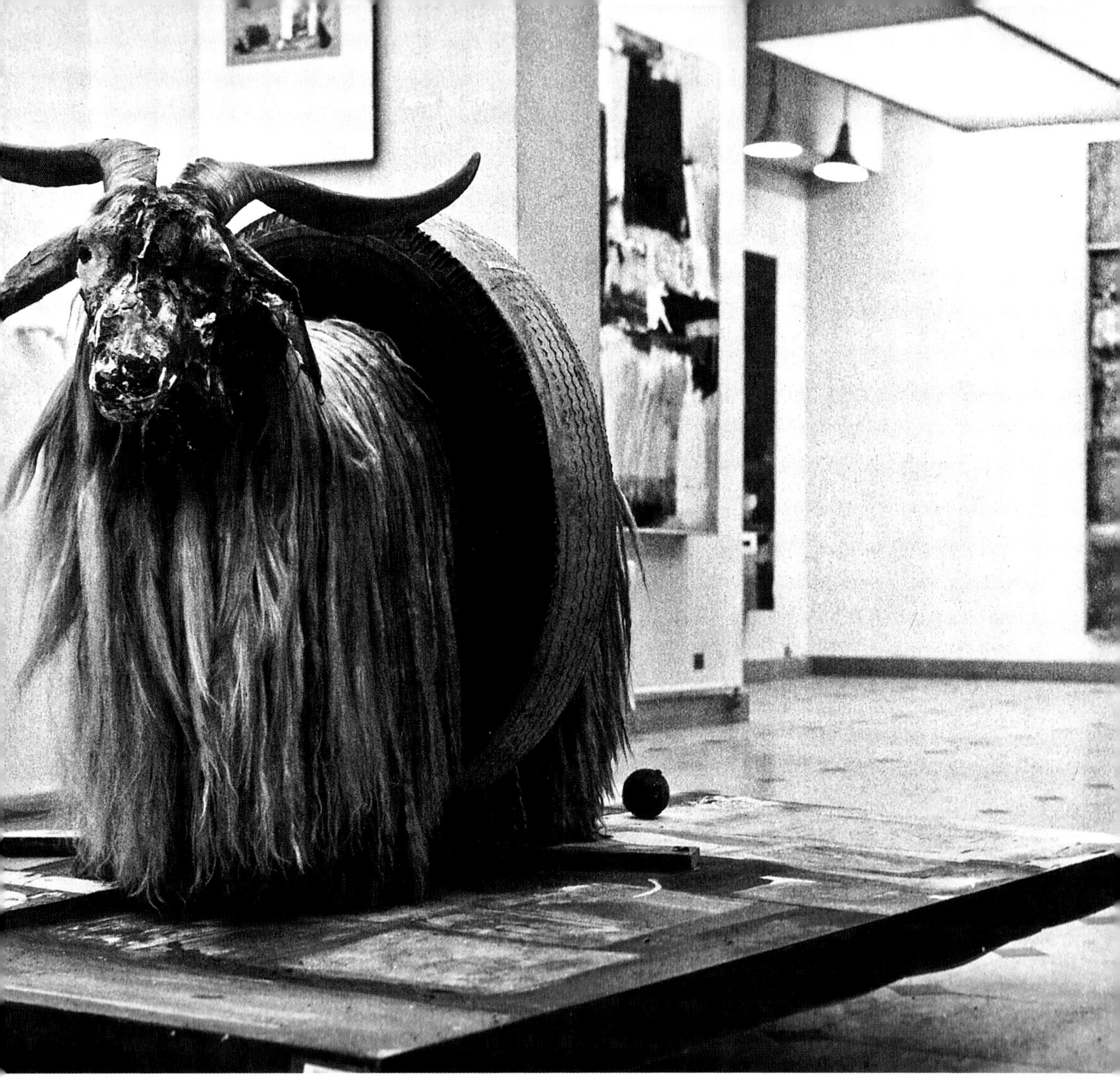

Figure 1.11
"Rauschenberg: Première exposition (oeuvres 1954–61)," installation view at Galerie Ileana Sonnabend, Paris, 1963. Photograph by Harry Shunk; Photo: Shunk-Kender, © Roy Lichtenstein Foundation.

> So at that point, there were lots of people in the gallery, lots of young people, lots of Swedes, Germans, and Dutch. And they were all very enthusiastic and he got a reception like a hero.... All the museum directors came by and looked at the work, and the director of the Stedelijk Museum was very enthusiastic and he immediately wanted to buy the biggest work called *Charlene*.... I didn't want to sell it to him because I hoped to keep it longer [laughs]. But he insisted very much and finally got it.... And Pontus Hultén bought the famous goat.[96]

Since both *Monogram* and *Charlene* were once considered for the Museum of Modern Art, New York, but never entered its collection,[97] the enthusiasm of European directors for Rauschenberg is quite noteworthy. Given such an unusually popular reception, it is not surprising that Sonnabend believed her series of shows prepared the way for Rauschenberg's winning the Grand Prize in the 1964 Venice Biennale. When asked what was so unique about Rauschenberg's work, Sonnabend once answered: "Well, it was much more apparent then that there was a break with Abstract Expressionism than it is now.... The fact he used paper—*found* papers, photographs, whatever, and incorporated it, also that he incorporated objects and *animals*, that was just unheard of! Also the way he worked with colors. It created quite a sensation. So indirectly, it prepared for the Biennale."[98]

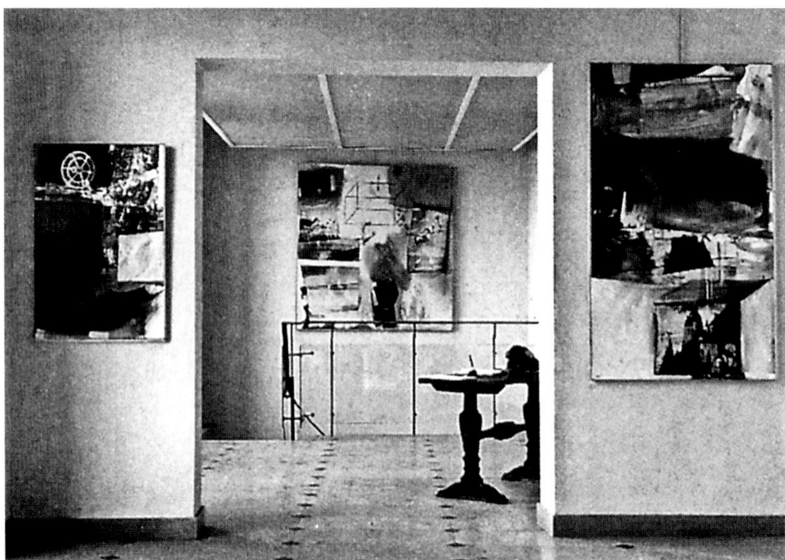

Figure 1.12
"Rauschenberg: Seconde exposition (oeuvres 1962–63)," installation view at Galerie Ileana Sonnabend, Paris, 1963. Photograph by Harry Shunk; Photo: Shunk-Kender, © Roy Lichtenstein Foundation.

By the beginning of 1964, then, Sonnabend was convinced that she had made a significant difference in the reception of American art in France. She discovered an article entitled "Pop Art and Happenings" by Otto Hahn in the literary journal *Les Temps Modernes*. In its January 1964 issue, Hahn presented Rauschenberg and Johns as the originators of Pop Art, affirming the relevance of this new trend from America: "For the first time, we are faced with a movement that extends the totality of the abstract heritage and attempts to elaborate a language in accordance with urban and industrial civilization. For that reason the experience is new and important."[99] Since the editor of *Les Temps Modernes* was Jean-Paul Sartre, whose anti-Americanism was widely known, the publication of this article was considered quite an achievement. Sonnabend wrote to Alan Solomon, who had just been appointed commissioner of the American Pavilion for that year's Venice Biennale: "This is a major change in thinking of European intellectual life and.... its repercussions will be felt and seen in six months from now"—that is, at the Venice Biennale in June.[100]

In this regard, Sonnabend's promotion of American Pop helped to create Rauschenberg's image as an established artist who already had a number of followers. Just before the Biennale opened, in May 1964, Sonnabend held another Rauschenberg show, which was again favorably received. Thanks to her efforts, Rauschenberg's critical reputation rose above those of the other American artists in Paris. Jouffroy published not only a long, eulogistic essay on Rauschenberg in the art monthly *L'Oeil*, but also a poem dedicated to his *Barge* (1962–1963)—a huge silkscreen painting produced in front of a television crew in New York—in another art journal, *Quadrum*.[101] Since Jouffroy's article came out in the May issue of *L'Oeil*, a month before the Biennale opened, Sonnabend could not have felt more convinced that her promotion of Rauschenberg prepared the way for his success in Venice.

Sonnabend's publicity campaign continued during the Biennale season. She put a full-page advertisement in the summer 1964 issue of *Art International* (figure 1.13), in which the back of a truck bears the names of the artists she handled. In September she placed another ad in the same journal, with an image of an envelope containing an invitation card with the names of her artists (figure 1.14). While the former ad provocatively represented the works by those American artists as commodities to be distributed in Europe, the latter cordially invited the European audience to see shows at her gallery. Taken together, the message was clear: "I am bringing these artists' work from America as a cultural gift to Paris. You are invited to see them." For the Biennale, she placed another full-page ad in *L'Oeil* (figure 1.15), in which the name "Rauschenberg" hovers in large print over the photogenic scenery of the Grand Canal of Venice, while the name of her gallery anchors the composition. If the two ads in *Art International* spoke about her mission, the one in *L'Oeil* predicted its result: thanks in part to Sonnabend's promotion of American artists in Paris, Rauschenberg would extend his triumph to Venice. The mission would be accomplished.

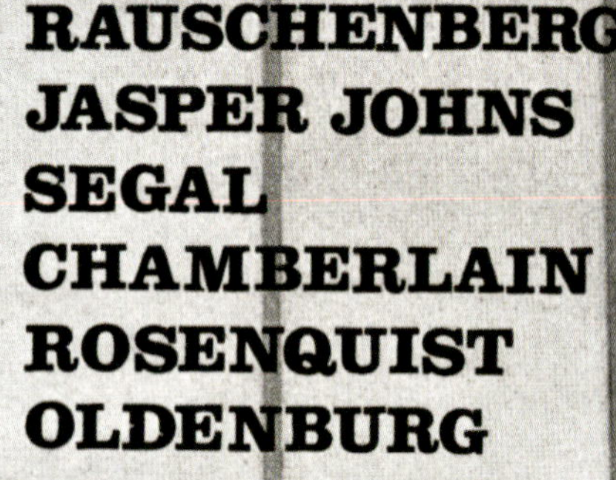
RAUSCHENBERG
JASPER JOHNS
SEGAL
CHAMBERLAIN
ROSENQUIST
OLDENBURG
DINE
WARHOL
LICHTENSTEIN
BONTECOU
PISTOLETTO
WESSELMAN
ILEANA SONNABEND
PARIS

75
3368
CG 13

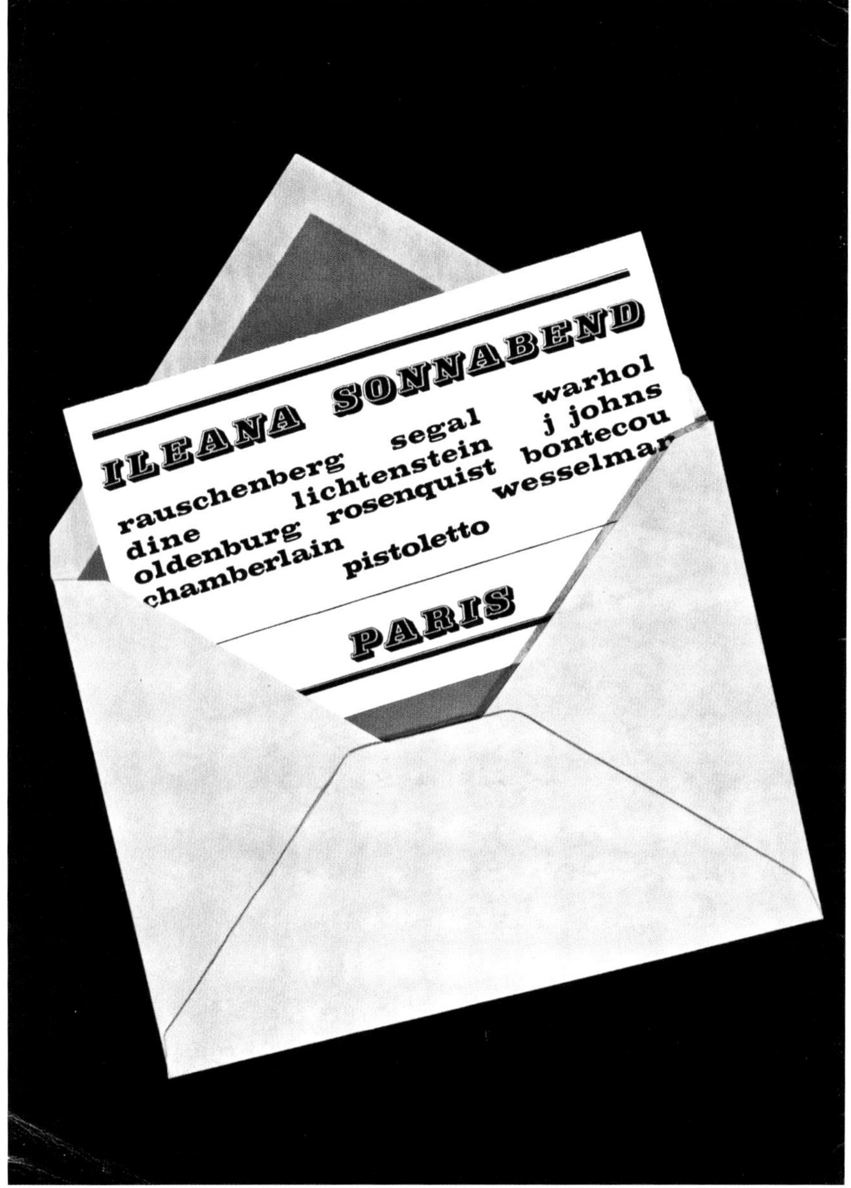

Figure 1.13
Advertisement for Galerie Ileana Sonnabend, *Art International* 8, nos. 5–6 (Summer 1964). Courtesy Sonnabend Gallery.

Figure 1.14
Advertisement for Galerie Ileana Sonnabend, *Art International* 8, no. 7 (September 1964). Courtesy Sonnabend Gallery.

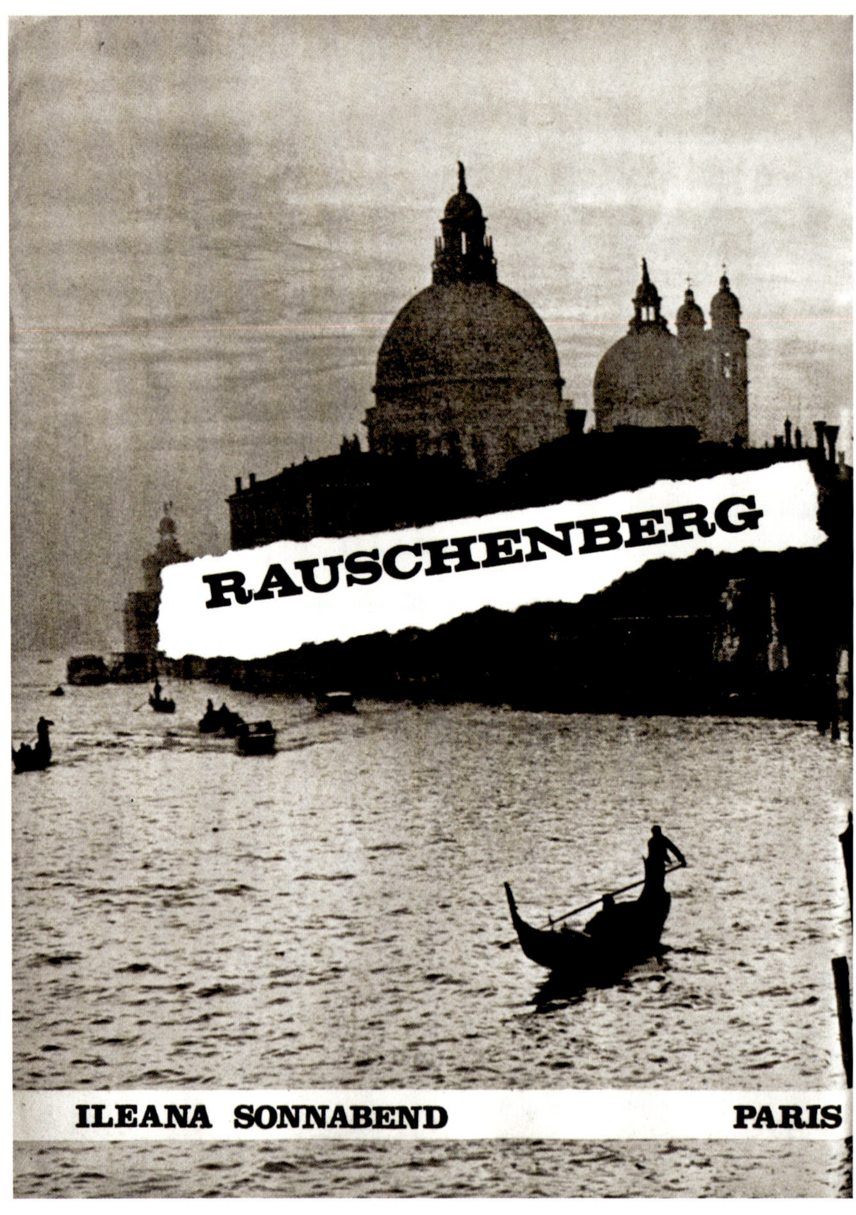

Figure 1.15
Advertisement for Galerie Ileana Sonnabend, *L'Oeil*, nos. 115–116 (July–August 1964). Courtesy Sonnabend Gallery.

RESENTING THE AMERICAN TRIUMPH IN VENICE: PARISIAN RESPONSES

As Sonnabend took the lead campaigning role with a firm belief in his art, Rauschenberg was a passive participant in his success in Paris. The same holds true for his winning of the Grand Prize at the 1964 Venice Biennale. As chapter 2 will elucidate, it was mainly Alan Solomon's strategic curatorship and publicity that engineered the American victory. When Rauschenberg returned to Paris in July on his way to England for Merce Cunningham's world tour, he was stunned by the French press's vehement reactions to his triumph in Venice. One day, a friend of Michel Ragon saw an elegant, young American man crying on the street in Saint-Germain-des-Prés, whom he recognized—with surprise—as Rauschenberg.[102] The artist did not expect such a negative response to his Grand Prize from a city that had previously embraced his art so adoringly.

In light of Rauschenberg's strong reputation in Paris at the time, the city's antagonistic response seems incomprehensible, especially because France did not participate in the competition for the Grand Prize in painting that year. Roger Bissière, the presumed French candidate, had asked to be placed outside the prize competition from the beginning.[103] In actuality, the French press was less resentful about Rauschenberg's winning the prize than about Solomon's aggressive tactics. In particular, his pronouncement of the "shift" of the world's art center from Paris to New York irked the French press, which took the statement literally as an American "declaration of war."[104] *Arts*, carrying the front-page headline "Venice Colonized by America," ran the most vehement review, Pierre Cabanne's "In Venice, America Proclaims the End of the École de Paris and Launches Pop Art to Colonize Europe" (figure 1.16), and the French press repeatedly insinuated that Rauschenberg's award was the payoff for the Americans' financial support of the Biennale (despite the lack of evidence for this assumption).[105]

Sonnabend was in fact gravely implicated in this "war," as she was present in Venice to help Solomon and very much involved with his game. At Caffè Florian on Piazza San Marco, where the Biennale crowd would often gather to discuss their business, she told her husband, Michael Sonnabend, "I hate this game of politics that goes on here, but I think if we are going to play it at all, we should play it right."[106] Perceived as part of the American plot, she became a target of French accusations, as she recollected: "At that point, all the French, well, not all of them, but many of the French officials that I knew were very upset with me.... They thought that it was the CIA who organized all this [laughs]. Some even came to me and said, 'How could you betray us like that?' but I didn't think I was betraying them. But they were crying, literally crying."[107]

French critics found American "cultural nationalism and artistic xenophobia" to be unfair, because the Parisian art scene had received American art with increasing interest and favor over the previous few years.[108] Furthermore, they found it outrageous that the other European countries seemed to join the American effort. While Alain Bosquet accused "American-German-Italian-Nordic armies" for "having killed" the École de Paris,[109] Restany claimed that the "Rome–New York axis"—in both ideological and aesthetic terms—

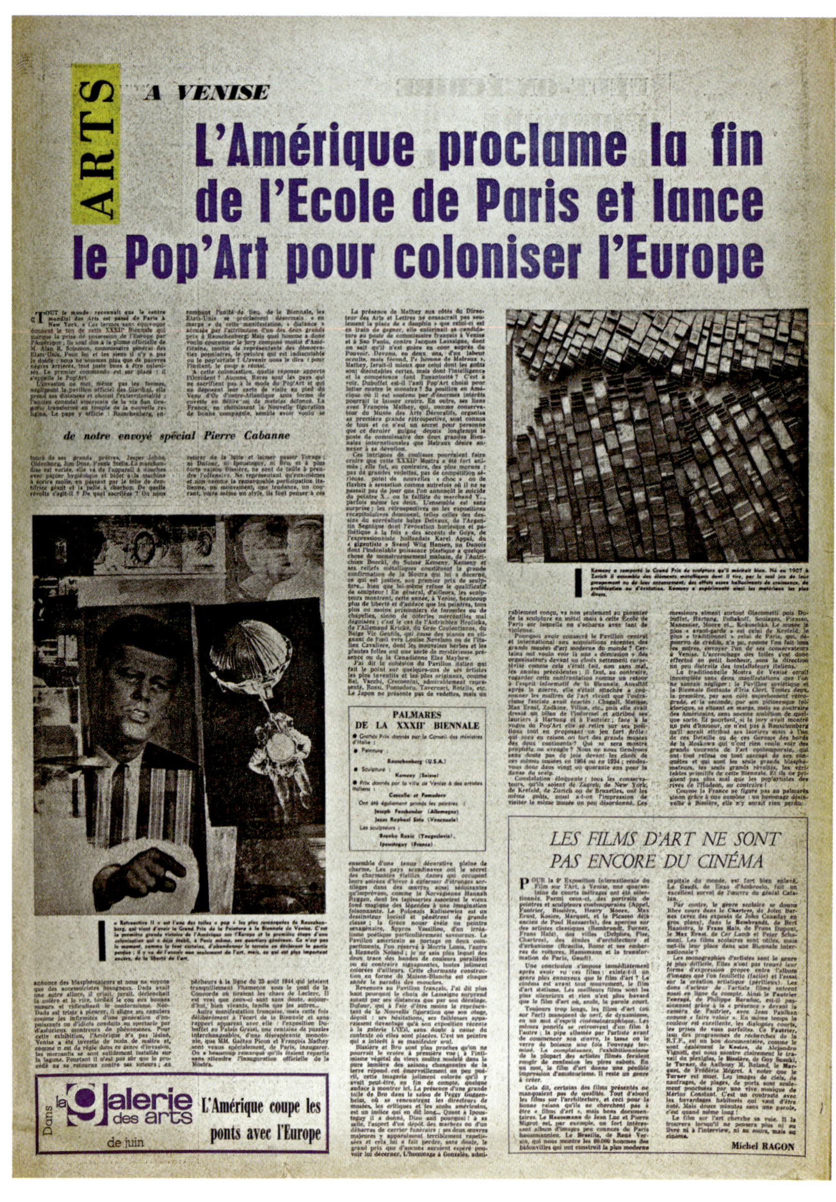

ARTS

A VENISE

L'Amérique proclame la fin de l'Ecole de Paris et lance le Pop'Art pour coloniser l'Europe

de notre envoyé spécial Pierre Cabanne

PALMARES DE LA XXXIIe BIENNALE

LES FILMS D'ART NE SONT PAS ENCORE DU CINÉMA

Michel RAGON

Dans la Galerie des arts de juin

L'Amérique coupe les ponts avec l'Europe

Figure 1.16
Pierre Cabanne, "À Venise, L'Amérique proclame la fin de l'Ecole de Paris et lance le Pop'Art pour coloniser l'Europe," *Arts*, no. 968 (June 24–30, 1964). © Photos Guy Carrard–Centre Pompidou–MnamCci–Bibliothèque Kandinsky.

had set the tone for the 1964 Venice Biennale.[110] A statement by Jean-Robert Arnaud in *Cimaise*, which happened to publish its third special issue on American art at the time of the Biennale, summed up the sentiment: "We at *Cimaise* were among the first to rejoice in the emergence of New York as a cultural center. But we saw in it only the beginning of a fruitful coexistence and not a fight to the death."[111]

What made the lack of a Grand Prize for France that year particularly painful was that it coincided with the decline of the Paris art market. As Cabanne reported in his article "How France Lost First Place in the International Art Market," the sales total of the art market in Paris was surpassed by that of London by the end of 1961 and continued to decrease, even though most of the works sold were French modern art.[112] In the market for contemporary avant-garde art, the situation was even worse. Just before the Biennale opened, Cordier closed his gallery. In a public statement that he released shortly afterward, Cordier blamed the Parisian art community for the demise of his gallery. Listing among the city's negative factors the conservative backwardness of French collectors, "the ridiculousness of the official Salons, [and] the irresponsible purchasing policy of the Musée d'Art Moderne," he complained that Paris "is not built to the scale of modern civilization, but is becoming a vacation spot and amusement center, and less and less a place for creation." He compared the situation in Paris to the lively environment in New York, concluding that such differences between the two cities "explain why New York, after having been a market, may become a preponderant cultural center."[113]

Ragon observed of the grim Parisian art scene as well: "Instead of fighting back, France falls into lack of confidence. Daniel Cordier closes his gallery, abandoning Paris to tourism in order to work for his gallery in New York. A certain number of young painters, no longer seeing American clients debarking on French land, go to install themselves in New York. In Paris, it's panic. No season was as calm and feeble as this year."[114] In this situation, Solomon's statement at the Biennale, precisely because it rang true, was interpreted as "rubbing salt in an open wound."[115] The American poet John Ashbery, who was working as an art critic in Paris at the time, pointed out that Rauschenberg's winning the Grand Prize had become "a scapegoat [that] was needed to account for the failures of the past season" in Paris.[116] Aware of the possible ramifications of Solomon's words, Sonnabend had advised him not to publish such a belligerent statement. After the Biennale, she wrote to him: "Here we are, back in Paris, submerged in the gallery business and almost drowned by the deluge of venom and resentment of the Press. Although I am still alarmed about the effect of all this on our existence here, I am beginning to see your point. The abscess had to be punctured. The shrieking reactions here make me appreciate your integrity all the more."[117] Appropriately enough, a touring exhibition of American art, "Art USA Now," was being shown then at the Musée d'Art Moderne de la Ville de Paris. According to a reviewer in *Cimaise*, the sight of Rauschenberg's work under the exhibition's banner "quickly convinced the viewer that our municipal museum of modern art has finally come to terms with reality."[118]

The 1964 Venice Biennale thus became an occasion for a reality check by Parisian critics. For instance, Ragon stated that the École de Paris was now being made to pay for its mistakes in having ignored the art of other countries,[119] while Hahn calmly opined that he was "for the Paris–New York battle, as far as it makes the public in France open their eyes to what goes on around them."[120] Even Restany, whose writing is usually tainted with nationalism, clearly recognized the situation: "Despite the presence of an active avant-garde and the warnings from some clear-headed observers, Paris is, in effect, becoming an isolated province in the international context, which is going through a radical revolution. This tendency toward isolation will only accentuate itself unless adequate measures are taken at all levels of organizations, in coordination with the structure of artistic life."[121] Faced with this crisis, *Arts* organized a special issue in which a variety of dealers, artists, and critics discussed the term "École de Paris" and its significance. The result was rather disheartening: the questionnaire revealed that there was no agreement on what the term meant or whether the term should be used at all to promote the post-1945 Parisian art scene. In fact, the debate over the definition and validity of the term was an old one; *Cimaise* had published a series of articles on the issue from 1955 to 1956.[122] The resumption of the same debate in *Arts*, involving more people this time, only confirmed the impossibility of solidarity among French artists and critics. The artistic and political positions of those in the Parisian art community were too diversified to create a unified front, even at a time of crisis in their own cultural milieu.

Parisians' negative responses to the American triumph at the Venice Biennale proved that there was a price to be paid for Rauschenberg's world success. After describing the episode of the artist's crying in public, Ragon questioned the French attitude toward his victory in Venice: "If, after all, there was an American conspiracy in Venice, wasn't there French machination? Why is it necessary to insult Americans because their methods were more effective than ours? And Rauschenberg in all of this, where is his fault? Being the winner, or being an American? We didn't even bother to learn whether he was a good painter or not."[123] But they had known he was a "good painter" since his first solo show in Paris in 1961—a reputation that never flagged until the scandal in Venice. In the end, therefore, Rauschenberg emerged triumphant out of this discursive debacle. In June 1965, exactly one year after the 1964 Venice Biennale, *Arts* ran a special issue on "The Ten Greatest Artists That Emerged during the Past Twenty Years," in which he was ranked as the "greatest."[124] *Arts* had asked one hundred well-informed people in the Parisian art community to list the most important living artists under the age of fifty. Rauschenberg, the sole American among the ten artists, scored more votes than any of his European peers. Thus, the virtue of his art was acknowledged in Paris even after the scandal in Venice.

As mentioned earlier, however, this success in Paris was by no means a commercial one, for there were no works by Rauschenberg or other American artists in public French collections as of 1965. Moreover, Sonnabend's monopoly on American art in the European market did not last long. During the latter half of the sixties, Castelli gradually gave in to increasing pressure from his European clients, who wanted to buy American artworks directly from him. With the demise of her monopoly, Sonnabend faced a crisis at the end of the 1960s because she was receiving few works from Castelli.[125] Although she would keep her Paris gallery until 1980, Sonnabend eventually went back to New York to devote herself to another mission, that of promoting contemporary European artists in the United States.

In the larger narrative, the importance of Paris for American art lay in its pivotal role as a way station to other cities in Europe. This was clearly manifested in the distribution of American art in European collections. By 1968, most American art in European public collections was housed in museums in Cologne, Stockholm, Amsterdam, and London, whereas Paris had only two pieces—one by Louise Nevelson and one by Mark Rothko.[126] Sonnabend's real contribution thus lies in her engineering the critical success of American art in Paris, which subsequently translated into commercial success elsewhere in Europe. She certainly did not plan it that way, but her effort contributed to the end of Paris's prominence as the capital of world art.

In this vastly changed map of the international art world, Rauschenberg emerged as a global celebrity after his Grand Prize in Venice. For him, this celebrity was in fact a double-edged sword. Although the prize established his reputation, the very concept of "being established" did not sit well with an artist who sought to be cutting-edge, avant-garde, and somehow outside the establishment. From then on, he was bound to carry the cultural and political baggage of being the "representative American artist" wherever he traveled—a burden that contributed to the tears he shed on the Paris street in July 1964. It is therefore necessary to turn the discussion to the 1964 Venice Biennale, the dynamics of which were far more complicated than has hitherto been assumed.

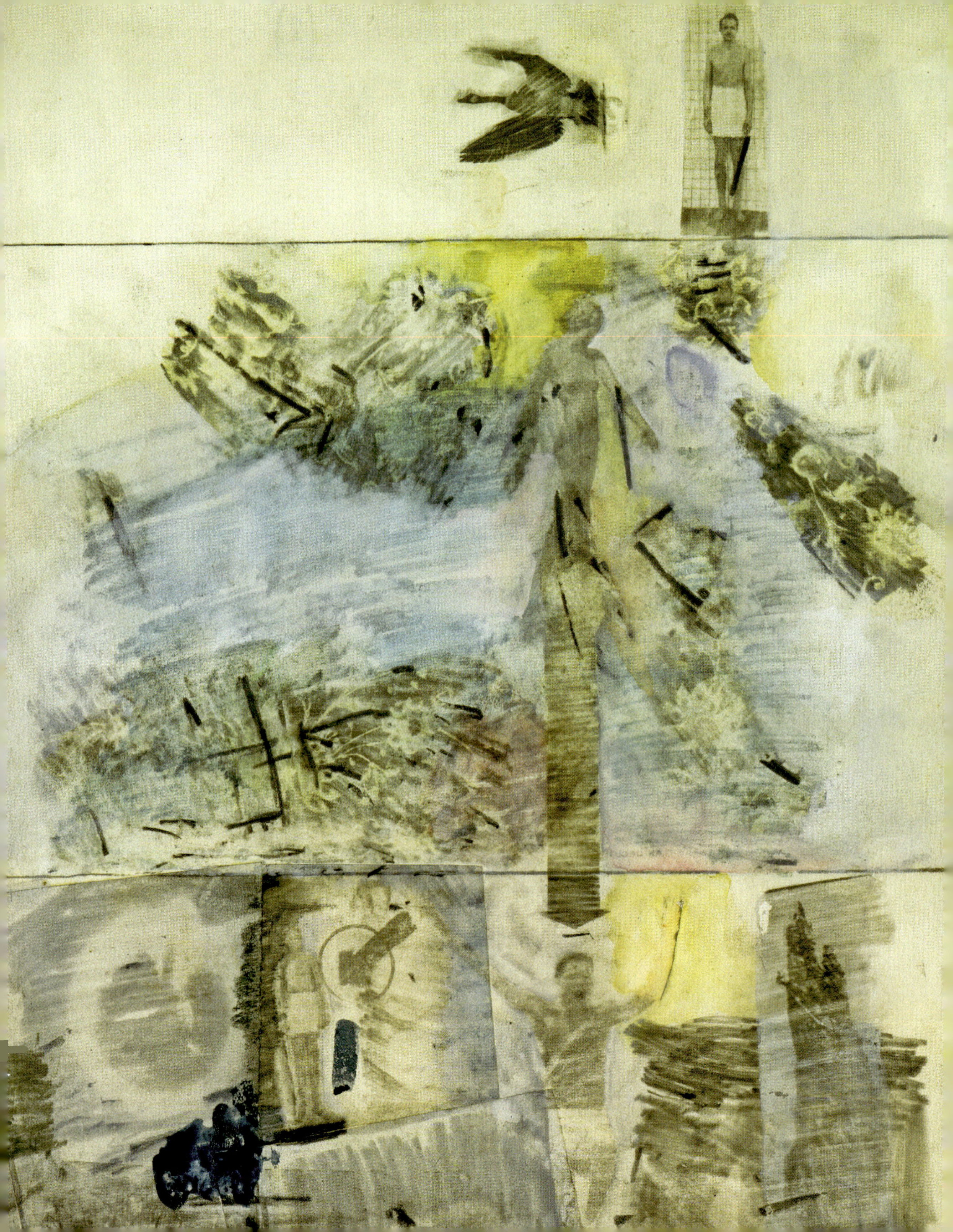

2

A SPECTACLE IN VENICE

INSIDE AND OUTSIDE RAUSCHENBERG'S VICTORY

When Rauschenberg arrived in Venice with the Merce Cunningham Dance Company on June 17, 1964, he was already the focus of attention at the 1964 Venice Biennale. The celebrated world art festival was to open in a few days and the jury was still discussing who should be awarded the International Grand Prize in Painting, for which the American artist was the strongest candidate. Under discussion was the question of Rauschenberg's eligibility, since most of his works were exhibited not at the American Pavilion in the Giardini, the official Biennale site, but at the former American Consulate. This irregularity caused a heated debate among the jury and others involved with that year's Biennale. Aware of the situation, Rauschenberg decided "to stay out of the politics": although he had been asked by Castelli to come to Venice a few days earlier to appear on a radio program, he deliberately did not participate.[1]

Despite the artist's efforts to stay out of the political fray, it followed him to the dance company's performance, which took place on the evening of June 18 at La Fenice, a grandiose rococo theater, the most prestigious venue in Venice. Calvin Tomkins, reporting on the Biennale for *Harper's*, described the event: "Booing, loud whistling, and passionate counter-cheering swept the exquisite, gilded theater during and after each dance."[2] Those voices "reached a new pitch, becoming positively warlike" when Rauschenberg appeared onstage with the dancers for one of many curtain calls.[3] Despite the jeering, the company's performance had a favorable impact on the Biennale jury's decision. Carolyn Brown, one of the *étoiles* of Cunningham's company, recollects how Rauschenberg's set and costumes stunned not only the audience but also the dancers themselves:

> The *Summerscape* pointillist drop cloth looked magnificent. *Story* was fantastic. Bob went wild: Trapdoors opened, stage levels rose and lowered, light bars flew in and out, the 'legs' disappeared into the flies, and stagehands moved about in the background, changing props, pushing brooms. The work, thus presented, took on a completely different dimension, not just visually but dramatically as well. We dancers were as amazed and dazzled by the spectacle as the audience was.[4]

Impressed by Rauschenberg's contribution as well as by his commitment as a stage manager and lighting director, the president of the jury, who had been opposed to giving the prize to the artist, conceded.[5] The jury decided in favor of Rauschenberg the next day on the condition that three of his paintings would be transferred from the Consulate to the Giardini. On June 20, Rauschenberg was officially announced as the Grand Prize winner—the first American recipient in the history of the Venice Biennale—at the award ceremony (figure 2.1).

That night, Tomkins witnessed the enthused celebration of Rauschenberg's victory by Italian artists:

> When Rauschenberg finally appeared there [Piazza San Marco] the whole group surged forward with a great shout. Seven or eight Italian artists reached him first, embracing him and shaking his hand and lifting him on their shoulders, and the young American was so surprised and so moved that for a moment he looked to be in some distress. "I hadn't expected that," he said afterward. "Butterflies in the stomach and a big lump in the throat. It really did mean something after all."[6]

Although Rauschenberg's personal experience of the 1964 Biennale by no means constitutes the whole story, these episodes point to the limitations of a currently prevalent interpretation of this landmark event in postwar art history. Since the 1964 Biennale was the first in which the United States government assumed official sponsorship for the American Pavilion, Rauschenberg's award has been considered an outcome of American cultural diplomacy during the Cold War.[7] However, as the Italian artists' embrace of Rauschenberg indicates, neither "Europe" nor "America" was monolithic in the art world's cartography in 1964. Even commissioner Alan Solomon was more than a vehicle of the American government or the American art community in general, as he had his own agenda to achieve in Venice. An examination of Solomon's role and idea for the American presentation is thus vital for understanding the global implications of the 1964 Biennale. His revelatory exhibition became what one could call an "American spectacle," in which numerous intersecting interests worked together to establish the preeminence of American art in the global art scene.

ALAN SOLOMON AND "THE NEW AMERICAN ART"

Alan Solomon was by far the most important player among those who engineered Rauschenberg's victory at the 1964 Biennale. Born in Massachusetts and educated at Harvard, Solomon began his career at Cornell University, where he founded the Andrew Dickson White Museum of Art in 1953 and served as its director until 1961. It was during his tenure at Cornell that he became aware of Rauschenberg: in 1958 he visited Rauschenberg's first show at the Leo Castelli Gallery and acquired a painting for the museum at Cornell. This purchase marked the first Rauschenberg work to enter a public collection.[8] Solomon's taste in post–Abstract Expressionist art came to the attention of the Jewish Museum in New York when it was planning to build a new gallery space for contemporary art. In 1962, Solomon accepted the museum's offer to be its director and launched a series of exhibitions under the rubric of "The New American Art." However, his initial idea of inaugurating the new gallery with a large Pop Art show was foiled by Sidney Janis's similar attempt, "The New Realists." He then decided to "go back to the beginning" with Rauschenberg, whom he considered the "old master" of the new art movement.[9]

In March 1963, a large Rauschenberg retrospective marked the opening of the new contemporary art program at the Jewish Museum. Besides being the centerpiece of Solomon's programming, it also brought about what Castelli called a "real explosion," in two senses.[10] First, Solomon surprised the art world by giving a relatively young, unestablished artist a major museum retrospective. Second, and just as importantly, the artist was not Jewish, nor did his art encompass any element of Judaism. The show established Rauschenberg's reputation in New York, with audacious works such as *Monogram* and *Canyon* (1959) causing both positive and negative reactions among visitors. Later that year, Solomon organized "Toward a New Abstraction," a group exhibition that featured Color Field painting. This exhibition was followed by the first museum retrospective of Jasper Johns in February 1964. Solomon then reached the pinnacle of his career when he delivered the Grand Prize to Rauschenberg at the 1964 Biennale.

Unfortunately, Solomon's career as a star curator was prematurely terminated by his sudden death in 1970. Equally unfortunate was that his writing—which consisted of general introductions for the art he promoted—had little influence on the subsequent, or even contemporaneous, discourse on American art. His legacy is thus largely forgotten today. However, it is necessary to resituate him in the history of post–World War II art, as Solomon is another key figure in the global rise of American art. While such influential critics as

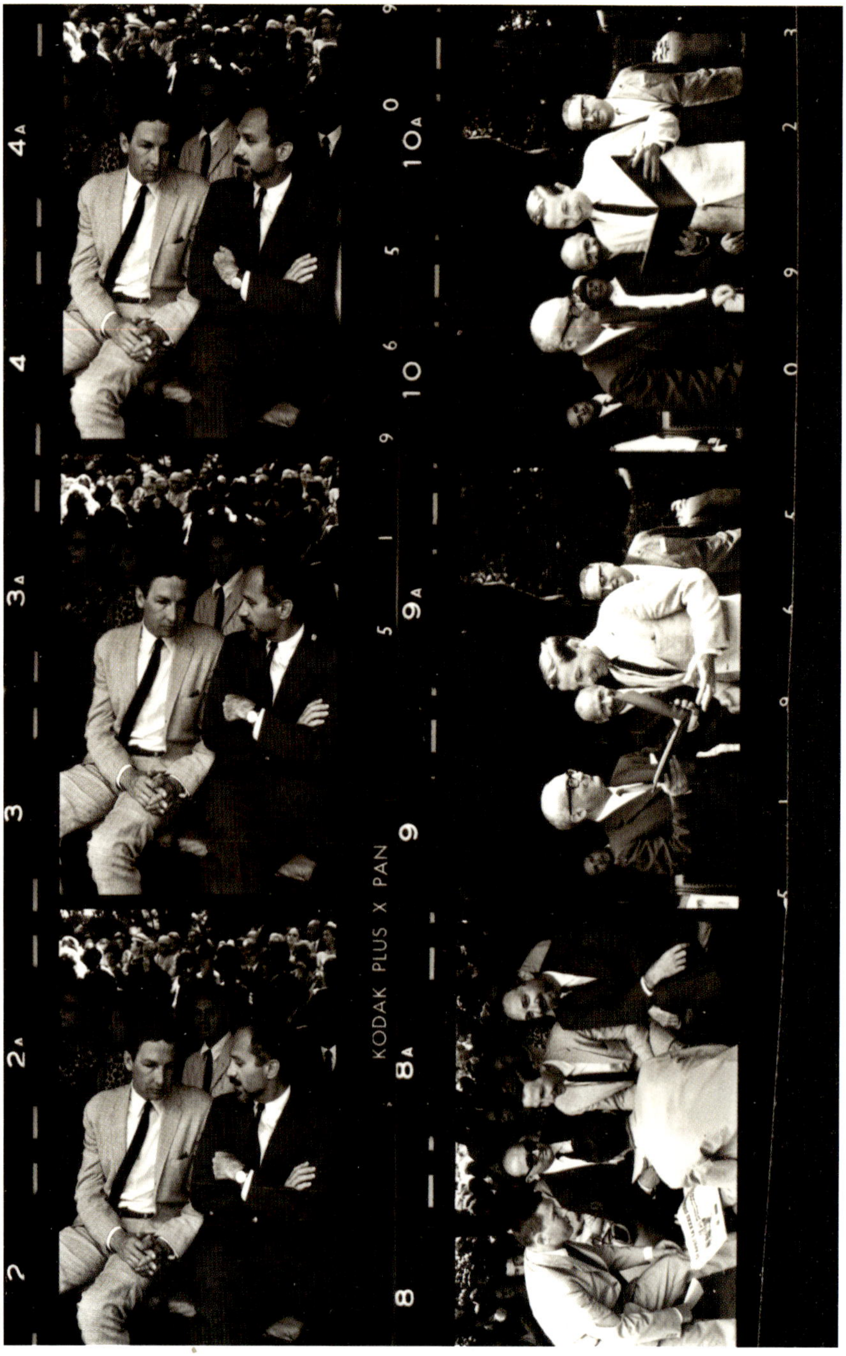

Figure 2.1
Thirty-second Venice Biennale awards ceremony, Venice, Italy, 1964. Contact sheet: black and white, 7 × 24 cm (cropped to show six images of Rauschenberg, Solomon, and others attending the ceremony). Courtesy Alan R. Solomon Papers, 1930–1972, Archives of American Art, Smithsonian Institution.

Clement Greenberg and Harold Rosenberg helped to cement the international status of American art through their writing, Solomon did the same through his spectacular exhibition of American art in Venice. In this sense, the entirety of the 1964 American presentation—from Solomon's ideas to his strategies to the actual displays—forms an independent text to be read and interpreted.

What Solomon characterized as "The New American Art" encompassed two distinct groups that emerged after Abstract Expressionism. One was the new type of abstraction usually called Color Field painting, and the other was the new form of figuration called Neo-Dada and Pop Art. Between the two trends, Solomon clearly favored the figurative camp, whose origin he located in the art of Rauschenberg and Johns. In a 1963 essay for *Art International*, he claimed that the pair represented two basic ideas common in the new art. While Rauschenberg endorsed "the new awareness of the mutuality of art and life" with his use of ready-made objects and images, Johns awakened interest in the "object and its new 'personality'" by questioning our daily perception of common products.[11] The so-called Pop artists—although Solomon did not use this term—followed this path and arrived at their own artistic production. He noted a shared sensibility among the new figurative artists: "Despite the differences in their styles, these artists share a common desire to intensify our perception of the image and to alter it in some way which complicates its effect.... They want us to share with them their pleasure and excitement at feeling and being, in an unquestioning and optimistic way."[12]

Although it was one of the first attempts to define what is now called the Pop Art movement, this essay nonetheless suffered inconsistencies in argument. For instance, Solomon did not explain how the new artists could "desire to intensify our perception and alter it" if they were merely "unquestioning and optimistic," as he claimed. Solomon's depoliticizing tendency was also evident in his essay for the Rauschenberg retrospective: "The new artists operate, by contrast [to Dadaists], in complete esthetic freedom, and politically they have disengaged themselves totally.... This new generation is wholly engaged in life and the process of art, in a direct, intense and optimistic way, without commitment to any of the familiar existing institutions."[13] Solomon believed the art he was promoting did not have any conflict with society at large because he saw the American artists' relationship to popular culture and society as more optimistic than pessimistic, and more accepting than oppositional—a view perhaps more indicative of his own temperament than the artists'.

In November 1963, Solomon received an invitation from the United States Information Agency (USIA) to serve as the U.S. commissioner for the 1964 Venice Biennale. His curatorial activities in post-Abstract Expressionist art made him a perfect candidate for the USIA, which was becoming aware of the increasing importance of American art in the world art scene. The letter of invitation explained, "Since American art for the first time in history enjoys the role of acknowledged leadership in international art circles, the U.S. exhibition should feature those vital aspects which have focused the attention of the cultural world upon us."[14] For Solomon, "those vital aspects" of course included works by Rauschenberg and Johns. The day after the Biennale's award ceremony in Venice, he confessed to Tomkins in an unpublished interview how he had felt when he accepted the offer from the USIA. The journalist took the following notes: "Way back last fall, when this started, Solomon had suddenly realized, that this time America could win Biennale with Rauschenberg. Solomon wanted Bob to win. He also wanted to put on a stunning show that would impress Europeans with the strength and diversity of American art—'do for Europe what the Armory show did for America.'"[15] To achieve this goal, Solomon enjoyed the cooperative attitude of the USIA, which left all the important decisions up to him, including the choice of artists. The USIA did require that he show them photos of works by selected artists in order to have his choices approved, but since "this [requirement] was purely to make sure there would be nothing obscene or political," Solomon saw "[n]o problem there—[the] current crop of artists are absolutely a-political, and by no means obscene."[16] Solomon's adamant denial of politics in works by Rauschenberg and others feels too resolute, and will be analyzed in the next section.

With the full support of the USIA, Solomon planned a large group show of "The New American Art" for the 1964 Biennale. His exhibition roster consisted of Rauschenberg, Johns, Kenneth Noland, and the late Morris Louis as "Four Germinal Painters," along with "Four Younger Artists": John Chamberlain, Claes Oldenburg, Jim Dine, and Frank Stella. Solomon traveled to Venice in late November to start preparing for the show. He was at the airport in Paris when he heard the shocking news of President Kennedy's assassination. With some hesitation, he went ahead to Venice with Lois Bingham, chief of the Fine Arts Section at the USIA Exhibition Division. Upon his arrival, Solomon immediately realized that the American Pavilion was simply too small to show works by the eight artists he had chosen. After negotiating with the Biennale officials and the U.S. State Department, he was allowed to use the former American Consulate, located on the Grand Canal next to Peggy Guggenheim's Art of This Century Gallery, as an official annex of the American Pavilion. He then "planned [the] space very carefully, put Noland and Louis in grounds [the Giardini] so as not to offend their feelings, and [because] that space was better esthetically for them,"[17] thereby saving the more spacious, centrally located Consulate for a large Pop Art show, with Rauschenberg and Johns as its main feature.

Solomon took great pains to renovate the Consulate building to make it an exhibition space. He installed appropriate walls, lighting, and furniture, and created many rooms of rather intimate size, in which he would hang only one work on each wall. A spacious structure, the Consulate allowed him to assign an independent room for each of the four younger artists after allotting more than half of the space to Rauschenberg and Johns, who were represented by twenty-two and twenty-one works, respectively. With governmental support, Solomon was able to transport the large and fragile works of art via the U.S. Navy plane Globemaster, the sight of which was quite a spectacle in itself (figure 2.2). He thus managed to realize a show that was "not only stunning" but also a "revelation," according to Tomkins: "The large, colorful, infinitely complex canvases of Rauschenberg and Johns

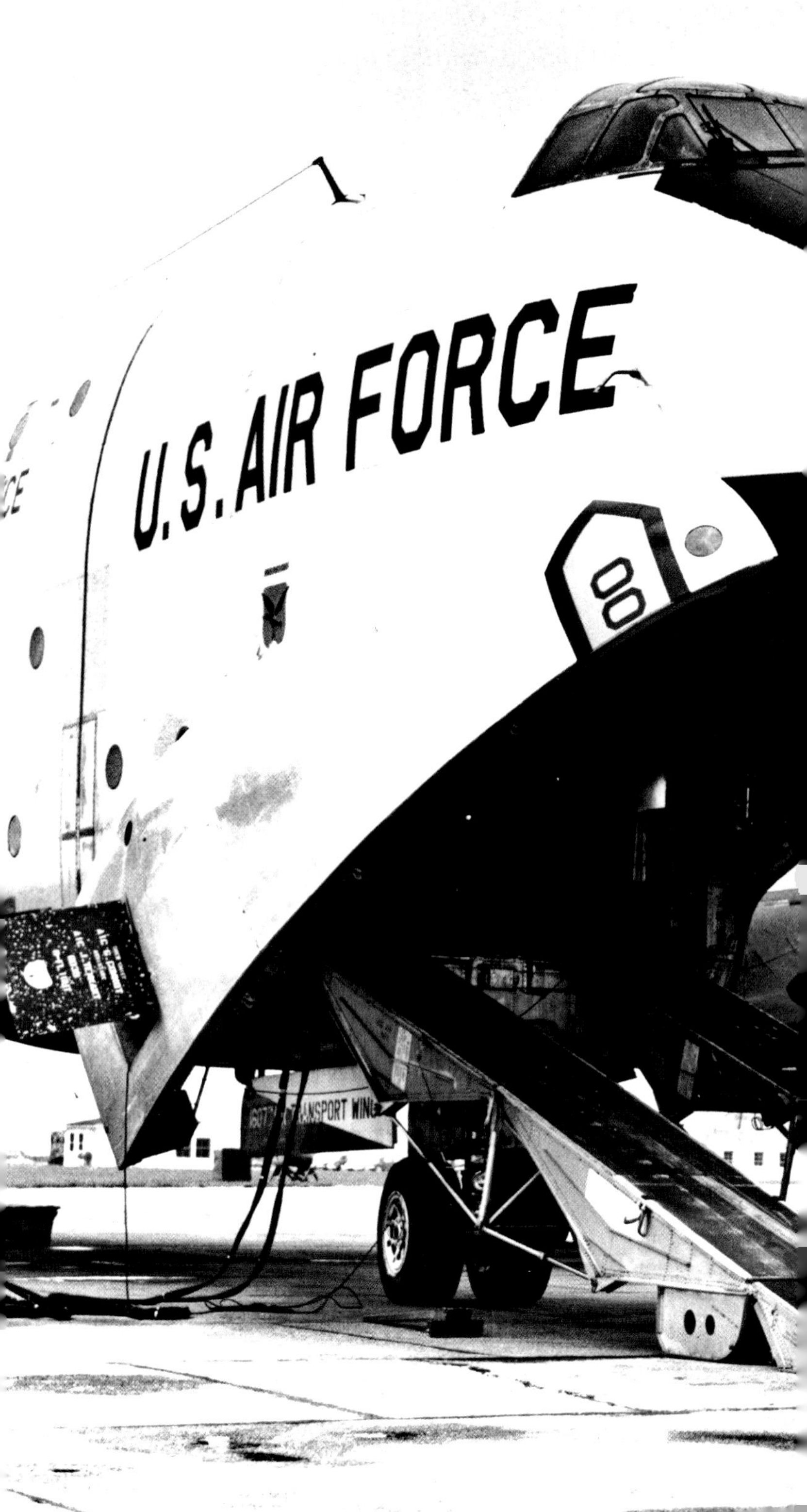
U.S. AIR FORCE

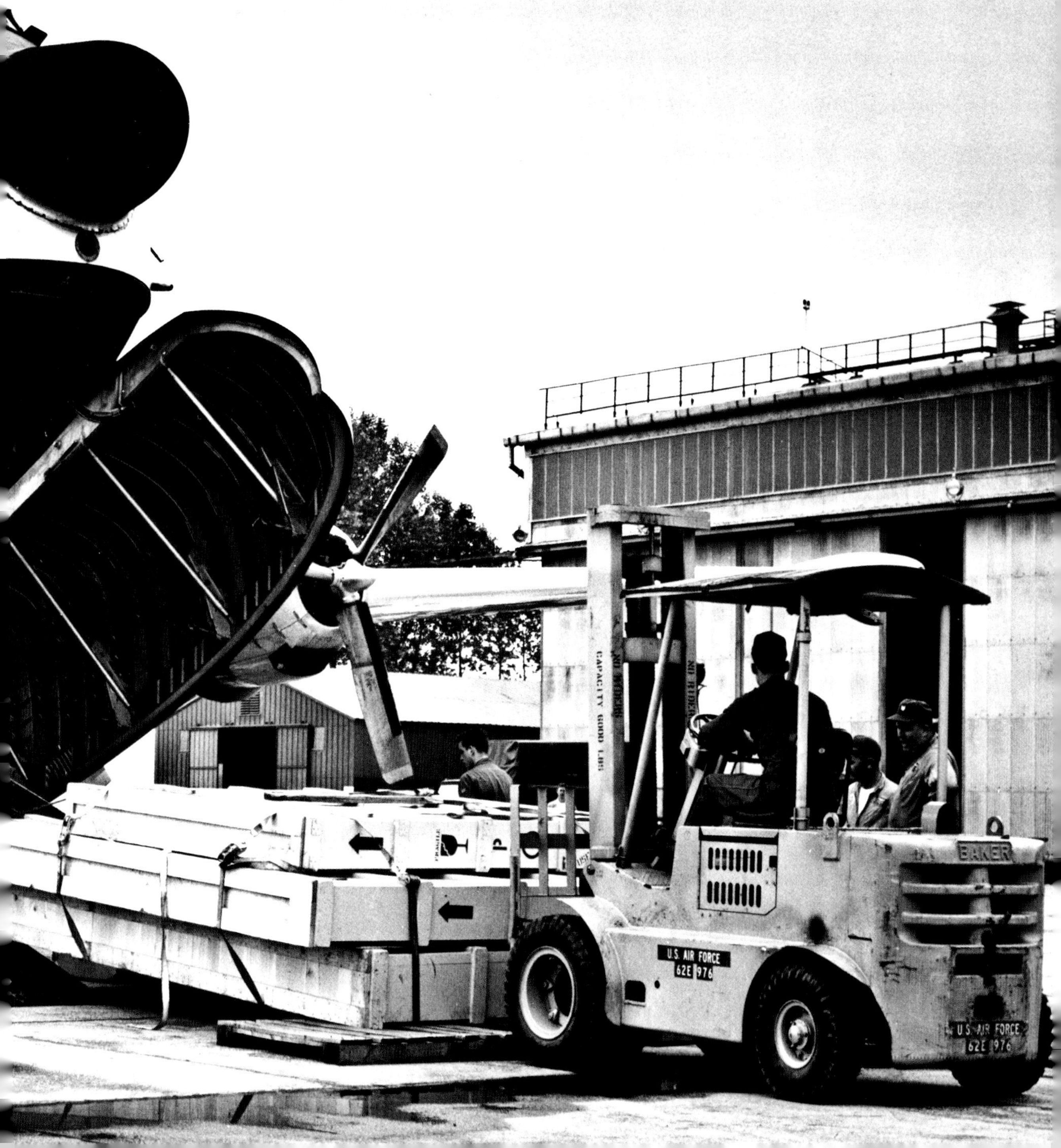

Figure 2.2
United States Air Force unloading art from a plane for the Venice Biennale, 1964. Photographic print: black and white, 18 × 24 cm. Courtesy Alan R. Solomon Papers, 1930–1972, Archives of American Art, Smithsonian Institution.

Figure 2.3
"The New American Art," installation views at the American Consulate at the Venice Biennale, 1964. Contact sheet: black and white, 25 × 21 cm. Courtesy Alan R. Solomon Papers, 1930–1972, Archives of American Art, Smithsonian Institution.

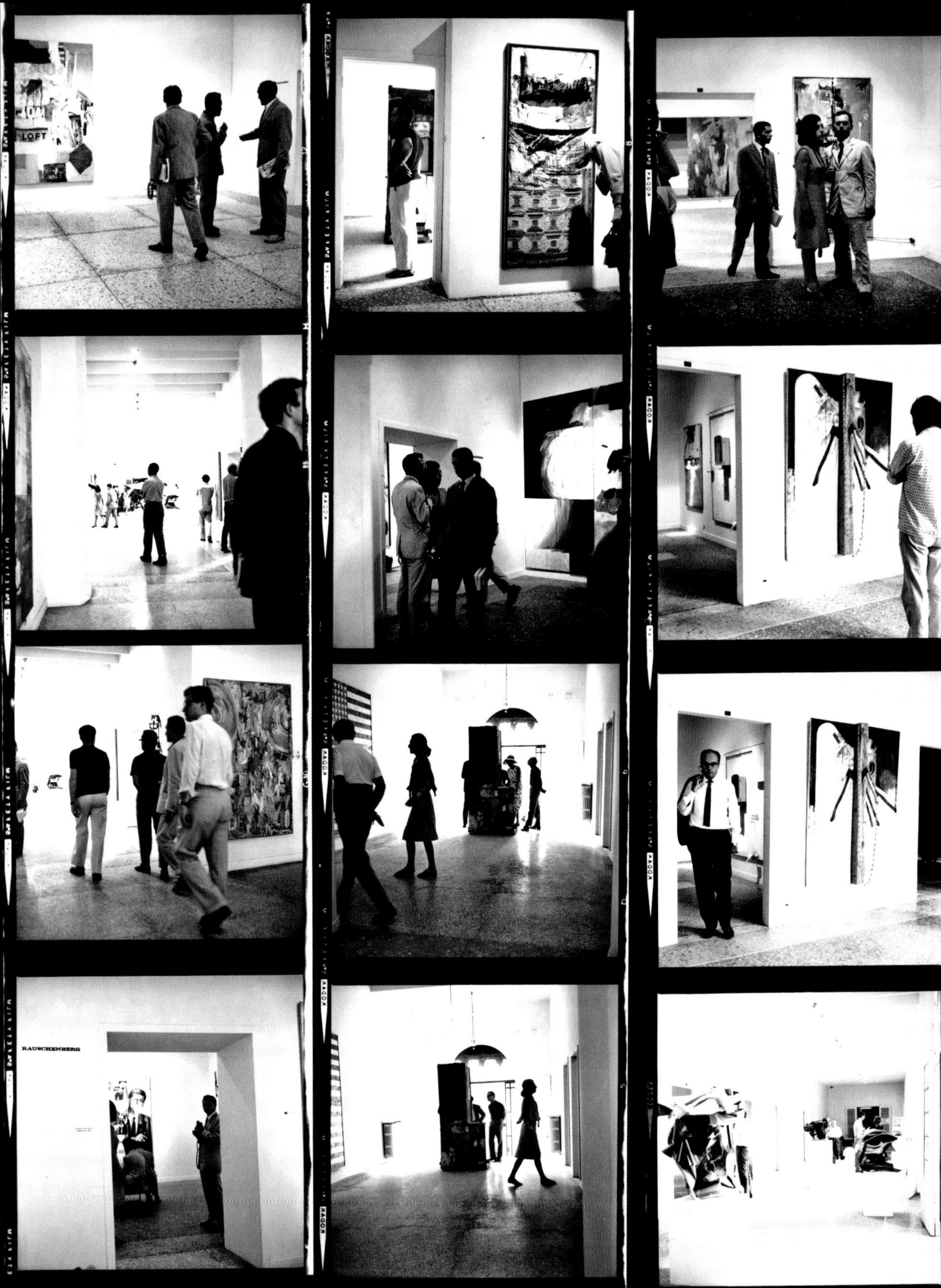
LOFT
RAUSCHENBERG

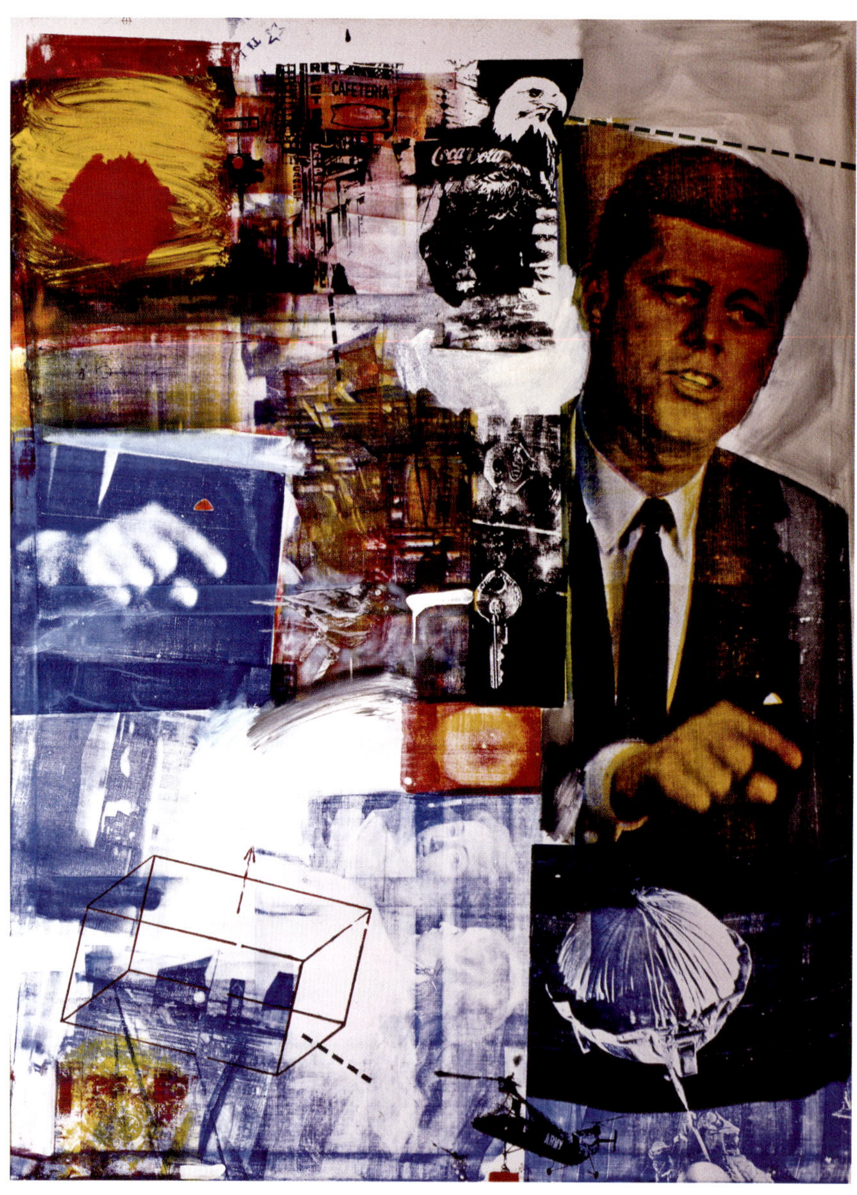

Figure 2.4
Robert Rauschenberg, *Buffalo II*, 1963. Oil and silkscreen ink on canvas, 96 × 72 inches (243.8 × 182.9 cm). The Robert B. Mayer Family Collection, Chicago; photograph by Christopher Gallagher.

had never looked better [than they did] in those small, rather intimate rooms.... In the Consulate, where they hung one to a wall and could thus be savored individually, pictures that I had seen many times before seemed to me entirely fresh and new."[18] Castelli also called Solomon's work as curator for the 1964 Biennale "his masterpiece" in every respect, describing the group show as even "better structured than just a mere one-man show of Jasper Johns or Rauschenberg."[19] Surviving photographs of the installation at the Consulate corroborate these statements, as they document the Biennale viewers exploring a variety of works that were carefully laid out and spaciously installed (figure 2.3).

These photographs also indicate that while Solomon went out of his way to deny any political elements in the exhibited works, he actually capitalized on the impact of the American motifs and materials incorporated in them. For instance, Rauschenberg's *Buffalo II* (1963) (figure 2.4), a silkscreen painting with an image of the late President Kennedy, was the first work to greet the audience in Rauschenberg's room. Johns's *Two Flags* (1962) was also given a conspicuous presence in the hallway across from a Rauschenberg *Untitled* Combine (1954–1955/1958), which contained popular imagery of America such as a postcard of the Statue of Liberty as well as fragmented pieces of the Stars and Stripes (see figures 2.6, 2.7). Moreover, these works were exhibited along with Dine's canvases containing bathroom fixtures and tools, Oldenburg's soft sculptures of banal objects such as a typewriter and a toaster, Chamberlain's works made of crushed automobiles, and Stella's hard-edged abstractions painted in industrial enamel paint. Despite the diversity in media and presentation, all of these works included aspects of contemporary American life in one way or another. As opposed to the serene and sophisticated abstractions by Louis and Noland shown at the Giardini, the works at the Consulate reminded visitors of American culture and lifestyle, which had already exerted an enormous impact throughout the so-called Free World by the mid-1960s.

Presenting the vigor of American art in relation to American popular culture was an effective mise-en-scène in an international art festival, since this popular culture was unique to post–World War II America and arguably its most attractive aspect, especially for those abroad. Even today, the impact of Solomon's 1964 curatorship seems to be remembered for this aspect. In the 2005 Venice Biennale, the Museum of American Art, an artists' group based in Berlin, presented an installation work entitled *Alan R. Solomon Gallery: "USA 64"* (2005) (figure 2.5). The installation consisted of two rooms at the Arsenale, the first of which featured hand-painted panels that reproduced pages from the 1964 American Pavilion's catalog, photographs of Rauschenberg and Solomon at the award ceremony, and a *Life* article on the 1964 Venice Biennale. It also included a small model gallery with hand-painted reproductions of works by Rauschenberg, Johns, Noland, and Louis. The model gallery, enlarged ten times, was also presented as the second room of the installation, including the four works which were also enlarged and hand-painted.

Founded in 2004 as an "educational institution dedicated to keeping memories of how Modern American Art shown in Europe during the 1950s and the '60s marked its dominance over the world art scene,"[20] the Museum of American Art effectively commented on Solomon's effort. Rather than reconstructing the entire 1964 American show, the group staged its *memory*, by hanging hand-painted—and thus imperfect—copies of the event, such as catalog pages and a journal article. Furthermore, the music playing in the background of the installation was precisely to the point: the song "America" from the 1961 musical movie *West Side Story*, which was a huge hit throughout the Western Bloc and beyond in the early 1960s.[21] Hearing the refrain of the song in an instrumental version, viewers were prompted to voice the lyrics:

> I like to be in America!
> O.K. by me in America!
> Ev'rything free in America!
> For a small fee in America![22]

The choice was indeed appropriate, as Tomkins remembers that the band at Caffè Florian on Piazza San Marco played tunes from *West Side Story* for tourists as well as the art crowd that summer.[23] The music thus seems to convey the essential impact of the 1964 American presentation: to many viewers, especially non-Americans, it represented not merely American art but American culture as a whole.

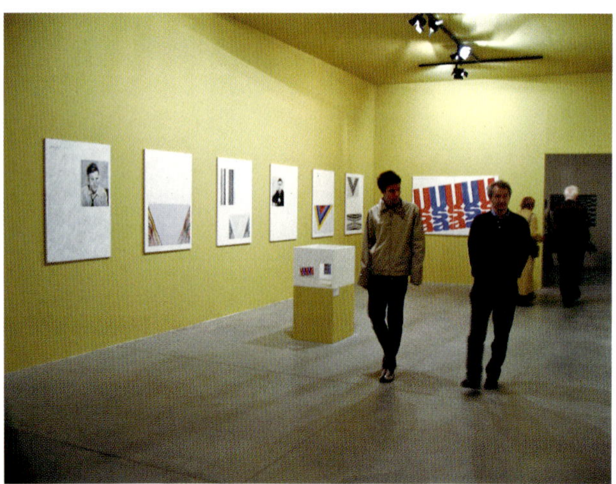

Figure 2.5
Museum of American Art in Berlin, *Alan R. Solomon Gallery: "USA 64,"* installation view at the 2005 Venice Biennale. Photograph by author.

Not satisfied with creating a spectacular exhibition of American art, Solomon completed his ambitious agenda through a daring publicity campaign. First of all, he placed a large banner on the facade of the Consulate to advertise the building as the U.S. Pavilion's annex. Secondly, he hired night guards for the site, so that people could visit the Pop Art show after the Giardini was closed. Last, but not least, during the press opening at the Consulate, he distributed a handout that contained his commissioner's statement (also printed in the Biennale catalog in Italian) as well as a few reproductions of works by the featured artists. Although Rauschenberg's works at the exhibition were primarily his Combines from the 1950s, Solomon chose for the handout *Buffalo II*, the eye-catching 1963 work with the image of President Kennedy, as well as Johns's *Three Flags* (1958). His commissioner's statement audaciously announced the international dominance of American art:

> A surprising number of exhibitions of work by post–Abstract Expressionist painters and sculptors have been held in England, Sweden, Holland, Germany, Denmark, Italy, and elsewhere, and they have been received with critical enthusiasm and a high level of public response. The fact that the world art center has shifted from Paris to New York is acknowledged on every hand.[24]

Prepared by the American-published *Art Gallery* magazine in cooperation with the USIA, more than two thousand copies of this handout were distributed during the Biennale period, making it impossible for anyone to miss his point. Together with the two-part exhibition at the Consulate and the Giardini, this statement completed what can be called the "American spectacle" that Solomon staged for the 1964 Biennale. In brief, he did almost everything he could to achieve his goal—to "do for Europe what the Armory show did for America"—and bring the Grand Prize to Rauschenberg.

RAUSCHENBERG'S "AMERICA" (1): *UNTITLED* (MAN WITH WHITE SHOES)

One thing Solomon did not—or would not—do for the 1964 Venice Biennale was to admit to any critical or political content in the popular imagery in the works he selected. In the catalog for the American presentation, he claimed that the artists employed such American icons as the national flag and the image of the president not to represent "chauvinism or satire," but simply "for their familiarity and their omnipresence." In his view, the artists were not, like Dadaists, flaunting destructive gestures against art and society but rather were interlopers in the realm of purely aesthetic experiences. In the case of Rauschenberg, Solomon claimed: "He has no interest in social comment or satire, or in politics; he uses his previously inappropriate materials not out of a desire to shock, but out of sheer delight, out of an optimistic belief that richness and heightened meaning can be found anywhere in the world, even in refuse found in the street." Willfully disregarding the potential sociopolitical content of the artist's work, Solomon continues: "Unlike other users of [found] objects, he divorces them completely from sentiment and nostalgia. If they are worn, or faded, or corrupted, their patina does not call up their past for him." In other words, Solomon

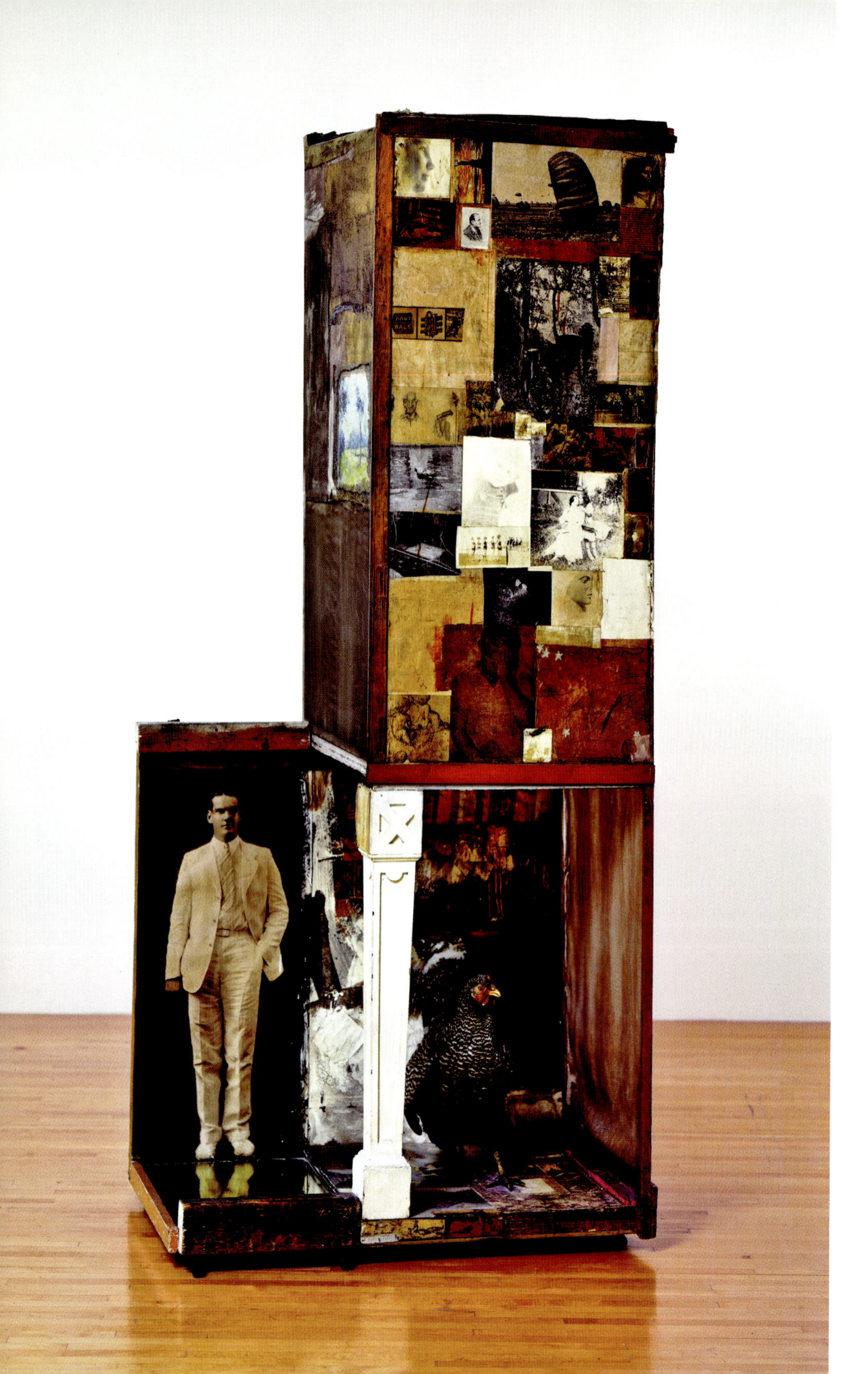
DONT
WALK

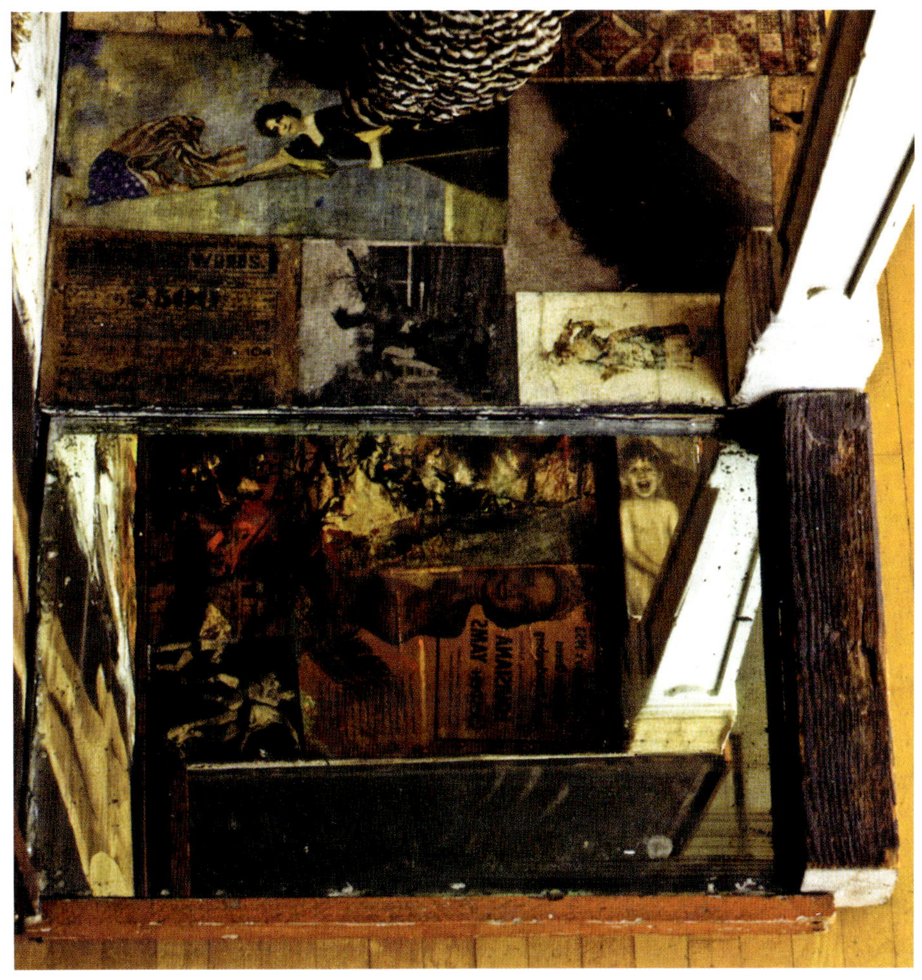

Figure 2.6 (detail, Figure 2.7)
Robert Rauschenberg, *Untitled*, ca. 1954–1955/1958. Freestanding Combine: oil, pencil, crayon, paper, canvas, fabric, newspaper, photographs, wood, glass, mirror, tin, cork, and found painting, with pair of painted leather shoes, dried grass, and stuffed Dominique hen, on wood structure mounted on five casters, 86 ½ × 37 × 26 ¼ inches (219.7 × 94 × 66.7 cm). The Museum of Contemporary Art, Los Angeles, The Panza Collection.

presents Rauschenberg's found objects as merely "elegant and beautiful, suggestive and seductive"—that is, as self-referential visual materials that offered no possibility of signification.[25] He thus reduces all of Rauschenberg's works to the same idea, repeated with minor variations, of the "gap between art and life."

Certainly, Rauschenberg himself talked about his work in terms of affirmation rather than negation; still, today Solomon's empty rhetoric of denial sounds simplistic and wanting against the diverse and complex manner in which the artist presented his "America." Since the appeal of "America" was part of Rauschenberg's international success, it is necessary to explore this aspect in his work. Although Rauschenberg's use of found images may sometimes appear heroic and celebratory in his silkscreen paintings, such as *Buffalo II*, his engagement with popular culture imagery was far more complex and ambiguous in his earlier Combines. For instance, the aforementioned *Untitled* (figure 2.6), the freestanding Combine customarily called "Man with White Shoes," uses found images as inventive thematic motifs that function as a mythic cross-referential network within the work. As Thomas Crow argues, the white-suited southern dandy with a mirror under his feet evokes the myth of Narcissus, while the mirror reflects a newspaper clipping announcing the artist's sister Janet as the winner of a beauty contest—another reference to Greek myth, this time to the Judgment of Paris (figure 2.7).[26] Intertwined with these associations are more references to the artist's family: a newspaper cutting about his parents' silver wedding anniversary and a photograph of his son Christopher, along with the boy's touching letter to his father.

These personal elements do not immediately cohere as an autobiographical narrative, as they are juxtaposed with other found images and objects as well as with the artist's painterly gestures. Nonetheless, it is noteworthy that *Untitled* includes a number of oblique references to America, such as an inverted postcard of the Statue of Liberty and fragments of the Stars and Stripes. In fact, the artist often called it "Plymouth Rock"—"the name of the long-assumed breed of hen that stands in the lower right corner, as well as a reference to the place where the Pilgrims first set foot in America"—as decoded by Paul Schimmel, another art historian who engaged in a thematic reading of the artist's work.[27] The stuffed bird stands on the picture of a woman holding an American flag, possibly on Independence Day, which seems to support this observation. In addition to these rather overt references, an allusion to contemporary America can be found in the image of a parachute and soldier in the upper right of the front wooden panel. In this photograph, the soldier seems to be running toward the inflated parachute. But what exactly is going on there?

This author's research uncovered the source of this image as a *Life* article from May 1958 (figure 2.8). This means that Rauschenberg continued working on this piece, which has previously been dated 1954–1955, until at least May 1958. (Another image from this article is used in *Monogram*, which demonstrates the artist's mode of working on multiple pieces simultaneously.) The article describes a tragic accident during a military parachute exercise, when a blast of wind inflated the soldiers' parachutes at the moment of landing, dragging them helplessly across the ground at high speed. In a desperate attempt to save his colleague's life, the soldier in the picture is "rac[ing] up to grab [the] chute in [an] effort to spill out its air" (figure 2.9).[28] The title of the article, "'It's What We Volunteered For,'" quotes a surviving soldier's words (figure 2.10). The article editorializes on the "freak accident" as the cost that the United States had to pay to maintain the post–World War II Pax Americana, which proved to be higher than expected.[29] The figure of the soldier can thus be seen as a surrogate for Icarus, another tragic protagonist of Greek mythology. It is hard to imagine that the artist added such a tragic image to the already somewhat self-reflexive work "out of sheer delight" and "optimistic belief," as Solomon argued in his catalog.[30] If *Untitled* is, as Schimmel suggests, a "veritable summa of Rauschenberg's life and art up to the time of its making,"[31] it could also be an allegorical commentary on the America of its time, a commentary that is far more nuanced than an outright critique or an optimistic celebration.

Insistently negating politics in "The New American Art," Solomon never acknowledged such complex ambiguity in Rauschenberg's work. Why did he need so adamantly to repress the "meaning" in the artist's work, even at the risk of being left with nothing significant to say about the art that he championed with such enthusiasm? One practical—and indeed, political—reason is that he needed to placate the USIA, which was intent on excluding political references from any and every Biennale work. A more fundamental reason, however, could be found in the critical landscape of the time. When Solomon started promoting "The New American Art," American art criticism was still dominated by Greenbergian formalism, which posited timeless, Apollonian clarity as the ideal state of a work of art. Greenberg's belief in the self-referential unity of a work of art was such that he demanded the "integrity of the picture plane" even in a medium like collage,[32] while finding "instantaneous unity" to be a pictorial feature shared by American abstraction and Renaissance illusionistic tableaux alike.[33] The enormous influence of Greenberg's theory on both the critical discourse and the painting practice of the time was crucial, especially because his writings reached the status of dogma when post–Abstract Expressionist art, of the kind that Solomon promoted, came to the fore.

Despite the circumstances, writing about the art of Johns and Rauschenberg allowed critics such as Leo Steinberg and Max Kozloff to challenge Greenberg's hegemony by formulating a nonformalist or antiformalist criticism.[34] Most famously, Steinberg coined the term "flatbed picture plane" to describe Rauschenberg's pictorial surface that received a variety of information from the outside world without hierarchy, which Steinberg claimed opened the door to a postmodernist painting.[35] Solomon might be seen as another postmodern critic in that he dismissed any coherent narrative or message in Rauschenberg's work. Unlike Steinberg or Kozloff, though, he did not challenge the dominant critical framework of the day by constructing an alternative critical tool with which to discuss such works. As a result, all Solomon could do was to *celebrate* "The New American Art." Extolling its openness, its playful and youthful spirit, and its optimism—all worn-out clichés of American virtues—he presented it as a symbol of America, while suppressing its allegorical nature.

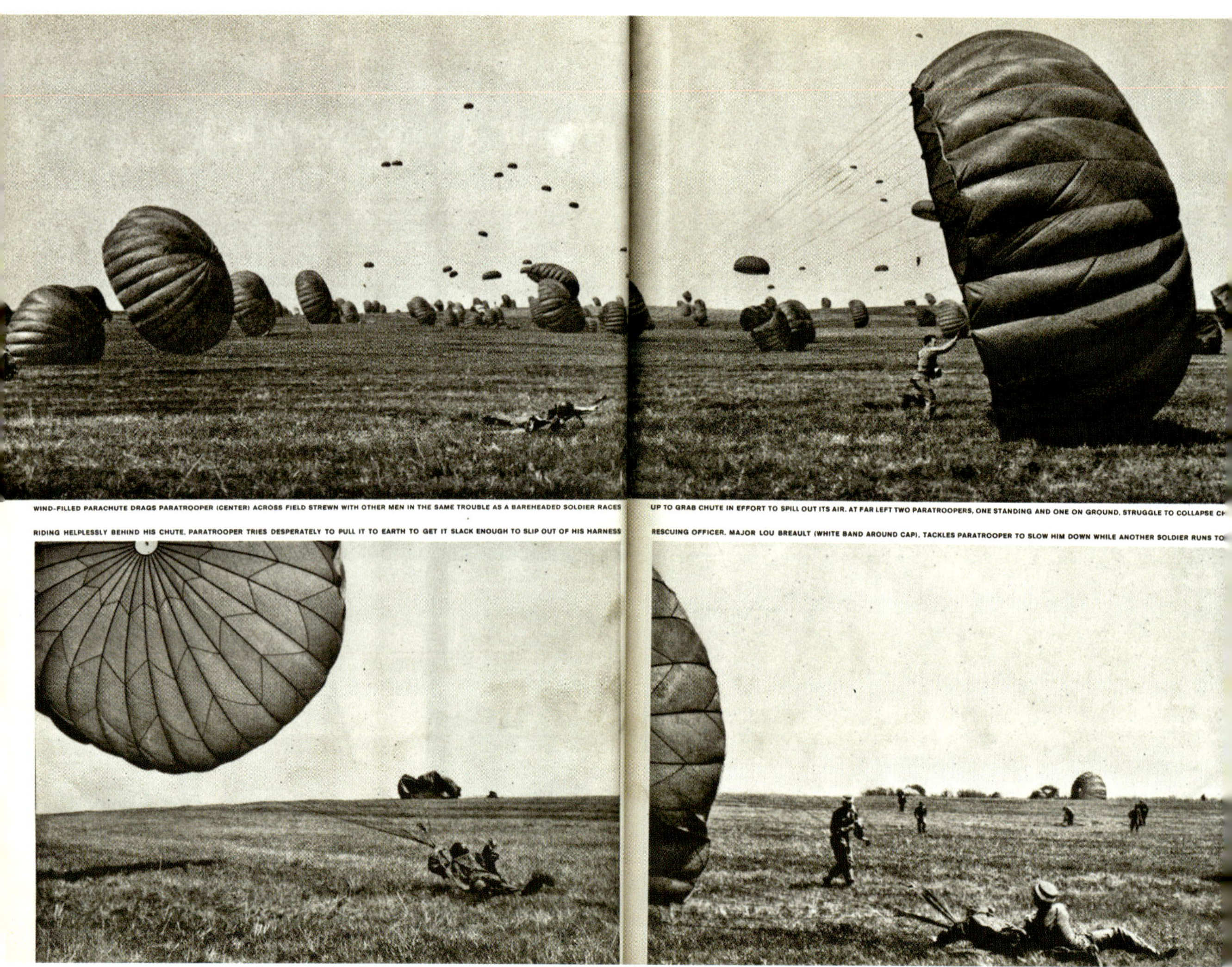

WIND-FILLED PARACHUTE DRAGS PARATROOPER (CENTER) ACROSS FIELD STREWN WITH OTHER MEN IN THE SAME TROUBLE AS A BAREHEADED SOLDIER RACES UP TO GRAB CHUTE IN EFFORT TO SPILL OUT ITS AIR. AT FAR LEFT TWO PARATROOPERS, ONE STANDING AND ONE ON GROUND, STRUGGLE TO COLLAPSE CH

RIDING HELPLESSLY BEHIND HIS CHUTE, PARATROOPER TRIES DESPERATELY TO PULL IT TO EARTH TO GET IT SLACK ENOUGH TO SLIP OUT OF HIS HARNESS RESCUING OFFICER, MAJOR LOU BREAULT (WHITE BAND AROUND CAP), TACKLES PARATROOPER TO SLOW HIM DOWN WHILE ANOTHER SOLDIER RUNS TO

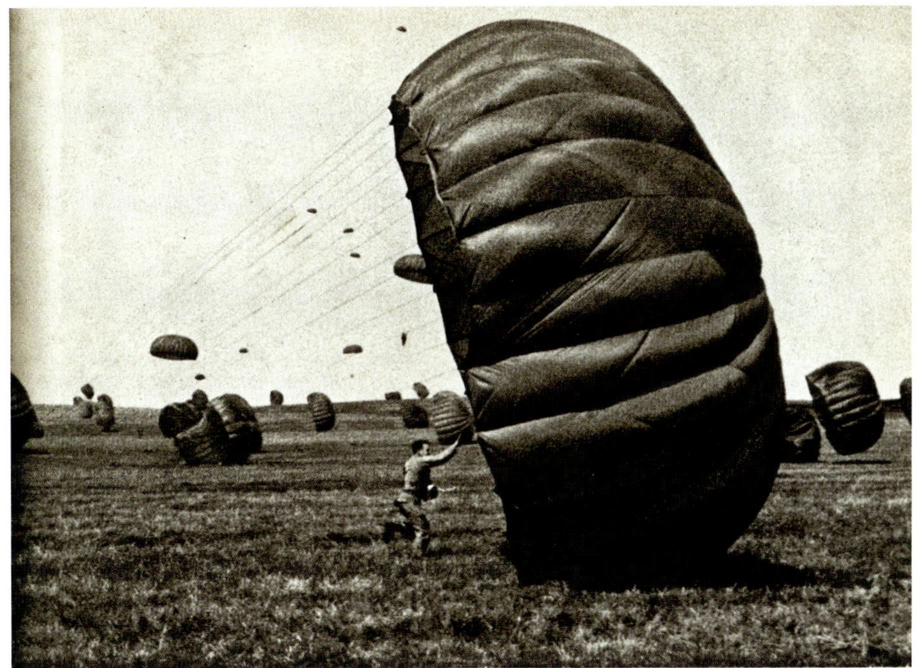

Figure 2.8 (detail, Figure 2.9)
"'It's What We Volunteered For,'" *Life* 44, no. 3 (May 5, 1958): 22–23. Text © 1958 Time Inc.; photograph © United Press International.

Vol. 44, No. 18

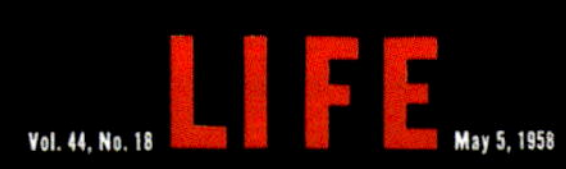

May 5, 1958

'IT'S WHAT WE VOLUNTEERED FOR'

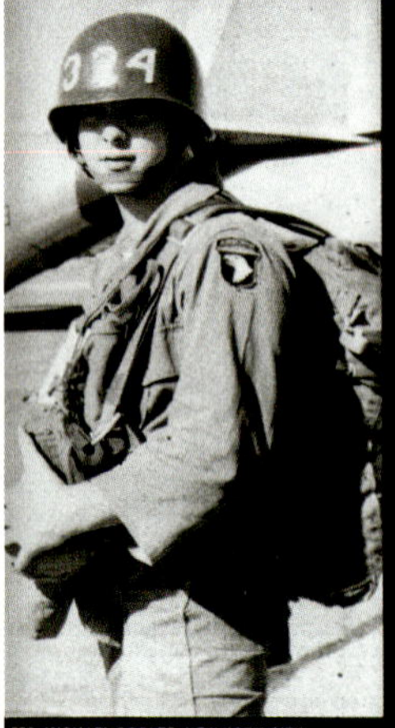

PFC. MICHAEL ROBLES, NEW YORK CITY

The price of U.S. military preparedness suddenly seemed tragically high last week. Five young airborne soldiers, shown here in pictures taken for their graduation to jump status, were killed in a freak accident which saddened the nation and demonstrated once more that combat troops must sometimes take the same costly risks in peacetime that they face in war. All five men were proud members of one of the U.S. Army's toughest and most elite units, the 101st Airborne Division, which was in Normandy and Bastogne. All had volunteered for the hazardous duty—and for the extra pay which goes with it. All were hardened, experienced paratroopers.

But as they and 1,300 other men took part in their unit's first mass jump, unpredicted gusts of wind blew across the drop zone in which they were landing. The men's chutes, instead of collapsing quickly on hitting the ground, were blown across the fields, dragging the men behind. Martinez was choked to death; Payne died from head injuries; Ruffin, Robles and Morley were strangled by their tangled suspension lines. Another 155 men were rushed to the field hospital with cuts, bruises and broken bones.

"Sure it was sad," said a sergeant, "but it's what we volunteered for." Some observers at the scene blamed the accident on a faulty measurement of the wind and a U.S. congressman demanded a House investigation. The 101st's commander, Major General William Westmoreland, himself had jumped with the men and been dragged 200 yards by the wind. "This was not a stunt," the general explained, "it was part of our business."

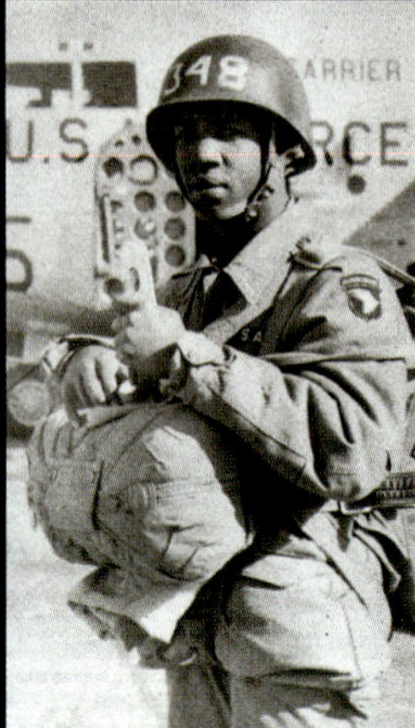

PVT. ELLIOTT MORLEY, MIAMI, FLA.

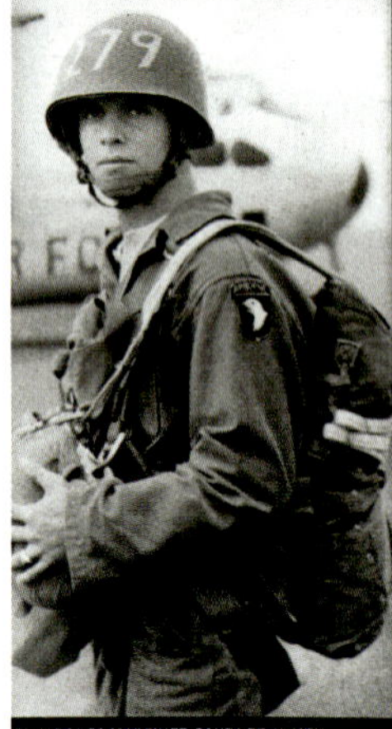

PFC. ALFONZO MARTINEZ, SANTA FE, N. MEX.

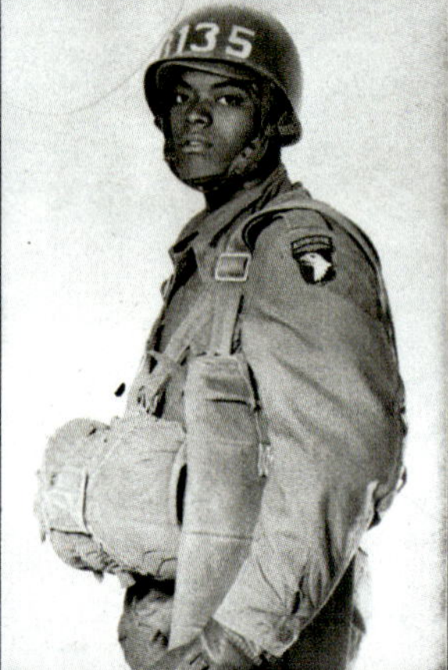

PFC. DANNIE RUFFIN, CLEVELAND, OHIO

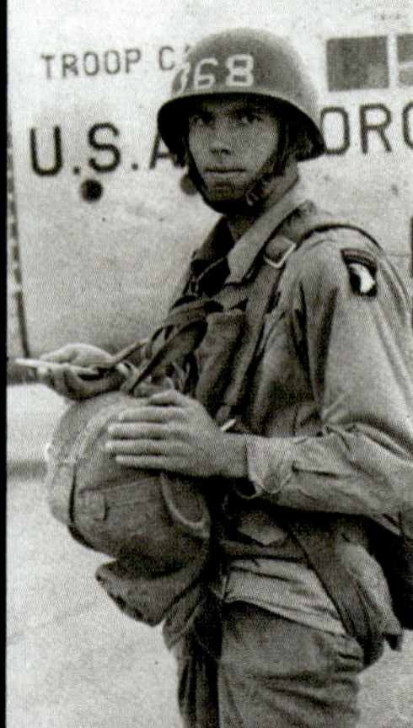

SP3/C CARL PAYNE, CLARKSVILLE, TENN.

Figure 2.10
"'It's What We Volunteered For,'" *Life* 44, no. 3 (May 5, 1958): 21. Text © 1958 Time Inc.; photographs by Craft Studio.

RAUSCHENBERG'S "AMERICA" (2): ALLEGORY IN THE DANTE DRAWINGS

Understanding the place of allegory in Rauschenberg's work is vital to understanding his "America," as it has been an object of controversy in previous studies on the artist. The debate originated with Craig Owens's landmark two-part essay "The Allegorical Impulse: Toward a Theory of Postmodernism," published in *October* in 1980. Owens traced the revival of allegory, which had been deemed an aesthetic error in modern aesthetics since the Romantic period, as one of the driving forces of postmodern art practice.[36] Situating Rauschenberg's work as one of the first instances of the revival of allegory, Owens announced, "it remains impossible to read Rauschenberg, if by reading we mean the extraction from a text of a coherent, monological message," and he criticized iconographers' "attitude toward reading as an unproblematic activity."[37]

This reproach on iconography led to what Crow calls the "rival notions of allegory" in Rauschenberg literature.[38] On the one hand, a group of iconographic scholars continued to interpret Rauschenberg's allegory as conveying prescribed—and often queered—meanings; for example, Laura Auricchio read the Dante Drawings as projecting a "camouflaged expression of homosexual longing into the predominantly heterosexual mores of the mid-century American avant-garde."[39] On the other hand, representing the so-called postmodern or poststructuralist critics, Rosalind Krauss openly despised such a reading as literal-minded, claiming, "It is precisely the message of uncertainty, slippage, of unreadability and fragmentation that allegory not only conveys but also, in a necessary act of redoubling, itself becomes."[40]

Acknowledging the merits and limits of both parties, Crow suggests understanding Rauschenberg's allegory in terms of the artist's own aesthetic needs in an era that found its ideal in the formal unity of the picture plane. In an attempt to flee from the lofty idealism of the "symbol" (even though Crow eschews the term, perhaps for justifiable fear of reducing the argument to simple binarism), Rauschenberg discovered the mode of allegory, largely forgotten and neglected for as long as two centuries, to be helpful for his artistic project. Crow extends his analysis of Rauschenberg's use of allegory: "In the mid-1950s, when there were next to no contemporary models to follow, fashioning an allegory proved to be a process of discovery for makers and viewers alike. The unfolding of the process could be described in stages: as a flight from compulsory unity as a master aesthetic toward a maximized proliferation and multiplicity of signs; then, as no condition of true randomness can ever be sustained, regularities begin to appear."[41]

This insight helps a further examination of the image of the soldier and parachute in *Untitled*. The tragic image of a frustrated flight assumes another significance when seen in relation to the "compulsory unity" imposed upon painters of the former generation of Abstract Expressionists. The self-destructive fate of painters such as Jackson Pollock was something from which Rauschenberg needed to flee, a fate echoed in the Icarus-like figure of the soldier. It is also important to note that he found the photograph in May 1958, probably shortly after he came across the image of the "great migrator" in *Sports Illustrated*. If he was inspired by the uplifting image of ascent in the article on the migrating bird, he found a gloomy image of descent in the *Life* picture. In these two pictures, the artist found the perfect embodiment of his allegorical theme of flight, in both literal and figurative senses.

The date of 1958 is significant as well, because in the late spring of that year Rauschenberg started the Dante Drawings, in which his engagement with the imagery of popular culture grew more intense than ever.[42] Although not included in the American exhibition at the 1964 Venice Biennale, the drawing series was traveling around Europe from 1964 to 1965 (including the period of the Biennale), thus presenting another occasion for the European audience to see Rauschenberg's vision of America. In fact, European critics saw an allegory of America precisely in his ambivalent treatment of mass culture imagery, rather than seeing it as an allegory of media (as postmodernists would) or the artist's sexuality (as iconographers would). As the Italian critic Paolo Barozzi wrote in praise of the drawings: "They represent the life and the spirit of the American people, but they go beyond the image of [Americans as] imperialist conquerors to reveal the secret fragmentation of loss, confusion, anxiety, crimes, and failures. In these illustrations, Rauschenberg breaks apart the image of America to investigate what hides beneath it."[43] A discussion of the series is thus indispensable here, for examining an allegory of America in the Dante Drawings would help us find a way out of the cul-de-sac of opposition in Rauschenberg literature.

When Rauschenberg embarked on the Dante Drawings, he still had major Combines such as *Untitled* (Man with White Shoes), *Odalisk* (1955–1958), and *Monogram* in his studio, as they were all unsold and probably not yet complete. If he gradually discovered the mode of allegory through creating them, he was more conscious of the allegorical nature of his drawing project by 1958. While Dante's *Inferno* was itself one of the most profound medieval allegories, the transfer drawing technique—which Rauschenberg discovered in 1952 and began deploying in earnest in 1958—was more overtly allegorical, for it allowed the artist to choose an image from his sources and use it for a different narrative.[44] Indeed, Rauschenberg chose to illustrate Dante's *Inferno* partly because he desired to prove himself a serious artist after Johns's successful debut had eclipsed his fame,[45] and partly because he wanted to make an extensive use of transfer and needed an appropriate theme for the purpose.[46]

The transfer technique basically involves cutting out a photographic image, wetting its surface with a solvent liquid (such as lighter fluid), placing it on a sheet of drawing paper, and rubbing its back with an empty ballpoint pen. The resulting image, transferred onto the paper, is a reverse of the original image. This method proved suitable for illustrating Dante's poetry, for, just as Dante had written his poem in his own Italian dialect and peopled Hell with his contemporaries, Rauschenberg used images from popular magazines such as *Time*, *Life*, *Newsweek*, and *Sports Illustrated* to express scenes and characters in the *Inferno*. For instance, his Dante was a towel-clad man taken from an advertisement for golf clubs (figure 2.11), "the most neutral popular image [he] could find in that scale."[47] Politicians such as John F. Kennedy and Adlai Stevenson also appear as stand-ins for characters in Hell, while athletes such as sprinters, tennis players, and Olympic champions are featured as sinners and monsters.

Among the Dante Drawings, *Canto II* (1958) (figure 2.12) is a good example of how Rauschenberg visualized Dante's poem. He divided the space into three horizontal sections to parallel the *terza rima* structure of the poetry, and also to indicate the downward direction in Hell. On the top section, Dante as the man with a towel stands alone, with the small version of the "migrating bird" (taken from the contents page of *Sports Illustrated*) indicating the start of his journey. In the section below, Beatrice is present as a classical statue, sending Virgil to Dante as his guiding hand in Hell. Her divine will is expressed as a vertical arrow that points to Virgil in the bottom section, represented as an uplifted runner. Another arrow then points to Dante, again in the figure of a towel-clad man, accepting the journey through Hell as his divine fate. This type of descriptive reading is not always self-evident in the series. On the contrary, despite the technical possibility of transferring an image as clearly as it is in its original source, Rauschenberg deployed the gesture of rubbing as indexical striations to express Dante's anxiety and the disquieting atmosphere in Hell.[48]

Furthermore, as Rauschenberg deliberately veiled his source photographs and used similar images to represent different figures in Hell, the identification of characters is often impossible, even when one looks intensely at the drawing. For instance, an image of a runner is repeatedly used to represent Dante and Virgil as well as sinners and monsters. While we have seen Virgil as a runner in *Canto II*, sinners are shown running on the plain of burning sand in *Canto XIV* (1959–1960) (figure 2.13), where Rauschenberg traces his own foot in place of a Giant of Crete, further complicating the chain of signification. In *Canto XXXI* (1959–1960) (figure 2.14), a runner used for *Course* (see figures 0.2, 0.3) appears again, along with Olympic champions, as a giant. In this drawing, it is even unclear which giant the runner refers to—although the artist assertively transfers his agonized face twice in this canto (one picture is taken from the article, and the other from the magazine's contents page). The duplication and fragmentation of the found image convey the ambiguous, almost troubled nature of Rauschenberg's involvement with popular culture in this series.

The most radical example of this procedure is the image of Thaïs in *Canto XVIII* (1959–1960) (figure 2.15). While Dante and Virgil appear as skiers and runners in this drawing, the image of the damned whore is taken from a picture in *Sports Illustrated*, in which a little girl is peeking out of a lake (figure 2.16). Rauschenberg appears to have found the image so intriguing that he not only transferred it but also drew it by hand in the illustration. While the clipped picture of the girl's face is clearly transferred toward the left of the bottom section, he drew the figure of Thaïs, with its reflection on the water, at the center bottom of the drawing by imitating the original photograph. In the source article, the image of the girl is accompanied by a caption: "I can sit here and Mommy doesn't mind. I can see everybody, but they can only see my nose and my head."[49] Rauschenberg isolated this innocent girl by taking her out of the original context, then transformed her into the whore who is permanently punished for her flattery in the pond of excreta in Hell.[50] The technique is thus clearly reminiscent of

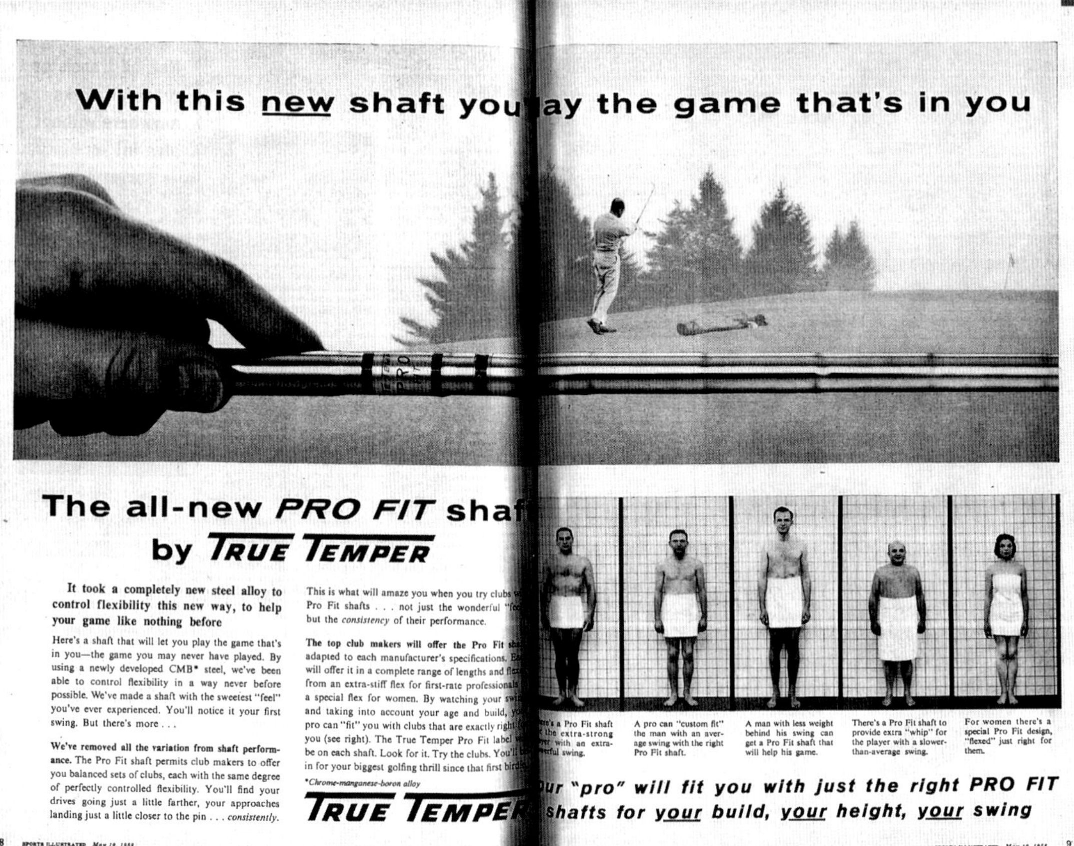

Figure 2.11
Advertisement for golf clubs in *Sports Illustrated* 8, no. 20 (May 19,1958): 8–9. Advertisement by True Temper Sports, Inc.

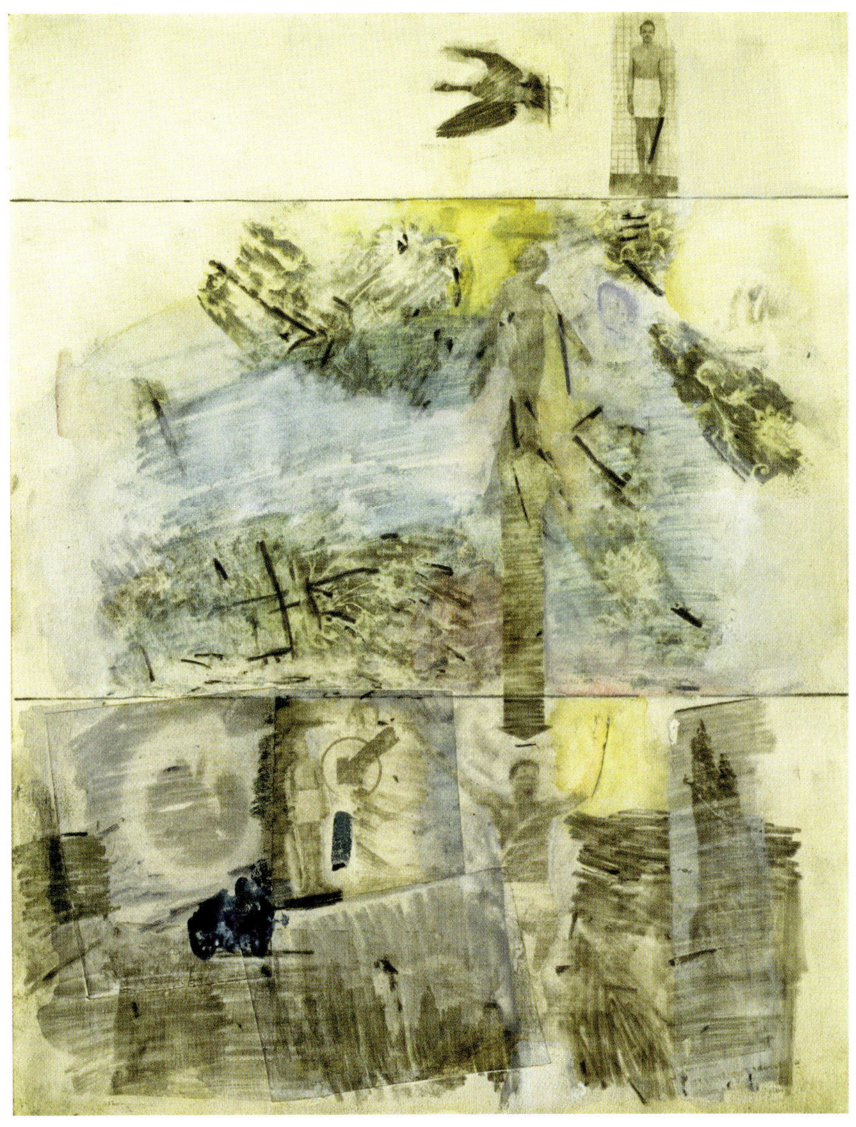

Figure 2.12
Robert Rauschenberg, *Canto II: The Descent*, 1958. Solvent transfer on paper, with cut-and-pasted paper, watercolor, wash, and pencil, 14 ½ × 11 ½ inches (36.5 × 28.9 cm). The Museum of Modern Art, New York. Given anonymously. Digital image © 2009 The Museum of Modern Art, New York/SCALA, Florence.

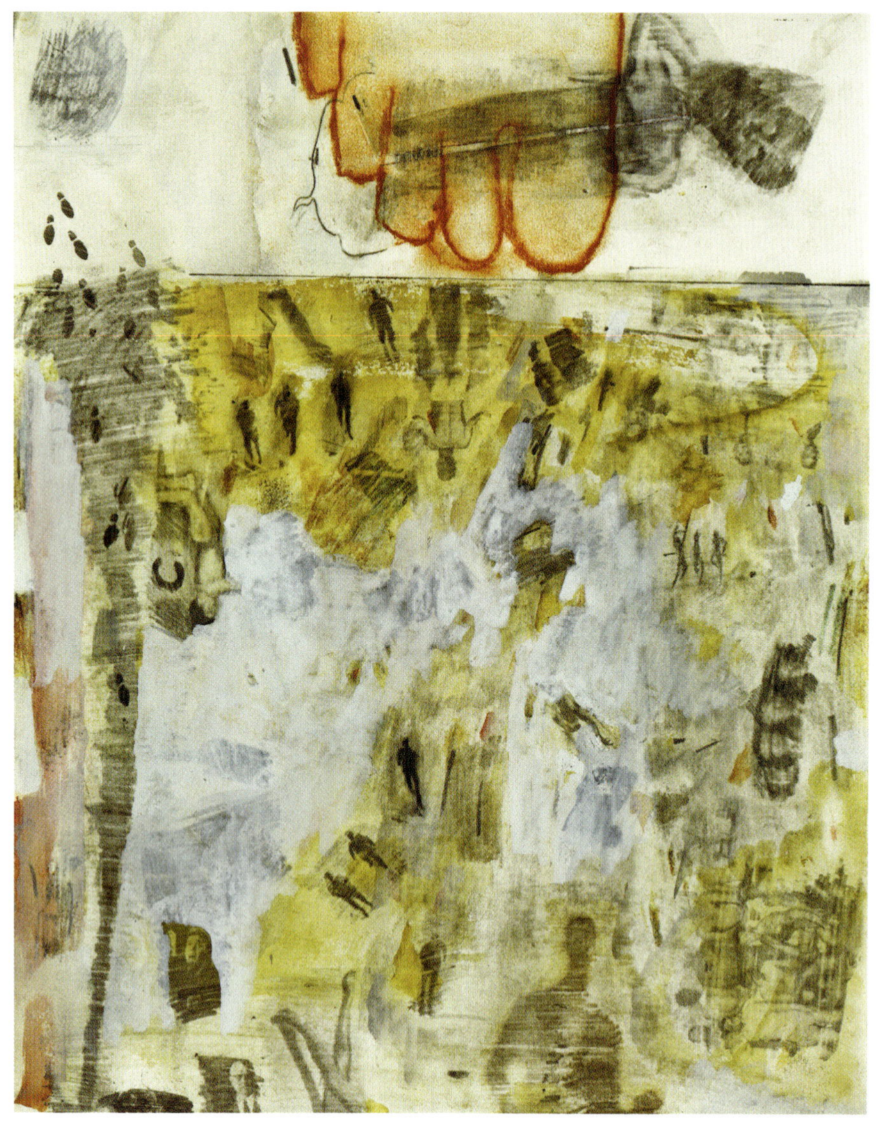

Figure 2.13
Robert Rauschenberg, *Canto XIV: Circle Seven, Round 3, The Violent Against God, Nature, and Art*, 1959–1960. Solvent transfer on paper, with watercolor, gouache, pencil, and red-chalk body tracing, 14 ⅜ × 11 ½ inches (36.5 × 29.2 cm). The Museum of Modern Art, New York. Given anonymously. Digital image © 2009 The Museum of Modern Art, New York/SCALA, Florence.

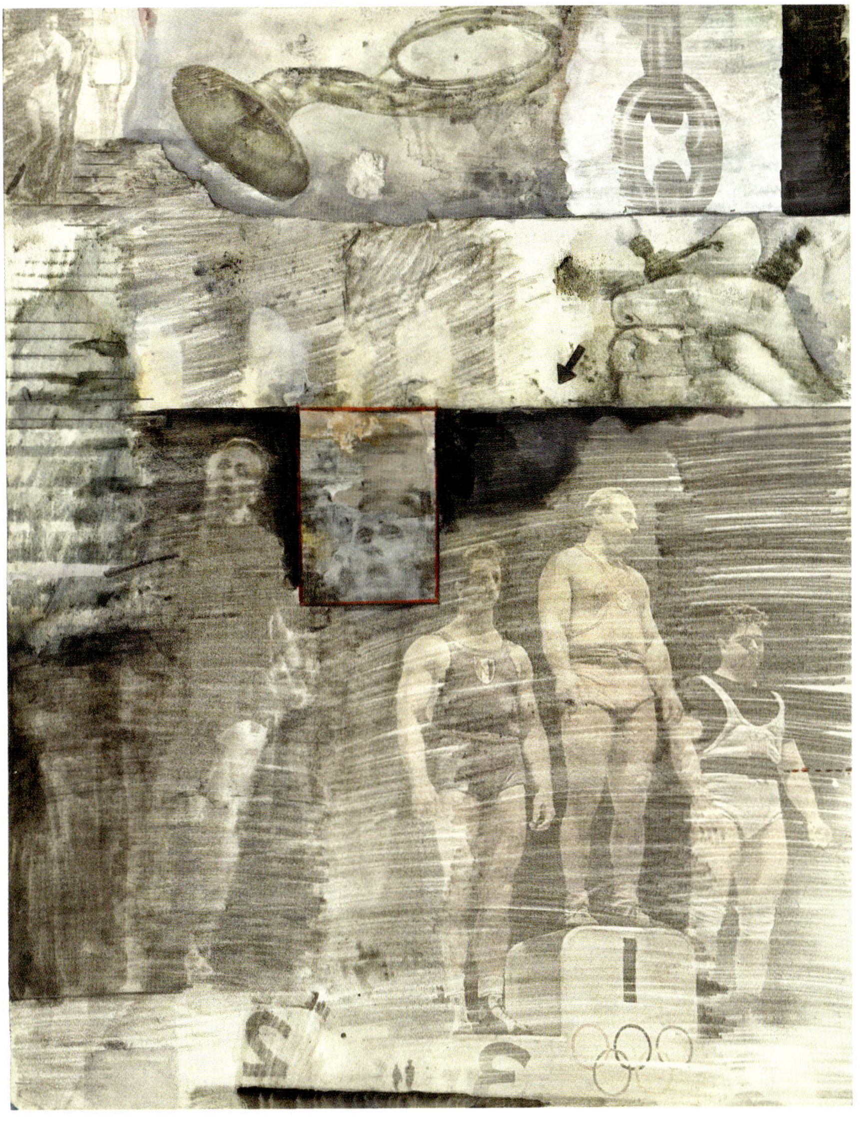

Figure 2.14
Robert Rauschenberg, *Canto XXXI: The Central Pit of Malebolge, the Giants*, 1959–1960. Solvent transfer on paper, with colored pencil, gouache, and pencil, 14 ½ × 11 ½ inches (36.8 × 29.2 cm). The Museum of Modern Art, New York. Given anonymously. Digital image © 2009 The Museum of Modern Art, New York/SCALA, Florence.

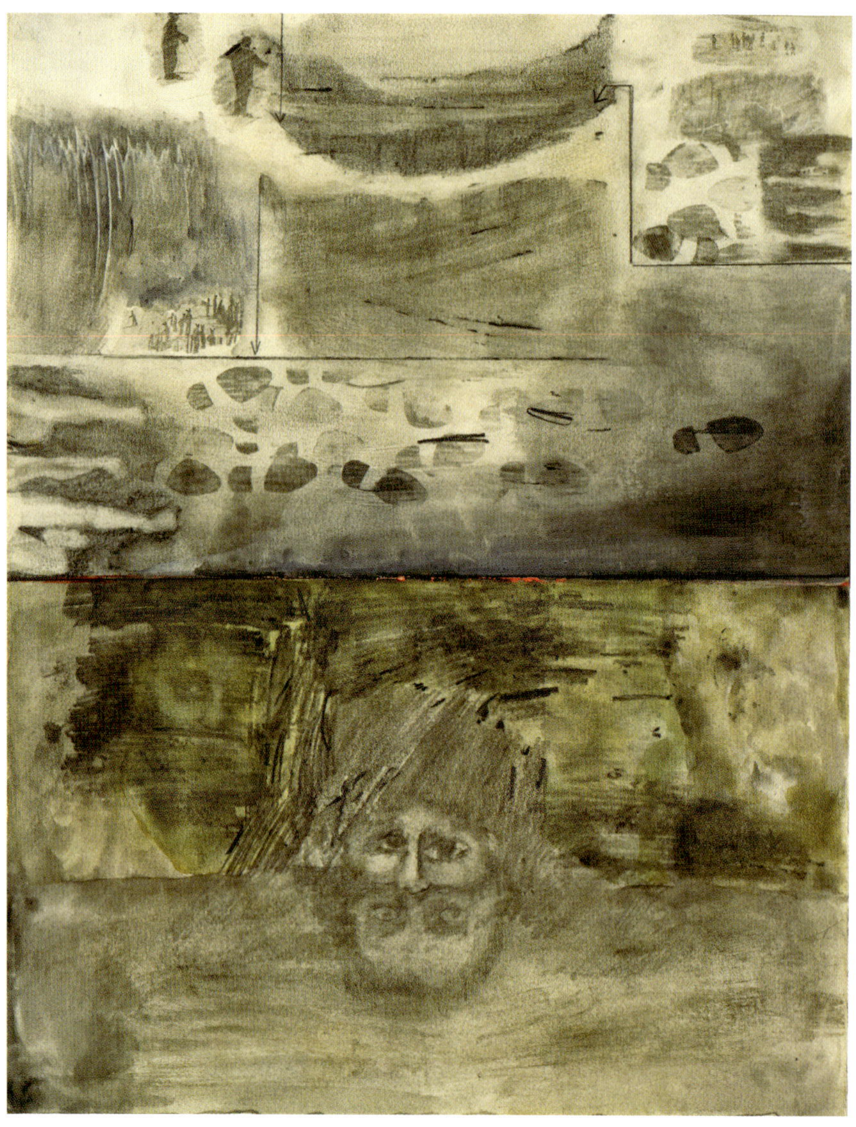

Figure 2.15
Robert Rauschenberg, *Canto XVIII: Circle Eight, Malebolge, the Evil Ditches, the Fraudulent and Malicious; Bolgia 1, the Panderers and Seducers; Bolgia 2, the Flatterers*, 1959–1960. Solvent transfer on paper, with wash, pencil, gouache, and crayon, 14 ½ × 11 ½ inches (36.8 × 29.2 cm). The Museum of Modern Art, New York. Given anonymously. Digital image © 2009 The Museum of Modern Art, New York/SCALA, Florence.

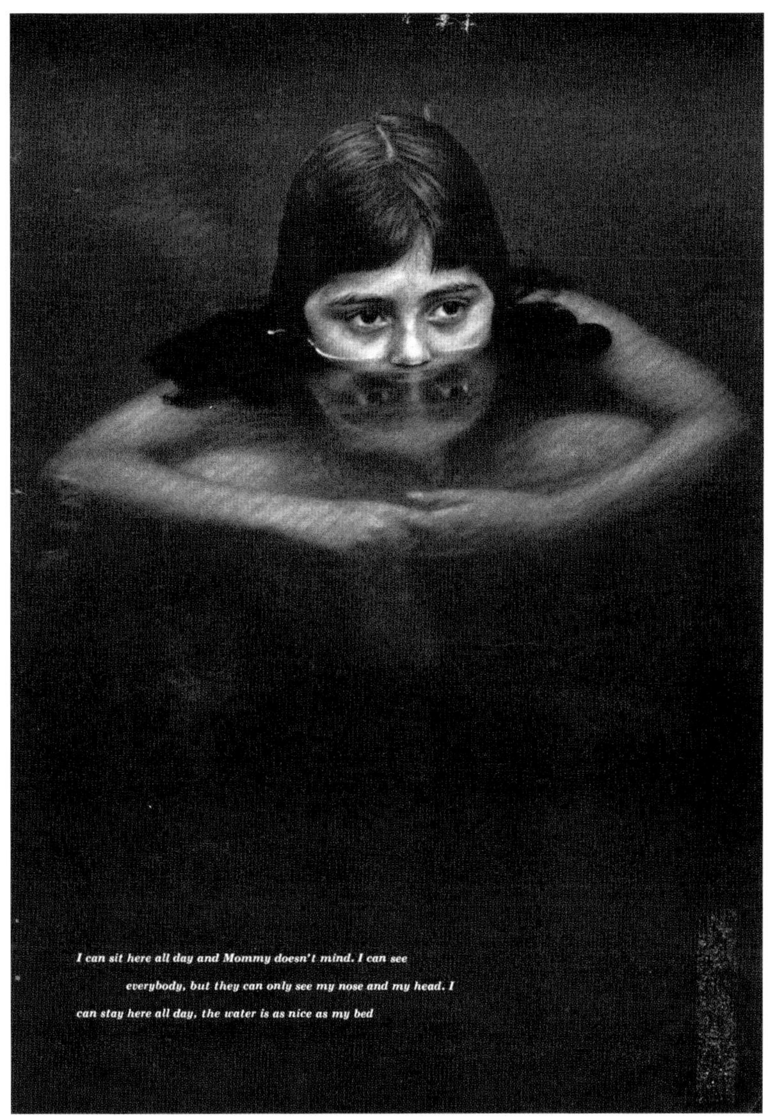

Figure 2.16
"The Endless Fascination of Water," *Sports Illustrated* 9, no. 9 (September 1, 1958): 37. Photograph by W. Eugene Smith © 1958, 2009 The Heirs of W. Eugene Smith. Reprinted courtesy of *Sports Illustrated*.

Owens's definition of visual allegory: "Allegorical imagery is appropriated imagery: the allegorist does not invent images but confiscates them. He lays claim to the culturally significant, poses as its interpreter. And in his hands the image becomes something other (*allos* = other + *agoreuei* = to speak)."[51]

It is to be noted, though, that Owens's Benjamin-based model of allegory does not entirely fit Rauschenberg's artistic practice. While Owens basically characterizes allegory as either a melancholic reflection on the irredeemable past or a postmodern appropriation as the authorship critique,[52] Rauschenberg often recovers the impact of found imagery in the present—that is, his work. In the case of *Canto XVIII*, the original photograph of the little girl, shot by W. Eugene Smith, is actually quite eerie in itself. By disconnecting it from its cloying caption, Rauschenberg redeemed the visual power of the original image and incorporated it into his vision of the modern inferno. The artist thus resisted the increasing power of the mass media over the visual in the late 1950s, as much as he was attracted to and felt pressured by it. While the Dante Drawings do not feature such obvious American icons as flags and Coke bottles, they include a number of uncanny and disquieting images from contemporary American society, which Rauschenberg complicated and problematized through his blurring transfer technique. By repeating the same process to express other scenes and characters in the *Inferno*, he wove a complex and powerful allegorical vision in which Dante, as a twentieth-century Everyman, passes through the contemporary hell of America.

As noted earlier, European critics keenly perceived this quality, perhaps because of their own ambivalent feelings toward the hegemonic American culture. Few critics in the United States pointed this out, however, as they were unaware of the aesthetic shift from a symbolic to an allegorical mode, and Solomon was no exception. While capitalizing on the visual impact of American imagery chosen by Rauschenberg, Solomon was not concerned that his work did not demonstrate much of the formal unity characteristic of the symbol. Lest the art he promoted be labeled as an "aesthetic error," he tried to rescue it by assuming there had been a symbolic unity between Rauschenberg's art and where it came from, that is, America. This empty rhetoric of denial encountered some reality checks in Venice, when he set out to obtain the Grand Prize for Rauschenberg—whose candidacy was in jeopardy because of the two-part exhibition.

ENGINEERING VICTORY

The question of Rauschenberg's eligibility started with a miscommunication between Solomon and the Biennale officials. While Solomon thought it had been agreed—albeit verbally—that the artists shown at the Consulate would be eligible for the prize, the Venice Biennale president, Mario Marcazzan, denied there was any such agreement.[53] This was an unexpected blow to Solomon, who had felt "they [the Biennale officials] have a certain obligation to us, particularly since they were very interested in the idea of an expanded American Exhibition, but were unable to provide us with any other space."[54] Since it was too late to change the presentation of the U.S. Pavilion in the Giardini, Solomon erected temporary plywood walls in its courtyard, hanging one work each by Rauschenberg, Johns, and the four younger artists as an appeal for their official candidacy.[55]

The international jury of that year's Biennale consisted of seven members nominated by Marcazzan: Arno Hammacher, director of the Kröller-Müller Museum in the Netherlands and the jury's president; Franz Meyer from Switzerland; Murillo Mendes from Brazil; Juliusz Starzyński from Poland; Giuseppe Marchiori and Marco Valsecchi from Italy; and Sam Hunter from America, the first American critic ever included on a Biennale jury. It must be noted that no juror was from France that year and that the juror selection process is unclear, with no surviving document on the matter.[56] The jury, whose members were not announced until June 14,[57] was still unable to reach an agreement on June 18, two days before the opening of the Biennale. To solve the problem, the jury suggested that the award be given to Noland in recognition of the superiority of American art, but Solomon responded that he would withdraw all the American artists if Rauschenberg were disqualified.[58] The jury then voted four (Hunter, Marchiori, Valsecchi, and Starzyński) to three (Meyer, Mendes, and Hammacher) to award the Grand Prize to Rauschenberg, but Hammacher, the president, threatened to resign because he insisted on abiding by the Biennale regulations.

The evening of June 18 was thus perfect timing for the Merce Cunningham Dance Company to perform at La Fenice. As noted earlier, Rauschenberg's work as set designer and stage manager favorably impressed Hammacher, who accepted the compromise the next day: with three of Rauschenberg's paintings transferred to the Giardini, Rauschenberg would be declared the winner and Hammacher would not resign. The next day, the works were moved in a Venetian vaporetto (figure 2.17), the sight of which was much publicized later as evidence of the American manipulation of the jury. Solomon and others then worked on the changed installation, removing works by Johns and the others and hanging Rauschenberg's work on temporary walls in the courtyard (figure 2.18). On June 20, when the award ceremony was held on the official opening day of the Biennale, many journalists photographed Rauschenberg in front of the improvised walls as the Grand Prize winner of that year's Biennale.

Rauschenberg himself felt that it was the dance performance that had clinched the award—the "idea of an artist really working, doing something in Italy, while others [were] politicking," as he told Tomkins.[59] Still, it was no coincidence that Cunningham's company performed in Venice on that particular day. Originally, there were no plans for the company to perform in Italy. As soon as Solomon was nominated commissioner in November 1963, he and Castelli asked David Vaughan, the company's tour manager, to include Venice in the world tour's itinerary.[60] Moreover, Solomon asked the Biennale officials whether Cunningham's company could be invited to perform at the opening gala of the Biennale on June 20.[61] When a traditional opera was chosen as a more suitable event for the opening gala, he suggested scheduling the dance company on the 18th, as a separate event from the

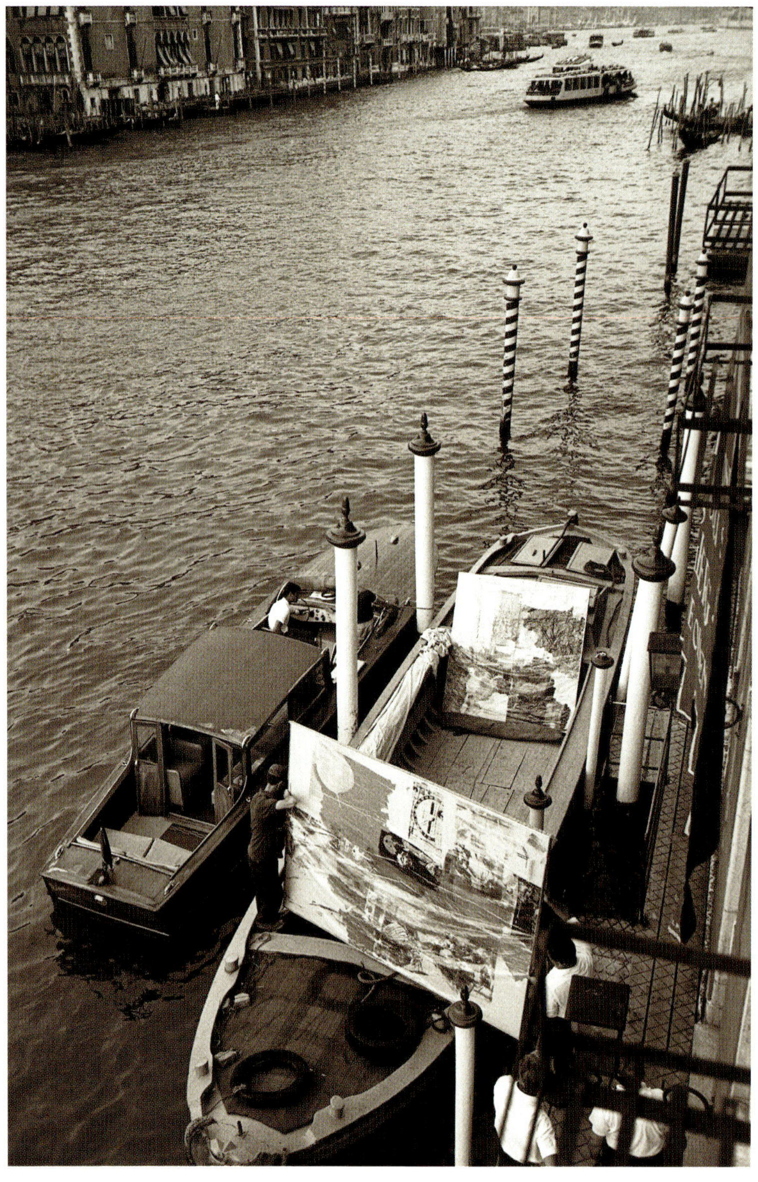

Figure 2.17
"The Pop artist's artworks being transported in the Laguna, XXXII Esposizione Internazionale d'Arte, 1964." Photograph Ugo Mulas © Ugo Mulas Heirs.

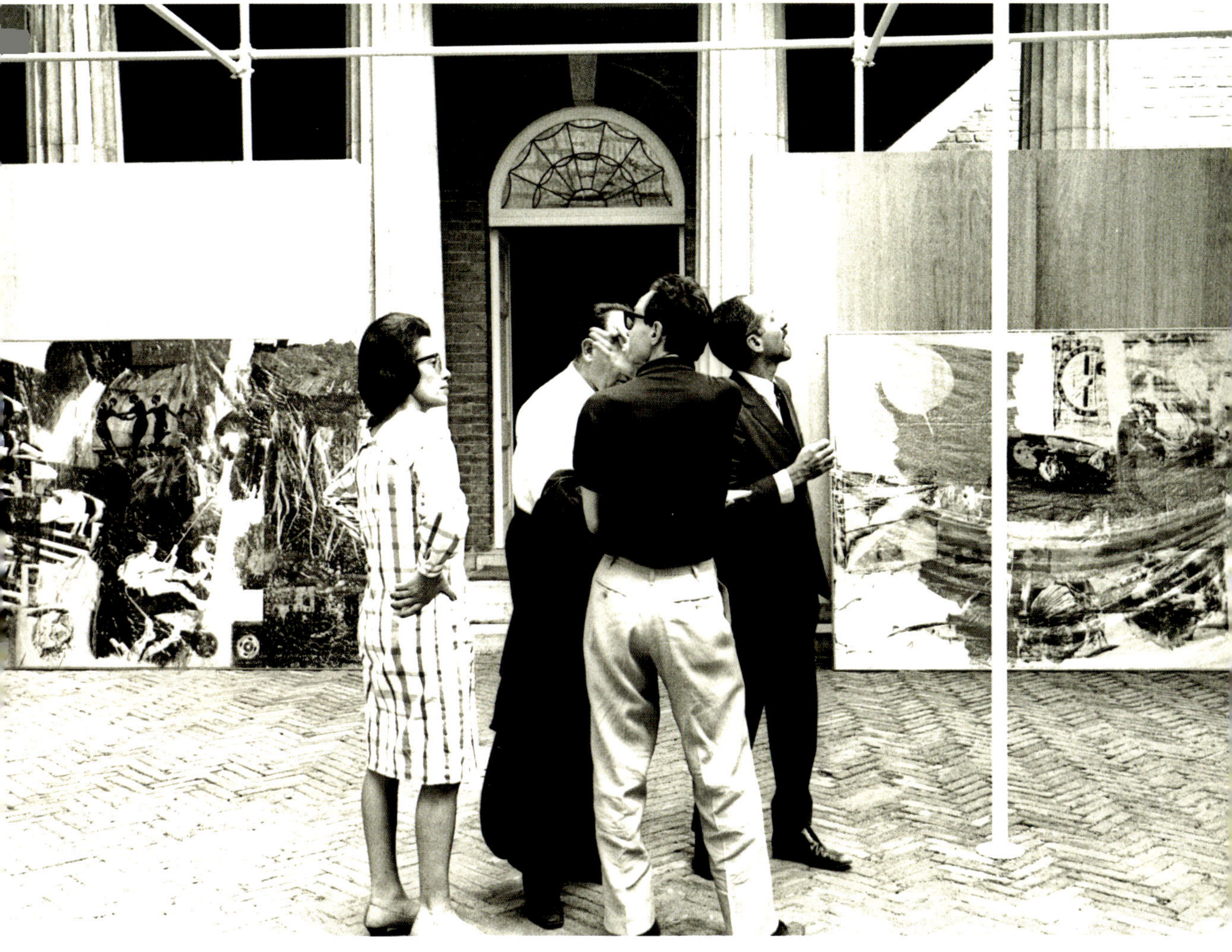

Figure 2.18
Alan Solomon and others working on the outdoor installation at the American Pavilion for the 32nd Venice Biennale art exhibition, 1964. Photographic print: black and white, 24 × 30 cm. Courtesy Alan R. Solomon Papers, 1930–1972, Archives of American Art, Smithsonian Institution.

Biennale. Marietta Stern, Solomon's secretary and interpreter in Venice, who made the theater arrangement on his behalf, wrote to him in New York: "Labroca [the artistic director of the theater] had at last consented to give us the Fenice for the evening of June 18, third day of the vernissage, a very good date, at the conditions you mentioned in your letter of March 19; if you pay the expenses of the John Cage [*sic*] company he gives the theater free, expenses for lighting, publicity, taxes, etc. to be paid by the box-office receipt."[62]

Although Solomon failed to secure the $3,000 performance fee from the State Department, he did not give up the idea of bringing the company to Venice. He explained to the art collector Ben Heller: "We tried to get the Government to send Merce Cunningham's company to Venice, not only because it seemed like a good idea, but also because I felt that Rauschenberg's presence and his sets and costumes might help to call attention to him and enhance the possibility of his getting a prize. The State Department declined and we have since decided to go ahead and schedule the concert anyway on our own."[63] In retrospect, June 18 proved to be the right day to influence the Biennale jury, because all the awards needed to be decided by the following day. Given the decisive impact that Rauschenberg's physical presence in Venice had on the jury's decision, Solomon did not exaggerate when he wrote to Bingham from Venice, "We might have won it anyway (apart from the question of merit) but we really engineered it."[64]

However, this victory was not the result of concerted efforts made by the American team. Although Solomon certainly received wholehearted help from the USIA staff and individual assistance from Leo Castelli and Ileana Sonnabend, he was in effect alone in his endeavor. The State Department at first resisted allowing the use of the Consulate and then refused to provide the performance fee for Cunningham's company. The New York art community also looked on the whole event with rather jaded eyes. Solomon was even hard pressed to find one American critic willing to serve on the jury. As he complained to Bingham: "There were some nightmares about this, including the unwillingness of people to serve on the jury, for personal reasons, which were apparently quite petty. One of them (and this I know to be true of Martin Friedman) was that they didn't want to help *me* win a prize. I think that Seitz had feelings like this, but more with respect to the museum, which after all had never won it."[65] This letter suggests that there were some mixed feelings on the part of the Museum of Modern Art, which had dropped its sponsorship from the Biennale for lack of funding but still expected the USIA to take care of the bill and hand the job over to the museum.[66] Sam Hunter, the founding director of the Rose Art Museum at Brandeis University, finally agreed to be a juror but was far from being a spokesman for Solomon, "to the point" (the latter complained) "where the Italian jurors wondered if he wanted the prize to go elsewhere."[67] This means that even in the United States, there was no consensus about how the American show should have been organized or even whether an attempt should have been made to win the major prize.

In this situation, the strong Italian support for Rauschenberg was the crucial factor in his winning the Grand Prize. As Solomon told Bingham, "It began with the simple pure fact that certain Italians wanted an American [to win the] prize for general altruistic cultural reasons, and proceeded to work for it."[68] Solomon further confided the backstage story to Tomkins: "Hunter was not too cooperative, spoke favorably of Johns and Noland. Marchiori and Santomaso, working together, really swung it. *Don't say this, though.* Can say that both the Italian jurors were strong for RR from the beginning, and that there was great enthusiasm for RR among Italian artists such as Vedova, Santomaso, Naveli [Novelli], and Casciella [Cascella]."[69] As discussed in chapter 1, Rauschenberg's work and attitude represented a way out of the dead end of Informel in Europe, an opinion shared by the art community of Italy. Tomkins even noted that Italian artists' adoration for Rauschenberg was such that they almost seemed to identify the artist with the late President Kennedy, who had also enjoyed immense popularity in Europe—a cultural dynamic Solomon had shrewdly exploited by opening Rauschenberg's section with *Buffalo II*.[70]

The Italian artists' "altruistic" support of Rauschenberg requires further examination, however, for it was tinged with their frustration at the French hegemony in the Venice Biennale after World War II. Since 1948, when the Biennale resumed after the interruption of the war, the Grand Prize for painting had almost always been given to artists based in Paris—Georges Braque in 1948, Henri Matisse in 1950, Raoul Dufy in 1952, Max Ernst in 1954, Jacques Villon in 1956, Jean Fautrier and Hans Hartung in 1960, and Alfred Manessier in 1962.[71] The Biennale officials were concerned with the situation, too, as the waning of Parisian dominance in the world art scene grew increasingly apparent. Importantly, Bingham recollects that a request came from the Biennale officials that Rauschenberg and Johns should be featured in the American Pavilion in 1964.[72] Solomon also commented on this point in his Biennale report submitted to the Congress: "It should be pointed out that the recent decline of European art had been reflected in the Venice Biennale, which was losing its traditional reputation as a rallying point for modern art, and about which there had already been predictions of decline and actual demise. This also accounted to a certain degree for the official enthusiasm toward us."[73]

In a nutshell, the Venice Biennale had to acknowledge and capitalize on the rise of American art in order to continue to be an up-to-date showcase of contemporary art.[74] Solomon and the Biennale officials thus shared a common interest in superseding the hegemony of Paris at the exhibition. While Solomon was determined to employ every means to bring the first Grand Prize to America, the Biennale officials also needed American art as a catalyst in order to rejuvenate the venerable international art festival. A geopolitical change in the world art scene had already been anticipated in the previous year. Giulio Carlo Argan, an influential art critic and art history professor at the University of Rome, organized the San Marino Biennale entitled "Oltre l'informale" (Beyond Informel). He explained that the title "does not imply polemical purposes or allude to the end of a historical phase." Rather, "by showing what happened afterward," Argan claimed, "the exhibition aims at demonstrating the historical validity of Informel."[75] Nonetheless, "Beyond Informel" did create a sense of the end of an era, as it included many post-Informel artists in Europe as well as a number of post–Abstract Expressionists in America.[76] Furthermore, by awarding the Gold Prize to the Japanese ex-Informel painter Hisao Dōmoto, the exhibition in effect announced that Informel was already entering the realm of history.

As though to continue in this direction, the Italian Pavilion at the 1964 Venice Biennale included a number of young Italian artists, many of whom had participated in the previous year's San Marino Biennale. Their works, presented under the term "Nuova Figurazione," were often compared to Pop Art.[77] For instance, the Italian literary and art critic Giorgio De Marchis described Gastone Novelli's painting as "nearer to Pop Art than to the 'New Figuration,'" observing that young Roman artists translated Pop Art vocabulary into an Italian dialect.[78] One of the artists, Mario Schifano, had earlier stayed in New York and was described as "adroitly keep[ing] abreast of the New York movement."[79] As discussed in chapter 1, Restany had seen something more than a haphazard artistic exchange in such parallel tendencies between the two cities. Calling the phenomenon the "Rome–New York axis," he claimed that this aesthetic and ideological connection set the tone for that year's Venice Biennale.[80]

Furthermore, the Italian Pavilion included a large section organized by Argan, entitled "Arte d'oggi nei musei" (Art of Today in the Museum). For this section, he invited eighteen modern art museums from various parts of the world to show "works of art produced after 1950" from their collections.[81] Although the locations of the museums varied from the artistic centers of Paris and New York to rather marginal cities such as Zagreb and Rio de Janeiro, Argan asked them "to emphasize the acquisitions of foreign works of art in a moment in which artistic movements have taken a marked global dimension,"[82] in order to achieve an accurate picture of the current state of the world art scene. Although some museums, such as the Musée National d'Art Moderne in Paris, still selected mostly Informel and École de Paris artists, this section reflected recent international art trends more directly than did the national pavilions.

For instance, the Moderna Museet in Stockholm showed Jean Tinguely, Alfred Leslie, and Richard Stankiewicz; the Tate Gallery in London sent works by Johns and César as well as such British Pop artists as R. J. Kitaj and Eduardo Paolozzi; the Galleria Nazionale d'Arte Moderna in Rome offered Cy Twombly and Arman; and the Krefeld Museum showed Alberto Burri, Lucio Fontana, and Yves Klein. Despite the quantitative predominance of "national" artists as well as those related to the École de Paris, these "foreign" works stood out as alternatives to the French model of action-based abstraction. This show, together with quasi-Pop works by young Italian artists shown in the same building, arguably made the Italian Pavilion the Venice Biennale's own attempt, with the help of Argan, to extend art "beyond Informel."

"DISBELIEF AND DISMAY": AMERICAN RESPONSES

Rauschenberg's winning of the Grand Prize was thus achieved through the unofficial joint effort of the Americans (Solomon, USIA staff, and art dealers) on the one hand and the

Italians (artists and critics) on the other. As examined in chapter 1, this American victory enraged the French press, whose hysterical reaction turned the 1964 Venice Biennale into an international scandal. One would imagine, though, that the award must have been celebrated in the United States, as the international dominance of American art was finally made official with Rauschenberg's victory. Strangely enough, that was not the case. As Castelli recalled, "Even here in America, where everyone should have been very proud about it, there was a feeling of disbelief and dismay practically at this having happened."[83]

Most of the American press focused more on the scandal than on the prestige of the award itself.[84] Like the French press, many American reviewers interpreted the transfer of Rauschenberg's work to the Giardini as proof of a secret deal between the Biennale officials and the Americans. While a *Newsweek* writer quipped that Rauschenberg "had to nail down his win with a fast maneuver,"[85] Milton Gendel of *ARTnews* also wrote mockingly that the artist "was saved for world celebrity by the presence of one combine at the American pavilion and the hasty importation of four [*sic*] from the Consulate."[86] The high reputation Rauschenberg enjoyed in Europe was occasionally mentioned but was mostly eclipsed by the criticism of the commercialization of the Venice Biennale. Writing for the *International Herald Tribune*, for instance, Gene Baro assessed Rauschenberg's prize as a "logical consequence" of "his own success with young Europeans, who see in his particular irreverence, in his wit, and in his taste, a way out for themselves," adding that his art was "ultimately conservative in design," and its radicalism a matter "of appearance."[87] He repeated this view in a longer review in *Arts Magazine*, dismissing the Biennale as a "trade fair of international art," which had "lost every artistic virtue."[88] A notable exception to this critical trend was Tomkins's sympathetic, well-researched report on the Biennale, which was inexplicably rejected by the *New Yorker* and published in *Harper's* only in April 1965.[89]

The most malicious response to the American Pavilion came from Emily Genauer in the *New York Herald Tribune*. In an article ironically titled "The Merchandise of Venice," she introduced the French perspective—endorsed by Paris art journals such as *Arts*—that "everyone in Paris knew Rauschenberg had it in the bag six months ago," while insinuating that the jury was part of a plot manipulated by art dealers, as their "commitments and enthusiasms were no secret to anybody."[90] Calling American works "junk art" and Solomon a "good showman," she attacked the American Pavilion as not only "completely and admittedly arbitrary" but also "infuriating." Since shameless commercialization had reduced the Biennale to "assemblages of what's new, rather than what's best," she even suggested discontinuing the event altogether. Two years later, Rauschenberg commented on Genauer's article: "Someone had sent me, I think it was a Genauer clipping where the merchants of Venice, something like that, where she exposed the whole set-up, and ... I don't know, I was feeling quite patriotic about it. I mean there's not many Americans who have won it and I felt like this, like if you're on the spot you have a real sense of this kind of international competition. And to find the most hostile criticism for my having won to be right in this country was just personally disgusting. There was very little celebration here about it."[91]

Aside from journalistic philistinism toward modern art, a cultural inferiority complex on the part of the American art community may have contributed to the negative reviews. As Castelli opined: "Nobody here had ever thought that one went to Venice in order to compete for a prize. That the prize was really perhaps reserved for … only for … squabbling younger Italian or other European artists, or for great masters. So that a young [American] man should get it was a surprise."[92] A more obvious reason for the critical reaction, however, was the press's antagonism toward the commercialization of the Biennale, which made the prize appear only financial—an award of $3,200 for the winner, followed by higher prices for his work on the market. In fact, Castelli's presence in Venice negatively affected the American reception of the Biennale. He was, after all, an art dealer who could expect significant profits from Rauschenberg winning the prize. As Castelli himself stated on the topic: "Obviously I didn't sit back and say 'I do nothing'[;] after all, I spoke better Italian than Alan.… But I never had any dealings with the jurors, who were already leaning to Bob. I never had any dealings with Sam Hunter. It was an easy victory because practically everyone was in favor of Bob.… But the conspiracy theory does not die."[93]

And indeed the conspiracy theory spread in New York. That summer, Solomon wrote from Venice to Castelli in New York: "He [Peter Selz] told me that the gossip in New York was that [William] Seitz did not accept [an invitation to serve as a juror] because the telegram of invitation was signed by you.… Barr told me the same thing and added that the talk in New York was that the poor souls at USIA and I, alone and innocent in Venice, had been taken in by you and Ileana, and that was why Bob got the prize.… I suppose a lot of this is attributable to the frustration and annoyance of the MOMA people."[94] Many art critics were curiously silent on the whole subject. Little wonder that formalist critics such as Clement Greenberg and Michael Fried were not very pleased to see Rauschenberg winning the prize over Louis and Noland—especially after Greenberg helped Solomon to view and select Louis's paintings, which were still unstretched and had never been exhibited after the painter died in 1962.[95] However, even the critics who had been sympathetic to Rauschenberg's art, such as Leo Steinberg and Dore Ashton, apparently published no comment on this event.

The exception was Annette Michelson, then contributing to *Art International* as a Paris correspondent. Although she discussed the hostile Parisian reaction to the Biennale, she rightly attributed its major cause to the panic that arose upon the closing of Galerie Daniel Cordier. She calmly argued that the scandal of the 1964 Biennale was a reality check: "The Biennale is and has been—since the war at least—nothing more than an enormously effective market mechanism. No deception is any longer possible."[96] Michelson further noted that the Pop style had already spread in Europe, which was evident in that year's Salon de Mai in Paris as well as in the Italian Pavilion in Venice. To her mind, the real problem lay in the challenge Pop Art posed to art criticism, which was unable to formulate new aesthetic criteria for Rauschenberg's "colonization of the 'gap between art and life.'"[97]

Michelson then made her own attempt "to formulate judgment" vis-à-vis Rauschenberg's works. On the one hand, she praised the tension between object and canvas in his earlier Combines as "undoubtedly a personal contribution, though generally of a conceptual interest." On the other hand, she criticized the artist's recent return to painting: "From now on, the face of President Kennedy, the ball players, the reproduction of the Rubens nude, will work as color areas, taking their places within a painting which derives its stylistic postulates from Hofmann, de Kooning—from the 'N.Y. School.' The gap between art and life has been abandoned. Rauschenberg has returned home from his colonial outpost."[98] This critique was a bitter blow to Rauschenberg, all the more for Michelson's cool and analytical tone, and she recalls Sonnabend's displeasure over the review.[99] In effect, Michelson declared that Rauschenberg's prize should be seen in terms of the "market mechanism" of the Biennale, and that his art itself was already in decline. Her criticism rang partly true, as Rauschenberg and his dealers did indeed subsequently reap the financial rewards of his status as a world celebrity. Nonetheless, it must be emphasized that the market mechanism alone could not create a star in the world art scene—at least not in the 1960s. Respect and adoration by fellow artists and art specialists were essential to sustain a long-term reputation. In Rauschenberg's case, he found such support in abundance outside his home country in 1964.

DISSENT AND ASSENT: INTERNATIONAL RESPONSES

The Italian reception of the American "spectacle" in Venice differed somewhat from those in France and the United States. The Biennale naturally had more press coverage in Italy than in any other country. In contrast to the Italian artists' strong support of American art, the popular press's reaction was predominantly unfavorable, not only to the American Pavilion but to the Biennale as a whole. *Il Tempo* compared Pop Art to the insolence "that comes to us like a slap from America";[100] ABC lamented that "everything is lost, even a sense of shame";[101] and *Epoca* complained that "we are paying for these jokes—these are the 'pearls' of the costly Venice Biennale."[102] The derogatory reports in the press worsened with time. *Avanti*, the journal of the Socialist Party, which initially attributed the success of the Biennale to American participation,[103] changed its tone and campaigned against Pop Art because it contained "the germ of a new fascism."[104] As the United States Information Service (USIS) in Rome reported to USIA in Washington, most of the articles more or less denounced "this new school now made 'respectable' by Mr. Rauschenberg's victory at Venice," and blamed American Pop for the international spread of "this new barbarism."[105]

Nonetheless, there were a few exceptions to this vitriol. *L'Unità* considered the American Pavilion "the most interesting of the foreign participants,"[106] and *Radio Corriere* opined that the prize awarded to Rauschenberg brought recognition to "the importance and the essential seriousness of an experiment which has already found bands of frantic followers in Europe, especially in Italy."[107] In addition, a number of reviews related the rise of Pop Art to the waning of Informel. ABC argued that Rauschenberg's prize "confirmed the deep fear of all those who are still dedicating themselves to traditional expressionism, that is to say, to Informel art,"[108] while *La Stampa* defended the value of Pop Art as animating the scene in the wake of the insipid and mannerist Informel that had pervaded the last Biennale.[109] This view was also predominant in the Italian literary and art journals. The critic De Marchis wrote in *Art International*: "Academic *informel*-ism, which in the works of some young and less young painters amounts to a supererogatory reelaboration of achievements in form, has been pushed to the side. By destroying the remains of and the manneristic complications of *informel*, Pop Art has made clear the significance of a poetics that has entered the tradition, saving what is authentic in it."[110]

Furthermore, this positive view of Pop Art found more company outside Italy. As will be discussed in chapter 3, the audience in Stockholm was already familiar with both Rauschenberg's work and Pop Art, thanks to Pontus Hultén's exhibitions of American art at the Moderna Museet. The news of Rauschenberg's prize was therefore received there not so much with surprise as with assent.[111] A Swedish critic described two national tendencies at the Biennale: "One is the USA's capacity to come constantly with a powerful and convincing presentation, the other one is France which consistently shows an inability to produce such a presentation."[112] The German press was even more positive. *Die Welt* enthused that "everything is brushed aside by the American youth, so full of vitality and exuberance,"[113] while *Der Tagesspiegel* in Berlin declared, "Rauschenberg truly deserves the prize he was awarded.... The Pop invasion of the Biennale is a clear-cut breakthrough."[114] Still, the German and Swedish press shared the French and Italian annoyance with Solomon's triumphant declaration of the shift in the world art capital from Paris to New York. *Dagens Nyheter* in Stockholm attacked the chauvinism of this remark,[115] and *Echo der Zeit* in Germany criticized such manipulative "opinion making" at the Biennale.[116] Solomon's audacious statement thus functioned as a double-edged sword. Although his chauvinistic posturing negatively colored the reception of the American presentation, he could not have achieved his goal without explicitly stating that the center of international art had shifted to New York.

Japan, the only East Asian country that participated in the 1964 Venice Biennale, contributed its own observations to this press compendium. Yasuo Kamon, that year's commissioner to the Japanese Pavilion, reported that most of the commissioners considered Solomon's two-part exhibit as a violation of the Biennale rules.[117] He also noted the marked contrast between the weak presentation of Informel painters in European pavilions and the strength of Rauschenberg's work, wherein "real American life was alive." Kamon found this kind of nonidealistic affirmation of reality strongly appealing, and thought it was possible only in work by an artist who actually lived urban American life. Kamon's Japanese colleagues who came to Venice for the Biennale shared his view. *Yomiuri shinbun,* Japan's leading daily, published an article entitled "American Art Is the Victor, Japanese Artists Are above Standard," which reported on a roundtable discussion held in Venice by Jun Ebara, an art critic who lived in Paris, Toshinobu Onosato, one of the four artists Kamon selected for his presentation, and Kusuo Shimizu, Onosato's dealer and the owner of the Minami Gallery, one of the few contemporary art galleries in Tokyo at the time. The three discussants began with a comment that the American Pavilion, including the Consulate, was the most lively and interesting in that year's Biennale, and that "commonplaces" of American art were more appealing to Japanese viewers than "paintings" of European art. They then agreed that a shift had occurred in the geopolitical power balance of the world art scene:

> **Shimizu:** From an art dealer's point of view, I can sense a big change in the rivalry between the European and American dealers. Before, it appeared that they were on an even keel. But now, American artists have increased eminence and the Europeans seem to have admitted the fact. . . .
>
> **Ebara:** You could already see that in the Salon de Mai exhibit this year. But it became decisive in this Biennale, where the Americans have overwhelmed the Europeans and triumphed.
>
> **Onosato:** The situation is this: the Europeans can no longer get along unless they accept American art. So it only makes sense that Pop Art is happening here as well.[118]

Shūji Takashina, a leading art critic and a curator of the National Museum of Western Art in Tokyo at the time, also felt that Rauschenberg's prize was awarded because it should have been awarded, for he believed Rauschenberg was one of the most talented artists of the day.[119] A graduate student living in Paris in the 1950s, Takashina had been involved with the introduction of Informel to Japan. His high praise for Rauschenberg's "strong will to elevate common everyday space into an artistic one" seems to signify that the traditionally Francophile Japanese art world was now officially ready to accept American art. When Rauschenberg arrived in Tokyo in November and participated in the event "Twenty Questions to Bob Rauschenberg," Takashina was onstage as his interpreter. Thus, in a wider international context beyond the Paris–New York axis, Solomon's "American spectacle" was generally accepted as the confirmation of the global rise of American art.

—

In the aftermath of the 1964 Venice Biennale, Solomon did not fare well, in striking contrast to the blessed Rauschenberg. The artist established himself as a world celebrity despite the scandal, and proceeded with his world tour with the Merce Cunningham Dance Company after Venice. By contrast, in the midst of the Grand Prize scandal Solomon was asked to leave the Jewish Museum. His modern art exhibitions, which had put the museum's name on the map, had created a serious conflict with the conservative Jewish Theological Seminary, the museum's parent institution.[120] After his resignation, Solomon organized the New York Theater Rally with Rauschenberg and his fellow dancers in 1965, and curated the American art section for Expo '67 in Montreal. He then joined the faculty of the

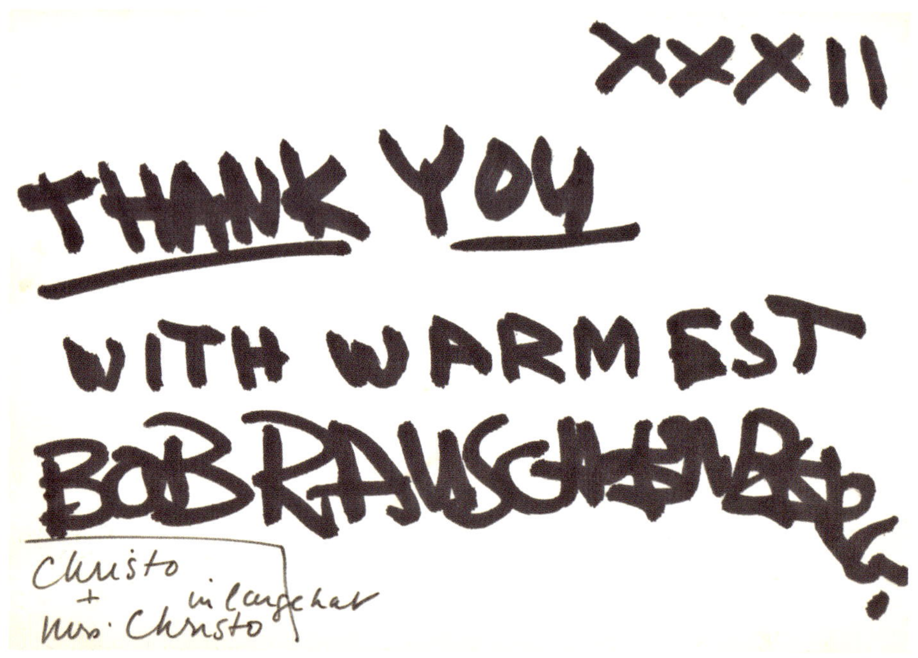

Figure 2.19
Robert Rauschenberg, postcard to Alan R. Solomon, ca. 1964. Handwritten sheet, 10 × 15 cm. Courtesy Alan R. Solomon Papers, 1930–1972, Archives of American Art, Smithsonian Institution.

department of art at the University of California at Irvine, but gradually lost his influence as a star curator, his name fading into oblivion after his premature death in 1970.[121] His last exhibition was "Painting in New York: 1944–1969," which he organized for the inauguration of the Pasadena Museum of Art in the fall of 1969.

However, the historical significance of Solomon's "American spectacle" should not be underestimated. From the vantage point of today's globalized art, the 1964 American exhibition played a crucial role in transforming the Venice Biennale from a pre–World War II world exposition model to a postwar global one. This, of course, had its own demerits, as Solomon's presentation furthered the already emergent trend of the spectacularization and commercialization of the international art festival. Still, by making an American artist the winner of the Grand Prize for the first time in the Biennale's history, Solomon succeeded in freeing the international art scene from Paris-centric values and opened up the field to artists from diverse backgrounds. Although its major players were still limited to male and white artists, it was a turning point nonetheless, and welcomed as such in the world art community.

To Solomon's chagrin, the American victory he engineered did not meet unanimous welcome in his home country; not only the popular press but his fellow curators and critics disparaged his achievement as theatrical showmanship. Disheartened and fatigued by these negative responses as well as by innumerable troubles he had to attend to in Venice, Solomon wrote to Bingham: "In the midst of all this we were going through the awful business about the work in the Consulate being qualified and the whole business about changing the exhibitions.... I can't tell you what hell I went through with the artists, and one thing and another. At this point I hate all artists and dealers."[122] Rauschenberg did not have to deal with the "awful business" himself. Two days after the Biennale's award ceremony, he left Venice for Vienna, moving on to the next performance scheduled for the dance company's world tour. At that point, Rauschenberg's "great migration" in 1964 had just started—he had another five months of traveling. Ever courteous, he did not forget to leave a thank-you note with Solomon for having brought the prize to him (figure 2.19).

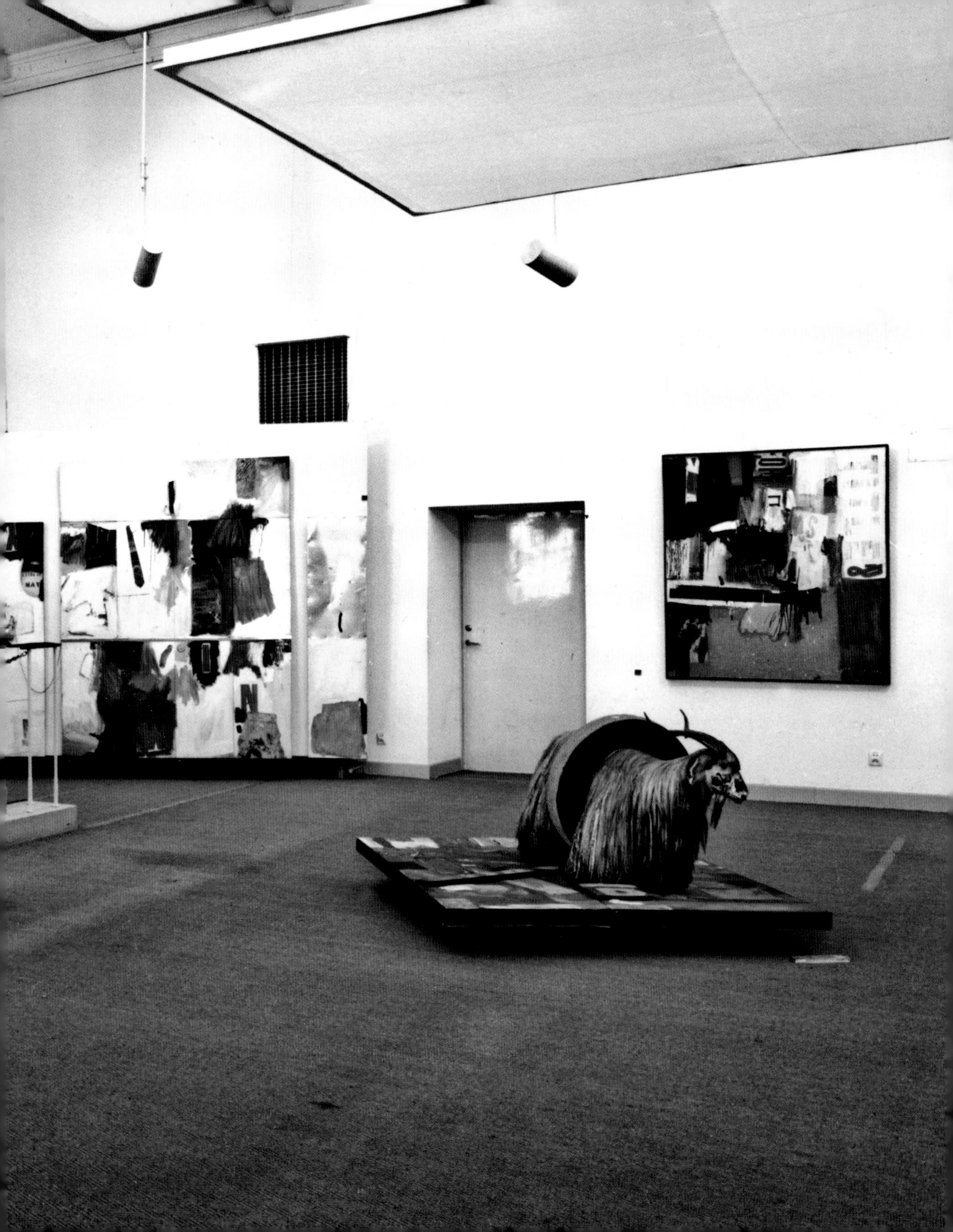

3

A CONFLICT IN STOCKHOLM

THE RISE AND FALL OF *MONOGRAM*

After much ado about the Biennale, the Merce Cunningham Dance Company toured a few more cities in continental Europe before moving on to England via Paris. Rauschenberg was already a star in London after his retrospective at the Whitechapel Gallery in February and March of that year, which had broken the gallery's attendance record. The London leg of the tour in July, which coincided with a photography exhibition of the company at the American Embassy, was such a critical success that it was extended for the month of August.[1] During one of the performances, Rauschenberg even created a Combine painting, entitled *Story,* on stage as part of his collaboration with the dancers. At the end of August, the company arrived in Stockholm for a brief summer vacation, after which it was scheduled to perform a series of events entitled "5 New York kväller" (5 New York Evenings).

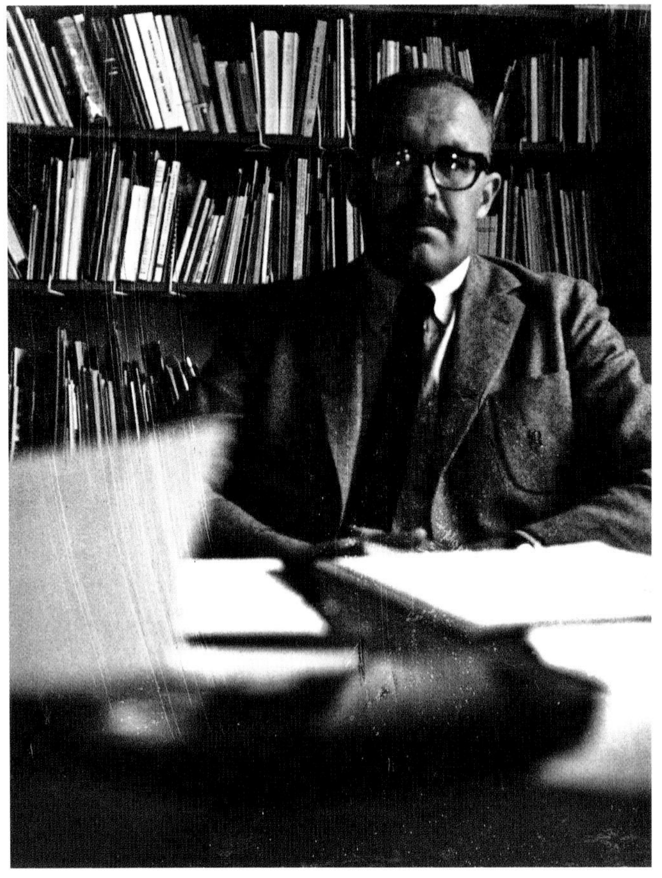

Figure 3.1
Pontus Hultén as new director of the Moderna Museet, 1958. Photograph: Moderna Museet, Stockholm.

Organized by an experimental music and intermedia workshop called Fylkingen, "5 New York Evenings" took place at the Moderna Museet, whose director Pontus Hultén had a strong connection with the New York art scene (figure 3.1). Instrumental in founding Sweden's first modern art museum in 1958,[2] Hultén organized a series of ambitious exhibitions that introduced the postwar avant-garde to Swedish audiences in the early 1960s. Aware of the marginal location of Stockholm within the modern art scene, Hultén planned to import the New York avant-garde so that he could promote his museum as a new artistic center in Europe.[3] Rauschenberg was a central figure in this agenda. Since creating a sensation with his Combine *Monogram* (figure 3.2) in the 1962 exhibition "4 amerikanare" (4 Americans) at the Moderna Museet, he had been considered a representative of the New York avant-garde in the Stockholm art scene.[4]

The Stockholm chapter of Rauschenberg's 1964 migration hinged upon *Monogram*, which at the time Hultén was trying to acquire for the museum's collection. The museum's representative for American artists in those days, Billy Klüver, a Swedish engineer at Bell Telephone Laboratories in New Jersey, worked to gain the artist's consent for the acquisition. Prior to Rauschenberg's arrival in Stockholm, Hultén received a promising note from Klüver: "Have spoken with Bob about *Monogram* etc. Bob very positive about you getting something before Sandberg. *OK* Be persistent and pound on him as soon as you see him (Bob R)!" (figure 3.3).[5] This note suggests that there was a competition over Rauschenberg's work between the Moderna Museet and the Stedelijk Museum—although Klüver seems to confuse the current director, Edy de Wilde, and his predecessor, Willem Sandberg.[6] Following Klüver's advice, Hultén was at the airport when the company arrived from London, not just to welcome the troupe but also to "pound on" his favorite artist, Rauschenberg. Hultén won the negotiation, and *Monogram* entered the collection of the Moderna Museet in 1965, while the Stedelijk Museum later acquired *Charlene* through Ileana Sonnabend.

As the first public European institution to organize postwar American art exhibitions on its own curatorial initiative, the Moderna Museet played a crucial role in the global rise of American art. By circulating the shows to other museums such as the Stedelijk Museum in Amsterdam, Kunsthalle Basel, and the Louisiana Museum in Humlebæk, Denmark, the Moderna Museet had a significant impact on the European art scene as a whole. What propelled Hultén's program were the cartographic dynamics of modern art. While New York needed another locale's support in order to replace Paris as a major center of world art, a marginal city such as Stockholm needed to take advantage of its connection with a central force in order to differentiate itself from other minor cities. This dynamic thus engendered not a unilateral but a reciprocal relationship, in which a major and a minor center of modern art complemented one another. As Patrik Andersson argues, it was precisely Stockholm's marginality—in both cultural and geopolitical senses—that enabled the Moderna Museet to play a critical role in the centralization of American art.[7]

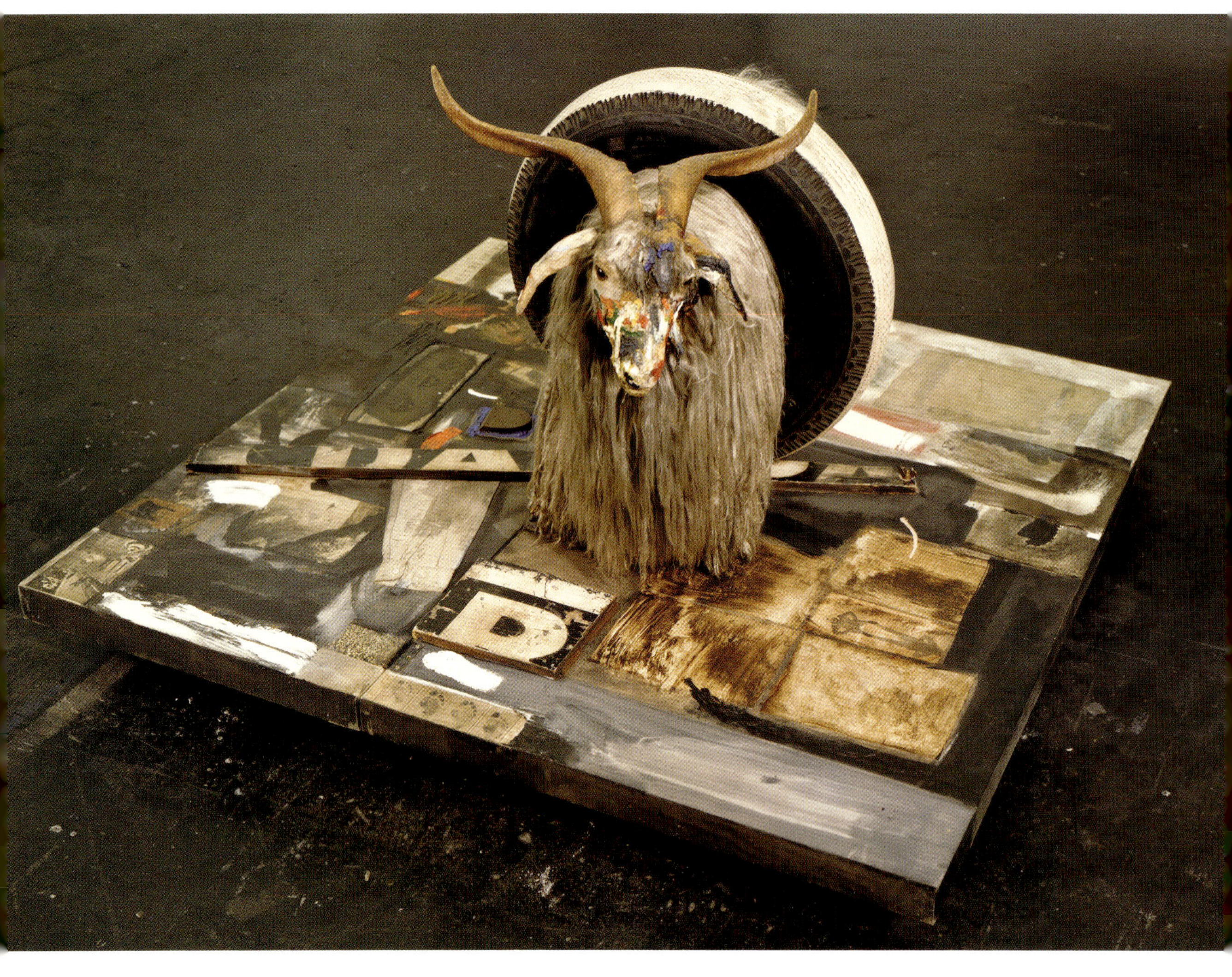

Figure 3.2
Robert Rauschenberg, *Monogram*, 1955–1959. Freestanding Combine: oil, paper, fabric, printed paper, printed reproductions, metal, wood, rubber shoe heel, and tennis ball on canvas, with oil on Angora goat and rubber tire, on wood platform mounted on four casters, 42 × 63¼ × 64½ inches (106.7 × 160.7 × 163.8 cm). Moderna Museet, Stockholm.

In this regard, Hultén's collaboration with Ileana Sonnabend was of critical importance. The two shared not only enthusiasm for Rauschenberg's art but also a practical common interest: Hultén needed Sonnabend's help to borrow American art works for his exhibitions, whereas Sonnabend welcomed an opportunity to show her artists in European museums. Hultén thus became part of Sonnabend's "team" to promote American art in Europe. However, the migration of the New York avant-garde to Stockholm created a conflict within the local cultural scene, with the Swedish audiences at times perceiving it as an American cultural invasion. Tracing the shifting reception of *Monogram* in Stockholm reveals how Rauschenberg's trips, while functioning as a link between the major and minor centers of modern art, also exposed the persistent asymmetry in world cultural currents.

THE "NEW YORK CONNECTION": PONTUS HULTÉN'S CULTURAL AGENDA

In 1959, a year after he became the first director of the Moderna Museet,[8] Hultén made his first trip to New York to establish what he called his "New York connection."[9] Traveling to the city after serving as a curator for the Swedish exhibits at the Bienal de São Paulo, he became acquainted with a number of American artists. Above all, according to Hultén, his meeting with Rauschenberg was like an epiphany: in the artist's studio he saw *Monogram*, which had been completed earlier that year after five years of trial and error. Falling in love with the work at first sight, Hultén immediately decided to purchase it for his museum and asked the artist to reserve it until the museum secured sufficient funds for its acquisition.[10]

At the time, Hultén was conceiving a large survey show of Kinetic Art to be titled "Rörelse i konsten" (Art in Motion), which he would realize in 1961 in collaboration with Willem Sandberg, Jean Tinguely, and Daniel Spoerri. In addition to Rauschenberg, Hultén also invited Jasper Johns, Richard Stankiewicz, and Allan Kaprow to contribute to the American section of the show. While in New York, he also reestablished contact with Billy Klüver, whom he had known during the engineer's student days in Stockholm. This proved to be an important connection, for Klüver would act as the museum's representative for American artists for many years afterward. Recollecting this trip, Hultén stated, "Seeing the new art in New York was a profound experience for me and I felt the show ['Art in Motion'] had a good theme that could encompass the almost violent dynamism of the period."[11] Since this would be the first major and ambitious modern art exhibition held in Stockholm, he was afraid that "show[ing] it to an unprepared Swedish public at the Moderna Museet in Stockholm as the museum's own product would have been too shocking."[12] He therefore arranged to first launch the show at the Stedelijk Museum, whose reputation was more established than that of the Moderna Museet at the time. "Art in Motion" thus opened in Amsterdam as "Bewogen Beweging" in March 1961 and then traveled to Stockholm in May, initiating Hultén's project to import the New York avant-garde to his city.

Hultén regarded Kinetic Art—or more precisely, "movement in art," the literal translation of "Rörelse i konsten"—as a critical and anarchistic way out of the dead end of both expressionistic and geometric abstraction. As the first international survey on this theme,

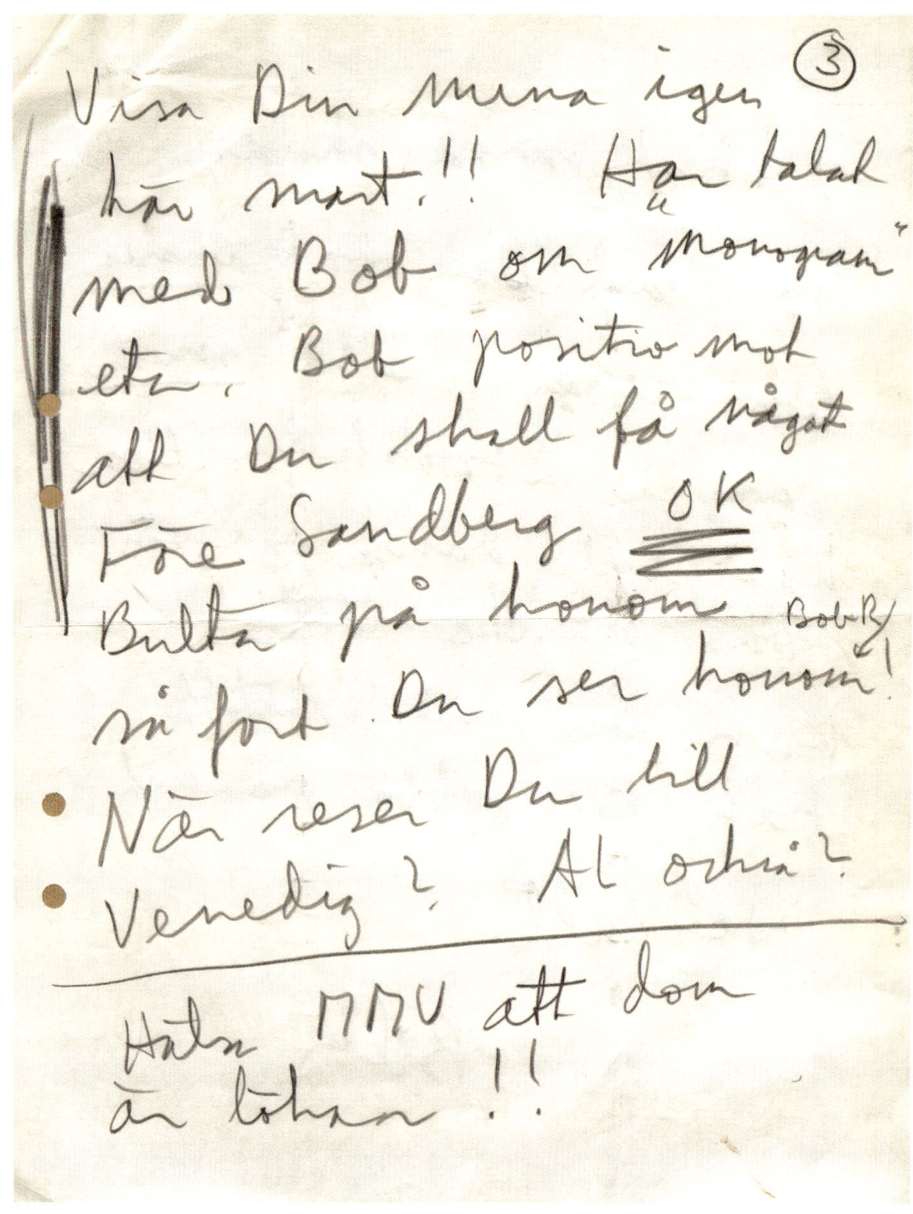

Visa Din mina igen ③
här mart!! Han talar
med Bob om "monogam"
etc. Bob positiv mot
att Du skall få något
Före Sandberg OK
Bulta på honom Bob R
så fort Du ser honom!
När reser Du till
Venedig? Al ochi?

Hälsa MMU att dom
är lökar!!

Figure 3.3
Billy Klüver, note to Pontus Hultén, June 3, 1964. Moderna Museet Archives. Photograph: Moderna Museet, Stockholm.

"Art in Motion" did not focus on American art per se, but ambitiously included more than two hundred works by eighty-three artists from twenty countries and spanning the twentieth century from the historical avant-garde to the most recent Kinetic Art.[13] Above all, the exhibition highlighted Duchamp as the father of "movement in art," with Jean Tinguely presented as his postwar successor. For the Stockholm showing, the Swedish art critic Ulf Linde painstakingly made a replica of Duchamp's *Large Glass* (1915–1923) with no specific instruction from the artist, as well as replicas of *Rotoreliefs* (1935) with the help of the artist Per Olof Ultvedt. To honor their endeavors, Duchamp himself flew from New York to Stockholm to attend the opening and signed the replica of *Large Glass*. As a representative of the postwar avant-garde, Tinguely was given a whole room, which was filled with dancing objects hung from the ceiling and a series of *Méta-Matics*, electricity-driven machine sculptures in steel that produced "automatic" drawings.

Although Rauschenberg was not a main feature of the show, he flew in from Paris, where he had just had a solo show at Galerie Daniel Cordier. Upon his arrival in Stockholm, he helped understaffed Hultén and Klüver install the show, even creating two new works: *Johanson's Painting* (1961) and *Door* (1961). The latter was a construction made of a real door and found objects, created as an entrance to Allan Kaprow's room-sized installation with cardboard boxes hanging from the ceiling. Rauschenberg also played a major role at the opening, which featured a number of programs including an "anti-fireworks" event by Tinguely and Ultvedt, a concert by Thelonius Monk, and a joint performance by Tinguely, Niki de Saint-Phalle, Ultvedt, and himself. However, the opening night turned into pandemonium. Tinguely and Ultvedt nearly killed themselves when the rockets, sent into the water instead of into the air as an "anti-fireworks" event, exploded too close to them; at the vernissage, a young woman remarked on Rauschenberg's work that Ingmar Johansson (a Swedish boxer) could have done that, which resulted in the artist's writing in the middle of the canvas "This is Johanson's painting"—hence the title of the work; Kaprow's installation was a total ruin as people took down the cardboard boxes and stamped on them; Monk refused to play until Rauschenberg persuaded him to; and finally, due to the mayhem, nobody remembered the details of the joint performance.[14]

Black Market (1961) (figure 3.4), a work Rauschenberg originally contributed to the show, had already produced an unexpected result in Amsterdam. The idea of this work was to invite viewers to take one of the objects from a suitcase below the canvas and replace it with something else in their possession. Because they were asked to record the exchange on a writing pad, the piece would constantly change over the period of the exhibition while maintaining traces of these exchanges.[15] Although it was not a piece of Kinetic Art per se, the work suited the theme of "movement in art," which attempted to transform the exhibition space into an open space for collaborative interaction between the artists and the audience. However, despite Rauschenberg's enthusiasm for the work's role as "an active cultural diplomat with an endless flow of art for anyone," he had to give up the idea of

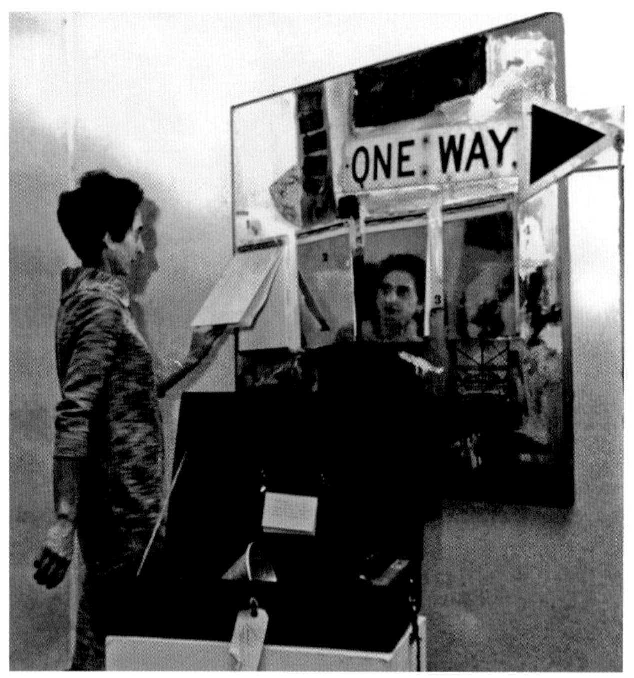

Figure 3.4
Installation view of *Black Market*, in "Rörelse i konsten" (Art in Motion), Moderna Museet, Stockholm, 1961. Photograph by Harry Shunk; Photo: Shunk-Kender, © Roy Lichtenstein Foundation.

viewer participation in Stockholm. As Hultén explained in a letter to Klüver, "All the objects in *Black Market* have disappeared [in Amsterdam]. Nothing is left.... People have taken them without replacing anything themselves.... Ask Rauschenberg to choose some new and curious objects, otherwise we will suffer in comparison to Amsterdam."[16]

With the idea of audience participation frustrated, "Art in Motion" represented a gap between the optimistic ideal of utopianism and the reality of transnational art exchange of the early 1960s. The exhibition nonetheless achieved Hultén's goal, breaking attendance records for the museums in Amsterdam and Stockholm. At the Stedelijk Museum, it was reported that the attendance even exceeded that of "The Family of Man," the blockbuster photography show organized by Edward Steichen of the Museum of Modern Art, New York, which traveled worldwide from 1955 to 1965.[17] In Stockholm, the exhibition drew as many as seventy thousand people.[18] Moreover, by opening at the Stedelijk Museum and circulating to the Louisiana Museum in Denmark after showing in Stockholm, the exhibition drew much international attention, thus firmly placing the Moderna Museet on the world art map.[19] As a whole, however, the global art scene at the time tended to center on the New York avant-garde. In the beginning of October 1961, when "Art in Motion" was still on view at the Louisiana Museum, "The Art of Assemblage" opened at the Museum of Modern Art, promoting Rauschenberg and other New York–based artists as legitimate successors of Duchamp. Unlike Restany in Paris, however, Hultén did not resist the tide of Americanization. On the contrary, he took a further step to confirm the trend and establish the bona fides of his "New York connection" by organizing another ambitious show, "4 Americans." For Hultén, promoting American art was tantamount to promoting his museum.

"4 Americans: Alfred Leslie, Jasper Johns, Robert Rauschenberg, Richard Stankiewicz" opened at the Moderna Museet in March 1962 (figure 3.5). Featuring works by the four artists, the exhibition focused on the post–Abstract Expressionist generation of New York art. In the foreword to the exhibition catalog, Hultén wrote: "Artists used to go to Paris to learn to paint and never left the city entirely. But this is not the case anymore.... After World War II, the greatest adventures in visual arts have played themselves out in America, with the most interesting painting coming out of New York. The generation of Pollock, Kline, and de Kooning is apparently only the beginning. The artistic activity in New York has an enthusiasm that has an inspiring effect on European art."[20] Today, this sounds like the familiar, America-centric narrative typically found in art history textbooks. In the early 1960s, however, it was a daring statement for any European art institution—or even for an institution in America—to make. As we have seen, when Alan Solomon made practically the same statement at the 1964 Venice Biennale, it caused an international scandal. Notably, the marginality of Stockholm afforded Hultén relative freedom to exercise his cultural agenda. By readily accepting the shift of the artistic center from Paris to New York, and by willingly "Americanizing" his own museum, Hultén cleverly secured a peripheral yet special position for the Moderna Museet in the postwar cartography of global art. As if to prove his statement, Hultén mounted numerous exhibitions of American art in the 1960s:

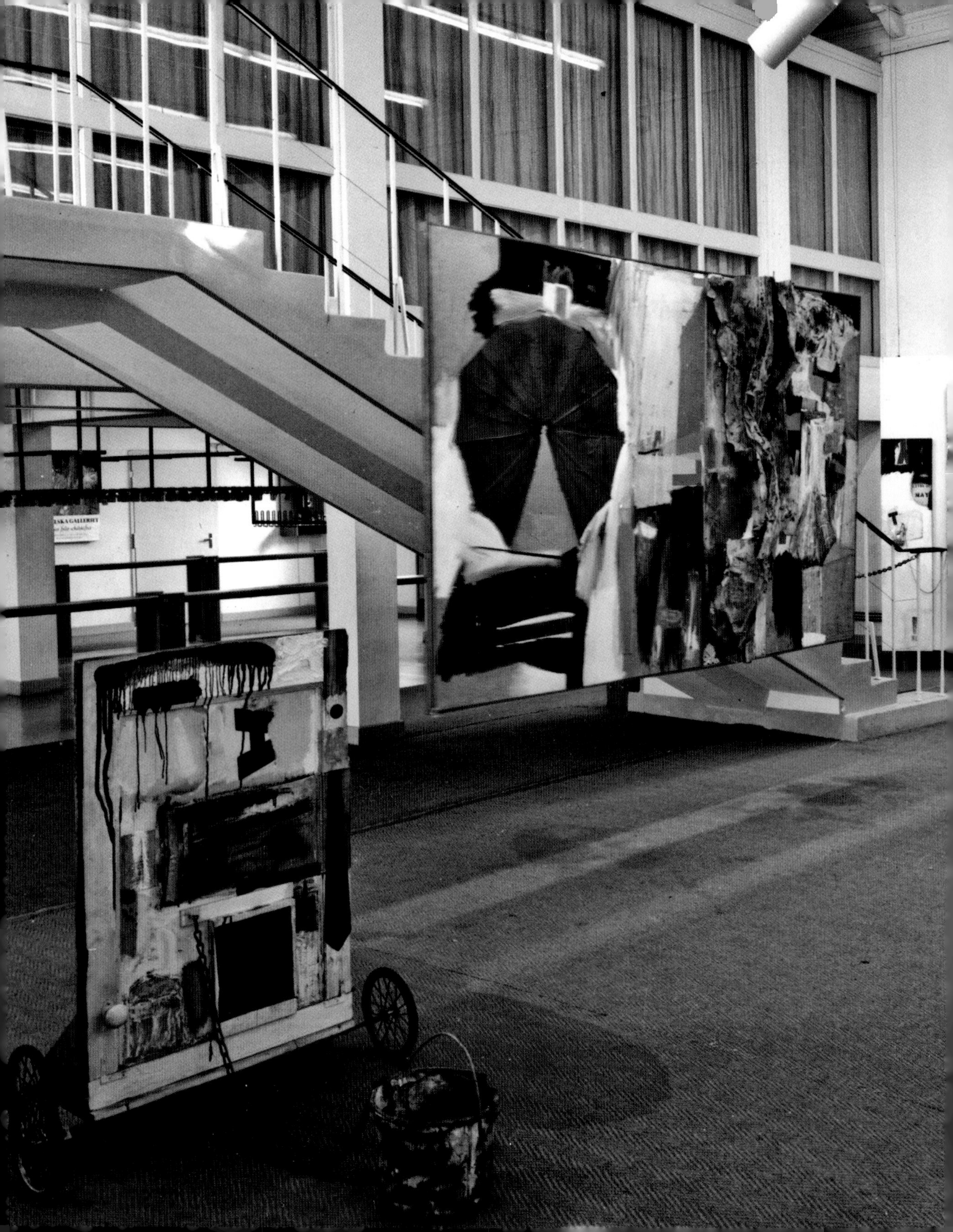

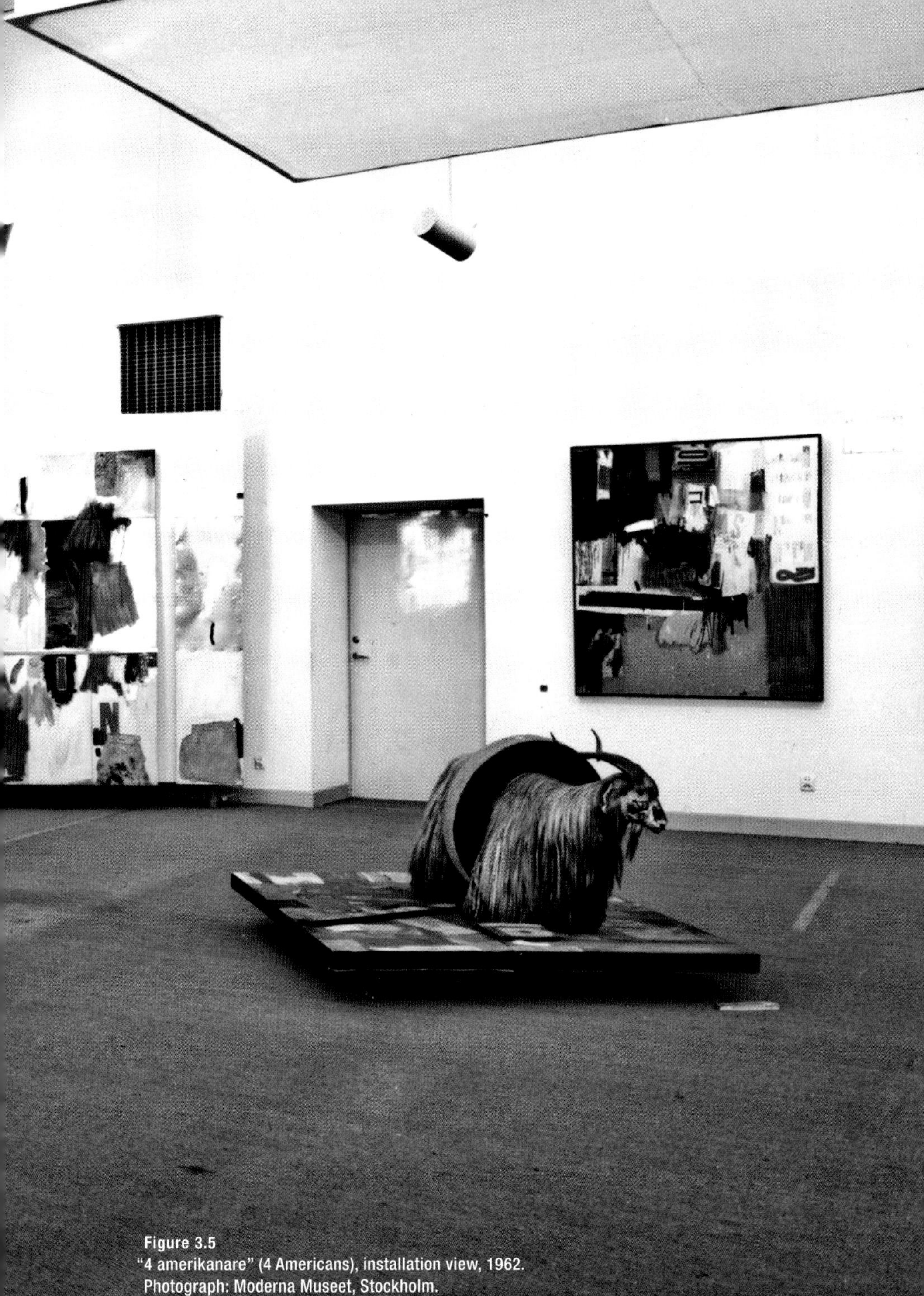

Figure 3.5
"4 amerikanare" (4 Americans), installation view, 1962.
Photograph: Moderna Museet, Stockholm.

1960 "Sam Francis"
1962 "4 Americans"
"Ben Shahn"
1963 "Jackson Pollock"
1964 "American Pop Art"
1965 "Robert Rauschenberg, Thirty-four Drawings for Dante's Inferno"
1966 "Claes Oldenburg"
1968 "Andy Warhol"

Hultén further promoted American art by circulating many of these exhibitions to other European cities, as he had done with "Art in Motion." For instance, "4 Americans" traveled to the Stedelijk Museum in Amsterdam and the Kunsthalle in Bern, while "American Pop Art" traveled to the Stedelijk Museum and the Louisiana Museum in Denmark. Hultén arranged the circulation in part because he wanted to share the exhibition cost with other museums, but largely because he found a lively interest in American art among the museum directors in other regional cities. By responding to the general desire for American art in Europe, the Moderna Museet functioned as an overseas clearinghouse of the New York avant-garde, the status of which boosted the museum's international recognition.

While preparing for "4 Americans," Hultén first established his important connection with Ileana Sonnabend, facilitated by Leo Castelli. Sonnabend was living in Rome at the time and was trying to find galleries that would be interested in showing American art. While Castelli took care of sending Johns's works, most of which were already in New York collections, to Stockholm, he asked Sonnabend to secure Rauschenberg's works for Hultén, since many of them were still in Europe after the artist's solo show at the Galleria dell'Ariete in Milan, held in October–November 1961.[21] Seeing a good opportunity to show Rauschenberg in a European museum, she sent such important works as *Pilgrim*, *Rebus* (1955), and *Hawk* (1960) from Milan to Stockholm, and loaned more from her own collection, including *Charlene* and *Odalisk*. Moreover, she prompted Castelli to lend *Monogram* and *Bed* to Hultén while securing *Gift for Apollo* (1959) and *Winterpool* (1959) from Giuseppe Panza, a key collector of Rauschenberg in Milan.[22] Thanks to Sonnabend's cooperation, Rauschenberg's room included a number of representative works by the artist from the 1950s. With Klüver's help, Hultén was also able to obtain major works by the other three artists in the show. Featuring as many as 118 works by Rauschenberg, Johns, Leslie, and Stankiewicz, "4 Americans" practically served as a retrospective of the four artists, with the degree of attention paid to them unprecedented even in their home country at the time. Thus, the Moderna Museet endorsed their art earlier than any other museum in Europe or America, preceding Rauschenberg's and Johns's retrospectives at the Jewish Museum in New York by one and two years, respectively. Although Rauschenberg and Johns did not make it to Stockholm for the opening, the exhibition hosted a series of events to introduce American culture to Swedish audiences.[23]

Of the four artists, Rauschenberg caused the biggest stir among the younger generation of local artists. As Hultén wrote to Calvin Tomkins in 1963: "Of course, Rauschenberg was the most shocking of the 4 Americans. People came to the museum only to see the *Bed* and the *Goat* [i.e., *Monogram*] and when they had seen those they left…. Rauschenberg has at the moment a certain influence on young Swedish art. If one is asking a young painter under 30 which artist impresses him the most, you would very often get the name of Rauschenberg."[24] Not everyone was happy about this sudden flow of American art into Sweden, though. Ulf Linde observed, for instance, that "4 Americans" was different from "Art in Motion" because the former packaged and put a label on postwar American art and thus felt like a promotional campaign. As far as Linde was concerned, the truly collaborative spirit that had characterized "Art in Motion" was already gone.[25]

Attracting about 28,000 people,[26] "4 Americans" elicited both positive and negative responses from the public. Although the museum could rely on support from the progressive youth, especially those familiar with the experimental Fylkingen, the reaction of the press, which reluctantly acknowledged the rise of New York art, varied from general skepticism to hysterical antagonism. One reviewer ridiculed the show as "pretentious presentations" that had an "air of Zen Buddhist loftiness, rising above both logic and rational contexts,"[27] while another opined that in New York "a work of art must be something like an anarchistic assassination or overwhelming attack in order to even have a chance."[28] One of the hostile critics called the exhibition a "new shock exhibit" and alerted his Swedish readers, "Beware of flirting with mental illness!… By all means, throw out a pair of dirty shoes and call it great art. Whoever wants to pay for it may do so. A healthy mind won't be taken in… this kind of art is dangerous!"[29]

Among the works exhibited in "4 Americans," *Monogram* became the literal scapegoat for these unsympathetic voices. The most eye-catching work in the exhibition, it was constantly reproduced in the newspapers to represent the shock value of the new American art. One art history professor at Lund University even mistook the stuffed Angora goat for a live one, and thus called for a boycott of the whole show.[30] Yet another reviewer referred to *Monogram* as specifically incompatible with the Swedish sensibility: "Faced with the most shocking and unsettling work in the grim collection—a stuffed goat from an old textile factory with his coat dragging on the floor, beautiful horns and a disgustingly painted snout, standing there on a painting instead of a pasture—all this is enough to make you surrealistically old-Swedish in your sensibilities…. The huge dimensions of the works, a typical expression of the American lifestyle, are incompatible with our own national ideas of art."[31] Revealing the typical apprehension held in a marginal nation toward hegemonic trends, this review is a reminder that the center-periphery relationship could cause a conflict when the local community positioned itself in opposition to the globalizing force. The conflict would be even more intense toward the end of the 1960s and early 1970s, as will be seen later in this chapter.

RAUSCHENBERG'S "GOAT"

Since three of the artists in "4 Americans" had already participated in "Art in Motion," Stockholm viewers often discussed their works in relation to movement. In fact, the Swedish title of the show, "4 amerikanare," carries a meaning of "4 large American postwar cars" as well as "4 American people," which indicates the Swedish perception of American culture at the time.[32] As if to reflect the larger cultural implication of the title, one review of the exhibition was titled "Americans in Motion,"[33] and in another Ulf Linde compared its vibrant quality to American popular culture such as jazz and driving.[34] *Monogram*—or "Goat," as Stockholm viewers would call it—would not have been misplaced in "Art in Motion" because it actually moves. With four casters attached beneath the canvas panel on which the Angora goat stands, the piece is a kind of vehicle: one push will set it in motion. Having previously seen "Art in Motion," the Swedish audience did recognize this quality in *Monogram*. For instance, a newspaper published a photograph of a little girl riding on the goat,[35] and Linde associated its horns with the handlebars of a motorbike, like the one that appeared in the 1953 Marlon Brando movie *The Wild One*.[36]

Curiously, this aspect has not received much attention in preceding studies on *Monogram*. As the best-known work by Rauschenberg, *Monogram* has been the focus of controversy between what Thomas Crow calls "iconophilia and iconophobia" in Rauschenberg literature.[37] The crux of the matter is exactly the same as the allegory debate outlined in chapter 2: To what extent—if at all—is it appropriate to find "meaning" in Rauschenberg's work? On the one hand, *Monogram* has been discussed mainly in terms of the artist's defiance of the traditional view of meaning in a work of art. For instance, Solomon stated in a catalog for the artist's 1963 retrospective at the Jewish Museum, "To take a specific example, the Angora goat surrounded by a tire in *Monogram* is without a doubt one of the most extraordinary images of the century. Its 'rightness' and clarity cannot be denied, and yet the goat absolutely defies any kind of rational explanation; it has no meaning, in the conventional sense."[38] As this view found its echo in the subsequent evaluation of the "unreadability" of Rauschenberg's work, *Monogram* has been a postmodern icon of indeterminate multiplicity.

On the other hand, the work has repeatedly been read as an icon of same-sex love.[39] In 1981, Roger Cranshaw and Adrian Lewis suggested that the "goat inside the tyre can be read as a sign of sexual penetration,"[40] while in the same year Robert Hughes succinctly articulated the homoerotic reading of *Monogram*: "Goats are the oldest metaphors of priapic energy. This one, with its paint-smutched, thrusting head and its body stuck halfway through the encircling tyre, is one of the few great icons of male homosexual love in modern culture: the Satyr in the Sphincter."[41] Although such a literal-minded reading is hard to accept, Leo Steinberg made a more convincing argument that homoerotic implications in *Monogram* could have worked as an insider joke in the late 1950s and '60s, and that the reading of the work "depends on the baggage you bring."[42] Significantly, Steinberg speculated on various images related to modes of transportation in the work during his first encounter with *Monogram* in the late 1950s. He recollects having asked himself, "Was he perhaps thinking of the evolution of travel—from walking, to the invention of the wheel, to motoring, to aviation?"[43] Although Steinberg quickly dismissed his own hypothesis—saying, "you can Rorschach this sort of thing into the work, but then it's the next patient's turn"—it is worth taking a closer look at this collage of images, for they do seem to revolve around a certain structure. The structure is governed not by the unlikely evolutionary narrative entertained by Steinberg, but by the dialectical tension between two parallel impulses, that is, an urge to move beyond and a force to resist such movement—a dynamic that looms large in Rauschenberg's work as a whole.

As Steinberg observed, *Monogram* includes many images and objects related to spatial movement: a tire around the goat's torso, a tennis ball, and pictures of astronauts and a tightrope in the air, among others (figure 3.6). A number of allusions to gravity are also present in the piece—footprints, a shoe sole, and a figure's reflection on water—which all represent the force that pulls objects to the ground (figure 3.7). Yet the references to motion and gravity are not mutually exclusive, as even the images related to aviation are an immediate reminder of gravity, or a fall to the earth. This is embodied in the photograph of parachutes pasted on the canvas panel, taken from the same *Life* article that the artist used for the *Untitled* Combine (Man with White Shoes). As examined in chapter 2, the image of a parachute that failed in landing condenses what Crow called "rise and fall" into one. Rauschenberg's interest in flight and gravity thus echoes in *Monogram* as well.

As if to confirm this point, Rauschenberg stenciled the words "EXTRA HEAVY" on the canvas panel (figure 3.8). These words probably refer to the goat's origin: the artist bought it from a secondhand furniture store whose owner had found it at a post office sale in an unclaimed crate, which would have borne similar stenciled words.[44] Although there is no telling how much the goat actually weighs, its visual weight was a major challenge for the artist: he took no fewer than five years to complete the work, in part due to his various ideas about where to place the goat within the work. It is thus arguable that *Monogram* is roughly structured around the dialectic tension between gravity as a physical principle and the artist's challenging such a force, which is abstract enough to contain a multivalent quality.

The development of this dialectic in *Monogram* can be observed in a series of sketches and photographs that record the early stages of the work.[45] The earliest preliminary study for *Monogram* (figure 3.9), from 1955, shows the goat with a ladder, a device for upward motion. Although no documentary photographs show the use of an actual ladder in any state of *Monogram*, the artist's attempt to give a sense of uplifting movement to the visually heavy material is evident in its first state—with the goat perching on a ledge that protrudes from the canvas (figure 3.10). In this photograph, which incidentally proves that the stuffed goat is relatively light, the goat looks like a flying animal, curiously deprived of weight. Rauschenberg also placed three light bulbs under the ledge of this version in order to "give it a lift," but the result was unsatisfactory, as he saw "the goat wouldn't give up, it wouldn't share with the rest of the imagery."[46] (The canvas panel used in the first stage of *Monogram* became an independent piece titled *Rhyme*, dated 1956.)[47]

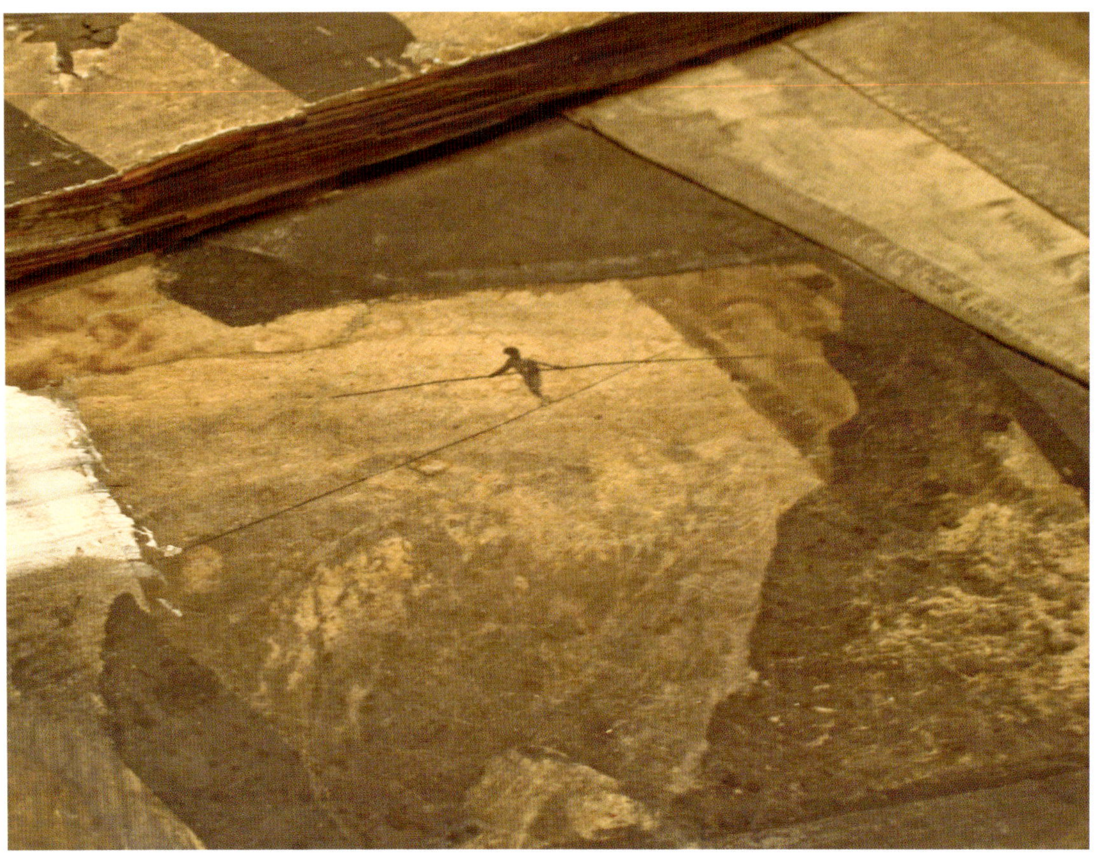

Figure 3.6 and 3.7
Details of *Monogram*. Photographs by author.

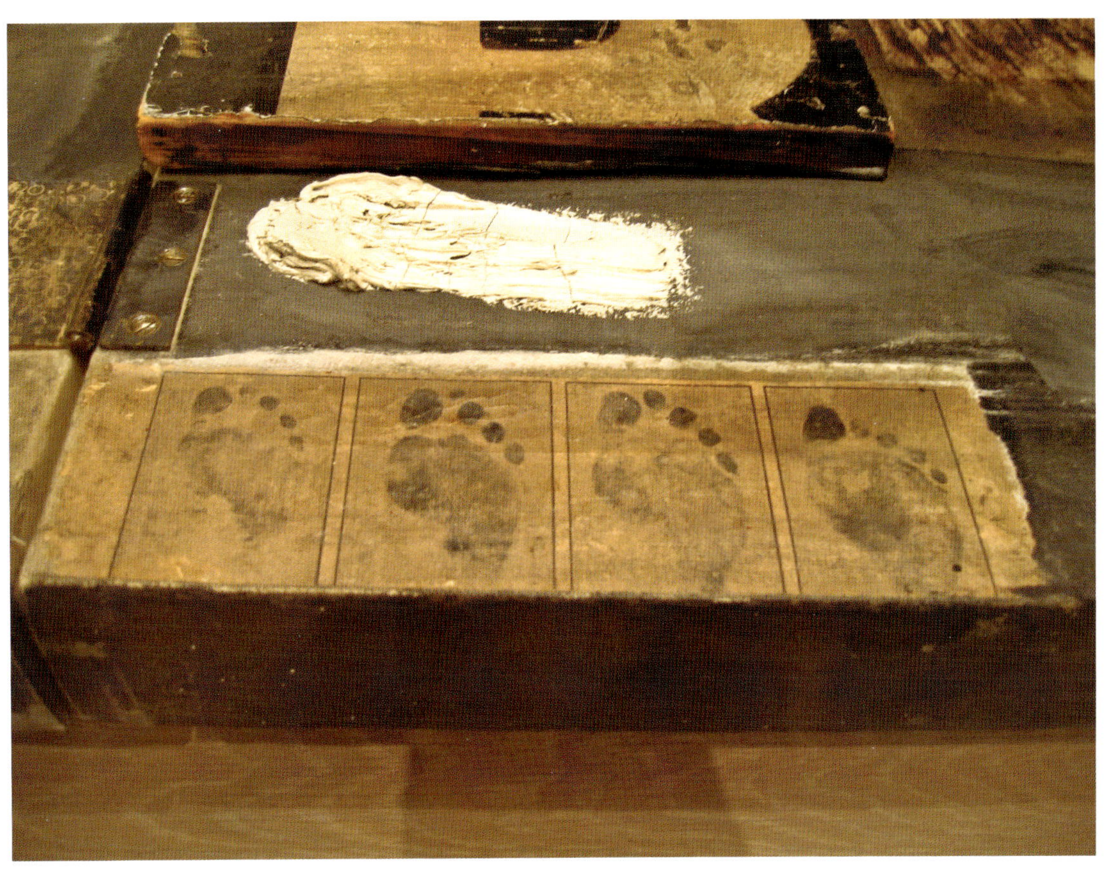

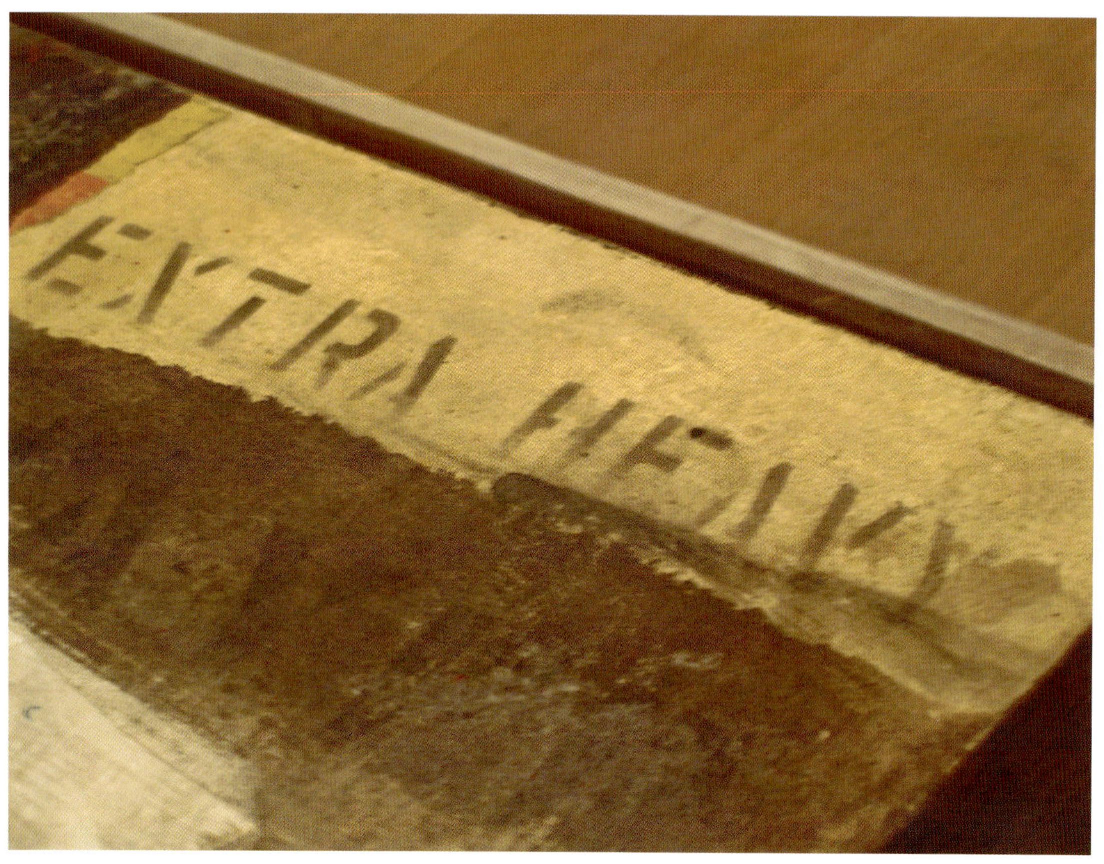

Figure 3.8
Detail of *Monogram*. Photograph by author.

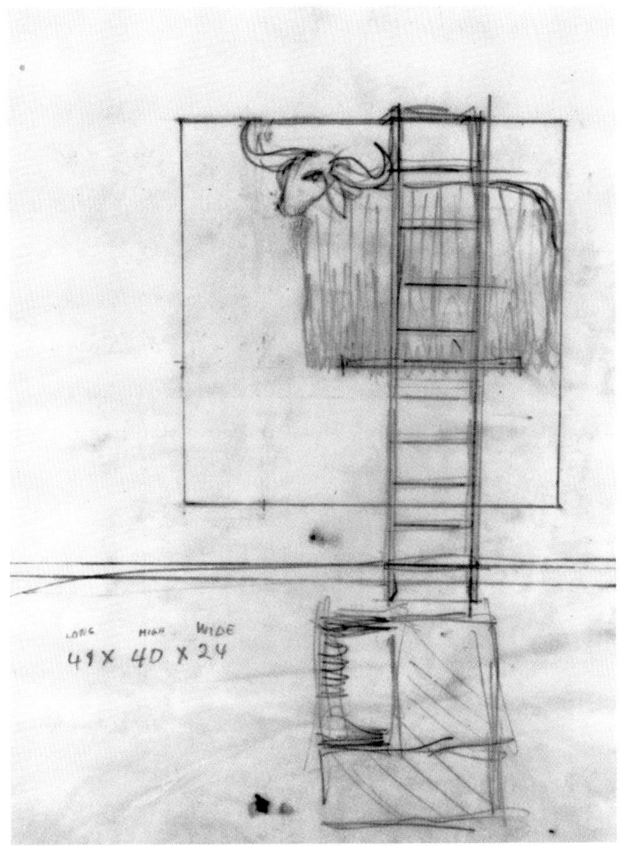

Figure 3.9
Robert Rauschenberg, *Monogram: Preliminary Study I*, ca. 1955. Pencil on paper, $11\frac{7}{8} \times 8\frac{3}{4}$ inches (30.2 × 22.2 cm). Jasper Johns Collection. Photograph by Glenn Steigelman.

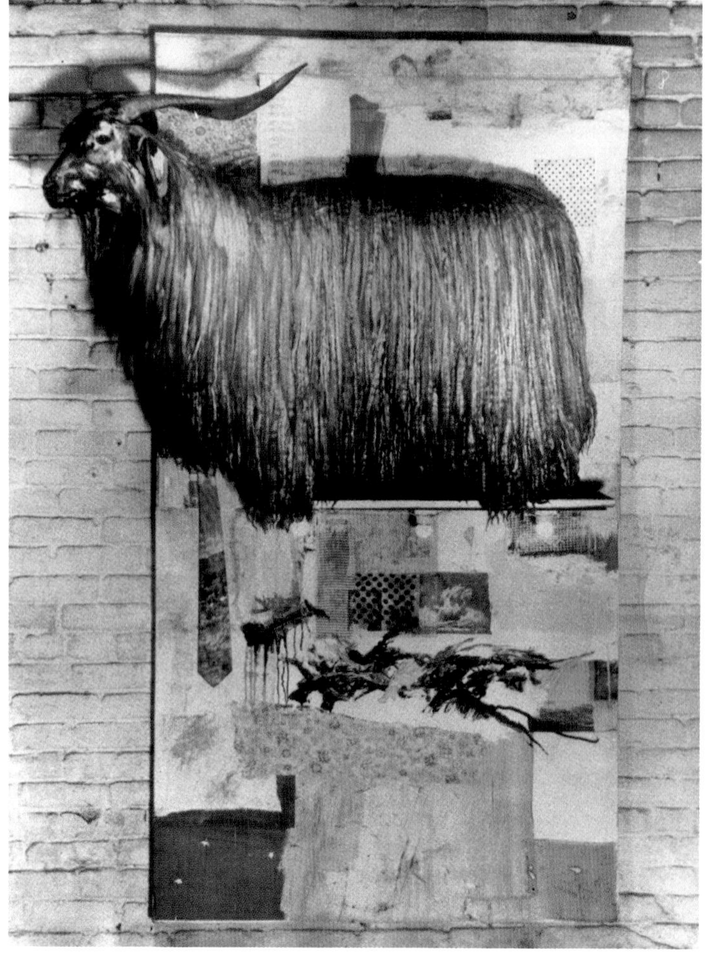

Figure 3.10
Monogram, first state, ca. 1955. Photograph by Harry Shunk; Photo: Shunk-Kender, © Roy Lichtenstein Foundation.

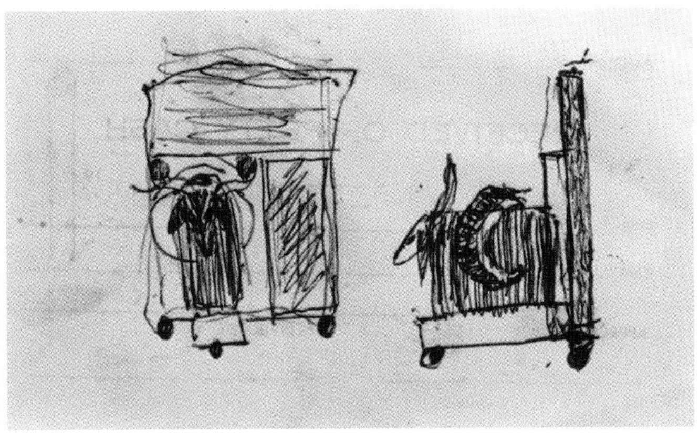

Figure 3.11
Robert Rauschenberg, *Monogram: Preliminary Study II*, ca. 1956. Ballpoint ink on paper, 3 × 5 inches (7.6 × 12.7 cm). Former Jasper Johns Collection. Location unknown.

The next study for *Monogram* (figure 3.11), from around 1956, shows the goat with the automobile tire around its torso as well as wheels beneath the structure on which it stands, drawn in a frontal and a side view. Yet the photograph of the second stage of *Monogram* from the same period is very different from the study: it includes the goat with the tire (painted white) and a taller, simplified ladder-like painting panel as its back support (figure 3.12). (This panel would later become a part of another painting, *Summer Storm*, dated 1959.) In this version, the goat is placed on a wooden base but not on wheels yet. This time, Rauschenberg observed: "It looked like the goat was a beast of burden. It looked like it was his job to pull this thing around, you know, and he was dead, he couldn't move, so that was sort of pitiful. So what the hell does this goat need? I said, it just needs a garden! It just needs a place to be! And so, that's how this piece came about, the final version."[48]

Accordingly, *Sketch for Monogram* from around 1959 shows how carefully the artist designed the final arrangement of the goat on the panel (figure 3.13).[49] Rauschenberg explained why he put a tire around the goat: "And one of the reasons that I used the tire is, because [in] the first place it fits, but [in] the second place, [in] nearly every place in the world you have used tires, I mean, just abandoned tires, just like cardboard boxes, rags, and I thought that was quite elegant. And when I put the tire around its torso, it had a kind of presence that it hadn't had when it was just a goat living alone."[50] Steinberg suggests that the round shape of the tire refers to a gesture of appropriation by Rauschenberg, who sometimes put circles around ready-made objects and images when incorporating them into his work.[51] It is true that the goat seems more sculptural with the tire, but neither Steinberg nor Rauschenberg himself mentions an important point: the tire did not just fit the goat without any manipulation; Rauschenberg made it fit *visually*, by painting it white. With the white paint, the tread of the tire becomes more conspicuous, making it analogous to the wave of the Angora's fleece, and the heavy industrial rubber is rendered much lighter. In addition, the white tire looks like a reversed, three-dimensional image of *Automobile Tire Print*, which Rauschenberg made with the help of John Cage in 1953. Just as the continuous trace of a tire created a beautiful ink scroll painting in that work, so does the white band around the tire in *Monogram* make it quite elegant, adding a kind of alchemical quality.

Hultén also regards the tire as a critical factor in *Monogram*. He once said, "Without the tire, the goat wouldn't take off, mentally. It has to do with the basic discipline of formal structure."[52] Observing the tension between "what's on the earth and [what's] in the sky" in *Monogram*, he further commented: "Yes, what's usually good for sculpture is not there, in the sense of equilibrium, the feeling of standing, or weight. Rather what is present is the opposite; the flying away, the taking off. Maybe that's something that's in the Combine with the goat. It seems to me that there is a lot about an absence of gravity, meaning that the elements, the parts do not appear to have a lot of matter, or be very material. It seems that he enjoys that, that they become poetic metaphors. They have no weight."[53] The final state of *Monogram* looks more comfortably "in motion," with the goat in its

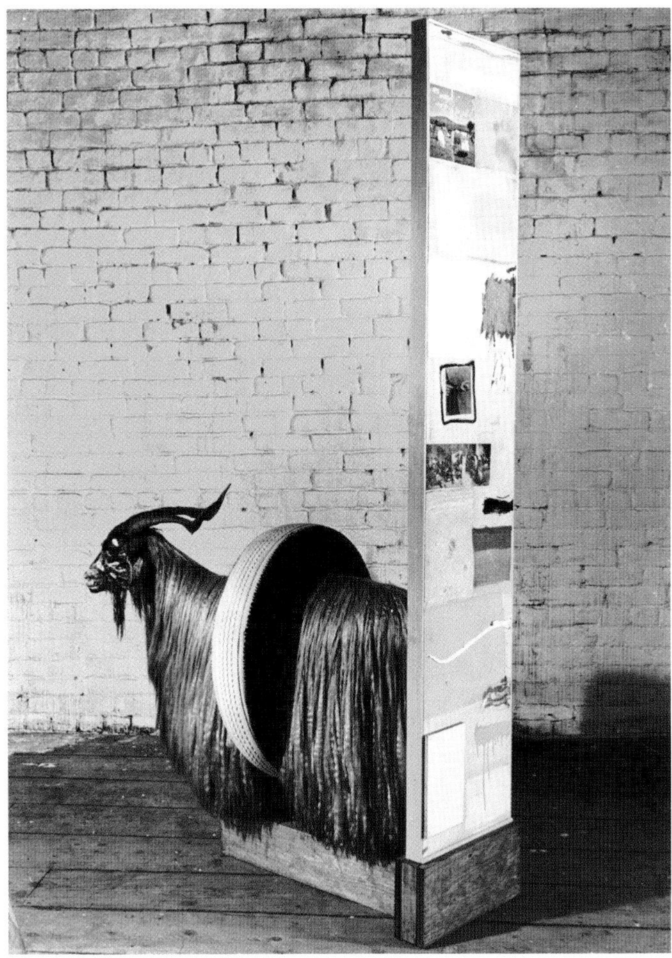

Figure 3.12
Monogram, second state, ca. 1956. Photograph by Rudy Burckhardt.

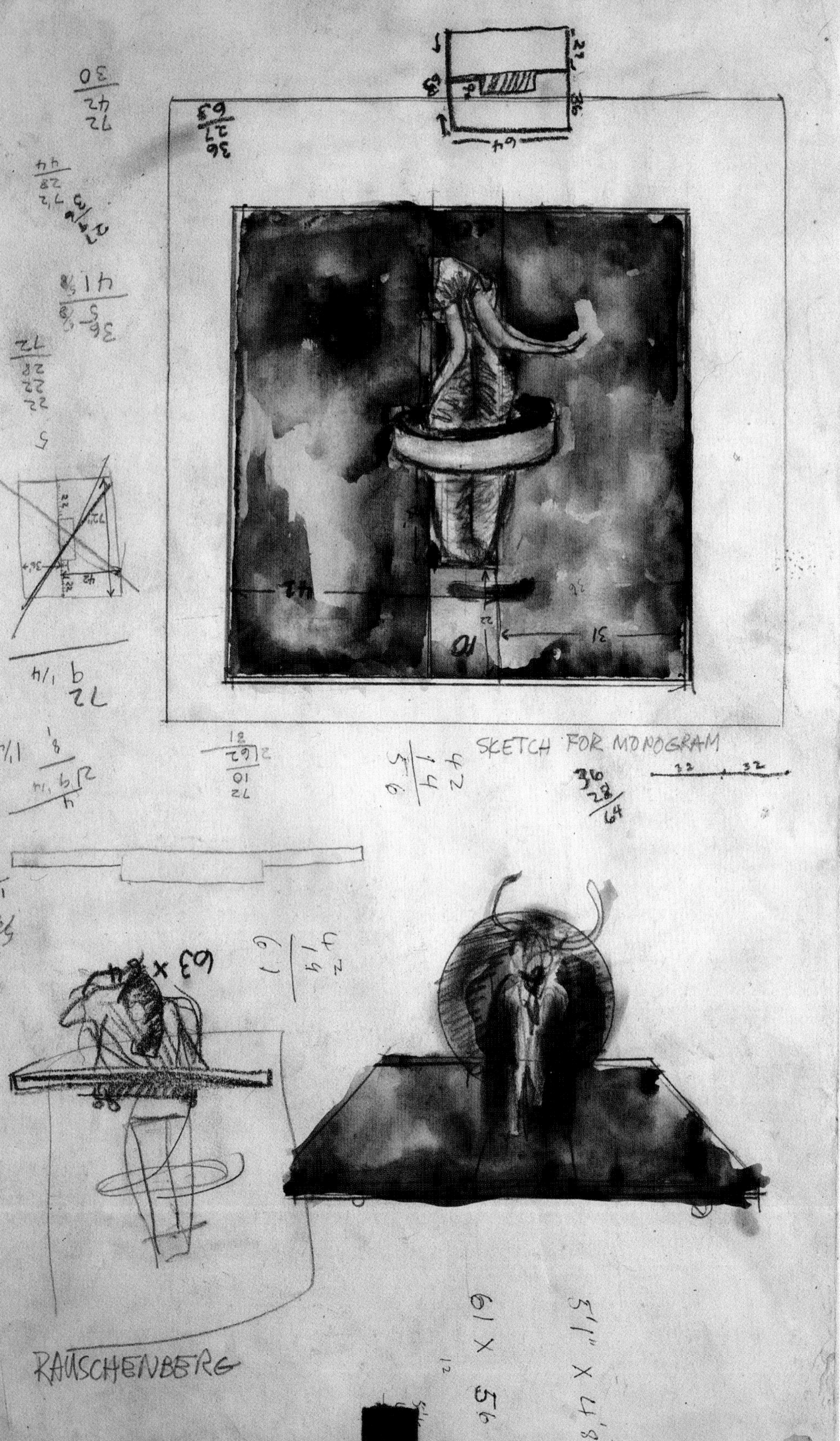
SKETCH FOR MONOGRAM
RAUSCHENBERG
5'1" X 4'8"

Figure 3.13
Robert Rauschenberg, *Sketch for Monogram*, ca. 1959. Watercolor and graphite on paper, 19 ⅛ × 11 ⅜ inches (48.6 × 28.9 cm). Estate of Robert Rauschenberg.

own garden. The installation view of "4 Americans" clearly reflects the quality of mobility in Rauschenberg's works (see figure 3.5). *Gift for Apollo*, which occupied the center of the display with *Monogram*, refers to the Greek god's celebrated chariot with four wheels. Combine paintings featured in the exhibition, such as *Allegory* (1960) and *Charlene*, also incorporated the motifs of an umbrella and a parachute. *Allegory* was in fact hung on the side of an open staircase, as if it were literally floating in the air.

In relation to the exhibition's presentation in Stockholm, Ileana Sonnabend once commented on Rauschenberg's own desire to float: "He doesn't believe in gravity, you know. At times he thinks he can float. After the Stockholm show, he was standing at the top of a beautiful staircase, and it seemed to him that he could just float down it, so he tried, and took a frightful fall."[54] While there is no confirmation that the staircase Sonnabend mentions is the one in figure 3.5—although it is tempting to think it is—her statement testifies to Rauschenberg's own attempt to challenge gravity. This theme of flight and motion would take on a different dimension when the artist started performing himself, physically becoming part of his work and migrating to various cities to enact his events and performances.

"AMERICAN POP ART" AND "5 NEW YORK EVENINGS"

Before the Merce Cunningham Company performed a series of events entitled "5 New York Evenings" in September 1964, Stockholm received another wave of American art. The Moderna Museet held a large show called "Amerikansk Pop-konst: 106 former av kärlek och förtvivan" (American Pop Art: 106 Forms of Love and Despair) from February to April. Featuring seven representative Pop artists—Jim Dine, Roy Lichtenstein, Claes Oldenburg, James Rosenquist, George Segal, Andy Warhol, and Tom Wesselmann—"American Pop Art" was the first large-scale Pop Art exhibition in Europe. Since the show traveled to the Louisiana Museum and the Stedelijk Museum, it marked a significant moment for the overseas promotion of not only Pop Art but also its forerunner Rauschenberg, whose successful retrospective in London coincided with the Stockholm showing of "American Pop Art." At the Louisiana Museum, which had not been a venue for "4 Americans," "American Pop Art" was mounted with additional works by Rauschenberg and Johns in order to reiterate the lineage. Moreover, in April 1964, the Tate Gallery also held a large exhibition that featured works by Rauschenberg and American Pop artists, and in June the Gemeentemuseum in The Hague opened an exhibition of Pop Art and Nouveau Réalisme, which traveled to Berlin and Brussels. With the Venice Biennale set to open in June, the flood of Pop-related shows in so many European museums must have helped to reinforce Rauschenberg's status as an artist who opened the door for Pop Art—an idea that Solomon forcefully argued in his catalog essay for the Moderna Museet's "American Pop Art" as well as for his Venice presentation.[55]

Sonnabend threw her total support to Hultén for "American Pop Art." After "4 Americans," they had become more conscious of the fact that they shared the project of promoting American art in Europe. Sonnabend made her sentiments explicit in response to Hultén's request to help him with "American Pop Art": "I'm afraid we're sailing in the same boat. Let's hope it doesn't sink!"[56] In helping Hultén, the Paris-based Sonnabend was in a much more advantageous position than Castelli in New York: she represented all seven of the artists featured in "American Pop Art." While Klüver had to deal with a number of galleries to collect works in New York for Hultén's exhibition, Sonnabend single-handedly secured works in Europe—including works from her private collection as well as those she had already sold to collectors. Eventually, she gathered one work by Rosenquist, seven by Lichtenstein, six by Segal, two by Oldenburg, two by Wesselmann, fourteen by Dine, and twelve by Warhol, sending them from Paris to Stockholm at the end of January.[57]

Hultén adopted a strategy similar to Sonnabend's in preparing publicity and producing a catalog. In addition to creating a series of postcards with works by the featured artists, he had Lichtenstein design an original poster for the exhibition, which also graced the catalog cover. The image provocatively featured a close-up of a man's right hand with its index finger pointing at the viewer in the manner of Uncle Sam in James Montgomery Flagg's "I Want YOU" Army recruiting poster. The catalog included texts on Pop Art by a variety of people such as Klüver, Solomon, Henry Geldzahler, and Hultén himself. Visually attractive (Sonnabend called it a piece of Pop Art, indeed) and substantive in content, the catalog quickly sold out while Hultén was still receiving requests for copies from overseas audiences.[58] With the rising international reputation of the Moderna Museet, Hultén endeavored to fortify its American art holdings, although he had to place priority on building a respectable modern European art collection.[59] To name just a handful of the American works he obtained, Johns's *Slow Fields* (1962) entered the museum in 1963; Oldenburg's *Ping Pong Table* (1964) and Rosenquist's *I Love You with My Ford* (1961) in 1964; and Warhol's *Marilyn in Black and White* (1962) and, most importantly, Rauschenberg's *Monogram* in 1965. In addition, Hultén was a major collector of modern art himself, and acquired a number of important works by these artists for his personal collection. For example, he had Rauschenberg's *Money Thrower for Tinguely's H.T.N.Y.*, Lichtenstein's *Foot Medication* (1962), Warhol's *Brillo Box* (1964), and Oldenburg's *Cheese Slice* (1964). Although not all of these works were purchased through Sonnabend, Hultén consequently became part of her "team" in Europe by creating a taste for the new American art through both his public and private collections.

Thus, when Rauschenberg arrived in Stockholm at the end of August with Cunningham's company, he was already famous there, with the Grand Prize at the 1964 Venice Biennale adding icing to the cake. His first visit to the city after participating in "Art in Motion" was a triumphal return. The dance company performed on the first and last nights of "5 New York Evenings," with individual events on the intervening three nights, such as Cage and Tudor's concert, a dance by Yvonne Rainer and Robert Morris—who flew from New York to join the event—and a performance by Rauschenberg, Öyvind Fahlström, and others. On his arrival in Stockholm, Rauschenberg made a collage-based poster for these events (figure 3.14), juxtaposing pictures of participants with images of objects such as a ladder and a tire that confirm the artist's continued interest in motion and gravity.

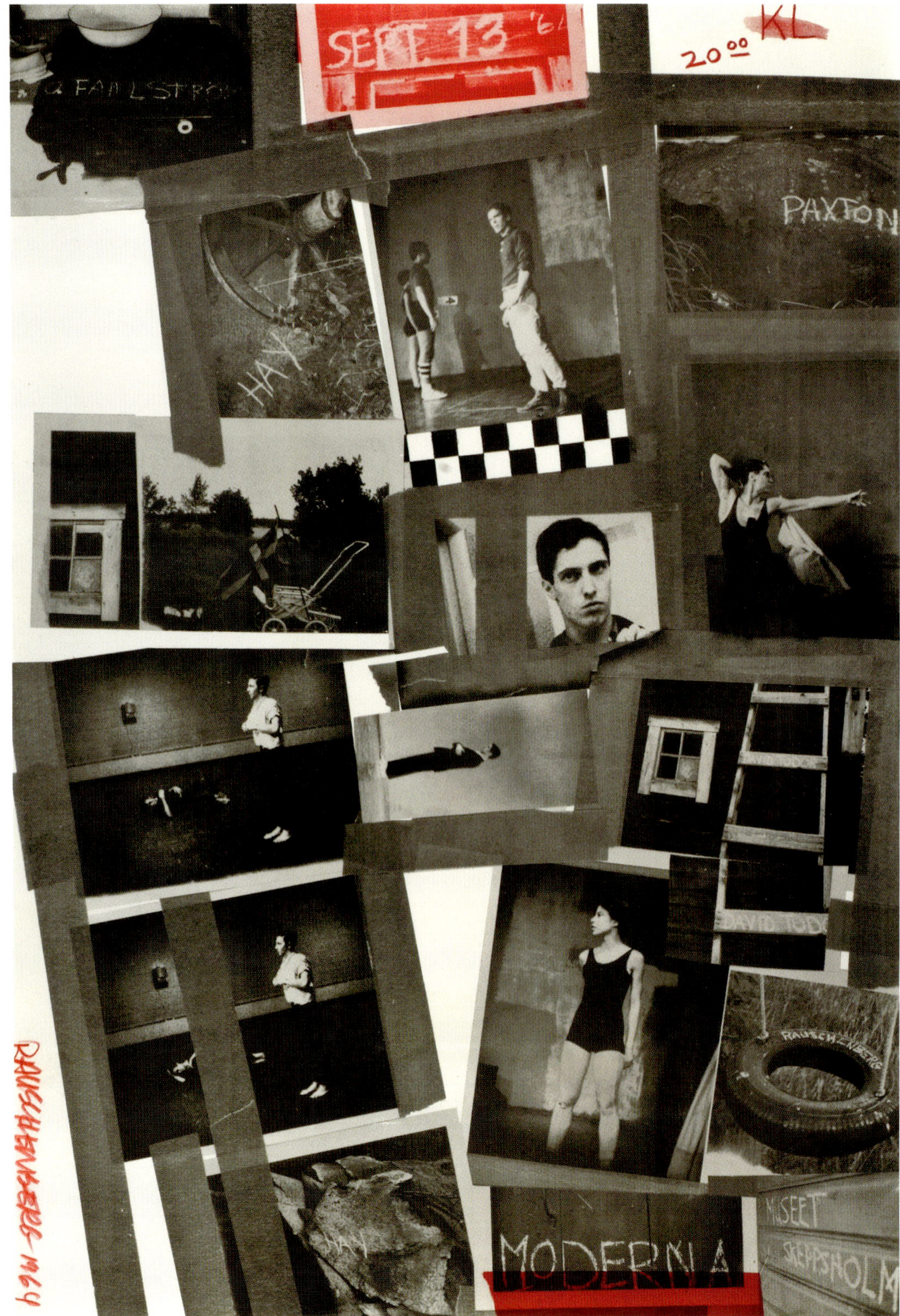
SEPT 13 '64
20.00 KL
PAXTON
HAY
RAUSCHENBERG
MODERNA
MUSEET
SKEPPSHOLM
RAUSCHENBERG 1964

Figure 3.14
Robert Rauschenberg, *Poster for "5 New York Evenings,"* 1964. Lithography on paper, 17 3⁄8 × 11 3⁄4 inches (44 × 30 cm). Moderna Museet, Stockholm.

Among his performance pieces, Rauschenberg's *Pelican*, the first piece he ever choreographed, in May 1963, had already prominently featured migration and aviation (figure 3.15). Dedicated to the Wright brothers, the inventors of the airplane, this dance piece involved a female dancer (Carolyn Brown) and two male performers (Rauschenberg and Per Olof Ultvedt, who was then visiting the United States for his solo show in New York)[60] outfitted with roller skates and parachutes. The piece was distinctly site-specific, as it was created for a "Pop Festival" that took place in a roller-skating rink called "America on Wheels" (quite a telling name, in the context of this study), where Rauschenberg became fascinated by roller-skating and started learning it. The festival was held in conjunction with the "Popular Image" exhibition at the Washington Gallery of Modern Art, the first Pop Art exhibition in a U.S. museum, with which Solomon and Klüver were also involved. Prompted by the exhibition's organizer, Alice Denny, Rauschenberg created the piece for the site and enacted it with a sound collage he composed especially for the piece.[61] Aptly called by critic Erica Abeel "Daedalus at the Rollerdome," *Pelican* gave a concrete expression to the artist's long-time fascination with flight and migration, generating a number of stunning visual images.[62]

Steve Paxton, a dancer who often collaborated with Rauschenberg in the 1960s, discussed Rauschenberg's choreographic method in terms of image production: "In his choreography, he animated people with tasks within images: the task of the men in *Pelican*, for example, was to wear the animating parachutes and skates and to kneel and wheel.... Movements can be generated in a number of ways, and he generated his by couching people within images and then allowing images to coexist, collide, or follow one another."[63] This insightful comment suggests that there is no fundamental difference between Rauschenberg's Combine production and his performance choreography: both operations are essentially based on a method of juxtaposition, in which combined images and objects produce another set of multiple, associative images. As Branden Joseph argues, the significance of Rauschenberg's performances should therefore be sought in the specific relationship between images and movements,[64] as seen especially in two performances the artist enacted for "5 New York Evenings" in Stockholm.

Rauschenberg performed *Shot Put* and *Elgin Tie* on September 13, the series' fourth evening, which also featured programs such as Alex Hay's *Colorado Plateau*, Öyvind Fahlström's *Ur Mellanöl* (Extract from Lite Beer), and Steve Paxton's *Jag vill gärna telefonera* (I Would Like to Make a Phone Call).[65] When his turn came, Rauschenberg first performed *Shot Put*, his second choreographic work which had premiered at the Judson Dance Theater in New York in January 1964 (figure 3.16), in which he moved around the darkened room with a flashlight tied to his right ankle. In addition to the flicking sound of a switch amplified and manipulated by David Tudor, Rauschenberg enacted *Shot Put* in Stockholm with Fahlström's sound piece entitled *Fåglar i Sverige* (Birdcalls in Sweden).[66] Rauschenberg's notes for this performance indicate a series of movements such as "open and close knee," "pull forward then do convulsive roll," and "do *some stomping* changing directions of the foot."[67]

These somewhat bizarre movements created a drawing made of light, reminiscent of photographs of Picasso's famous *Space Drawing* from 1949. However, unlike Jackson Pollock—who reportedly cried out, "Goddamn it, that guy has done everything. There's nothing left," upon seeing Gjon Mili's photographs of *Space Drawing*[68]—Rauschenberg did not suffer from competition anxiety with the Spanish master. The abstract and inorganic shapes Rauschenberg blindly drew in the dark with his right leg marked a striking contrast to Picasso's virtuosic skills of representation. With his own figure completely hidden in darkness as opposed to Picasso's maestro presence looming behind his light drawing, Rauschenberg's drawing is closer to a heavenly constellation, an abstract shape that migrates in the sky. The movement *is* the image in this piece, created when the two were realized at the same time, thereby collapsing the boundary between them.

Immediately after performing *Shot Put*, Rauschenberg rushed out in the dark to the back of the museum and climbed to its roof to begin the next performance, *Elgin Tie* (figure 3.17). This was a site-specific piece that he newly conceived in Stockholm, inspired by the Elgin Marbles—whose history presents another salient case of cultural conflict caused by the migration of artifacts[69]—he had seen at the British Museum in London. Hiding on the roof, he could not be seen by the audience when the lights were turned on. All they saw was a rope hanging from the skylight, ending in a barrel filled with water on a large farm wagon, placed in the middle of the performing area during the interval. First, a cardboard box descended from the ceiling and landed on the bed of the wagon. The artist then appeared from above and started to descend the rope. He was outfitted with various objects, including a plastic bag filled with water, a flashlight, and a mouton coat that belonged to Hultén, who cheerfully told this author, "I hope he returned it!"[70] The performer maneuvered through a series of tasks with these objects, as he attached one after another to the rope while descending.[71] Reaching the end of the rope, Rauschenberg went inside the barrel on the wagon, where he realized he had not planned a way out. He later recollected his miserable state in the barrel: "And going in was quite simple. But I hadn't figured out getting out was going to be that difficult. But it's the opposite kind of movements. I mean, you slip in, but you have to have action to get out. And I stayed in there a little too long. Not long enough to actually drown but it did cross my mind, 'You know what? I think I'm gonna drown!' So this piece, I never did again. But I always took it very seriously."[72] After he emerged soaking wet from the barrel, Rauschenberg slipped into a pair of boots nailed to the wagon, which allowed him to bend forward at a nearly impossible angle. The performer then took out a white tie and tied it around his neck, which was a cue for Hultén's brother-in-law, who was a farmer, to bring in a cow (figure 3.18).

Rauschenberg had originally planned to ride the cow during the performance, in imitation of scenes on the Elgin Marbles, the Parthenon friezes he admiringly called "that fantastic combination of men and animals."[73] Learning that Swedish cows were much wilder than those in his home state of Texas, he gave up the idea that "[he]'d be carrying a bag of flour, and the flour would join [him] and the cow together."[74] He thought instead of

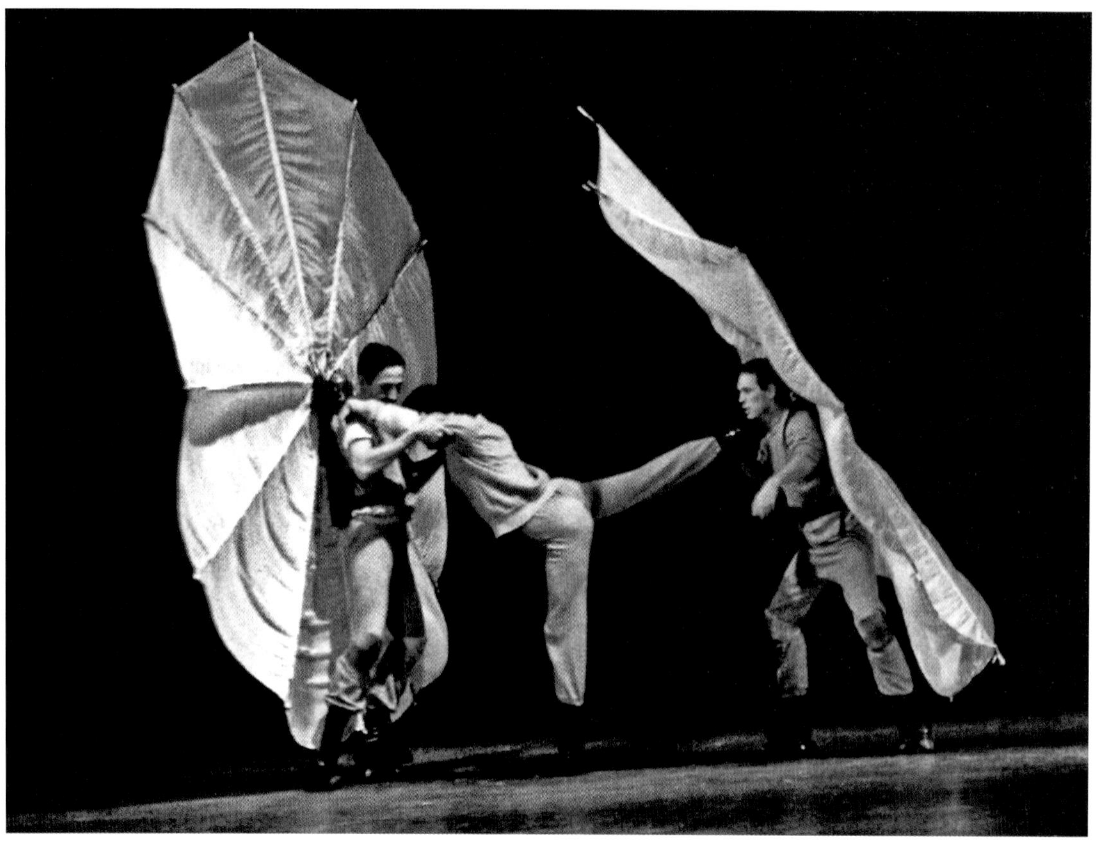

Figure 3.15
Rauschenberg performing *Pelican* (1963) with Alex Hay and Carolyn Brown for the First New York Theater Rally, at an abandoned television studio (Broadway and 81st Street), New York, 1965. Photograph by Elisabeth Novick.

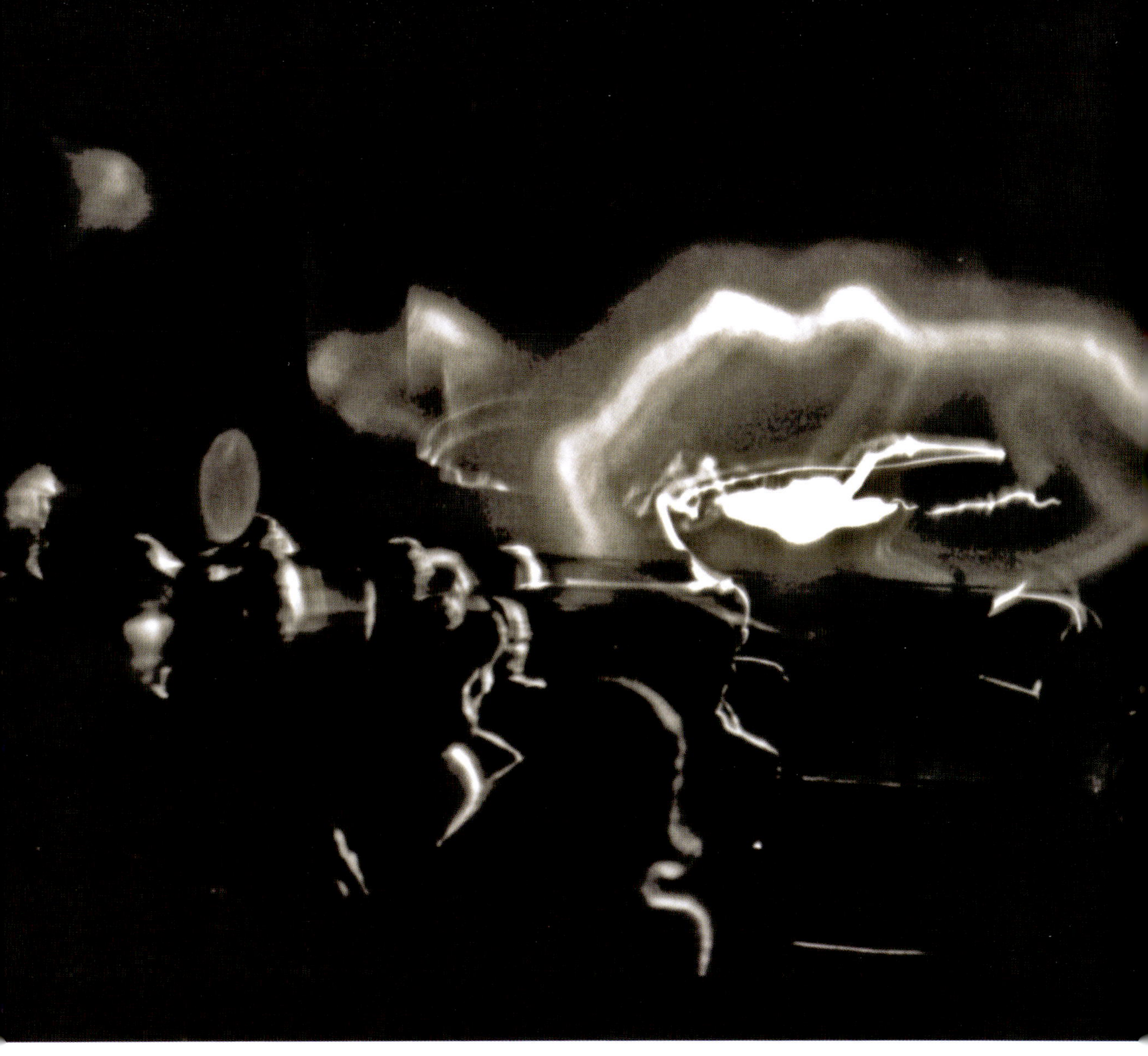

Figure 3.16
Rauschenberg performing *Shot Put* (1964) at the Surplus Dance Theater, February 1964. Photograph by Hans Namuth.

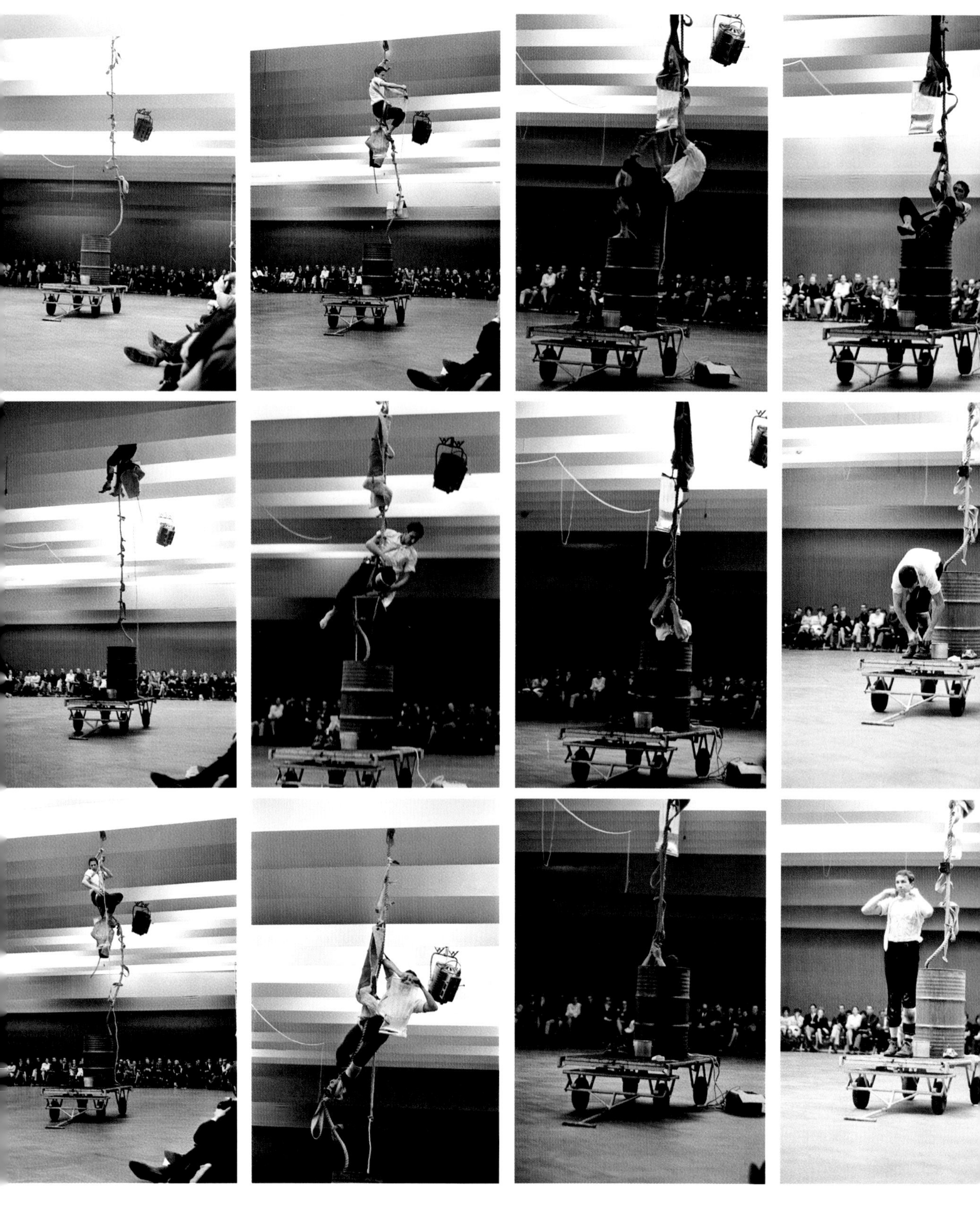

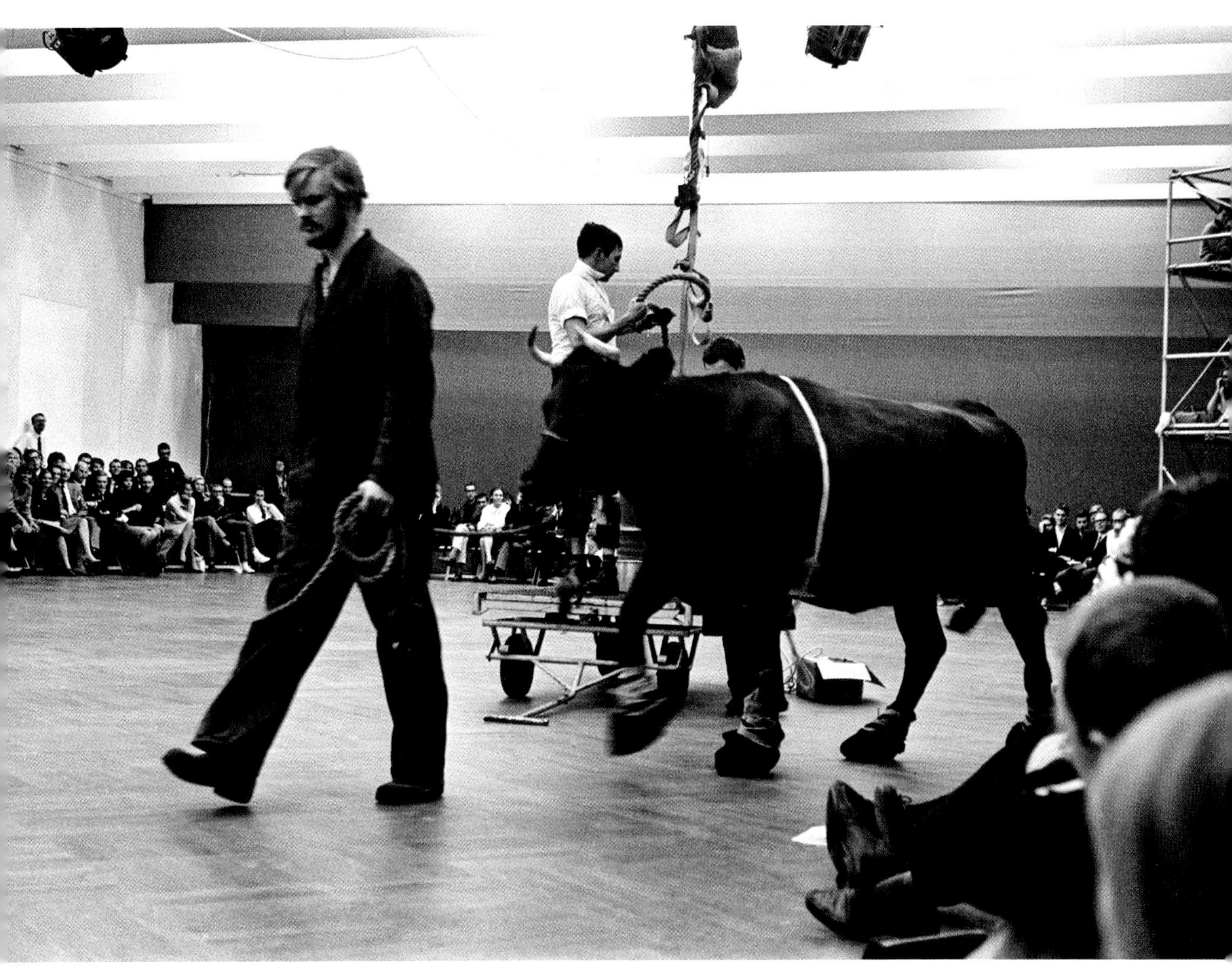

Figures 3.17, 3.18
Robert Rauschenberg performing *Elgin Tie* at the Moderna Museet, 1964. Photographs by Stig T. Karlsson/Moderna Museet, Stockholm.

harnessing the cow to the wagon so that the cow would pull it to the exit, but this did not work either, since the museum floor was too slippery for the cow's hooves. In the realized scene, the farmer led the cow, which wore socks over its hooves to avoid slipping, off to the exit and an assistant pulled the wagon, in which Rauschenberg stood and kept tying, untying, and retying his tie.[75]

Despite Rauschenberg's failure to literally illustrate the Elgin Marbles in *Elgin Tie*,[76] the work reveals its own internal structure on closer examination. Echoing the artist's view that he took the piece very seriously, Hultén recalled that it was "very much prepared, and quite a complicated performance."[77] If *Elgin Tie* was a site-specific performance structured around the principle of the Combines, an argument can be made that it indeed referred to a specific Combine, one most associated with the Moderna Museet—namely, *Monogram*. In fact, the acquisition of *Monogram* by the Moderna Museet was under negotiation when Rauschenberg performed *Elgin Tie* at the very site. Originally, *Monogram* could have entered the Museum of Modern Art, New York, in 1959, when Robert Scull offered to buy it for the museum.[78] Alfred Barr Jr., not an enthusiast of Rauschenberg's work, declined the offer, asking Castelli uneasy questions: "Wouldn't the piece disintegrate rather soon? Were there vermin in it?"[79] Accordingly, *Monogram* was still available in 1964. With the rising esteem of Rauschenberg, however, his work was in high demand among art collectors and museum directors, creating some rivalry among them. As Klüver's note to Hultén, quoted at the start of this chapter, was dated June 3, 1964, right before Rauschenberg set off on the world tour, Hultén probably did not have a chance to discuss the matter with the artist until his visit to Stockholm. It is therefore highly likely that they finalized the purchase of *Monogram* during Rauschenberg's stay in the city. In fact, the official invoice of fifteen thousand dollars for *Monogram* was sent from the Leo Castelli Gallery to the Moderna Museet in December 1964, after Rauschenberg went back to New York at the end of the tour.[80] Thus, Rauschenberg must have been aware of the final destination of *Monogram* when he performed *Elgin Tie*.

Indeed, many factors in *Elgin Tie* correspond to those in *Monogram*. Ulf Linde already noticed the parallels between the two works at the time of the performance. The presence of a cow, a mouton coat, a barrel, and wagon wheels in *Elgin Tie* have their counterparts in *Monogram*: the Angora goat, its fleece, the tire around its torso, and the casters beneath the platform.[81] Although it wasn't realized, the initial plan to include flour in *Elgin Tie* is analogous to the use of white paint in *Monogram*, which brought the tire into harmony with the color of the goat's fleece. As a medium intended to visually combine the artist and the cow, the white flour would have aligned the performance with a procession of Greek gods, like those on the Parthenon frieze. If the cow had let Rauschenberg ride on its back or had pulled the wagon as alternately envisioned, the artist would have appeared as a deity or demon. Finally, Rauschenberg's gesture of entering the barrel can be seen as an enactment of the most iconic element in *Monogram*, mimicking the goat in the tire. At once absurd and erotic, the gesture seems to straddle the divide between homoerotic and postmodern interpretations of *Monogram* in Rauschenberg literature. When the two pieces are examined together, *Elgin Tie* can be interpreted as a commentary on *Monogram*, the work that took the artist five years to complete and had just found its home at the Moderna Museet at the time of the performance.

ANTI-AMERICAN TURN

According to Hultén, "5 New York Evenings" marked "the last big organized event in what had been the springtime of collaborations with the New York artists."[82] In reality, the relationship between the art worlds in Stockholm and New York had already been somewhat soured by the time the Merce Cunningham Dance Company arrived. Hultén originally planned another large international art project in conjunction with "5 New York Evenings." In April, he wrote to David Vaughan, a manager for the company's world tour: "The time you suggest, second week of September, is very good. We are planning to open on the 4th of September the big collective exhibition 'Dylaby II' with the participation of Robert Rauschenberg, Jean Tinguely, Niki de St Phalle, P. O. Ultvedt, Claes Oldenburg, Öyvind Fahlström and others."[83] Although this exhibition would have offered an excellent backdrop against which to present the company's performance, "Dylaby II" was not realized. As seen in chapter 1, the original "Dylaby" project, held at the Stedelijk Museum two years before, created much conflict and tension between Rauschenberg and the European artists, making any further collaboration difficult.

In 1966, when a similar collective exhibition project did take place at the Moderna Museet, Rauschenberg was intentionally left out. During the preliminary discussion for the collaboration project, called *Hon* (She), Tinguely and de Saint-Phalle wrote to Ultvedt in Sweden:

> **de Saint-Phalle:** I'm glad that you like the idea of an enormous collaboration. But there are problems . . . it would have to be an enormous castle. Jean and I both feel that this collaboration would be something sufficient in itself.
>
> **Tinguely:** What's the use in a large Pop hot dog? Don't you feel the four of us would be enough since the castle would become a unity. Why have an enormous hamburger next to it?
>
> **de Saint-Phalle:** Rauschenberg also may be unnecessary.[84]

This exchange clearly points to the discomfort that Tinguely, de Saint-Phalle, and Ultvedt felt from the sudden international prominence of American art—especially works by Rauschenberg and Pop artists—that left little room for their own works. Hultén must have found himself in a difficult position, torn between his strong connections to the New York art world and his friendship with the European artists. Since the Moderna Museet had gained significant public recognition by that time, he had to make a more conscious and careful effort to balance European, American, and Swedish art exhibitions to avoid criticism from both the general public and the artistic community in Sweden. Such effort became increasingly imperative from the mid-1960s on, when Swedish citizens gradually developed an anti-American sentiment, stirred by the intensifying war in Vietnam.

Notably, "5 New York Evenings" coincided with the beginning of what is called the "Swedish-American conflict over Vietnam."[85] Torsten Nilsson, then foreign minister of Sweden, voiced his concern about the growing presence of the United States in Vietnam for the first time in September 1964. With the beginning of the bombing of North Vietnam in February 1965, editorials critical of U.S. foreign policy began appearing in the Swedish press. Amid these geopolitical events, Rauschenberg's Dante Drawings were exhibited at the Moderna Museet in March 1965 with the recently acquired *Monogram*. Although the political context did not seem to have a direct impact on the reception of "5 New York Evenings" or the Dante Drawings exhibition—both events still received a generally positive response—the relationship between the New York and Stockholm art worlds was becoming visibly tense.

Ulf Linde was instrumental in shaping the anti-American turn that the Stockholm art scene took in the mid-sixties. He had already developed a critical view of Rauschenberg in 1963, when he wrote from Stockholm to Ultvedt, who was then visiting New York: "The fact that Rauschenberg has begun working with silkscreen stuff I find upsetting. It is, after all, Andy Warhol who has the patent on silkscreening. Is there no Restany over there to keep an eye on what artists are doing?"[86] Before the artist began his silkscreen paintings, Linde had held a higher opinion of his work: he considered the Dante Drawings to be among Rauschenberg's best works,[87] because their literary structure controlled the artist's otherwise random creative impulses. It was precisely this lack of control that Linde criticized in what he called the "open art" of America. From March to May of 1965, he published a series of articles in *Dagens Nyheter* (Daily News) attacking Alan Solomon, who promoted such art.[88] In the first of these, entitled "The Open Art: The Inheritance from Munich," Linde described Solomon's attitude toward art as being irresponsible, quoting Solomon from *Art International* in October 1964:

> Instead of protesting, or satirizing, they [Pop artists] are telling us that anything goes, and that the mystery of art does not depend on *any* imaginable preconception. This openness, so much a determinant in the attitude of the new American generation . . . is absolutely incomprehensible to Europeans oriented toward Cartesian rationalism.[89]

Solomon had good reason to make such an admittedly chauvinistic comment. Writing (most likely) during the 1964 Venice Biennale, he was countering the hostility of the European press against American art. Linde nonetheless accused him not only of anti-intellectualism but also of dogmatism, asserting that his Americanism intimated an attempt to sever any link with European artistic tradition. Linde went on to debunk the importance of John Cage, whom he considered the father of "open art" in America, by casting doubt on the originality of the composer's thought. Linde emphasized Cage's study with Schönberg, who had been acquainted with Kandinsky in Munich around 1916. Stressing the apparent similarity between writings by Kandinsky and Cage, Linde proposed a genealogy of open art: "Kandinsky-Schönberg-Cage-Rauschenberg."[90] Although this unlikely scenario only seems to prove Linde's own European chauvinism, it appealed to certain Swedish intellectuals at the time, who felt alarmed by the expansion of Americanism in both culture and politics.

Meanwhile, the Swedish-American conflict was heating up. Foreign minister Torsten Nilsson again addressed his concerns about the Vietnam War in May 1965, and two months later Olof Palme, then a young minister of transport and communications, delivered a harsh critique of American militarism in Vietnam. This caught the attention of Washington, which requested that Palme clarify his speech. Responding to this incident, the two leading newspapers in Sweden, the conservative *Svenska Dagbladet* (Swedish Daily Paper) and the liberal *Dagens Nyheter*, demanded that Palme be reprimanded, but Nilsson protected him. The summer of 1965 thus marked a turning point in the Swedish-American conflict. After this date, Swedish officials, especially Palme, who would become the next prime minister in 1970, took a more active approach in criticizing American militarism.[91]

It is important to note that political and cultural debates took place in the same discursive arena in Sweden. Linde's criticism of open art and the preceding debates over the exhibitions at the Moderna Museet appeared in widely circulated newspapers such as *Dagens Nyheter* rather than in monthly art journals. In other words, readers of these papers could read about political issues and art debates in one sitting. Well informed on the stakes in both politics and art, Stockholm's citizens could raise a collective voice against the museum's activities if they found it necessary to do so. To avoid such criticism, Hultén organized a series of exhibitions that would reorient the position of the Moderna Museet in Swedish society. In the winter of 1965, he began this reorientation by showing James Rosenquist's *F111* (1964–1965), a work unmistakably critical of the American government's military policy. At the end of the year, Hultén opened "Den inre och den yttre rymden" (The Inner and the Outer Space), a thematic survey of modern art. Unlike "Art in Motion," this exhibition emphasized a more geometric and monochromatic tendency in modern art, focusing on such artists as Malevich, Naum Gabo, and Yves Klein; the Americans included in the show were Barnett Newman, Mark Rothko, Kenneth Noland, Donald Judd, and Rauschenberg, whose *White Paintings* (1951) were recreated for the exhibition.[92] From June to September 1966, he showed *Hon* (She), a woman-shaped cathedral built in the museum by de Saint-Phalle, Tinguely, and Ultvedt, followed by a solo exhibition by Oldenburg, an American Pop artist of Swedish descent. By stressing the European heritage of modern art, Hultén tried to strike a balance in the museum's activities.

Still, New York and Stockholm had another falling out in 1966. By that year, Rauschenberg and Klüver had been intensely involved in an exploration of the interaction between art and technology. After completing *Oracle* (1962–1965), a mobile sculpture made of five pieces each containing a radio that could be manipulated by remote control, they wanted to organize an event that would involve collaboration between artists and engineers on a larger scale. Klüver proposed it for the Stockholm Festival, an annual art festival organized by Fylkingen. Since "5 New York Evenings" had filled the entire 1964 festival, and Americans Robert Morris and Yvonne Rainer had been featured as the main performers in the 1965 festival, the 1966 festival was expected to be another collaborative project between Swedish and American artists. But the art and technology project required a much grander budget, which became a problem. Although Fylkingen sent three thousand dollars to New York as part of the agreed-upon budget of ten thousand dollars, it refused to pay the rest when the American group demanded additional payment without explaining how the initial money had been spent.[93]

Eventually, the conflict over funding the art and technology project led to the cancellation of the 1966 Stockholm Festival. In a long letter addressed to the American artists, Fylkingen criticized the unacceptable nature of their demands, which included extensive publicity in the Swedish press and a reception ceremony with King Gustav VI Adolf as a guest. The letter concluded, "You Americans seem to expect us in Fylkingen to pay large amounts of money just in order to create a platform for your own future work in [the] USA, and … we have to be content with any crumbs of fame that may fall from your table."[94] Franklin Königsberg, the lawyer for the American group, responded with an equally harsh message: "Unlike Fylkingen, we have the courage of our convictions. We intend to try every means to make a reality of the Festival of Art and Technology."[95] The project for the aborted 1966 festival did indeed become a reality in New York in October 1966, as "Nine Evenings: Theater and Engineering," the inaugural event for Experiments in Art and Technology (EAT). Meanwhile, Fylkingen stopped inviting American artists for its international events after 1966. As the Swedish-American relationship worsened, the presence of American artists in Stockholm diminished significantly in the latter half of the 1960s.

"THE NEW YORK COLLECTION FOR STOCKHOLM"

The love-hate relationship between New York and Stockholm did not end without one last big project: "The New York Collection for Stockholm" in 1973. This originally started as an EAT project without any predetermined destinations. After organizing a series of EAT projects, Rauschenberg and Klüver came up with the idea of assembling a collection of contemporary art for a museum or a corporation to purchase. When Klaus Kertess of the Bykert Gallery, New York, became unavailable to select the works, they asked Hultén to be the curator. Klüver explained the nature of the job to him: "Bob R will work with you to make up the collection.... Your commission will be 10% of the net, which is what we get when costs are paid.... Your 'duties' will be to select what the collection will contain, negotiate with the artists, set prices, sign contracts for us, find a buyer, make a catalogue if necessary, handle the press conference, set up an exhibition at Automation House if we decide it's necessary."[96] Acquiring an important American art collection for the Moderna Museet had been Hultén's dream from the very beginning of his career. Although the museum acquired a few important pieces in the sixties—in addition to those mentioned

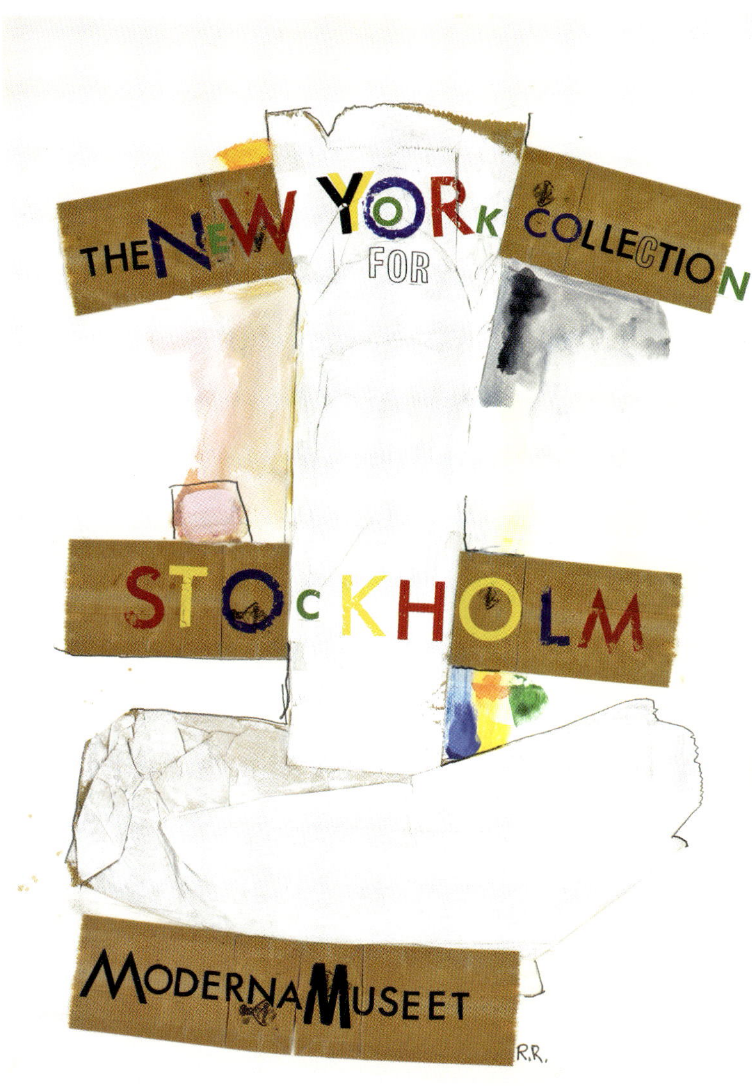

Figure 3.19
Robert Rauschenberg, *Drawing for the New York Collection for Stockholm Poster*, 1973. Collage, press type, watercolor, and pencil on paper, 30¾ × 21⅝ inches (78.1 × 54.9 cm). Moderna Museet, Stockholm.

earlier, works such as Jackson Pollock's *The Wooden Horse* (1948), Frank Stella's *Claroquesi* (1964), and Donald Judd's *Untitled* (1965) entered the museum later in the decade—it did not possess a sufficient number of works to represent the larger scope of postwar American art. As soon as he was involved with the project, Hultén sought ways to bring the collection to his museum.The timing could not have been worse, however, given the increasingly anti-American sentiment of the Swedish public. The Swedish-American conflict over Vietnam exacerbated toward the end of the sixties, as the Swedish government began sheltering American draft evaders in 1968. Moreover, when Sweden became the first nation to recognize North Vietnam in 1969 by providing economic aid to Hanoi, the U.S. government even considered economic sanctions against Sweden. At the end of 1972, the conflict between the two countries reached its peak with Palme's public speech against the Christmas bombing of Hanoi. In this speech, which received worldwide publicity, Palme went so far as to associate the Hanoi bombing with the bombing of Guernica during the Spanish Civil War, infuriating American officials.[97]

In this context, it is hardly surprising that the proposed grand-scale migration of the "New York Collection," which included thirty works by artists based in that city, caused a heated debate in the press even before the collection arrived in Stockholm. Part of the problem was that the project's funding was not clear to the public. Although the collection was officially called a "gift," participating artists did receive the usual 50 percent of the sales price of their work, while their galleries waived the commission fees.[98] Accordingly, when it became apparent that the Educational Department of the Swedish government would contribute one-fifth of the $1.5 million budget, Swedish artists raised a collective voice against it. Among them was Per Olof Ultvedt, who had supported and collaborated with Hultén and New York artists in the previous decade. Now feeling snubbed by the system that favored his American colleagues, he coauthored an article with four other artists in *Dagens Nyheter* to criticize Hultén's museum directorship. Since all of the artists were associated with institutions such as the State Art Board, National Artists Organization, and Arts Academy, their criticism represented not only the artists' individual opinions but also a collective view of the Swedish art establishment in general: "We criticize the New York Collection because we find it to be limited in geography and in content. For us, the 1960s New York avant-garde is not important enough to defend another acquisition at this level. We therefore blame the museum leadership for provincial thinking, albeit 'New York Provincialism.'"[99]

The debate intensified when the exhibition "The New York Collection for Stockholm," for which Rauschenberg created a poster, opened at the museum in October 1973 (figures 3.19, 3.20). Although most American military forces had retreated from Vietnam by then, the political tension in the preceding years between the United States and Sweden—let alone the cultural tension between New York and Stockholm—inevitably shaded the reception of the collection. In effect it became an unwanted gift in Stockholm, as Ultvedt and the others published another critique in the same newspaper (figure 3.21). Under a caricature

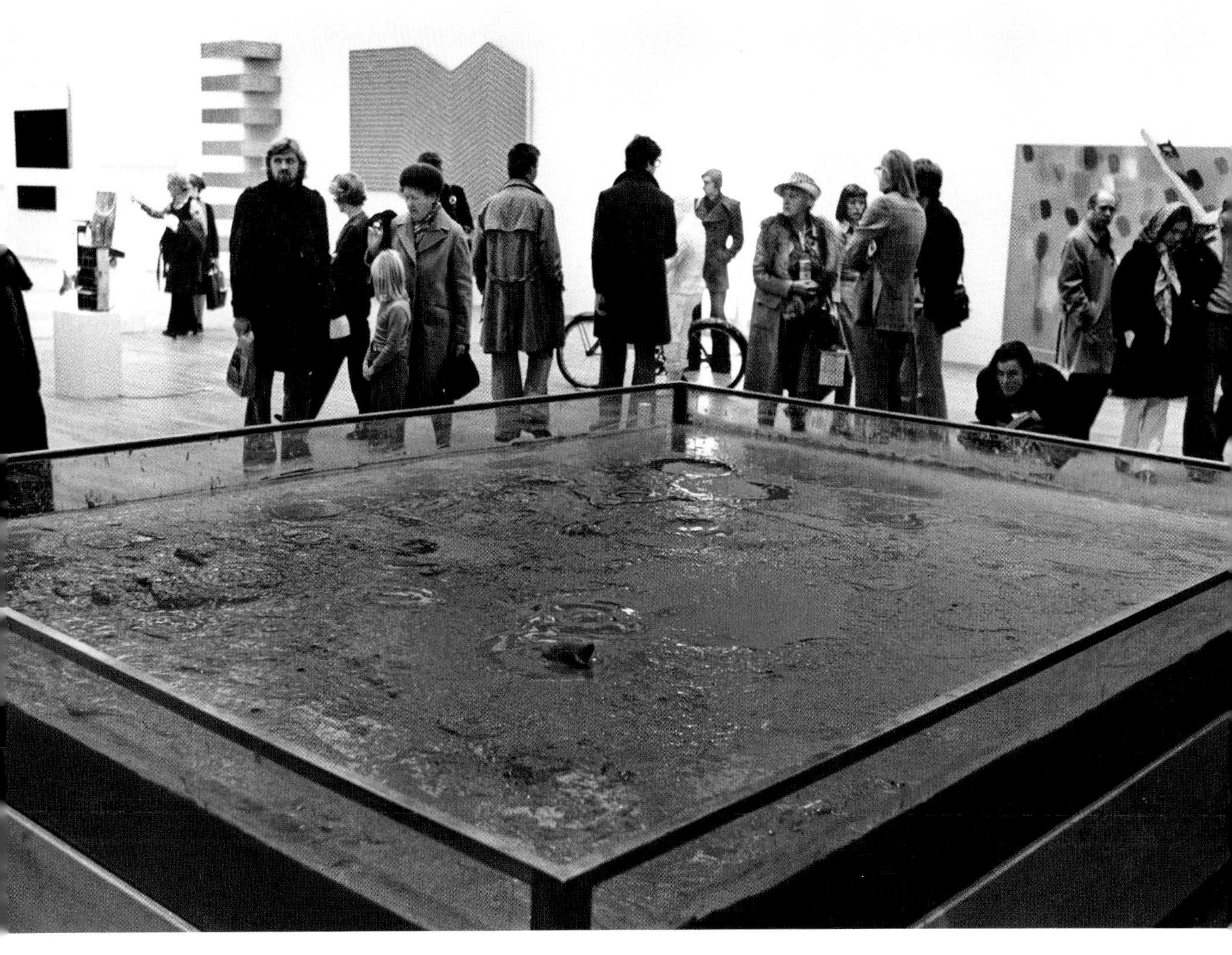

Figure 3.20
Robert Rauschenberg's *Mud Muse* (1968–1971), installed in "The New York Collection for Stockholm," Moderna Museet, Stockholm, 1973. Photograph: Moderna Museet, Stockholm.

drawn by Ultvedt, a caption read, "Donation on a big scale, or what is happening under the table?" The caricature insinuates that the Americans bribed the director of the Moderna Museet; Hultén, depicted with his trademark glasses and a bowtie, is shown receiving the collection on the table while receiving something else underneath. Neither Hultén nor EAT made an effort to clear up the public's doubts. When a Swedish artist questioned whether the American artists had really donated the works as stated in the press release, the EAT attorney blithely responded, "It was a donation from many sources."[100]

The American artists' involvement with industrial technology only made the matter worse. Since many works in the "New York Collection" involved collaboration with engineers, including Rauschenberg's *Mud Muse* (1968–1971), the whole collection was negatively received as a reflection of the American military technology used in Vietnam.[101] This criticism may sound arbitrary, since many of the artists in the collection were actively against the Vietnam War. For instance, Rauschenberg anonymously financed a large portion of the Artists Peace Tower built in Los Angeles in 1965 and boycotted the 1970 Venice Biennale along with Warhol, Lichtenstein, and others as a protest against the war. Still, the skepticism in Stockholm was not entirely off the mark. Teledyne Corporation in Los Angeles, which provided technical assistance for *Mud Muse*, reportedly made such tools as a night sniper gunsight and miniature sensors that were dropped along the Ho Chi Minh Trail to trace troop movements.[102] Even in the United States, Rauschenberg and Klüver were criticized for working with the defense contractor by American artists whose antiwar feelings made them suspicious of any collaboration with an industrial corporation.[103] Although this particular fact may not have been known in Sweden, the technology utilized in works in the "New York Collection" provoked the ire of Stockholm's citizens, who were already sensitive to political and military issues. It was therefore no coincidence that Ultvedt and his fellow artists, feeling neglected by their own national institution, concluded their protest with the following sentence: "We hope that *Geometric Mouse, Scale A5/5, Aluminum, 3.6m high* [a 1969 work by Oldenburg in the collection] will be the final monument over the period which began with the goat with the tire."[104] From their perspective, *Monogram* was the beginning of the whole problem, a symbol of the American cultural imperialism that had invaded Sweden after the end of World War II. Thus, *Monogram* was a scapegoat once again; the object that initiated the migration of American art to Stockholm was now seen to reflect not only the cultural but also the political and hence military expansionism of post–World War II America, and was loathed as such.

In the end, the "New York Collection" became Hultén's parting gift to the Moderna Museet, as he left Sweden to become the founding director of the Centre Georges Pompidou in Paris at the end of 1973. While Hultén migrated literally from a minor to a major center of the European art scene, the Moderna Museet redirected itself, mounting retrospectives of Torsten Renqvist and Evert Lundquist, two representative Swedish modern artists, before closing for renovation in 1974–1975. The new director of the museum, Swedish painter Philip von Schantz, made it clear that he was not going to adopt the "internationalist"

Debatt om New York Collection –

"Restlager på Moderna museet"

I ONADENS ÅR 1973, en dag i början av november (DN 4/11), vaknar en något förvirrad Olle Granath och finner tiden mogen att bemöta den kritik som några av oss för ett och ett halvt år sedan riktade mot Pontus Hulténs förvärv av New York Collection till Moderna museet. Vid den tiden innehade f ö Granath ett vikariat i ledande ställning på museet under Hulténs tjänstledighet. Efter så lång tystnad hade man kunnat vänta sig ett mera vederhäftigt debattinlägg. Vi finner det nu nödvändigt att friska upp hans minne genom att rekapitulera några av huvudpunkterna i vår kritik.

① Vår kritik gällde Moderna museets ensidiga inriktning på konst från axeln Paris—New York, som redan före New York Collection var starkt representerad i samlingarna. Den nu aktuella utställningen, där man även visar det tidigare innehavet, är ett talande bevis för riktigheten i vår kritik.

② Vi reagerade starkt mot museichefens odemokratiska sätt att bakom ryggen på publik och konstnärer och med rädsla för eventuella opinioner driva fram ett så stort förvärv av en av honom handplockad konst. Vi anser fortfarande att museichefens befogenheter måste begränsas så att demokratisk insyn i verksamheten möjliggörs.

③ Vi menade också att den typ av manifestationer utan pedagogisk uppföljning som New York Collection representerar i mycket tillhör en förgången tid. Ett modernt museum ska inte som huvudambition ha att resa monument över diverse passerade epoker.

Av alla slag

Det auktoritära elitmuseet tillhör 1800-talet eller borde göra det. Vi anser att publiken ska ha möjlighet att se bilder av alla slag och från alla delar av världen, även om en del av dem inte är börsnoterade i Paris eller New York för ögonblicket. Publiken ska själv få möjlighet att ta ställning utan förmyndare som talar om vad som är värt att se.

Vad sker just nu i Afrika, Asien, Sydamerika och Australien? Vad sker i alla de ateljéer och verkstäder som aldrig får besök av konsthandlare och med dem befryndade museichefer? Och vart har alla andra bildformer tagit vägen?

Ingen av dessa punkter har Granath brytt sig om att bemöta. I stället försöker han på känt översittarmaner försvara en sjuk sak genom att förlöjliga och snedvrida kritiken. Varför insinuerar han så enfaldigt att det finns "en opinion som vill se ett uttryck för reaktionär stormaktspolitik i allt som kommer från väster"? Och varför insinuerar han på samma sätt som Hultén att kritiken skulle bottna i egoistiskt gruppintresse? Här redovisar Granath dessutom på ett beklämmande sätt sitt tidigare dokumenterade förakt för KRO:s fackliga arbete. Vi antar att KRO kommenterar den här saken på egen hand.

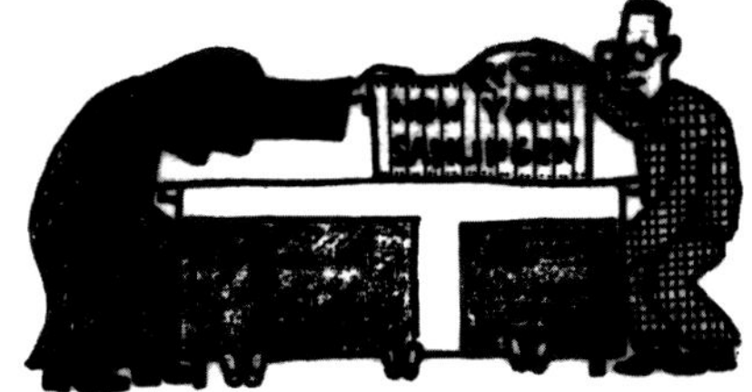

DONATION PÅ HÖG NIVÅ, ELLER VAD HÄNDER UNDER BORDET?

Per Olof Ultvedts syn på donationen.

Den aktuella utställningen och förvärvet har enligt vår mening kommit att utnyttjas av politiker såväl svenska som amerikanska, i ett försök att genom "gåvoköpet" bereda väg för utväxlingen av nya ambassadörer. Detta är obehagligt och rent 1800-talsmässigt. Men för Granath framstår det bara som en dumhet. Dumhet eller inte — faktum kvarstår. Till och med en av "donationens" fanbärare, Emile de Antonio, framhöll i en DN-intervju att "vissa högt uppsatta personer nu gärna ser att det blir en avspänning mellan USA och Sverige igen".

Fel slutsats

Granaths försök att rättfärdiga "donationen" ideologiskt har vi ingen anledning att gå in närmare på. Hans prat om bl a action painting har ingen relevans för New York Collection.

I slutet av sin artikel ger Granath en beskrivning av utställningen som i stora delar överensstämmer med vår uppfattning, men han drar helt andra och enligt vår mening felaktiga slutsatser. Det är säkert riktigt att New York Collection visar "rester av redan förbrukade möjligheter" som "oåterkalleligt" tillhör det förflutna.

Givetvis kan det vara av värde att göra en sådan utställning för att publiken ska få möjlighet att konstatera om liket lever eller inte. Detta är dock något helt annat än förvärv av utställningens samtliga föremål. Och det är just mot detta vi har opponerat oss. Låt vara att vi fått restlaget för realisationspris, motsvarande 10 à 20 procent av ett förment marknadsvärde. Men det är ändå fråga om en för svenska förhållanden betydande satsning, som hittills kostat staten ca 500 000 kronor då ännu inte alla räkningar är betalda.

Om man ena dagen stillatigande låter en utåtriktad verksamhet av Filialens typ strypas därför att den anses för kostsam men andra dagen förvärvar föremål som det redan finns nog av på museet för mångdubbelt större belopp, måste det vara något fundamentalt fel i målsättningen.

Oroande

Vi upplever det faktum att New York Collection nu finns på [illegible] vilket den kommit dit som oroande. Oroande därför att det kan uppfattas som ett hot mot den nya kultursyn som utvecklats under de senaste åren av enskilda människor (författare och konstnärer) och grupper (centrumbildningar, fria teatergrupper och kulturarbetarnas fackliga organisationer). Denna kultursyn har även börjat märkas på ett mera officiellt plan, t ex i vissa statliga utredningar (kulturrådets betänkande), utbildningsenheter och museer.

"Donationen" (dvs förvärvet) aktualiserar det krav på en öppen diskussion om Moderna museets målsättning och den framtida verksamheten som framförts bl a av KRO, KLYS och Konstakademin. Det är nödvändigt att den kommer nu, i samma ögonblick som museet byter chef, ges nya resurser i samband med den omfattande tillbyggnaden och innan man tar ställning till MUS 65:s förslag om dess framtid.

Vi hoppas att "Geometrisk mus. Skala A 5/5. Aluminium, 3,6 m hög", ett av verken i New York Collection, ska bli det slutgiltiga monumentet över den epok som inleddes av geten med bilringen.

BO AHLSÉN, konstnär, lärare. Ordförande i KLYS (Konstnärliga och litterära yrkesutövares samarbetsnämnd)

MARGARETA CARLSTEDT, konstnär, ordförande i KRO (Konstnärernas riksorganisation).

KARL OLOF BJÖRCK, konstnär, lärare vid Teckningslärarinstitutet.

STEN DUNÉR, konstnär, lärare vid Teckningslärarinstitutet, ledamot av NUNSKU (Nämnden för utställningar av nutida svensk konst i utlandet)

PÄR STOLPE, museikonsulent, f d föreståndare för Moderna museets filial.

PER OLOF ULTVEDT, konstnär, professor vid Konsthögskolan, [illegible]

Replik:

NÄR DET GÄLLER kritiken mot museets organisation och de befogenheter som gjort det möjligt för dess chef att skaffa New York Collection på det sätt som skett finns det ingen anledning för mig att gå i svaromål. Att Moderna museets organisation diskuteras öppet inför de ändringar som följer med MUS 65 och nybyggnaden finner jag lika angeläget som undertecknarna av vidstående artikel. Däremot ser jag ingen anledning använda verken i samlingen som slagträn i den diskussionen.

Vad som menas med att verken inte kommer att få "pedagogisk uppföljning" vet jag inte. Räknas inte museets dagliga och omfattande visningsverksamhet?

I begreppet "huvudambition" under punkt tre döljs förmodligen en undermening. Men jag anser det självklart att Moderna museet skall ha en så bra och fullständig samling modern konst som det är möjligt att skaffa med de begränsade medel som står till buds.

Det låter riktigt att man bör bevaka de uppräknade världsdelarnas konstproduktion. (Moderna museet visar just nu en utmärkt utställning från Colombia.) Men det är inte självklart att alla kulturer formulerar vitala delar av sig i bild i någon större omfattning, traditionerna kan ha dragit åt andra håll.

Om artikelförfattarna dessutom vill påstå att museet helt försummat konst från andra håll än "axeln Paris—New York" har de fel. Det finns gott om exempel på motsatsen i både utställningsverksamheten och förvärven till samlingen (vävnader från olika delar av Afrika, måleri och affischer från Kuba, naivism från Israel m m). Man frågar sig dessutom om någon av artikelförfattarna föreslagit museet någon av alla de glömda ateljéerna och verkstäderna utan att vinna gehör för sitt förslag.

Ett museum av detta slag kan aldrig bedriva någon form av kvantitativ kulturantropologi. Resultatet behöver för den skull inte bli ett "auktoritärt elitmuseum".

KRO bedriver facklig politik och skall så göra. Men när den politiken strävar efter att sätta alltför snäva nationella ramar på kulturlivet finns all anledning att opponera sig. Organisationen har ett snart femton år gammalt horn i sidan till Moderna museet för dess betoning av internationell information. Den informationen menar jag att vi hade varit fattigare utan!

Till sist: Min förvirring som människa och kritiker är något ständigt pågående. En rad av de konstnärer som representeras i den aktuella samlingen har emellertid hjälpt mig bringa en viss reda i den förvirringen. Därför finner jag dem värda ett bättre öde än att bara bli tillhyggen i en debatt som rör svensk kulturpolitik.

OLLE GRANATH

Figure 3.21
"Debate on New York Collection: 'Left-over Stock at Moderna Museet,'" coauthored by Bo Ahlsén, Karl Olof Björck, Margareta Carlstedt, Sten Dunér, Pär Stolpe, and Per Olof Ultvedt, *Dagens Nyheter*, November 18, 1973. Illustration by Per Olof Ultvedt. Reply by Olle Granath. © Dagens Nyheter.

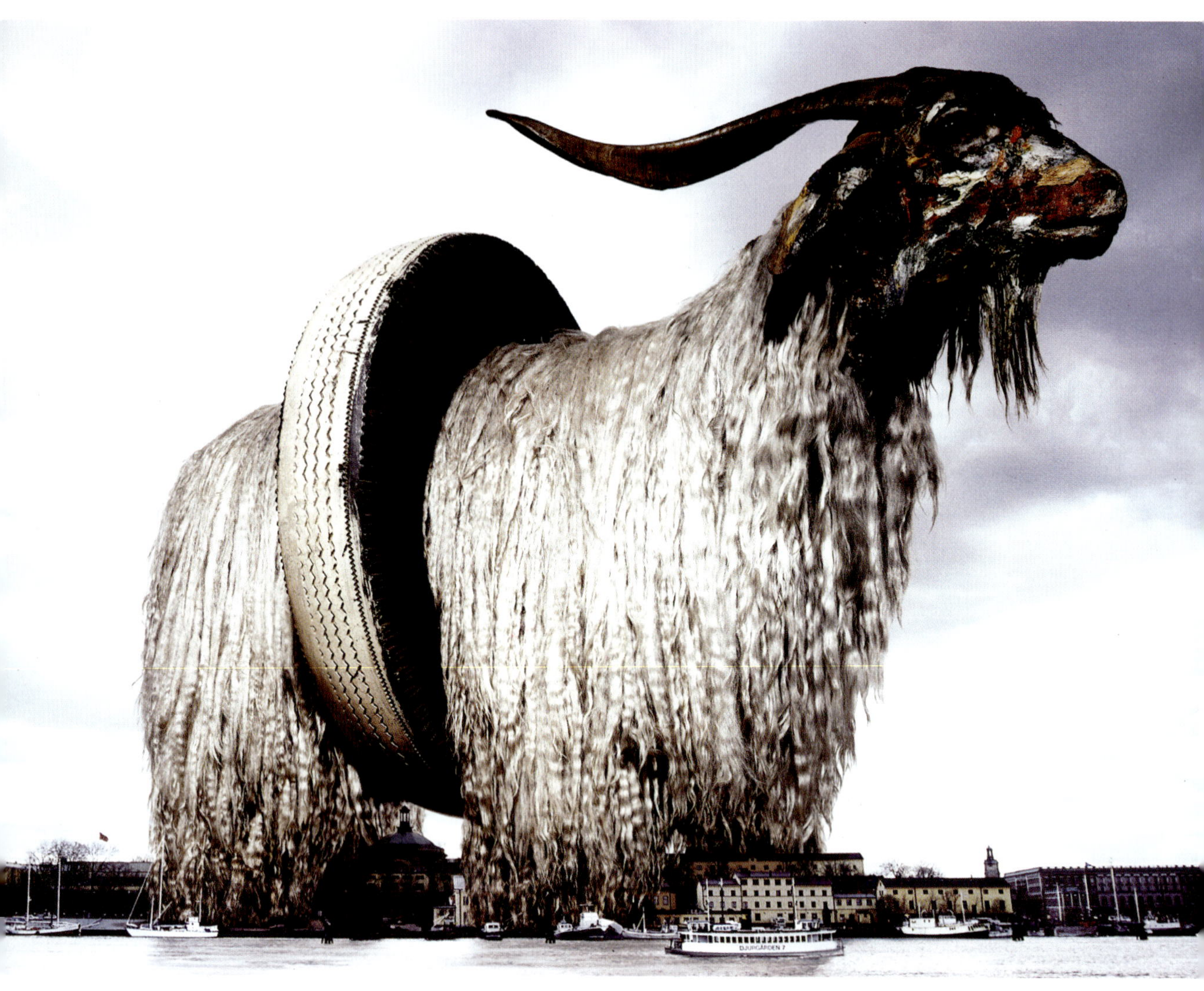
DJURGÅRDEN 7

Figure 3.22
Photograph for a billboard advertisement to raise interest in the new architecture for the Moderna Museet, 1991. Photograph: Moderna Museet, Stockholm.

stance taken by Hultén: "That contemporary art should be shown at a museum of modern art is obvious, but why be in such a hurry to expand the collections?... Why are the acquisitions of international contemporary art by the modern museums so appallingly conformist? Does the intimate collaboration between curators from different countries have to result in exhibitions and collections being almost identical?"[105] Although this claim sounds surprisingly familiar and even universal today, the Moderna Museet had to pay a price for its "national" turn. Severing its connection with the New York art scene, the museum quickly receded into the margins of the European art world. As critic Ludvig Rasmussen retrospectively described the decline of the Stockholm art scene in the 1990s: "At the end of the sixties, Stockholm had lost its luster as art capital, becoming gradually more provincial. The Moderna Museet gave up its position as a center for renewal and has never regained it.... [During the rise of commercialism in the art of the 1980s] the Moderna Museet sat there as a stone-dead mausoleum for second-rate American avant-garde rejects."[106] This assessment suggests another insight into the dynamics of geography in world art. Although major and minor forces in the global art scene complement one another, the relationship is essentially asymmetrical as long as there is only one major center and numerous minor centers. In other words, the "New York connection" was a necessary condition for Stockholm to partake of the world art scene, whereas the "Stockholm connection" was only one of many relationships, albeit an important one, for New York in the 1960s. The same can be said of Rauschenberg's 1964 world trip. Despite his enthusiasm about artistic interchange and collaboration with the Stockholm art scene, he visited twenty-nine other cities during the trip and engaged with a number of local art communities. As chapter 4 will elaborate, Tokyo is one such place where he created works of art by collaborating with the cultural other—another critical factor in examining the global rise of American art.

A POSTSCRIPT: *MONOGRAM* TODAY

After the end of the fruitful yet contentious Stockholm–New York relationship, *Monogram* lived its own life in Stockholm.[107] Today, the early years of the Moderna Museet and Hultén's leadership during the 1960s are remembered as its most heroic period. After the backlash against American art during the Vietnam era, Hultén's activities were recognized in the 1990s as having situated Stockholm within the global art scene. As a consequence, *Monogram* became *the* symbol of this period. The work is now the most beloved object at the museum, affectionately called the "Goat"—in Swedish, *geten* (the goat) or *en get* (a goat)—by Stockholm's citizens. It is perpetually called upon as the museum's symbol in times of need. In 1991, it was even featured as a billboard image in an appeal for the construction of a new museum building (figure 3.22). Björn Springfeldt, then serving as museum director, said as much when he wrote to Rauschenberg to ask for his permission to use the image: "*Monogram* is a totem for Moderna Museet and immediately tells people what it is about."[108]

In the billboard poster, an enlarged image of *Monogram* triumphantly stands over Skeppsholmen, the island on which the museum is located. The picture also seems to promote the foresight of the museum, which recognized the importance of Rauschenberg even before New York's Museum of Modern Art had. Once a scapegoat symbolizing American expansionism, the work has been resurrected as an icon of the museum. In 1994, when the museum moved to a temporary location during the construction of its new building, Springfeldt reported to Rauschenberg that "the newspaper even came [up] with a goat named Sigge as [the] symbol for the museum moving."[109] The work was also used on postage stamps to celebrate the museum's reopening in 1998. It was therefore not an exaggeration when Rauschenberg stated that *Monogram* "works very hard in Sweden, and it is a kind of national icon."[110] The work underwent such an extraordinary reception in Stockholm that it seems the Moderna Museet came to identify itself with the piece—and hence with its creator, Rauschenberg. As if to prove this point, when the new museum building reopened in 2004 after some architectural defects were fixed, the Moderna Museet embraced a new logo based on Rauschenberg's handwriting (figure 3.23). The logo was originally part of the catalog cover he had designed in 1981 for *Le Moderna Museet de Stockholm à Bruxelles*, and was used again for *Moderna Museet: 1958–1983*, a publication celebrating the museum's twenty-fifth anniversary. It was then chosen to be the official mark of "The New Identity Programme" for the museum's 2004 reopening.[111] The new logo can thus be seen as another kind of "monogram," a combination of Rauschenberg's American (which translates as global) handwriting and the museum's public (thus local) identity. What began as international open art and later met local resistance as a symbol of American invasion has now been completely assimilated into the Stockholm cultural scene, becoming the Moderna Museet's "glocal" icon.

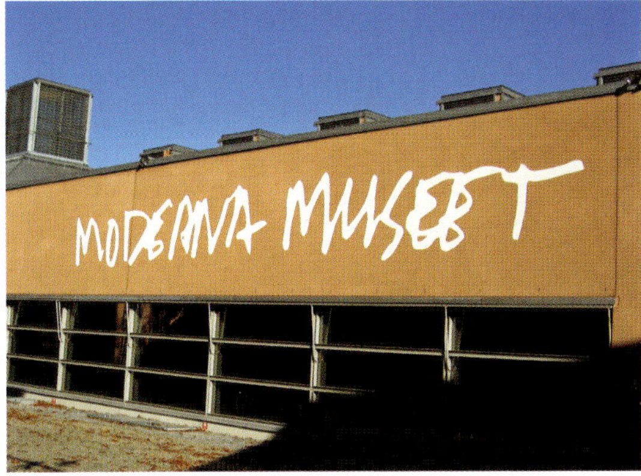

Figure 3.23
Robert Rauschenberg and Stockholm Design Lab, logotype of the Moderna Museet, in use since February 2004. Photograph by author.

ht to a pure
body, even a
-Painter",
artists are
ke an original

if
e someone paints
oe Portrait on ~~same~~
ey say it is a creative
if I paint "Mona Lisa"
it is an imitation.

?

4

A DIALOGUE IN TOKYO
RAUSCHENBERG MEETS THE JAPANESE AVANT-GARDE

After Stockholm, the Merce Cunningham Dance Company danced in Turku and Helsinki in Finland and then in four cities in Eastern Europe, where it experienced a response from authorities that was peculiar to the Cold War period. In Prague, for instance, the poster for the company carried neither Cage's nor Rauschenberg's names—possibly because they were perceived as decadent—and advertised its program as "American ballet in the style of *West Side Story*." In Poznań, the American vice-consul implied that the Polish authorities had the dancers watched.[1] The audience behind the Iron Curtain was nonetheless attentive and engaging on the whole, as Cunningham did an impromptu workshop in both cities. After a few more stops in Western Europe, the company embarked for Asia on the last leg of its world tour. The party flew to India from Paris on October 13 at the invitation of the Sarabhai family, one of whose members had studied with Cage in New York. The tour progressed through Bombay, Ahmedabad, Chandigarh, Delhi, and on to Bangkok in Thailand, where they performed for King Bhumibol and Queen Sirikit. Finally, on November 5, the company landed in Tokyo for the final stop.

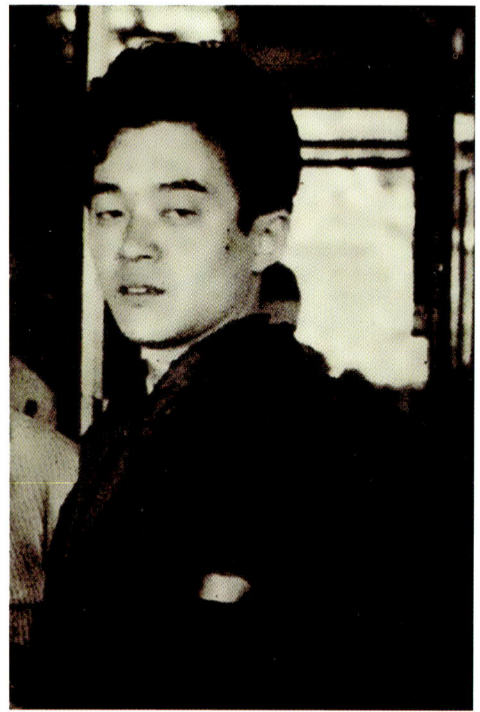

Figure 4.1
Yoshiaki Tōno, ca. 1962. Photo courtesy Ari Imai.

At the airport, the company received an enthusiastic welcome by a crowd of the press, artists and critics, and members of the Sōgetsu Art Center, an experimental art forum that hosted the company's Tokyo visit. Among them was art critic Yoshiaki Tōno, who had befriended Rauschenberg in New York in 1959 and had since introduced his works in Japanese art journals (figure 4.1). Tōno was eager to show him around Tokyo, because unlike Paris, Venice, or Stockholm, the city was an entirely new place to the American artist. By the time of his arrival, Rauschenberg was already an object of adoration in the city's art community. Aside from Tōno's publications, his award of the Grand Prize at that year's Venice Biennale had profoundly impressed Japanese avant-garde artists. Artist Ushio Shinohara, one of the most active figures in the local art scene of the time, described the New York artist vividly: "Gilt-edged sunglasses and a khaki jumper. He's such a cool Yankee that he doesn't quite look like a modern master. He's dressed so well that the wannabe Ivy Leaguers in Ginza would immediately want to imitate his look."[2] To Shinohara's eyes, Rauschenberg embodied the trendy pop culture of America, as a celebrity on tour to convey not only his art but American culture in general (figure 4.2).

In fact, Rauschenberg's status as a global celebrity had created considerable tension within the dance company: after winning the Grand Prize in Venice, he tended to attract all the media attention wherever they traveled. This did not please Cage and Cunningham, although Rauschenberg's contribution saved the company from its financial plight more than once, making it possible to continue the world tour at all. Moreover, a basic difference in artistic attitudes between Cage and Cunningham on one side and Rauschenberg and a few young dancers on the other became increasingly apparent, making further collaboration difficult.[3] Upon his arrival, Rauschenberg asked the music critic Kuniharu Akiyama, who served as his coordinator during his stay in Tokyo, to arrange a meeting place for him to discuss the situation with his coworkers Steve Paxton, Barbara Lloyd, Deborah Hay, and Alex Hay, whom Rauschenberg had hired as his technical assistant. In the quiet restaurant where Akiyama took them, they all decided to leave the company at the end of the world tour.[4]

Many of Rauschenberg's activities in Tokyo thus took place apart from the official program of Cunningham's dance company. Although he was committed to his work as the company's stage manager, he participated in a U.S.-Japan dance exchange workshop that Akiyama arranged for Rauschenberg's team and Japanese modern dancers.[5] He also created three works of art during his three-week stay in Tokyo, which was a rather rare occurrence throughout the world tour. The most notable event of all was the program entitled "Twenty Questions to Bob Rauschenberg," during which the artist created the Combine *Gold Standard* (figure 4.3). Originally planned by Tōno as a public interview with the artist, the program turned into a performance, for Rauschenberg ignored all the questions from Tōno, as moderator, and from the audience's representative, Shinohara. He instead responded by silently and intently working on his Combine, as the baffled audience nonetheless politely watched. A legendary incident in the history of postwar Japanese art, it is perhaps better remembered today than the dance company's performance itself.

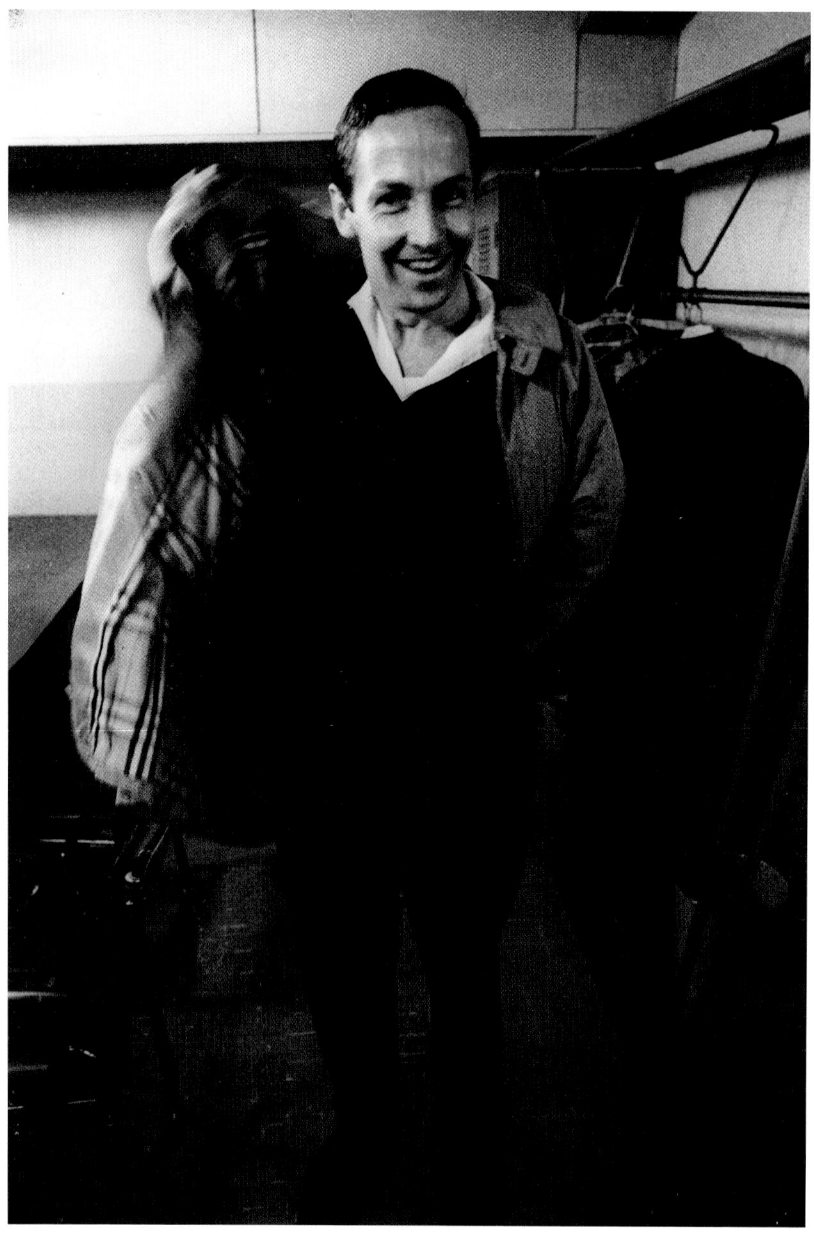

Figure 4.2
Robert Rauschenberg in Tokyo, 1964. Courtesy Sōgetsu Foundation Archives, Tokyo.

However, while in Tokyo, Rauschenberg was first and foremost a tourist himself, trying to make some sense out of this foreign city, where he did not speak the language. In this sense, his interchange with the art community of Tokyo was a case of cross-cultural interaction. The interchange involved two intertwining agencies: that of Rauschenberg as an outsider in the city and that of Japanese artists (and to some extent critics) in confronting the star artist from America. These agencies, each oriented according to its own interests, did not quite meet. The American artist was interested in visualizing his response to the Asian metropolis, whereas Japanese artists actively interpreted and reinvented the American Pop Art vocabularies to suit their own artistic purposes—sometimes even to Rauschenberg's discomfort. This cross-cultural encounter and the resulting failure to communicate offer another critical case study in the global rise of American art. The American artist's encounter with the Tokyo avant-garde reveals the complexities of the phenomenon, with local artists at once idolizing *and* destabilizing the dominant cultural discourse—Rauschenberg's, in this case.

YOSHIAKI TŌNO AND "FANTASTIC NEW FACES OF THE WORLD"

Like Ileana Sonnabend in Paris, Alan Solomon in Venice, and Pontus Hultén in Stockholm, Rauschenberg found a local advocate in Tokyo: Yoshiaki Tōno, a young critic who forcefully promoted postwar American art in Japan. Having emerged in the late 1950s, Tōno was a representative voice of the post-Informel generation in Japan. To understand the significance of his work—especially his 1959 essay "Madness and Scandal: Fantastic New Faces of the World,"[6] which for the first time introduced Japanese readers to the work of Rauschenberg along with Jasper Johns, Jean Tinguely, and Yves Klein—it is necessary to briefly examine how the post–World War II Japanese art scene regained its contact with Western modern art.[7]

Despite the rapid flow of American culture into Japan in the years immediately after the end of World War II, the Japanese art scene generally looked more toward European modernism than that of America, as it had always done in the prewar period. As very few Japanese citizens were allowed to travel abroad at the time, imported art journals were a major source of information and inspiration for those interested in Western modern art. Anything new from Europe, and particularly from France, looked overwhelmingly refreshing to Japanese artists and the general public alike, who had been denied any contact with the outside world during the war. Even color reproductions of works by such painters as Picasso and Matisse were deemed worthy of public display: in 1948, the exhibition "Reproductions of French Paintings" was mounted to great enthusiasm; some artists even copied those reproductions during after-hours of the exhibition.[8]

In the 1950s, Japan started receiving real works of art from overseas. In 1951, solo shows of works by Matisse and Picasso were held in Tokyo, while the exhibition "Salon de mai in Tokyo" also made a sensation, presenting works by contemporary French painters who elaborated on the stylistic innovations of these two modern masters. In the same year,

Figure 4.3
Robert Rauschenberg, *Gold Standard*, 1964. Combine: oil, paper, printed reproductions, clock, cardboard box, metal, fabric, wood, string, shoe, and Coca-Cola bottles on gold folding Japanese screen, with electric light, rope, and ceramic dog on bicycle seat and wire mesh base, 84¼ × 142⅛ × 51¼ inches (214 × 361 × 130.2 cm). Glenstone.

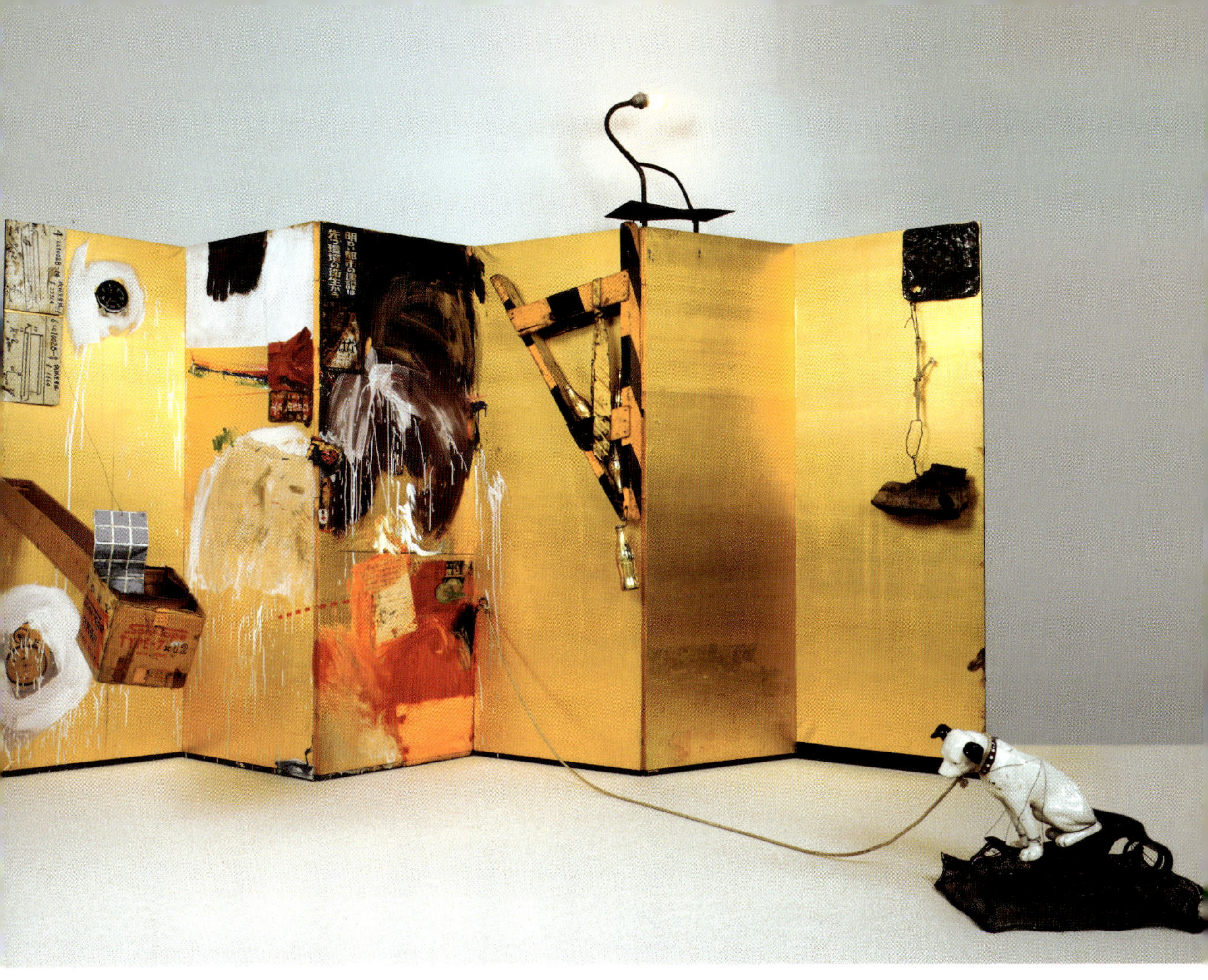

the Yomiuri Independent Exhibition (hereafter the Yomiuri Independent), a legendary "no jury, no prize" annual exhibition sponsored by Japan's leading newspaper company,[9] organized two special sections respectively for contemporary French and American paintings. Notably, this marked the first occasion for such representative Abstract Expressionists as Jackson Pollock and Mark Rothko to be shown in Japan. Jirō Yoshihara, who would found the Gutai Art Association a few years later, applauded the free and vivid spirit of the American paintings exhibited at the exhibition, which convinced him of the "universality of abstraction as a pictorial language."[10] The avant-garde calligrapher Shiryū Morita demonstrated a similar recognition when he reproduced an image of Franz Kline's painting on the cover of the first issue of *Bokubi* (Ink Beauty), an avant-garde arts magazine he launched in 1951.

However, the Japanese generally associated gestural abstraction more with Paris than with New York. The 1956 exhibition "Art of Today's World" decisively effected this perception. Critic Shin'ichi Segi, who had a connection with the Parisian art scene and often contributed to *Cimaise* in the 1950s, organized the exhibition partly in collaboration with Michel Tapié. Including works by Europeans (Jean Fautrier, Karel Appel, and Georges Mathieu, among others) as well as some Americans (Willem de Kooning and Sam Francis), the show presented contemporary abstract paintings under the label of Informel for the first time in Japan.[11] "Art of Today's World" offered many young artists in Tokyo an eye-opening experience. Describing the rich content of the show as a "smorgasbord," Shinohara recollected, "I devoured it in haste. It was filled with all kinds of color, style, and method. It was only a question of which one to imitate."[12] As if to prove this comment, gestural abstraction flooded the following year's Yomiuri Independent, which created a phenomenon called "Informel whirlwind."

In September 1957, Tapié and Mathieu came to Japan, at the invitation of Jirō Yoshihara and Sōfū Teshigahara (hereafter Sōfū),[13] a modern-spirited flower arrangement artist and avant-garde sculptor who founded the Sōgetsu *ikebana* (flower arrangement) school in 1927. The four people formed a close relationship, as they shared a similar international ambition: while Tapié and Mathieu sought to open a market for Informel paintings in Japan, Yoshihara and Sōfū also wanted to promote their work and school abroad.[14] Of all the activities of the French team in Japan, the most notorious was Mathieu's creation of a mural-size action painting, which he enacted in both Tokyo and Osaka (figure 4.4). Dressed in a *yukata* (informal cotton kimono) with a red *hachimaki* (headband), holding a paintbrush in his left hand and a paint tube in his right, Mathieu looked as if he were impersonating a *samurai* inflicting vengeance upon the canvas. The dynamism and speed of his performance amazed the large number of viewers and the press it attracted. As a wealthy art patron, Sōfū bought one of these paintings and also commissioned Mathieu and Sam Francis to create mural paintings for Sōgetsu Hall, the *ikebana* school's new headquarters, to be inaugurated in 1958.

The collaboration between the Informel camp and Sōgetsu/Gutai seemed mutually profitable.[15] On the one hand, gestural abstraction became hugely popular in Japan, creating

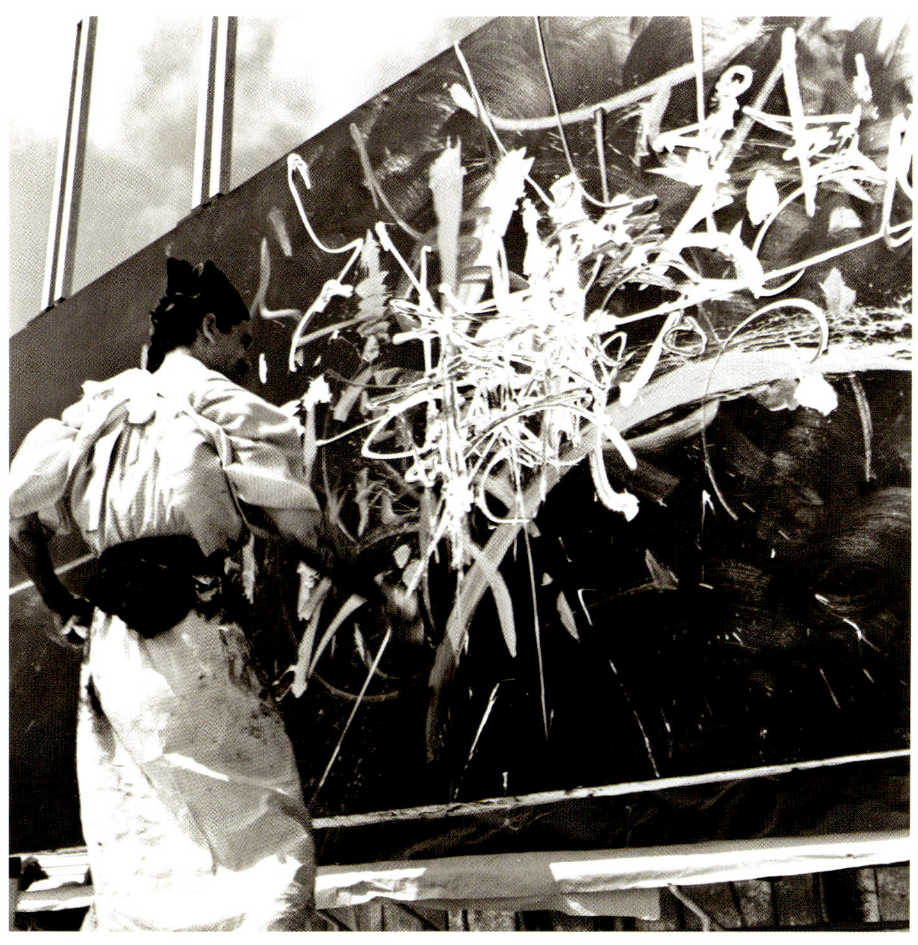

Figure 4.4
Georges Mathieu creating *Toyotomi Hideyoshi* in public on the rooftop of Daimaru Department Store, Osaka, September 12, 1957. Courtesy the former members of the Gutai Art Association and Ashiya City Museum of Art & History.

a market—albeit a small one—for Informel paintings in the country. Through Tapié's connection with the art scene in New York, on the other hand, Yoshihara was able to hold "The 6th Gutai Art Exhibition" (known as "Gutai's New York exhibition") at the Martha Jackson Gallery there in 1958,[16] while Sōfū embarked on an international tour of his flower arrangement shows in 1959. However, Japanese critics started feeling uneasy with Tapié's economic motives. For instance, the critic Segi turned his back on Tapié and reproached him for his manipulative promotional strategies,[17] while the elder critic Shūzō Takiguchi was concerned about the mindless imitations of Informel by young Japanese painters.[18] Meanwhile, as an artist Shinohara reacted with ambivalence: inspired by Mathieu's speed and action, but unimpressed by the French painter's resulting finely balanced compositional painting, Shinohara developed his own boxing-based style of painting (figure 4.5).

Against this background, Tōno emerged as a young critic at a time when Informel was still dominant in the Japanese art scene yet starting to lose its glamour. Although Paris retained a tremendous allure for the Japanese art audience, he surely saw that New York was becoming one of the essential places to visit as a rising art center. At the end of the 1950s, Tokyo was still economically far behind, making overseas travel a rare luxury. Tōno thus seized on the opportunity to travel when he was nominated a subcommissioner, under commissioner Takiguchi, for the Japanese Pavilion at the 1958 Venice Biennale. After completing this job, he went on a grand tour of Europe, America, and Mexico, visiting major art venues. Given that very few Japanese people could take such a trip at the time, Tōno's report of what he saw abroad functioned as a precious mediator between the major art centers, Paris and New York, and the far margin of modern art, Tokyo.

During his trip, Tōno discovered artists who would lead the next trend of world art, which roughly corresponded to Neo-Dada and Nouveau Réalisme. In Paris, he met Jean Tinguely and Yves Klein, and in New York he became friends with Johns and Rauschenberg. Upon his return to Tokyo, Tōno published the essay mentioned earlier, "Madness and Scandal: Fantastic New Faces of the World," in the art monthly *Geijutsu shinchō* (New Trends in Art) to introduce works by the four artists. The article described three scandals that Tōno had encountered during his grand tour. The first took place at the Biennale's section for international young artists, where Johns's *Flag* baffled a number of viewers. The second was the *succès de scandale* of Tinguely and Klein's joint exhibition in Paris, which closed after only one day because the tremendous noise of their work provoked the arrival of firefighters. The third was at the Leo Castelli Gallery in New York, where Rauschenberg's *Monogram* caused a great sensation. Tōno was quick to notice the new artistic sensibility shared by these artists. He noted that they all had a kind of "open, adventurous spirit," unlike many other young artists who were still struggling with the legacy of such postwar masters as Jean Dubuffet and Jackson Pollock.[19]

Tōno's report was a breath of fresh air to those who had grown tired of Informel and awaited something new from abroad. The critic continued to promote the new generation of American artists. In 1960, he wrote on Cage and Neo-Dada artists as well as the second generation of Abstract Expressionist painters, and in 1962 he published a long article with a specific focus on Rauschenberg in *Mizue* (Watercolor).[20] Entitled "Robert Rauschenberg, or the New York Inferno," the article included many illustrations of the artist's work. As Rauschenberg had not yet received such extensive attention in American art journals,[21] Tōno's promotion of his work at this early date is noteworthy. And the essay had a significant impact on Japanese artists: Shinohara found a full-page, black-and-white reproduction of *Coca-Cola Plan* (1958) so inspiring that he made a copy of it in 1963 under the rubric of "Imitation Art." Shinohara's act of imitation saliently illustrates the moment at which the Tokyo art scene was shifting its source of avant-garde inspiration from the French model to the American one.

Meanwhile, the Sōgetsu Art Center, established upon the inauguration of Sōgetsu Hall in 1958, was becoming an important avant-garde venue for artists based in Tokyo. Its director, Hiroshi Teshigahara, an avant-garde filmmaker and Sōfū's son, was eager to introduce his audience in Tokyo to the cutting-edge arts of America such as jazz, avant-garde film, modern dance, and experimental music. Comparable to Fylkingen or the Moderna Museet in Stockholm, the Sōgetsu Art Center was a modestly scaled institution that effected important changes in the local art scene by inviting artists from abroad; in fact, the foreign artists involved with Stockholm and Tokyo overlapped to a great extent. Sam Francis, a friend of Pontus Hultén, had had close connections with both places since the 1950s, and Cage and David Tudor performed in both cities in 1962 at the invitation of Fylkingen and the Sōgetsu Art Center. Tinguely also showed in both Tokyo and Stockholm. A good friend of Tōno, Hultén visited Japan in 1962, and was shown around Tokyo by Sam Francis.[22]

Around the same time, Japanese artists were actively creating their own branch of avant-garde art in Tokyo.[23] The short-lived group called Neo Dada, of which Shinohara was a member, was active from March to October in 1960,[24] and Hi Red Center, an experimental art group formed around Genpei Akasegawa, Natsuyuki Nakanishi, and Jirō Takamatsu, was founded in May 1963 and active through October 1964.[25] Most of these artists were involved with the Yomiuri Independent, which presented an annual occasion for them to exhibit anything they created, however chaotic or outrageous the work might be. Many of the submitted works were increasingly Happening-based and involved transient, mundane objects. Seeing such disorder at the Yomiuri Independent upon his return to Tokyo, Tōno coined the term "Han-geijutsu" (Anti-Art), a concept he had developed in relation to works by Rauschenberg and Johns, whose use of ready-made materials invalidated the traditional categories of painting and sculpture.[26]

Tōno was also instrumental in bringing the "fantastic new faces" to Japan, although his original plan of organizing a group show of work by the four artists did not materialize because of Klein's premature death in 1962.[27] Tōno instead arranged Tinguely's solo show at the Minami Gallery, one of three commercial galleries specializing in contemporary art in Tokyo at the time,[28] for which he was acting as consulting advisor. Tinguely arrived in Tokyo in February 1963 to prepare for the show, scheduled in March. He was introduced by Tōno to Shinohara, who became his assistant and helped create a series of

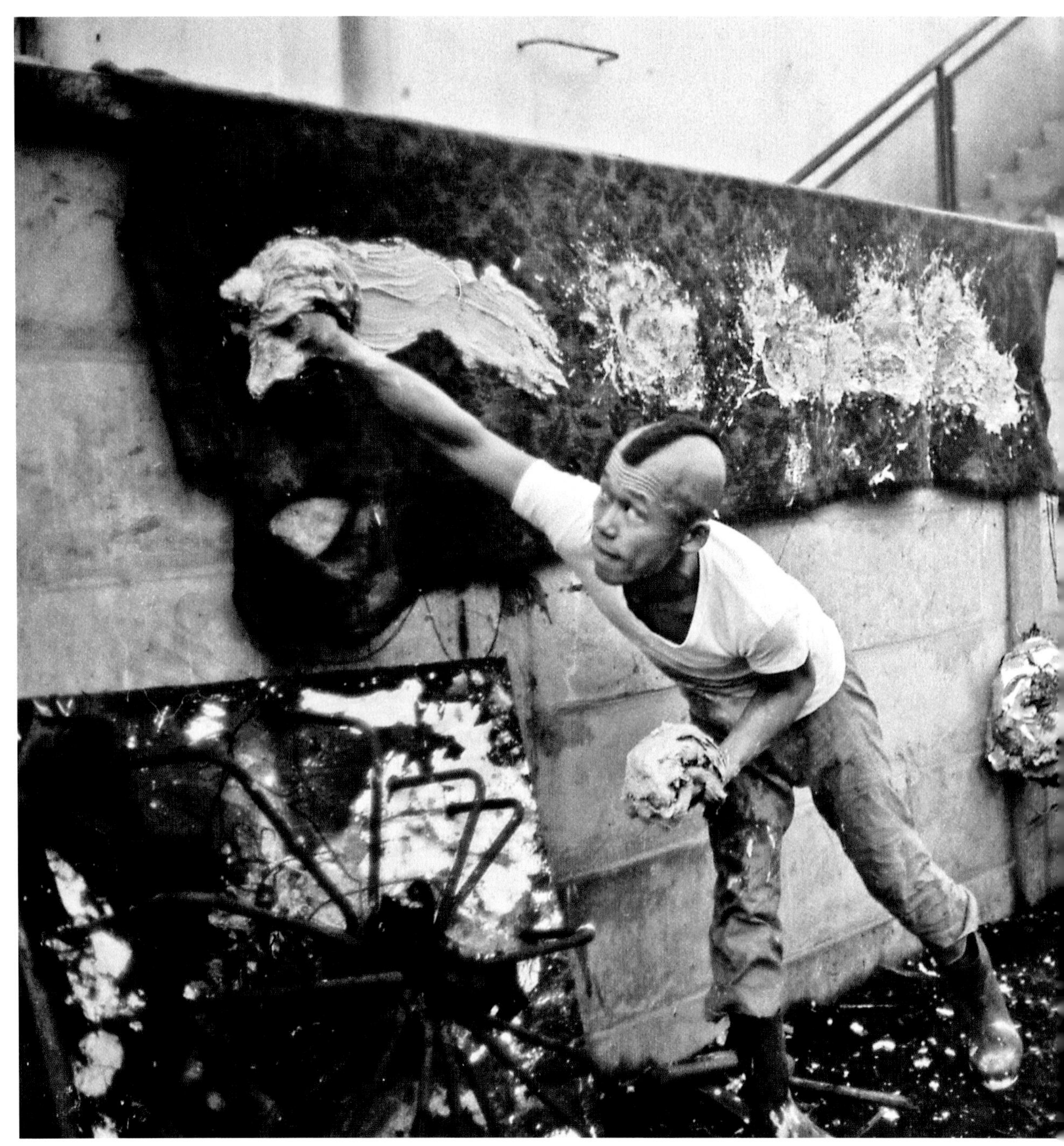

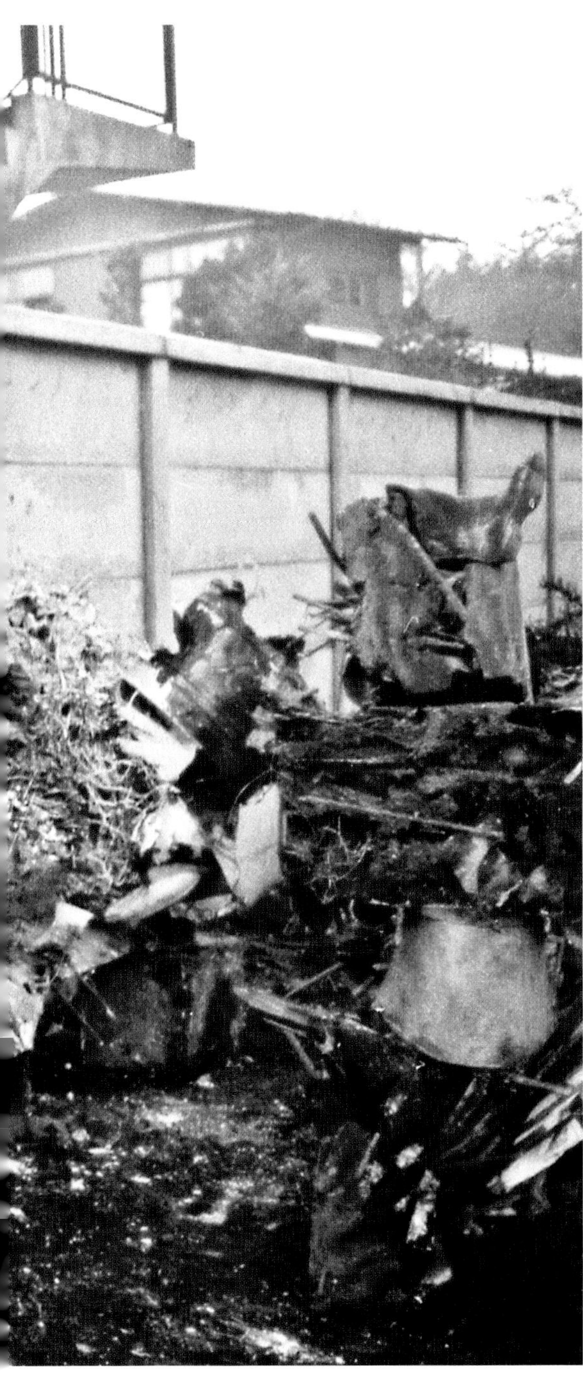

Figure 4.5
Ushio Shinohara, *Boxing Painting*, 1960. Photograph by Meiji Fujikura; copyright 1960 Akiharu Meiji Fujikura, Japan.

Méta-Matics in the city. He also had a chance to look at the Yomiuri Independent, which shocked him with its unbridled energy and the apparent absence of censorship. Indeed, the 1963 Yomiuri Independent achieved the apex of chaos by hosting so many works involving principles of indeterminacy. Nakanishi's work incorporated numerous clothing pegs attached to stretched canvas or scattered around on the floor throughout the exhibition space, and Takamatsu's rope piece extended into Ueno Park outside the museum. Some artists even organized a "miniature restaurant," cooking tiny dishes within the exhibition space and selling them to museum visitors. Other artists presented their own performing bodies—some unclothed—as works of art, which museum guards judged to be obscene.[29] Although the chaos of the show impressed Tinguely as proof of the truly democratic nature of the exhibition, it was becoming a serious problem in the eyes of the sponsor, the Yomiuri newspaper company, which decided to discontinue the exhibition at the beginning of 1964. Artists were shocked to lose the only public venue where they could show anything they wanted to, but they quickly rebounded by holding on their own initiative such group exhibitions as "Off Museum," which comprised a series of outdoor performances and an exhibition organized by Shinohara at the Tsubaki Kindai Gallery in Shinjuku.

In May 1964, Jasper Johns arrived in Tokyo at the invitation of the Minami Gallery, which was again arranged by Tōno. He stayed in Tokyo for two months to produce a number of works, such as *Watchman* and *Souvenir*, which were shown with his earlier works at his solo exhibition at the gallery in 1965. Interestingly, during his stay in Tokyo Johns encountered things that Rauschenberg would see six months later. He saw both Shinohara's "Imitation Art" works and Nobuaki Kojima's *Standing Figure* (1964), which would be onstage alongside Rauschenberg during "Twenty Questions to Bob Rauschenberg." One day, Tōno took Johns to the Tsubaki Kindai Gallery where Kojima was showing his figures. Each of Kojima's figures was customarily called "Man with a Flag," as they were covered with cloth that looked like the Stars and Stripes. This impressed Johns—who was known as the quintessential *Flag* artist—so deeply that he even posed for a photograph with these objects (figure 4.6). On his second visit to the gallery, Johns saw the group exhibition "Off Museum" and on this occasion Shinohara showed Johns his works. The latter seemed indifferent, except when Shinohara showed an imitation of Rauschenberg's *Coca-Cola Plan*. The excited American artist started discussing the work with Tōno and was further taken aback by an imitation of his own work, *Three Flags,* painted in complementary colors. Shinohara even presented a sample of his "Imitation Art," entitled *Drink More* (figure 4.11), as a gift to Johns. According to Johns, he actually took an inspiration from these works and created *Flags* (1965), which he presented at the Whitney Annual of 1965. It was a large vertical painting with two flags on a gray background. One was painted in green and orange in the upper part of the work, while the other was a real canvas of flag painted in gray, attached to the lower part. The idea was that the viewer would get a spectrum of red and blue after looking at the first flag, which could be superposed on the monochrome flag below.[30] He thus complicated the relationship between the imitated and the imitator.

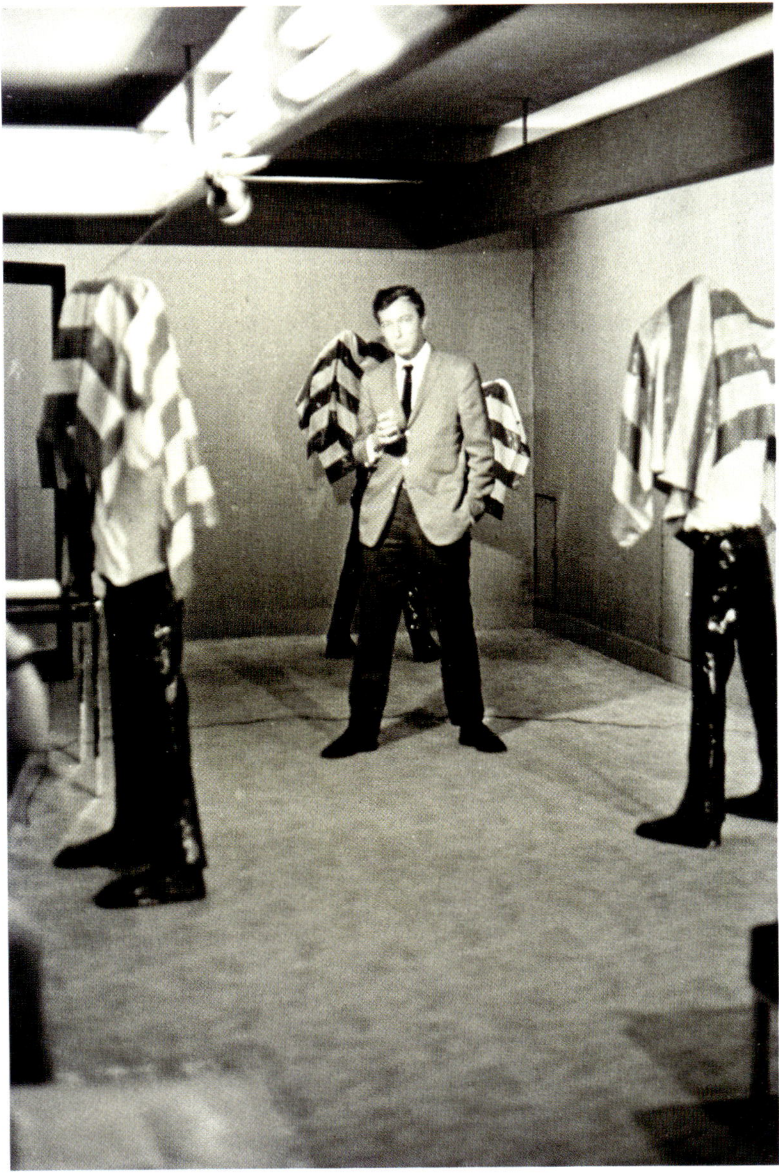

Figure 4.6
Jasper Johns posing with Nobuaki Kojima's *Standing Figures* at the Tsubaki Kindai Gallery, Tokyo, 1964. Photograph by Jun'ichi Takeishi; courtesy Kazutada Tsubouchi.

Rauschenberg was the last of the four "fantastic new faces" to come to Japan. His visit coincided with a transitional period of the Japanese art scene. The abrupt discontinuation of the Yomiuri Independent had created a sense that an era had ended in Tokyo. A number of ambitious artists in Japan—especially former members of Neo Dada—had already started migrating to New York, to try their luck and abilities in the new art center of the world.[31] Seeing his fellow artists departing Japan, Shinohara felt "left behind" in Tokyo.[32] However, such mobility was not easy for the Japanese artists, especially compared with their American counterparts. With the exchange rate of one U.S. dollar pegged to 360 yen, migrating to America, or even just traveling there, was so expensive that it required a "do-or-die" determination. This imbalance of cultural and financial power between American and Japanese artists would reveal itself during Rauschenberg's encounter with the avant-garde art scene in Tokyo.

RAUSCHENBERG'S "TOKYO"

What Rauschenberg saw as an outsider-tourist in Tokyo in 1964 can be found in the first work he made in the city, a collage entitled *For John Cage* (figure 4.7). The ground of the collage is an aerial photograph of Shinjuku, a recently redeveloped ward in Tokyo. In this photograph, Tokyo was already fairly large and dense, but still decades away from being the high-tech futuristic city that it is today. Nevertheless, the whole cityscape of Tokyo had a new look when Rauschenberg arrived in November 1964. The Olympic Games had just taken place there in October, in preparation for which the government had constructed the Olympic Roads and the Tokyo Metropolitan Expressways.[33] Rauschenberg's eyes thus adroitly responded to a city that had just undergone extensive modernization. His collage was used to illustrate the Sōgetsu Art Center's small brochure of events that featured his interview program, "Twenty Questions to Bob Rauschenberg," and a concert by Cage and Tudor.

As mentioned, Cage and Tudor had visited Tokyo two years earlier, as the first international artists invited by the Sōgetsu Art Center.[34] This invitation was made possible in part by Toshi Ichiyanagi, a composer who had studied with Cage in New York and had performed his music in Tokyo the previous year. On his 1962 visit, Cage performed *Theater Piece* and also premiered *o′oo″ dedicated to toshi ichiyanagi and yoko ono* at the Sōgetsu Art Center. In the former piece, he cooked, read a book, and moved around onstage as he would do in his everyday life, but with the sound of his actions amplified and delivered to the audience through a number of speakers. In *o′oo″*, Cage amplified the subtle noise of writing out a score while smoking from time to time.[35] After about forty minutes of this action, he descended into the auditorium to receive a kiss from Yoko Ono (who was married to Ichiyanagi at the time), which indicated the end of the performance. These performances brought about what is now remembered as "John Cage shock" among contemporary musicians in Japan.[36] After attending the performance of *o′oo″*, art critic Yūsuke Nakahara commented that he saw "a way of subverting modern art" in Cage's indeterminacy and chance principles, which were "the rules that dominate our real life, not art."[37]

While Nakahara's statement could be applied to Rauschenberg's artistic practice as well, it should be noted that Cage developed these principles out of his dialogue with Zen Buddhism, which he had studied with D. T. Suzuki at Columbia University.[38] In contrast, Rauschenberg, while very sympathetic to Cage's ideas, did not have such a committed engagement with Japanese aesthetics. In the collage *For John Cage*, he seems to accept the fact that he was merely passing through Tokyo and thus makes no excuse for his "touristic" engagement with the foreign metropolis. First of all, the ground of the collage is an aerial photograph, likely from a postcard or a sightseeing brochure. In addition, as artist Fujiko Nakaya (an assistant for Rauschenberg's Sōgetsu event) recollected, the American artist acquired a tourist's phrase book specifically to create this work.[39] By pasting cut-out words and phrases onto the image, he recreated the kind of linguistic chaos that might surround a tourist in a foreign city. Japanese words and phrases sprinkled over the picture form a few distinct groups. The lower left is concentrated with a random selection of individual words such as "interesting" and "horrifying" in parentheses, while tourist-like phrases such as "I would like to take the table by the window" and "Please show me the seat chart" gather around the upper and the bottom center. Rauschenberg may have used another, more in-depth phrase book to assemble the Japanese sayings—such as "Out of sight, out of mind" and "So many men, so many minds"—that occupy the upper right corner, as these would be rather unusual for a tourist's elementary use.

Since phrase books are usually bilingual, Rauschenberg must have known what those Japanese fragments meant in English. However, though there is a sense of compositional flow, with the name "Cage" situated at the top and "Rauschenberg" at the bottom of the railway lines, the words and phrases do not form a coherent statement. On the contrary, as they are effectively suspended in the air without speech subjects, there is no communication at work in this collage. Rather, the linguistic syncopation that visually pulses over the image of Tokyo functions as Cagean urban noise. It acts in much the same manner as the noise that might daunt a tourist's aural perception in a city where he or she does not understand the language. Rauschenberg seems to be lightheartedly mocking the tourist fantasy of having a firsthand experience of the cultural other, by showing that this experience is in fact mediated by a standardized guidebook and phrase book. While the disembodied language over the image of Shinjuku seems to resonate with the restless transformation of Tokyo, its syncopated rhythm actually corresponds to Rauschenberg's description of Tokyo as "staccato," the word he used when Tōno asked about his impression of the city. He added, "Tokyo is not like New York, which is always in a hurry, but rather is a city with many powerful centers dispersed all over."[40] Rauschenberg thus presented his first impression of Tokyo as a greeting card to the Japanese audience.

However, his engagement with the foreign metropolis was not free from the problematics of representing the cultural other. *Tokyo* (figure 4.8), the second collage he created

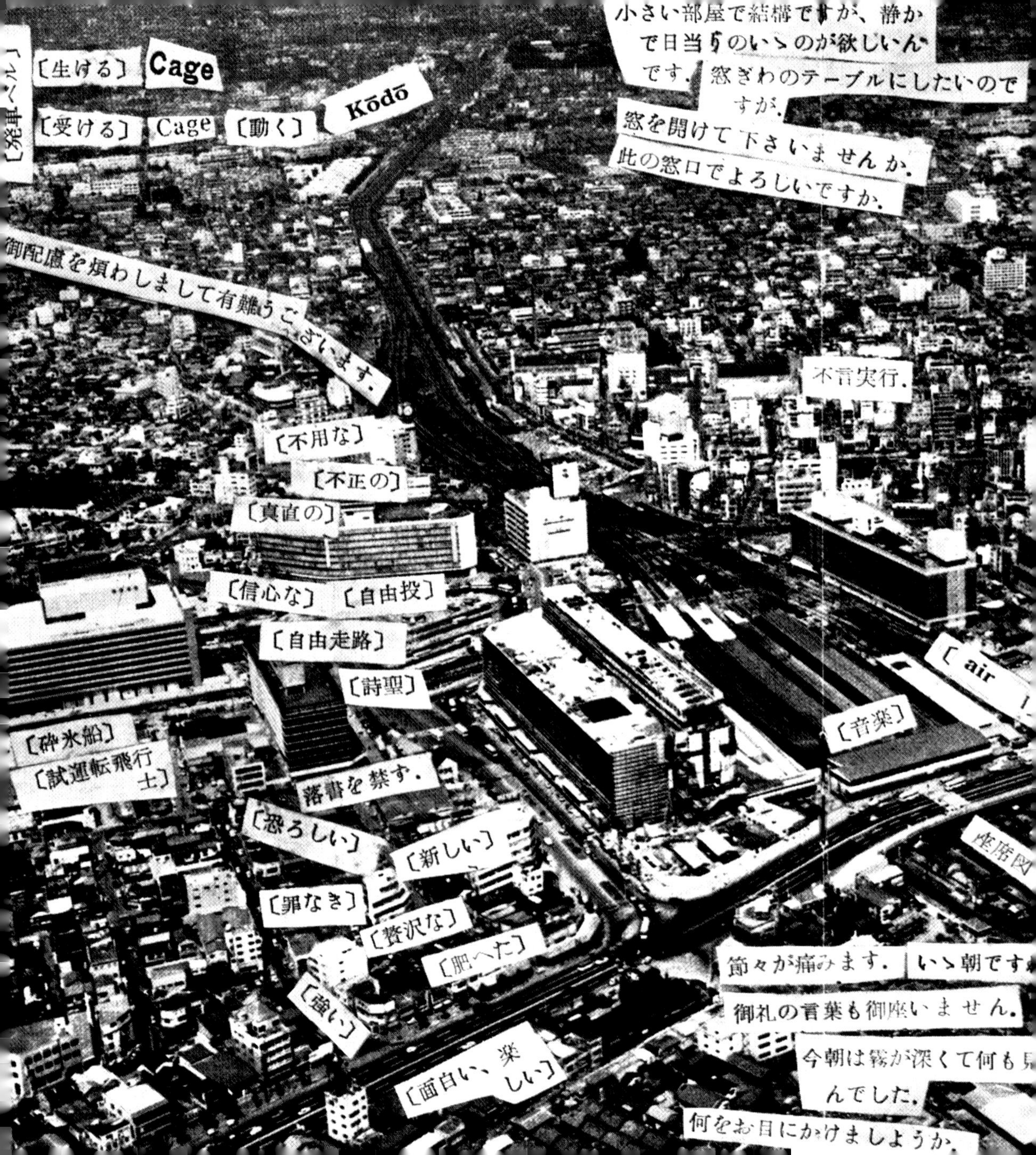

〔生ける〕 Cage

〔受ける〕 Cage 〔動く〕 Kōdō

小さい部屋で結構ですが、静かで日当りのいゝのが欲しいんです。

窓ぎわのテーブルにしたいのですが。

窓を開けて下さいませんか。

此の窓口でよろしいですか。

御配慮を煩わしまして有難うございます。

不言実行。

〔不用な〕

〔不正の〕

〔真直の〕

〔信心な〕 〔自由投〕

〔自由走路〕

〔詩聖〕

〔air

〔音楽〕

〔砕氷船〕

〔試運転飛行士〕

落書を禁ず。

座席図

〔恐ろしい〕

〔新しい〕

〔罪なき〕

〔贅沢な〕

〔肥へた〕

〔強い〕

〔面白い、楽しい〕

節々が痛みます。 いゝ朝です

御礼の言葉も御座いません。

今朝は霧が深くて何も見えませんでした。

何をお目にかけましょうか。

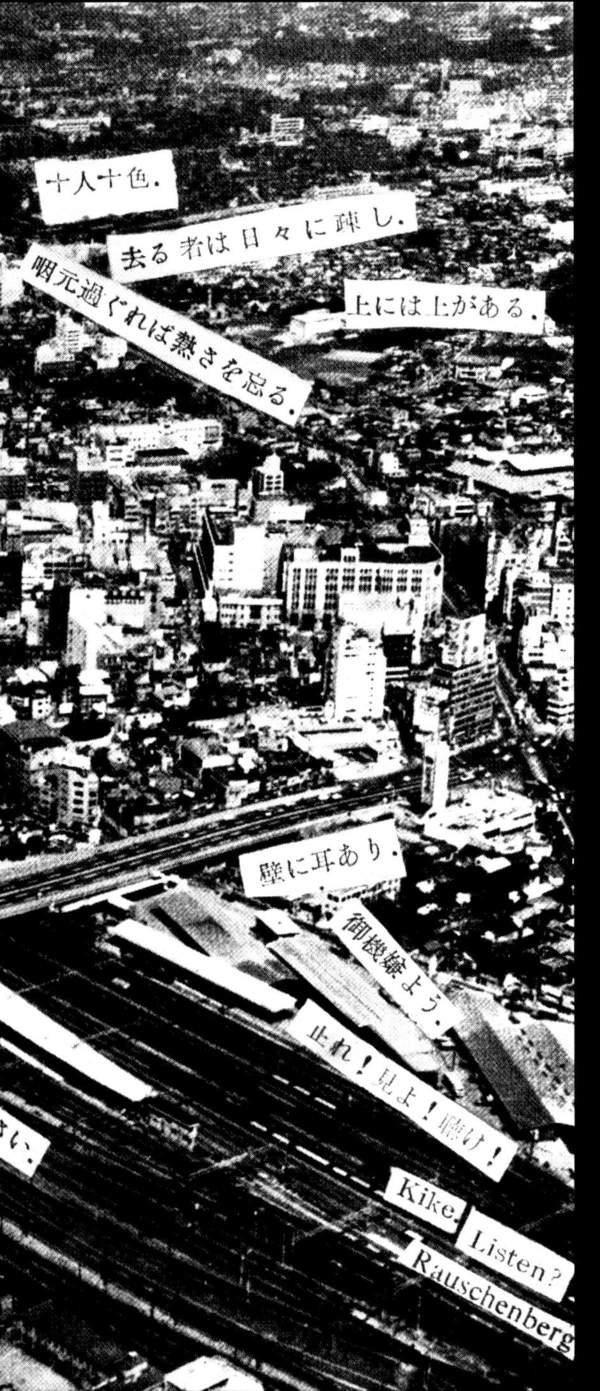

Figure 4.7
Robert Rauschenberg, *For John Cage*, 1964, collaged paper on photograph. Location unknown. Reproduced from the Sōgetsu Art Center's brochure of events that featured "Twenty Questions to Bob Rauschenberg" and a concert by Cage and Tudor.

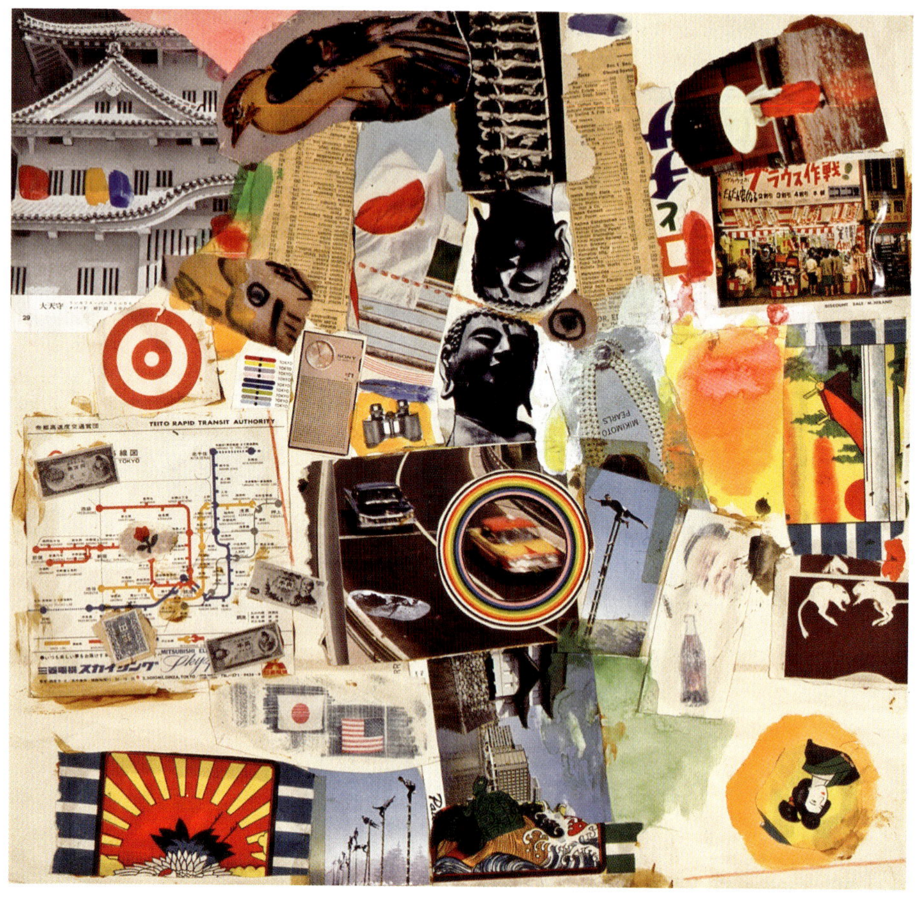

Figure 4.8
Robert Rauschenberg, *Tokyo*, 1964. Solvent transfer, paint, and collage on paper, 18⅞ × 20 inches (47.9 × 50.8 cm). Estate of Robert Rauschenberg.

in Japan, at the request of the newspaper *Yomiuri shinbun*, provides quite a different take on the city. In this work, Rauschenberg cut out pictures from popular magazines to juxtapose traditional and urban images of Tokyo that equally attracted his eye as a tourist. While the images of a Great Buddha, a castle, and a scene of acrobatics are included as exotic elements, the images of highways, a subway map, and a discount sale in a shopping arcade convey a sense of busy and modern urban atmosphere. Although this juxtaposition of the old and the new of a foreign metropolis might seem simplistic, the collage was not meant to be complete in itself as a work of art; it was intended for publication on the front page of *Yomiuri shinbun*—a project that was never realized. The newspaper's editorial staff originally asked Rauschenberg to write an essay with a collage,[41] but the artist came up with a plan on his own, which he explicated to Tōno: "My essay is a collage and I said I wanted it to be printed surrounded by the news of the day in the paper, on the front page, if possible. It's a very colorful collage, and it would be resolved into four colors with a rotary press and be printed on the page as a four-colored collage. Then I wanted the surrounding articles to be printed in various colors as well, as opposed to the usual black ink. I wanted one article printed in blue, the other in red, and the editorial in yellow." Involving a number of unpredictable factors, this project would have been a kind of Cagean composition in print, as Rauschenberg continued: "I have no idea how it will turn out. Nobody knows what kind of news will be published nor is it possible to predict what kind of color it will be finally printed in. But the whole page—including articles—would be my essay on Tokyo."[42] He praised the Japanese newspaper company for taking on such a bold plan:

> When it's printed, people would open the paper as they normally do, read the colored news of the day and also read a work of art. Wouldn't that be wonderful? It would not be a thing that belongs to just art fans anymore but it would be a thing that is just there. So if you treated this picture as a reproduction of an artwork in an art journal or something, it would be far from my intention.... You might think I'm crazy to ask such an outrageous thing of a big newspaper company, but it's great that it was accepted. It could never happen with the *New York Times*.[43]

Although *Yomiuri shinbun* at first agreed to Rauschenberg's unorthodox layout scheme, the newspaper did not carry out the project in the end. A possible reason becomes evident when one looks at its actual front pages from the period of Rauschenberg's departure for New York. From the end of November to the beginning of December 1964, they were filled with articles on foreign affairs. For instance, Japan's role in the Organization for Economic Cooperation and Development (OECD), its relationship to South Korea and China, and its space development program were under debate, while America's bombing in Vietnam was also frequently reported. Surrounded by these articles, Rauschenberg's *Tokyo* would have emerged as a piece of local news on the front page.

In theory, this art/paper had the critical potential to subvert the traditional idea of originality and authorship, as Rauschenberg would have let the actual situation of any given day determine the final status of the work. Moreover, by being distributed by the newspaper company with the highest subscription rate in Japan, the work would have achieved a truly public nature that would have directly engaged millions of newspaper readers. In practice, though, the project could have come across as the privatization of public media, transforming what Marshall McLuhan once acclaimed as "a collective work of art"—i.e., a page of news—into a work of art that bore the artist's signature style.[44] While McLuhan praised the newspaper as a "daily 'book' of industrial man, an Arabian Night's entertainment in which a thousand and one astonishing tales are being told by an anonymous narrator to an equally anonymous audience," Rauschenberg would have disrupted the very anonymity of the paper by inserting his own collage and turning the whole page into his "essay on Tokyo." The daily newspaper would have lost its objective neutrality by being literally "colored" by the individual artist. As his statements demonstrate, the newspaper project pointed to Rauschenberg's own idealistic incomprehension of the foreign culture. Tokyo was a marvelous place for him, one where he could realize projects such as this, which he would not have been able to do at home. Juxtaposed with the article on bombing in Vietnam, this "essay on Tokyo" would have revealed Rauschenberg's utopian or even quasi-colonial optimism by literally invading, if unintentionally, the public sphere of discourse in a foreign land. This elicits the question: If Rauschenberg was an agent of the cultural dominant, what strategy was left for Japanese artists, who needed to wrestle with the prestige of American art in creating their own branch of the avant-garde?

SHINOHARA'S "RAUSCHENBERG" (1): "IMITATION ART"

A key to answering this question is how we interpret Shinohara's "Imitation Art" and the issue of originality in Japanese art. Shinohara made his 1963 *Coca-Cola Plan* based on a reproduction of Rauschenberg's 1958 original (figures 4.9, 4.10). Just as when he freely adapted Mathieu's action for his own *Boxing Painting*, Shinohara was not mindlessly imitating Rauschenberg as his cultural superior. Seen side by side, the difference between the original and the imitation is clear. For instance, because he could find them more easily, Shinohara used Coca-Cola bottles made in Japan, which had Japanese logos in *katakana* (the syllabary used to phonetically represent foreign words) on one side and English logos on the other. In addition, he hand-made a mold from clay to cast the wings in plaster, as ready-made cast metal wings were not available in Japan. He made the round object (a wood newel cap in the original) by the same method. Finally, he painted the work with Day-Glo paint, because he was working with a black-and-white reproduction of Rauschenberg's Combine and didn't know what colors had been used in it. Importantly, too, Shinohara understood the "point" of *Coca-Cola Plan* while imitating it: the work is structured around the number "3." First of all, three Coke bottles are used; secondly, the height of the work is roughly three times that of a Coke bottle; and thirdly, the "plan" in the upper part of the work is also predicated on multiples of 3. He also found it smart that Rauschenberg added his own gesture to the ready-made objects, by splashing paint on two of the three bottles and shaving off the surface of the newel cap. He found the process of imitating so interesting that he ended up making ten copies.[45] Thus, the resulting work indicates that Shinohara was likely playing with these altered details. This playful quality makes his work not so much a copy as a parody of the original.

As mentioned earlier, Shinohara had found the reproduction of *Coca-Cola Plan* in Tōno's essay in the art journal *Mizue*.[46] Given the scarcity of information on overseas art movements at the time, art magazines were extremely important as a source of inspiration for Japanese artists throughout the 1960s. Without Tōno's article, Shinohara might not even have known about *Coca-Cola Plan*. Since expensive art catalogs were accessible only to the cultural elite, such as art critics and gallery owners, Shinohara and like-minded fellow artists devoured any foreign magazines that reproduced or described new artwork being made overseas—and according to his recollection, even those art magazines would arrive only a couple of times a year.[47] In fact, some avant-garde artists in Tokyo were so eager to learn about and absorb the new art movements that were appearing one after another in New York that they felt they barely had enough time to develop their own style. Shinohara discusses this impatience to keep up with the latest New York art movements in his autobiography *Avant-Garde Road*, which he serialized in the art journal *Bijutsu techō* (Art Notebook) from 1966 to 1967.[48] In this memoir, he candidly relates his amazement at the quick pace of shifting styles in New York when he and his friends saw the January 1963 issue of *Art International*. Declaring the arrival of Pop Art, this issue featured two articles related to the show "The New Realists" at the Sidney Janis Gallery and one essay on Claes Oldenburg.[49] The impact of American Pop was so enormous that Shinohara did not even mention its French counterpart, Nouveau Réalisme, which Restany tried so hard to promote in the same issue (see chapter 1). To the Japanese artists, it was clear that they would have to respond to the new trend in America, not the one in France. "The sooner the better, if you imitate this style" was Shinohara's excited reaction.[50] Abandoning his performance-based *Boxing Painting*, he decided to create a work of Pop Art to submit to the Shell Art Award Exhibition in July 1963.

Shinohara then faced a dilemma: although Pop Art was certainly a new style, its imitation by a Japanese artist wouldn't qualify as new anymore. As he explains in his autobiography, "If you used food, that would be an Oldenburg, while human figures are taken by Segal, comics by Lichtenstein, flags by Johns, paint-pouring by Rauschenberg. There is no new style anywhere anymore. Shit! Why don't I do all of them at once then!"[51] He thus made his first work of "Imitation Art," titled *Drink More* (figure 4.11), an assemblage painting with the Stars and Stripes in the background, from which protruded a plaster hand holding a Coca-Cola bottle. The work was an attempt to emulate Johns, Rauschenberg, and George Segal all at the same time in a single work. He then went on to produce a more exact copy of an original work, based on the full-page reproduction of Rauschenberg's *Coca-Cola Plan* in Tōno's essay. He recalls the embarrassment and exaltation that he simultaneously felt at the completion of the imitation:

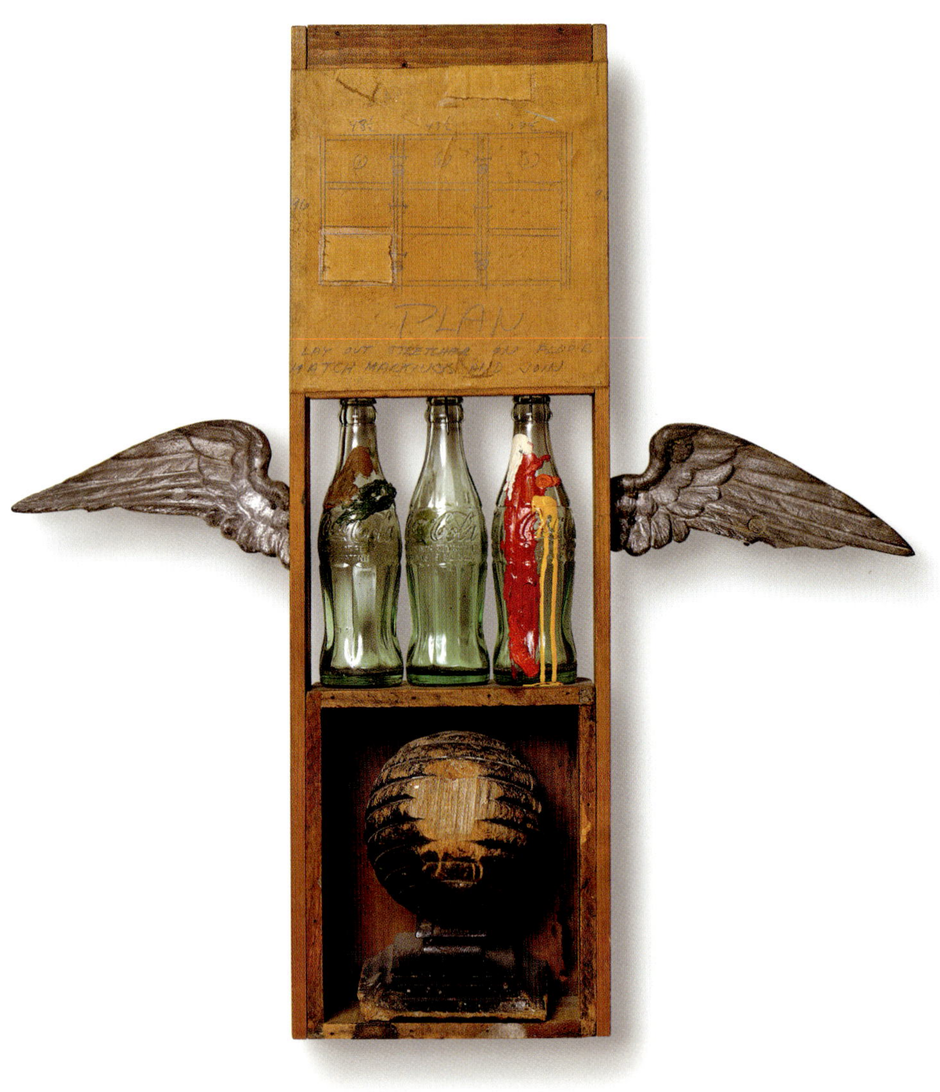

Figure 4.9
Robert Rauschenberg, *Coca-Cola Plan*, 1958. Combine: pencil on paper, oil on three Coca-Cola bottles, wood newel cap, and cast metal wings on wood structure, 26¾ × 25¼ × 4¾ inches (67.9 × 64.1 × 12.1 cm). The Museum of Contemporary Art, Los Angeles. The Panza Collection.

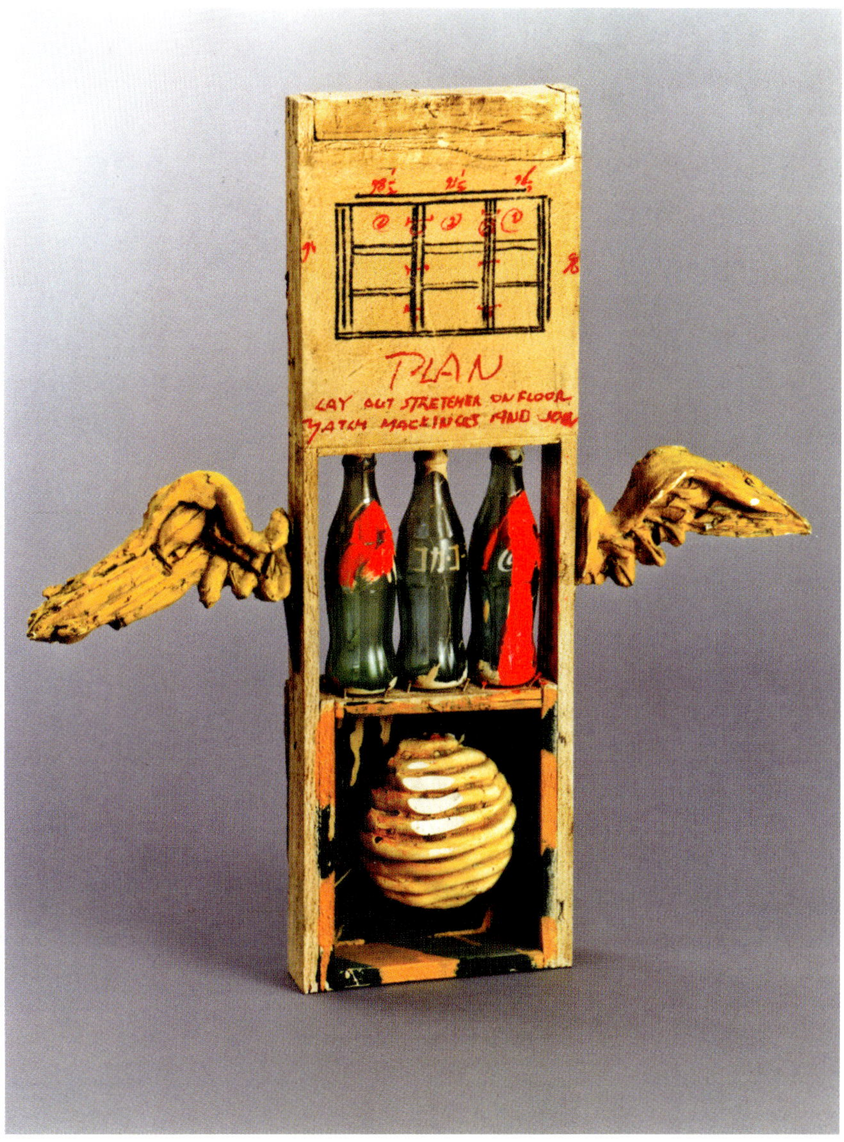

Figure 4.10
Ushio Shinohara, *Coca-Cola Plan*, 1964. Fluorescent paint, three Coca-Cola bottles, pegs, nails, and plaster wings on wood structure, 28 ⅛ × 25 ¾ × 2 ½ inches (71.5 × 65.5 × 6.5 cm). Toyama Prefectural Museum of Modern Art.

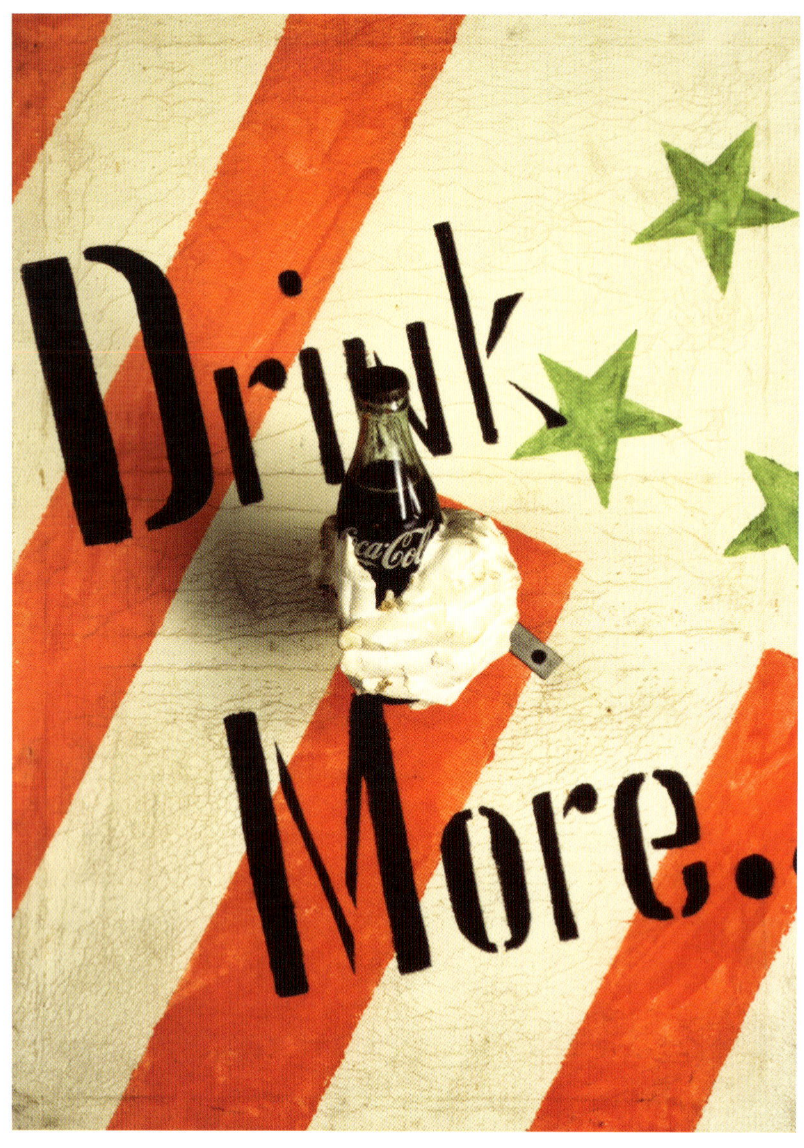

Figure 4.11
Ushio Shinohara, *Drink More*, 1964. Fluorescent paint, lacquer, plaster, and Coca-Cola bottle on canvas, 61 3⁄8 × 74 5⁄8 × 9 1⁄2 inches (156.0 × 190.0 × 24.0 cm). Yokohama Museum of Art.

> Around that time, I saw a black-and-white reproduction of *Coca-Cola Plan* by Robert Rauschenberg, the American Neo-Dada artist. I said to myself, "OK, let's imitate this," because the same Coke bottles were scattered around in the backyard. So I made its imitation within less than half an hour. I could not figure out the color from the reproduction so just painted bright color on my own. My mother yelled at me, "What a shame to copy someone's work!" but I was filled with excitement to complete the work while feeling guilty.[52]

The reaction of Shinohara's mother, who was a painter herself, shows her belief in the importance of originality in art, precisely the concept that the young Japanese artist was questioning. In those days, Shinohara was discontent with Japanese academic art education, which called for students to develop their own original style yet had not changed its traditional teaching method of requiring students to copy old masters and plaster models. Enclosed within the tradition of *yōga*—Western-style oil painting—the model of originality in Japanese art schools was still that of French modernism, exemplified by such painters as Cézanne, van Gogh, and Gauguin, or Picasso and Matisse for a more contemporary version.[53] Shinohara called this approach to art "cultural seclusion," which he ironically associated with Japan's "island-nation" attitude toward foreign cultures during its period of national seclusion from the seventeenth to the nineteenth century. Against this background, his imitation of Rauschenberg can be seen as an ironic three-dimensional copy of a modern master as opposed to the reverent two-dimensional copying of old masters required by the art school. Theorizing on his "Imitation Art" series after the fact, Shinohara declared: "After all, imitation art denies originality. In other words, there is no more time to pursue form or self in modern times. It's more interesting to copy someone's work in this situation."[54]

What Shinohara describes as a phenomenon unique to his own times was in fact an ongoing problem in Japanese art. The question of originality has always been an issue in the discourse of Japanese art history, for Japanese art had developed by responding to information and techniques brought from abroad: Chinese influence (often via the Korean Peninsula) in its premodern era, European influence in its post-seclusion period, and then American influence after World War II. This history resulted in a perpetual identity crisis in Japanese art—especially in the modern era, when the system of "art" and the concept of "originality" imported from the West required Japan to create both its own unique art and its own art history. Since the Meiji era (1868–1912), therefore, many Japanese artists had gone to Europe to learn oil painting techniques and the latest currents of modern art, passing the information on to the Japanese art community upon their return home. Much Japanese modern art thus developed in response to Western modern art, the perceived cultural superior. This dynamic of response to a foreign source posed an impossible dilemma for many Japanese artists, as it made it difficult for them to achieve "originality," a prerequisite of modern art. In order to become practitioners of modern art, they first needed to acquire its basic vocabularies and keep up with its development, but doing so made them perpetual followers of Western art, which kept them from becoming equal and original participants in the world art scene. As we have seen earlier, this dynamic remained unchanged after the end of World War II. Shinohara's version of *Coca-Cola Plan* is thus a visual embodiment of this most fundamental problem in Japanese art, while simultaneously serving as a critique of the myth of originality that haunted its discourse. Ironically, "Imitation Art" proved that the "avant-garde road" in Japan might actually lie in *imitation* rather than *originality*, and thereby radically debunked the concept of originality as a sustaining myth for the avant-garde.

In fact, Rauschenberg himself had been critical of the myth of originality from the early stage of his career. For instance, his *Erased de Kooning Drawing* (1955) notoriously capitalized on the ineffaceable aura of the elder artist, while *Factum I* and *Factum II* from 1957 questioned the Abstract Expressionists' belief in the unique value of a spontaneous, expressive brushstroke. How did Shinohara's "Imitation Art" appear to Rauschenberg, then, when he actually encountered these objects? Although Shinohara never imagined that Rauschenberg would come to Tokyo and see his imitation *Coca-Cola Plan*, the American artist was already aware of Japanese Pop, most likely via Tōno. In 1963, he told a Japanese journalist in New York that he wanted to go to Japan to see the imitations of Pop Art that he heard were increasingly being made there.[55] Tōno thus granted his wish by taking him to Shinohara's home the day before Rauschenberg's interview program. Shinohara recollects the encounter: "I showed my works one after another to Bob, who remained silent; *The Beatles, Lovely Lovely America, Don Shorander with Four Gold Medals, Air Mail*.... It was as if I were reproducing American Pop. But it was just like Rauschenberg that he never said anything lame, like he wanted to see something more originally Japanese. Japan as a Zen country did not matter to him. What mattered was an encounter between works of art." Shinohara then asked Rauschenberg a "special question" about "Imitation Art":

> "May I imitate your works?"
>
> I asked my special question. I wanted to show my *Coca-Cola Plan*, too, but didn't have the courage to do so. I'd bring it to the stage of tomorrow's program anyway.
>
> "Sure."
>
> I was a little disappointed by this immediate OK. I was expecting a blow in the face or at least a little pause. Well, I will make as many imitations as I like since I got the OK in person. However, I lost interest in "Imitation Art" after this encounter with Bob.[56]

In an interview with this author, Shinohara told a different version of this story, claiming that he did show Rauschenberg the imitation of *Coca-Cola Plan* during his visit. Shinohara said the American artist was overjoyed and held the work adoringly in his arms, calling it "my son."[57] Whatever the case may have been, Rauschenberg was happy with the imitation as long as there was only one. Shinohara recalls that when Rauschenberg found out that the Japanese artist had actually made ten copies of *Coca-Cola Plan*, he seemed disturbed. As Shinohara himself said, "One imitation is philosophy, but ten of them makes it production!"[58] Perhaps Rauschenberg acutely sensed that multiple copies could turn the original—*his* work, that is—into a mere commodity.

One must remember, however, that the "original" from which the imitation of *Coca-Cola Plan* was made was already a reproduction, for Shinohara created his work based on a photograph in an art journal. Moreover, the logic of mass production is already evident in Rauschenberg's own *Coca-Cola Plan*, because he put not just one or two but three Coke bottles in the work. By emphasizing the underlying logic of the original, Shinohara somehow disturbed Rauschenberg, which speaks for the critical power of imitation. In this sense, "Imitation Art" was a precedent of postmodernist appropriation—just like Rauschenberg's *Erased de Kooning Drawing*—in which the imitator destabilizes the authority of the original. The irony is that, this time, Rauschenberg's work was put in the position of the original. This irony loomed even larger during the event "Twenty Questions to Bob Rauschenberg," in which Shinohara participated with his multiple imitations of *Coca-Cola Plan*.

"TWENTY QUESTIONS TO BOB RAUSCHENBERG"

Within the history of post-1945 Japanese art, "Twenty Questions to Bob Rauschenberg" is a legendary incident. The event was originally planned and advertised as a public interview by Tōno, who had called for questions to the artist on the pages of *Bijutsu techō* prior to Rauschenberg's arrival in Japan.[59] On the day of the interview, however, Rauschenberg did not respond to any questions, instead creating the Combine *Gold Standard* onstage by painting and placing objects on a gold Japanese folding screen offered by Sōfū. Despite its fame, this interview-cum-performance event has never been examined in detail before. According to Fujiko Nakaya, Rauschenberg's assistant for the event, it was Sōfū who prompted the artist to produce a work on the gold screen. As a sponsor for Cunningham's tour in Japan, Sōfū had held a party one night for the entire troupe at a high-class Japanese restaurant. On this occasion, Sōfū told Rauschenberg about the traditional, though no longer common, Japanese custom that a guest would paint a picture or write a piece of calligraphy as a token of gratitude for the host. Seeing that Rauschenberg was inspired by the story, Sōfū offered him a gold folding screen, which Rauschenberg decided to use for his public interview since he did not really like the idea of participating in an ordinary interview program.[60] Following this decision, the coordinator Akiyama helped the artist to collect materials on the streets of Tokyo.

"Twenty Questions to Bob Rauschenberg" took place at the Sōgetsu Art Center, for which Sōfū had commissioned works from Mathieu and Francis (figure 4.12). When Rauschenberg appeared on the stage in front of a capacity crowd, he was flanked by their murals, painted some seven years before. In contrast to Mathieu's bombastic impersonation of a *samurai*, Rauschenberg was dressed in a simple worker's outfit, ready to work

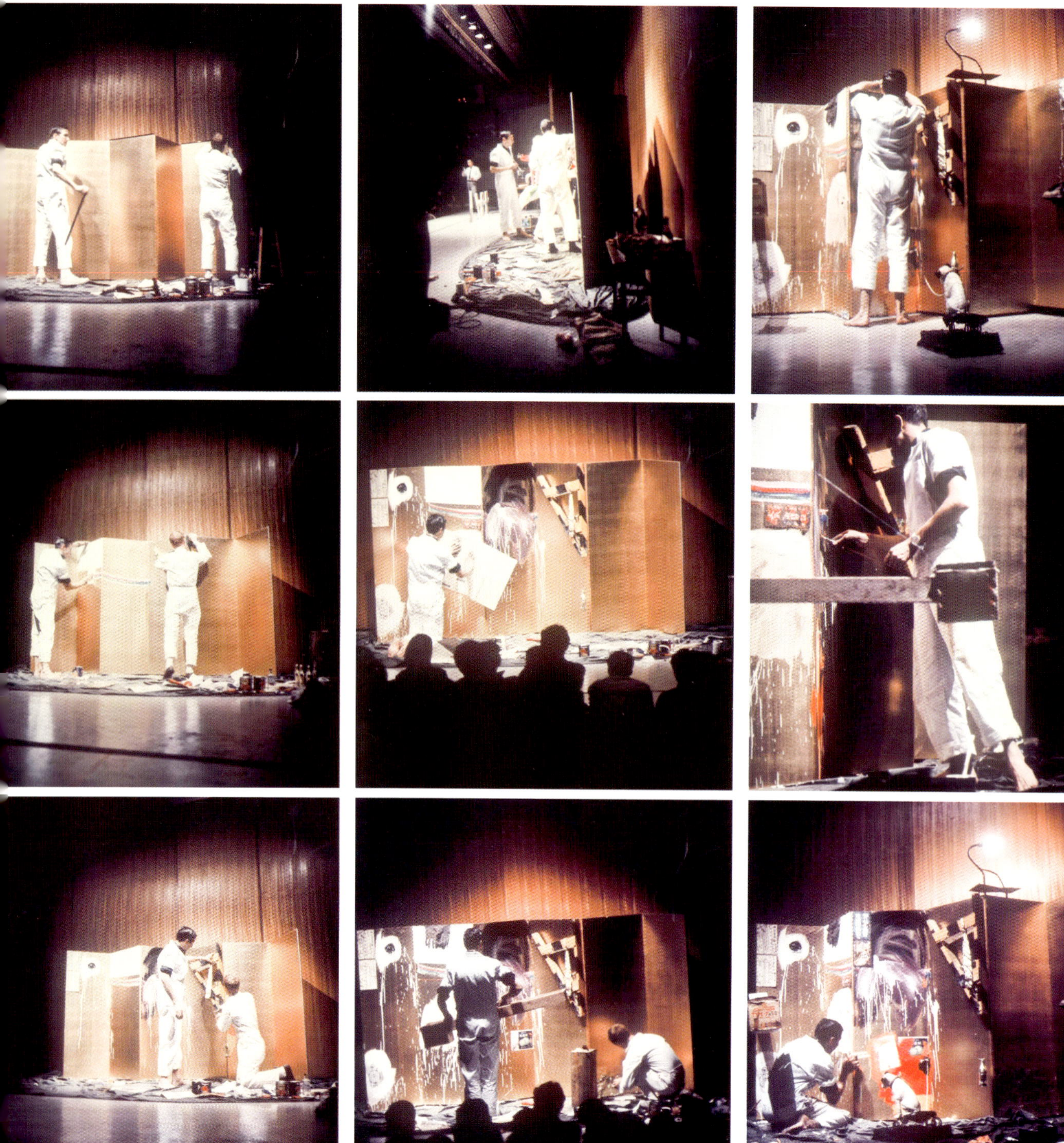

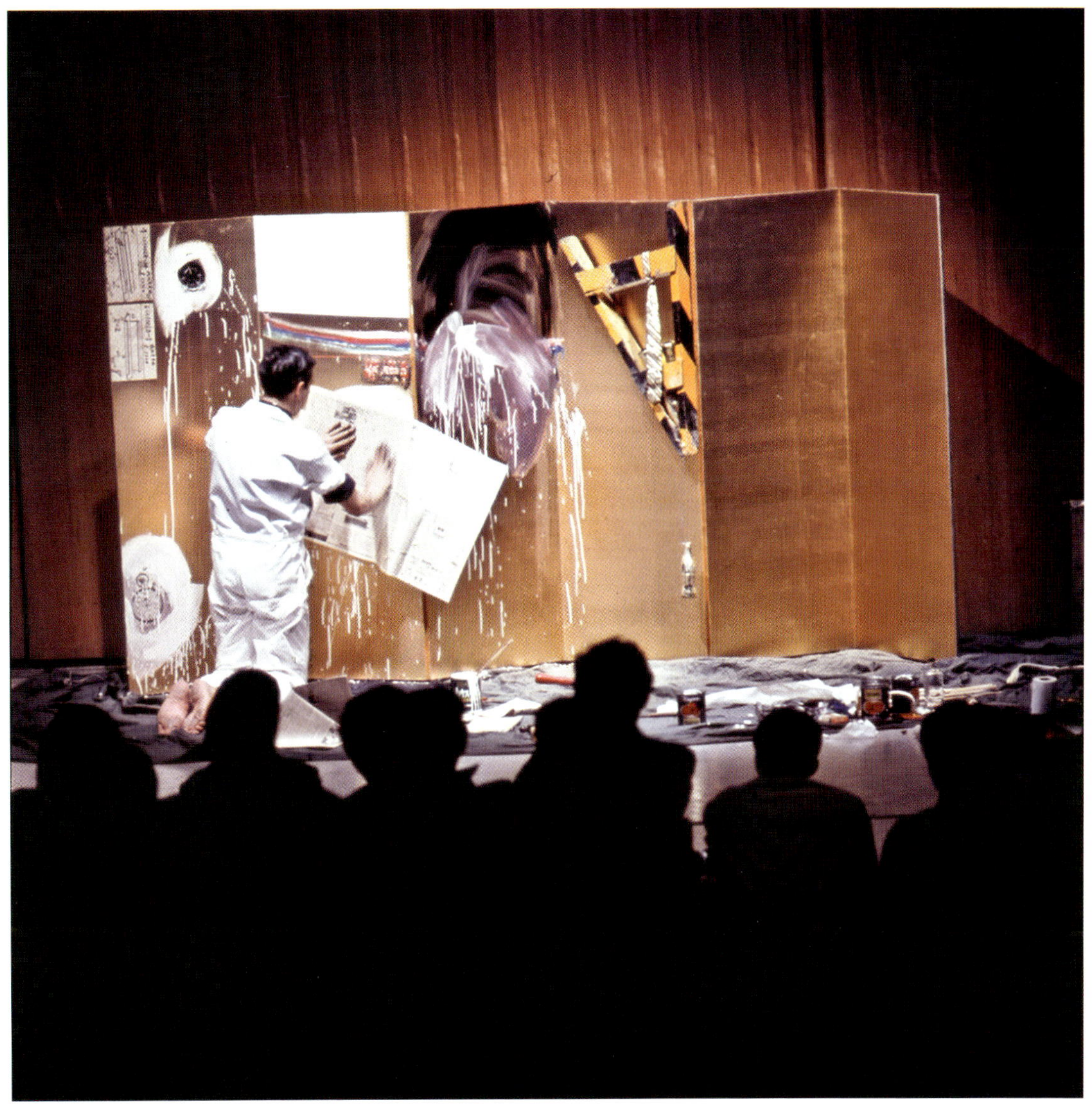

Figures 4.12, 4.13
Robert Rauschenberg creating *Gold Standard* during "Twenty Questions to Bob Rauschenberg," at the Sōgetsu Art Center, Tokyo, November 28, 1964. Photographs by Masaaki Sekiya; courtesy Sōgetsu Foundation Archives, Tokyo.

on the "oriental" support given to him. When the program began, Rauschenberg started working on the screen, with Alex Hay as his main assistant and additional help from Deborah Hay and Steve Paxton. They began by removing the black frame from the upper edge of the screen to create a kind of free, open space. This was a typical gesture for Rauschenberg, who always presented his work as an open field, with which a viewer could be engaged. He then accentuated its surface with paint while Paxton affixed a road barrier from a construction site. Splashing white and black paint over the screen, Rauschenberg went on to attach items such as a speedometer, an image of a clock, Coca-Cola bottles, and a tie painted gold—all typically Rauschenbergian objects—and also created an improvisational transfer drawing with a page of the *Japan Times* (figure 4.13).

While the baffled audience patiently and politely watched the proceedings, the critic Tōno, who had known what the artist would do in advance, presented his own "happening" by constructing questions from Rauschenberg's own writing and others' essays on his work. Thus, the artist's famous statement "Painting relates to both art and life. Neither can be made. (I try to act in the gap between the two)"[61] was turned into: "Does painting relate to both art and life? Can neither be made? Do you try to act in the gap between the two?" Appropriated in this way, Rauschenberg's original statement is transformed into a different form of information, just as the reversed image in a transfer drawing is no longer the same as the original. However, the audience was unable to hear what Tōno was saying because the questions were processed through an electronic sound distorter made by composer Ichiyanagi and delivered as electrical noise. Although Tōno was attempting to create a kind of metaphysical Combine by treating his own medium—words and logic—as ready-made materials, the idea was not clearly communicated to the audience, whose incomprehension was thereby doubled.[62]

In addition, Tōno had invited Shinohara and Kojima in advance to pose questions to Rauschenberg directly. When Tōno raised his hand twice as arranged, the two artists went onstage, dragging Shinohara's sculpture *Marcel Duchamp in Thought* (1964), his imitations of *Coca-Cola Plan*, and Kojima's *Standing Figure*, the last of which held a placard that said "QUESTION" (figure 4.14).[63] Shinohara read out his questions in both Japanese and English, with the help of the interpreter Shūji Takashina, a leading art critic and a curator at the National Museum of Western Art at the time.[64] According to Takashina, Rauschenberg looked back in spite of himself when addressed by the interpreter in English as "Mr. Rauschenberg," but he immediately went back to work, recognizing that Takashina was asking a question.[65] Frustrated, Shinohara placed a sheet of paper bearing a translated question at Rauschenberg's foot. The question read:

> Everybody has a right to a pure creative act. Everybody, even a so-called "Sunday painter." Nevertheless, only artists are required to make an original creative act. For instance, if someone paints a Marilyn Monroe portrait on canvas, they say it is a creative work of art. And if I paint "Mona Lisa," they say it is an imitation. Why?

Reading the question silently, Rauschenberg pasted the sheet of paper onto the third panel (from the left) of the gold screen (figure 4.15). He actually considered Shinohara's question significant and later answered it in an interview he had with Tōno:

> Both of them [a portrait of Marilyn Monroe and a copy of *Mona Lisa*] are fresh works of art. There is no difference between them. I have always used other people's work myself. I have included in my work a photograph taken by somebody else, a reproduction of silkscreen, and an oil painting painted by another painter. I have even used a mirror, which imitates everything as it is. Everything is fair.[66]

Onstage, however, Rauschenberg responded to the question by continuing to work on the gold screen. With help from his assistants, he attached to the screen other objects such as a Sony cardboard box, a figure of the RCA Victor dog (customarily called "Victor's dog" in Japan), a worn-out pair of black leather shoes, and an electric light. When the piece was finally completed, more than four hours had passed since the start of the event and most of the audience—including Cage and Cunningham—had already left the hall.

The resulting work, *Gold Standard* (see figure 4.3), has the appearance of a collection of random improvisational gestures enacted with objects the artist had found on the streets in Tokyo. Upon closer inspection, we can see that Rauschenberg actually sought to achieve a compositional balance within the work. Traces of white paint on the three left panels connect and balance a variety of found objects such as Coke bottles and a striped tie hung from the road barrier, while retaining the spontaneous quality of Rauschenberg's splashing gestures and drips. In the three right panels, where there is virtually no trace of paint, the white of the electric light and the Victor dog are set off against the three left panels. In a similar way, the artist paired the traditional quality of the gold folding screen with urban debris from Tokyo's streets, as each of the six panels has at least one characteristic modern or urban material. For instance, the cardboard Sony box protrudes from the first panel on the left, and the second panel bears the transferred image of the *Japan Times*. The Victor dog is tied to the third panel, the fourth one has Coke bottles, the fifth includes an electric light, and the sixth an old pair of leather shoes. In this way, the gold screen, a traditional object of Japanese culture, is made into a support for modern figures of both gestural brushstrokes and found objects.

Such juxtaposition of the traditional and the modern was (and remains) what makes Japan attractive as a tourist destination: it is timeless and traditional, but with the familiarities and comforts of modern urban life. Rauschenberg's work thus capitalizes on the stereotypical image of Japan as a country where tradition and technology can coexist without friction. The Victor dog, placed on the bicycle seat and tied to the gold screen, seems quite lost in this rather disorienting landscape of Tokyo. With the quizzical expression on its inclined head, the figure reads as a kind of surrogate tourist in an unfamiliar place—where a clear order does not exist, let alone "His Master's Voice," as the company's ad caption read. The dog, however, is not a surrogate of Rauschenberg himself, for this juxtaposition of the

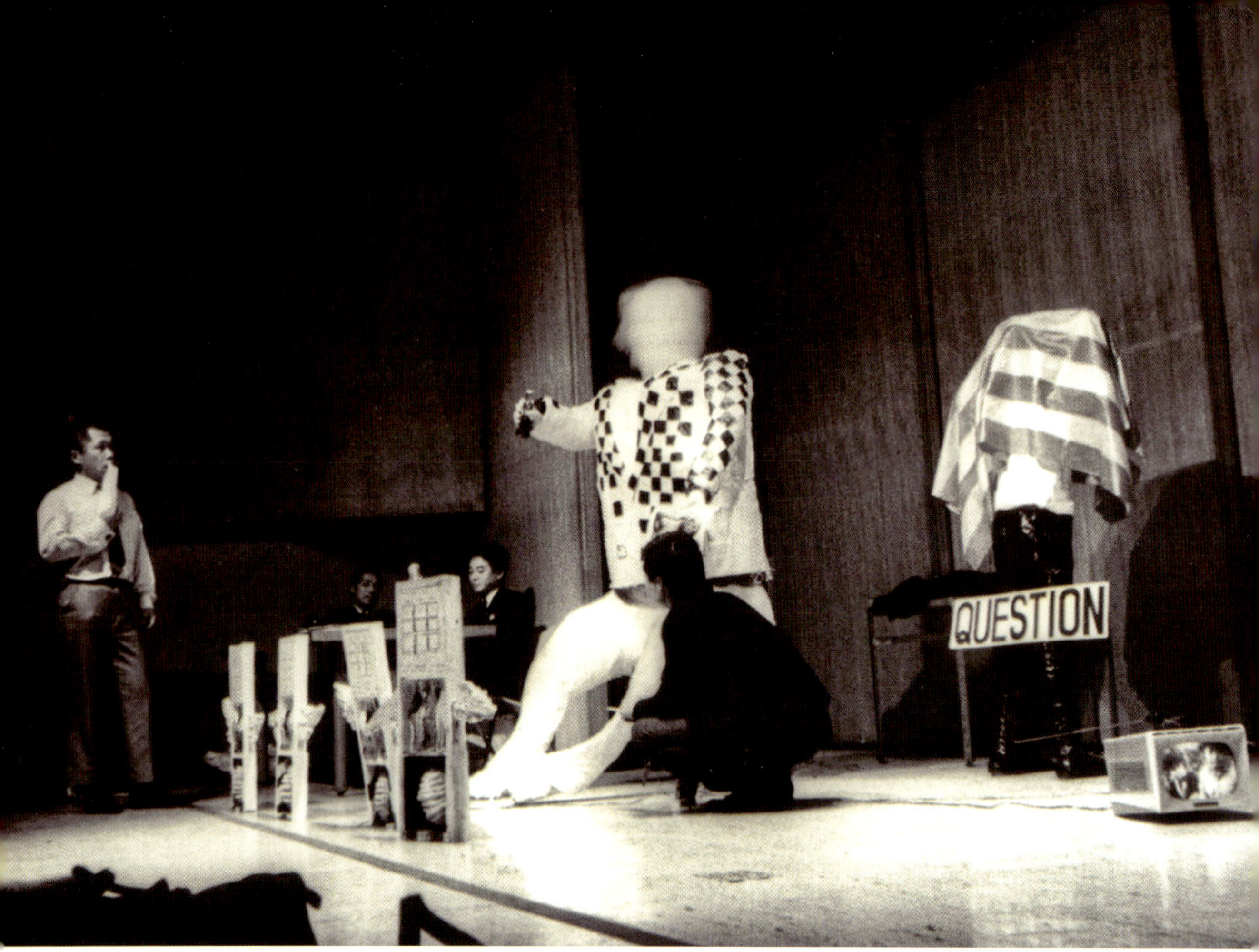

Figure 4.14
Ushio Shinohara asking Rauschenberg questions onstage. Photograph by Masaaki Sekiya; courtesy Sōgetsu Foundation Archives, Tokyo.

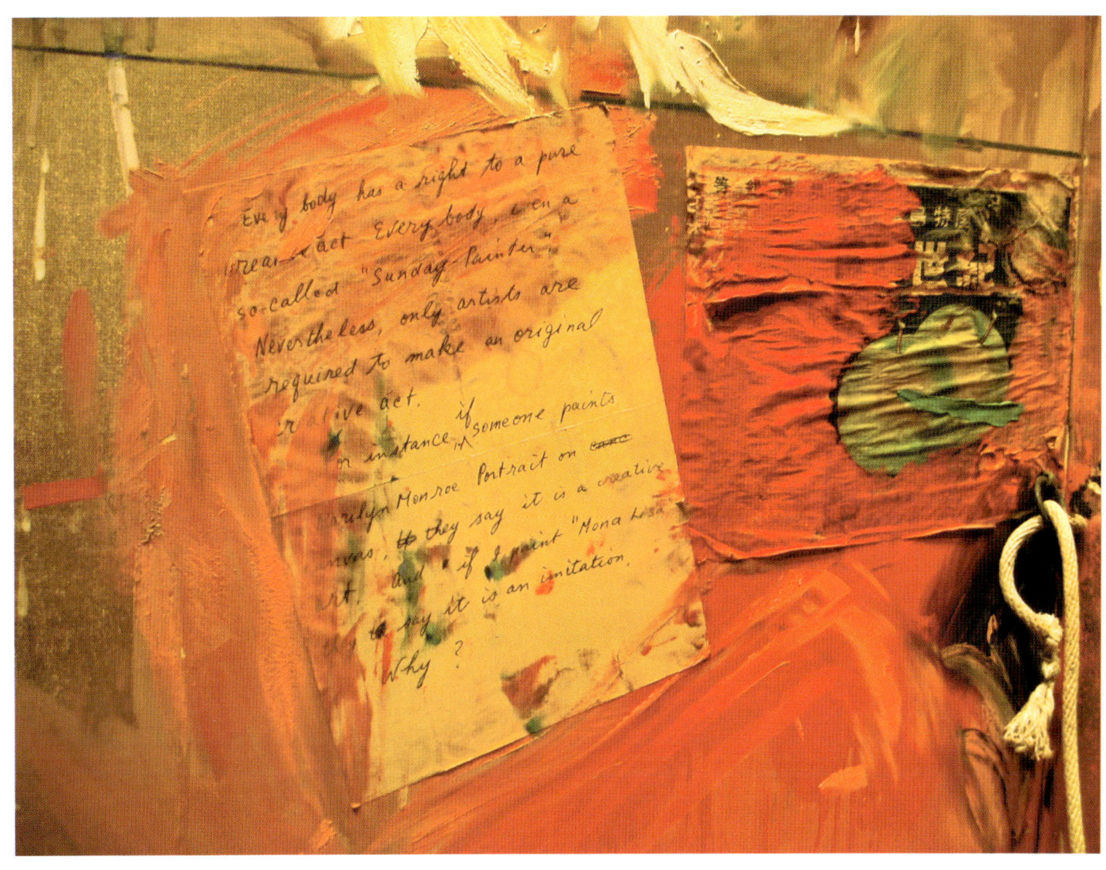

Figure 4.15
Detail of *Gold Standard*. Photograph by author.

old and the new of the foreign metropolis is executed with the artist's own established Combine method. The confusion of the dog might thus allude to the befuddlement of the other participants and the audience of "Twenty Questions to Bob Rauschenberg," who were denied any sort of verbal interaction with the artist.

In an interview with Tōno on the night before he returned to New York, Rauschenberg said that he had tried very hard not to answer any questions during the program because that would have entirely changed the significance of the whole event.[67] Tōno also recalled that when Rauschenberg arrived in Tokyo, he was already skeptical about the idea of an interview. According to Tōno's reconstruction of their conversation, Rauschenberg had confronted the critic with the question: "What is dialogue anyway?… Can you just call it dialogue or interview if a critic and an artist discuss issues with words and the artist states his opinion? Maybe there is a trap in that idea, a trap that you somehow assume you will be understood after all. I do wonder if communication should make such coherent sense."[68] Rauschenberg's doubt about the meaning of "dialogue" may partly be explained by the fact that he had been traveling around the world for six months by then. During the trip, he experienced a number of communication problems within and outside of the dance company, the most troubling of which were his worsening relations with Cage and Cunningham. Given his distrust of words in general, it was no coincidence that he pasted the Japanese saying *Fugen jikkō*—literally "Act it without saying it" and corresponding to the English aphorism, "Actions speak louder than words"—onto the middle of the collage *For John Cage* (see figure 4.7). It is as if the saying predicted Rauschenberg's determination not to rely on words during the performance. This deep suspicion about communication is what differentiates Rauschenberg from more one-dimensional Orientalists such as Mathieu, who never risked or questioned his subjectivity in an encounter with the cultural other. In contrast, Rauschenberg kept his own agency at bay, by playing out onstage the cross-cultural discommunication.

Yet Rauschenberg's creation of *Gold Standard* was not entirely silent; it was accompanied by image and sound from a small television onstage that was kept on throughout the program, as if to make up for the absence of verbal interaction (figure 4.16).[69] Formally, the TV was a constitutive element of the performance: a "modern" screen that emanated light from within, as opposed to the traditional gold screen that reflected light from outside. (Interestingly, the screen offered by Sōfū was not a traditional version with real gold leaf, but a modern, standardized version coated with gold paper and covered by a piece of translucent, silky fabric.) But the TV meant much more than that for Rauschenberg. According to Nakaya, putting the TV onstage was his form of resistance to the pressure of the public production of a work, as he was actually quite frightened by the self-assigned challenge.[70] The artist later confessed to Tōno: "I had never made a painting before in front of the public that way, which scared me very much, but I did not want to make a big deal out of it. So the best way to kill the fear was to practice the very thing that frightened me."[71] The television was thus expected to keep Rauschenberg company onstage while also mediating between the artist and the audience as a tool of mass communication.

The nature of Rauschenberg's fear must be carefully examined at this point. The public he feared in this case consisted mostly of Japanese people, who regarded him as representing the authentic frontier of the American avant-garde. His anxiety might have been derived from the weight of the role imposed upon him in a country where the influence of American art and culture had been immense in the postwar years. In this respect, it is no coincidence that the works that Shinohara and Kojima brought up to the stage included such American icons as Coca-Cola and the Stars and Stripes. The cloth over Kojima's *Standing Figure* does not include any stars but makes an obvious allusion to the American flag with its thirteen stripes in red and white (figure 4.17). Although the artist was initially interested in the formal play of hide-and-seek between the cloth and the figure's ever-invisible head, the uncanny quality of the blinded figure has been interpreted to represent the oppressive presence of America in postwar Japan.[72] When Johns posed for a portrait with these figures earlier that year, he seems to have correctly understood both the formal and sociopolitical tensions within the work (see figure 4.6). Looking straight into the camera, the American artist appears willing to take on the challenge presented by the figures' morbid aura. It is equally important that both Shinohara and Kojima made *multiple* copies of these works that imitated American symbols. In *The Location of Culture*, Homi K. Bhabha theorized the logic of mimicry as a strategy to challenge colonial authority by multiplying imperfect copies of its culture:

> What they all share is a discursive process by which the excess or slippage produced by the *ambivalence* of mimicry (almost the same, *but not quite*) does not merely "rupture" the discourse, but becomes transformed into an uncertainty which fixes the colonial subject as a "partial" presence.... The success of colonial appropriation depends on a proliferation of inappropriate objects that ensure its strategic failure, so that mimicry is at once resemblance and menace.[73]

To paraphrase Bhabha's dense rhetoric, mimicry, with its inevitable failure to fulfill its desire to become "authentic," paradoxically produces a difference from the thing that it imitates and enacts a hybridization of the original discourse. Of course, there is a clear difference between Japan as a once-aggressive imperialist colonizer and colonial India, which Bhabha discusses in his essay. It is nonetheless true that Japan's defeat in World War II and the seven years of occupation by U.S. forces had in effect transformed the country into America's cultural colony. It is thus arguable that another kind of postcolonial paradox was at work when Rauschenberg, onstage as the authorial American avant-garde, felt ill at ease surrounded by these hybridized and multiplied American icons. Through being imitated by the cultural other in Tokyo, the American artist—despite his own critique of originality and authorship—was ironically made to represent the "original," the authority of which was then destabilized by the multiple copies. Rauschenberg's creative agency as the cultural dominant was thus simultaneously made secure *and* insecure by the Japanese artists' strategic employment of imitation.

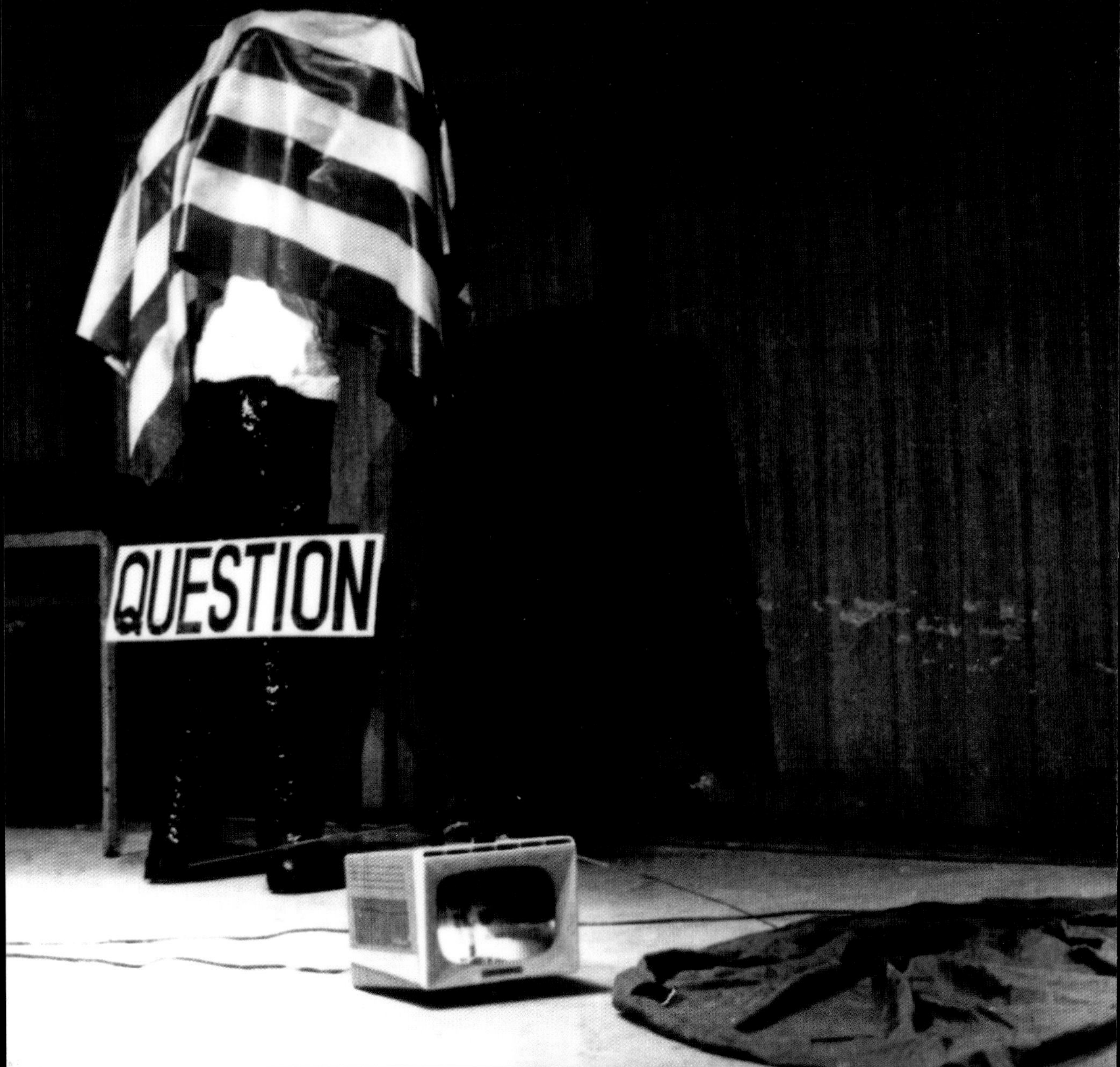
QUESTION

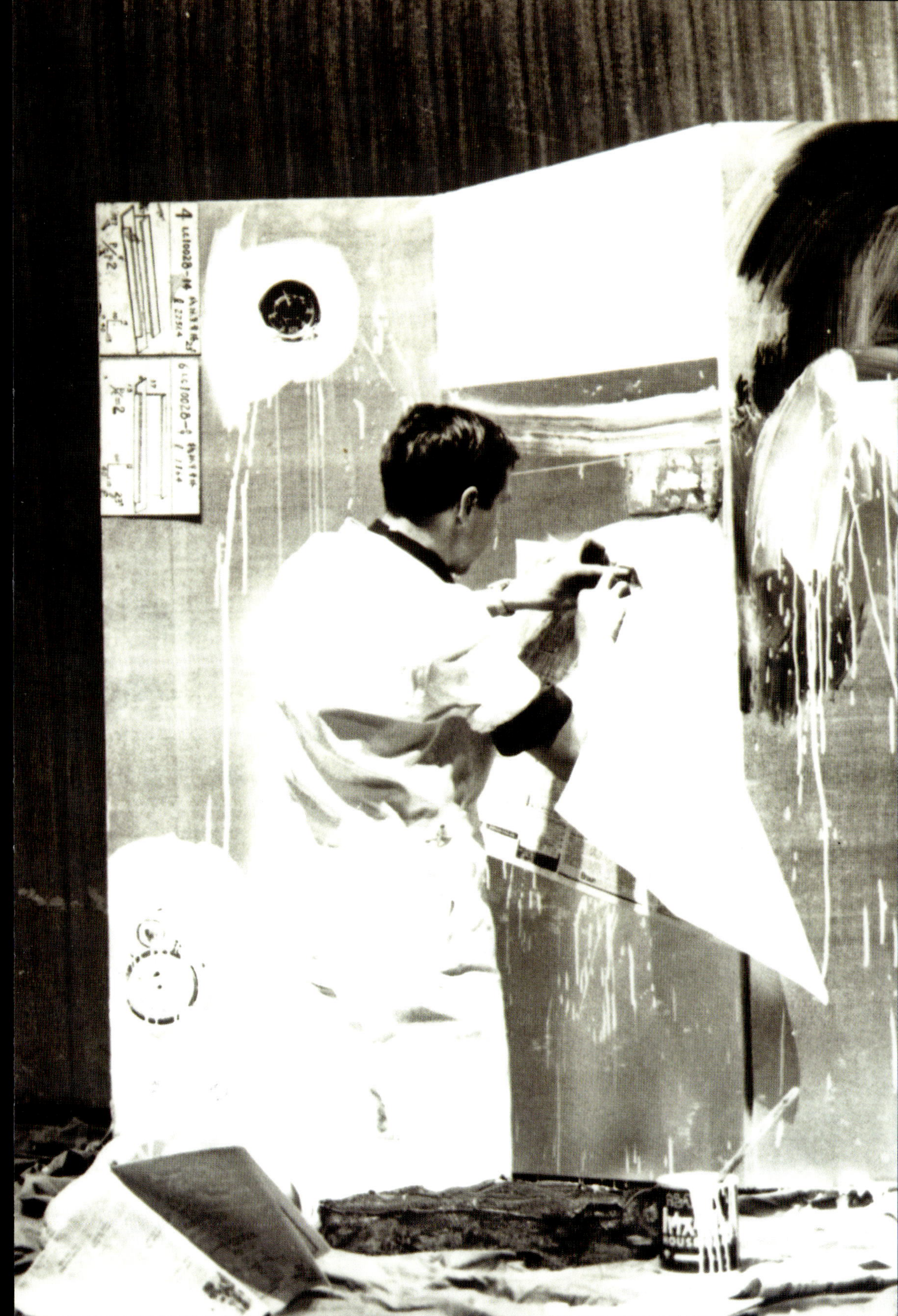

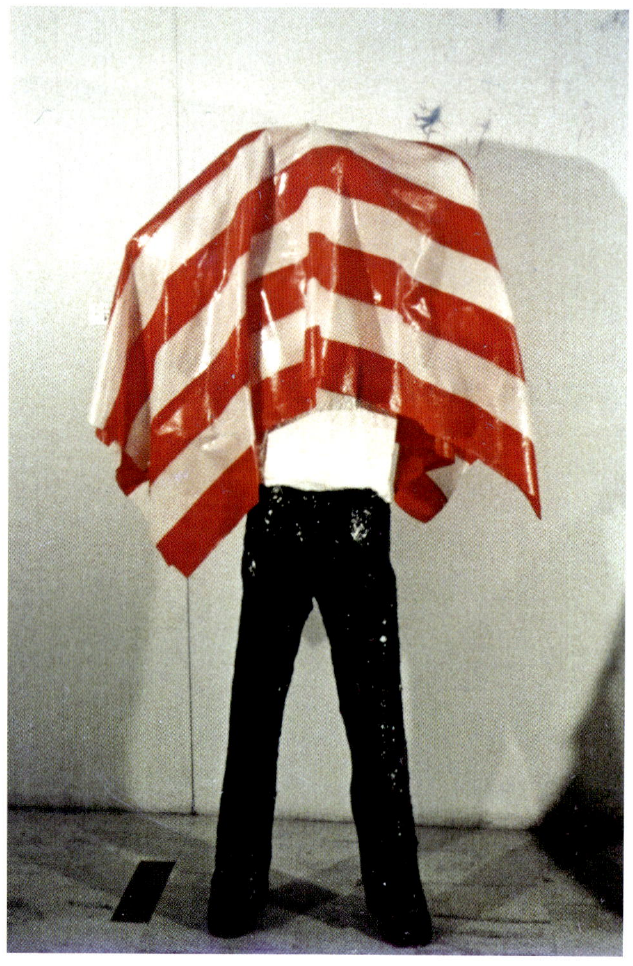

Figure 4.17
Nobuaki Kojima, *Standing Figure*, 1964. Installation view at the Tsubaki Kindai Gallery. Photograph by Jun'ichi Takeishi; courtesy Kazutada Tsubouchi.

The title of his work, *Gold Standard*, must be read closely as well. Rauschenberg chose this title specifically, "First of all, because it [the screen] is gold, and second of all, because it stands, and also because I think this work is the standard itself."[74] As an economic term, "gold standard" refers to the system of using the value of gold as the standard on which to base the value of money. Rauschenberg's title thus implies that there is such a foundational standard in this work as well: the "standard" would be the artist's affirmative belief in his own artistic capacity, which enabled him to complete the work despite the great anxiety he suffered onstage. Yet the title can also be read as a reference to the cultural and economic hegemony of postwar America: the gold standard under the Bretton Woods Agreement was in fact the gold-dollar standard, in which U.S. dollars, as a privileged international currency, had the same exchange value as gold. The gold-dollar standard was not an unshakable system, however, because its stability depended solely upon the steady growth of the American economy. French president Charles de Gaulle repeatedly criticized it in the 1960s as an unfair system because it allowed the United States to print and spend more dollars than the country's actual reserve of gold.[75] As the economist Milton Gilbert warned in 1968, it had become increasingly clear by the mid-sixties that the system would be untenable due to the ever-increasing outflow of U.S. dollars in the midst of the American involvement in Vietnam.[76] Just as Rauschenberg's authority as the cultural superior was shaken onstage in Tokyo, the very paradigm that the gold standard symbolized in the postwar world—that is, Pax Americana—was just starting to crumble. Perhaps without being fully aware of this larger implication of the title, Rauschenberg demonstrated his refusal to be "lost in translation" in this threatening situation in a foreign land.

The significance of the TV onstage, then, goes beyond that of mere companionship for Rauschenberg during the performance. Arguably, the artist presented it as "the master's voice" for the event, in which the whole idea of communication was put into question. Seen this way, the TV stands in for the ultimate failure of communication—the failure not only of cross-cultural communication (whether verbal or mass-mediated) but also, disquietingly, of artistic communication. For the inclusion of a television onstage seems to proclaim that, with the arrival of the "society of the spectacle," TV might replace art as a universal tool of communication: at the very least, watching TV should be as good as watching Rauschenberg's live performance. Japan was just taking the first steps toward becoming such a society, since color television became popular in most households because of the Tokyo Olympic Games in 1964. The international sports festival transformed Japan's capital into a newly made city. The government had not only constructed the inner-city highways but also employed every means to clean up the city before the Olympic Games, which would be the first occasion for Japan to show its face to the international community since the defeat of World War II. The collective obsession to beautify Tokyo was so intense that members of Hi Red Center mocked it in a street performance titled *Cleaning Event*, in which the performers, dressed as public sanitation workers, obsessively and impeccably cleaned a Ginza street, using dusters and toothbrushes (figure 4.18).

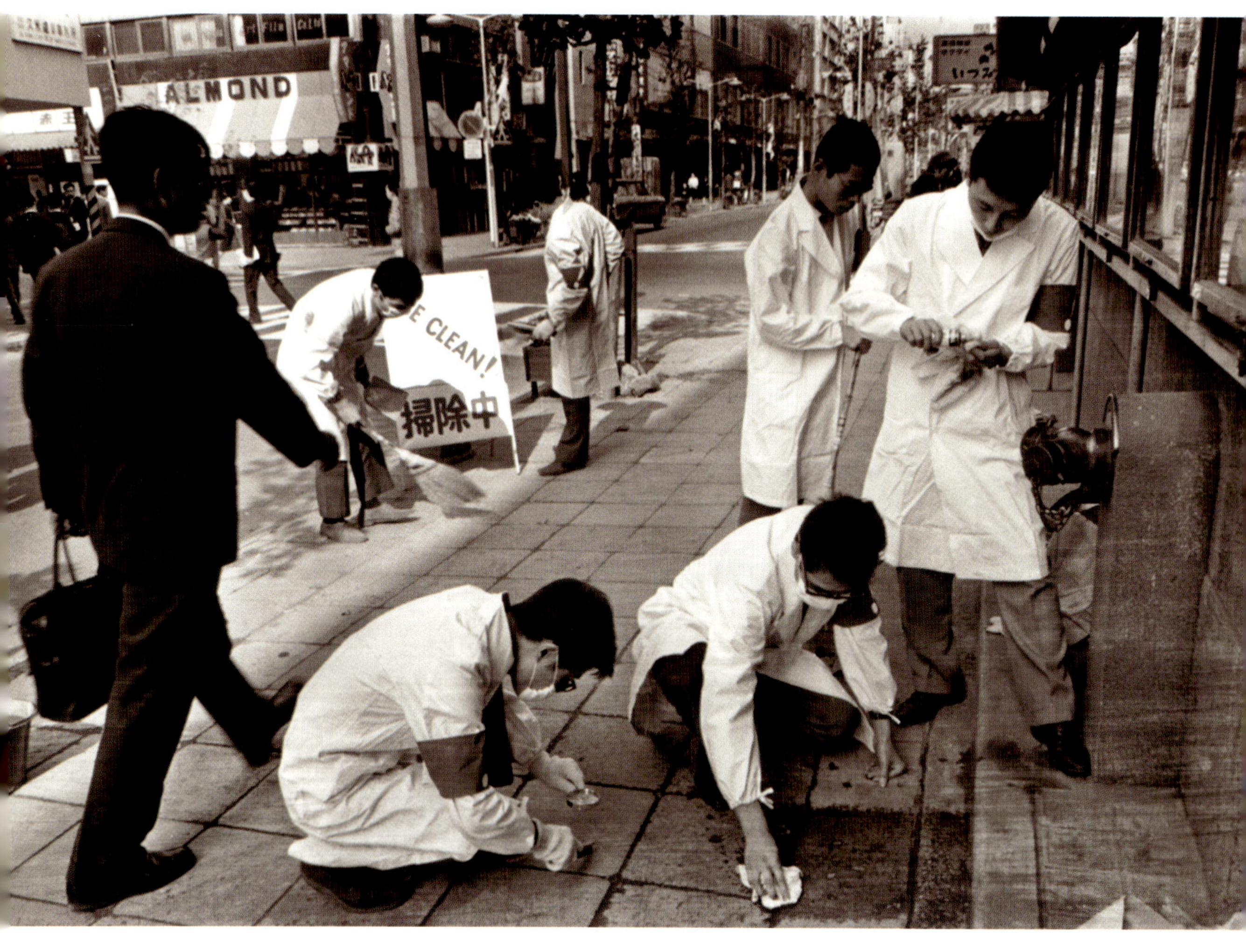

Figure 4.18
Hi Red Center, *Cleaning Event*, 1964. Street performance.
Photograph by Minoru Hirata.

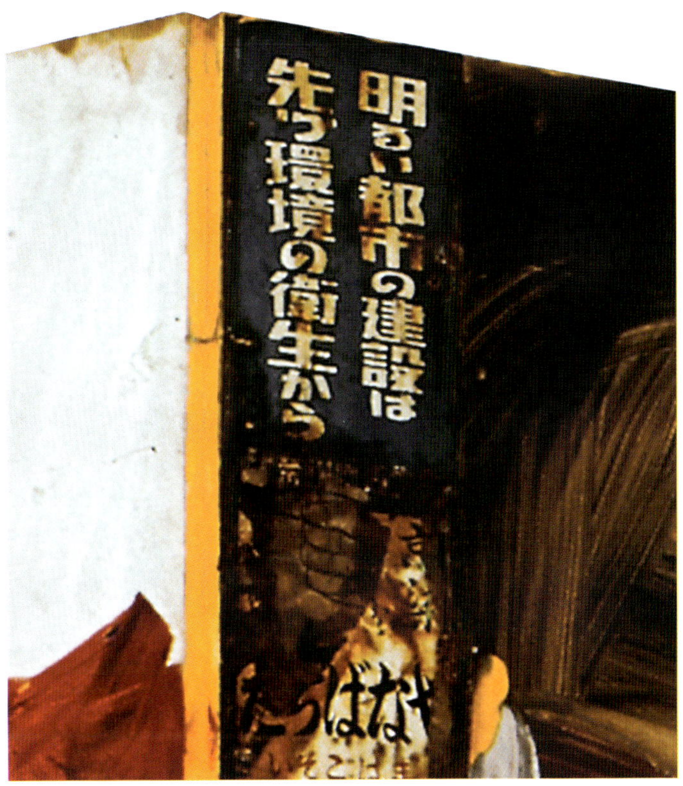

Figure 4.19
Detail of *Gold Standard*. Photograph by author.

This situation explains why the two right panels of *Gold Standard* are relatively empty except for the electric light and the old pair of shoes dangling from the top. Rauschenberg actually found it difficult to collect enough materials for his work in a city so clean and devoid of litter; he ran out of objects to complete the last two panels of *Gold Standard*.[77] As a result, these last two panels bear traces of Rauschenberg and Hay's almost tautological gestures: they attached an extra layer of gold leaf onto the lower part of the fifth panel and then painted another black bar above the black frame of the bottom edge of the sixth panel. In this context, a street sign that Rauschenberg attached to the top of the third panel from the left reads as his ironic gesture. It says, "Let's start with making a hygienic environment in order to construct a bright city" (figure 4.19). The work is thus another of Rauschenberg's deliberately touristic views of Tokyo, in which the artist does not claim an authentic experience or profound understanding of the cultural other—because he is aware that any communication could beome just another form of miscommunication.

SHINOHARA'S "RAUSCHENBERG" (2): BETWEEN TOKYO AND NEW YORK

"Twenty Questions to Bob Rauschenberg" was thus a half-staged, half-improvised performance arising from the tense interaction between Rauschenberg and members of the Tokyo avant-garde. Although Shinohara lost interest in "Imitation Art" after obtaining permission from Rauschenberg to imitate his work, he concluded the series with *Imitation Box* after the American artist went back to New York. In December 1964, Shinohara and his fellow artists organized a group exhibition titled "Left Hook" at the Tsubaki Kindai Gallery, in which Shinohara exhibited *Imitation Box* and *Marcel Duchamp in Thought* along with Kojima's *Standing Figure* in a boxer's outfit (figure 4.20).[78] *Imitation Box*, which has since been destroyed, was a self-contained mini retrospective of the "Imitation Art" series, featuring Shinohara's own works such as *Drink More* and *Coca-Cola Plan*, along with many others (figures 4.21, 4.22).[79] Within a discarded mini refrigerator—itself a container of consumable products—he placed two of his *Coca-Cola Plans*, and used all the other flat planes to display other works. For instance, the back space of the refrigerator, which originally housed a radiator, was used to present an imitation of Johns's *Three Flags* and *Painted Bronze*, while the side panels functioned as supports for *Drink More* and *The Beatles*. The front of the door also displayed *Air Mail*, an imaginary letter from Rauschenberg, with a sign reading "Imitation Box" below it; a study of *Coca-Cola Plan* was mounted on the back of the door. Furthermore, the back panel of the refrigerator bore images of Johns's *Painted Bronze* and an installation view of his exhibition, painted by hand. Upon closer inspection of a photograph of the work, we notice that the panel bears another smaller panel that holds a magazine in which the original page for Shinohara's inspiration can be found.[80]

In its incorporation of other artists' works, Shinohara's *Imitation Box* resonates with Rauschenberg's *Short Circuit* (1955), which also questioned the traditional idea of authorship by inviting a viewer to open a lid to find works by Johns and Susan Weil beneath. The difference is that Shinohara was in no position to include *real* works by Rauschenberg and

Johns, as he had not even seen those works in person at the time. He imitated their works from reproductions and then multiplied them, as copies without the original. This image of an endless regression of American art seems to demonstrate *Imitation Box*'s logic of self-proliferation. The refrigerator is in fact a perfect "box" for carrying these objects, as a sign of modern efficiency and consumer convenience. The refrigerator was one of the three electric appliances, or "three regalia," that Japanese people dreamed of owning in the 1950s, along with a black-and-white television and a washing machine. In the 1960s, commodities called the "3 Cs"—a color television, a cooler (air conditioner), and a car—replaced the three regalia. The model of this ideal domestic life was, of course, American. Japanese people followed trends of American life just as Shinohara tried to keep up with the latest currents of the New York art scene.

Seen in this way, Shinohara's *Imitation Box* aptly embodies what Bhabha calls the "ambivalence of mimicry," an effect created by imitating the original and ending up multiplying something "almost the same, *but not quite*."[81] Containing a number of imperfect copies of American art, *Imitation Box* demonstrates the difference between "being American" and "being Americanized." The work is reminiscent of the ways in which Japanese consumers willingly hybridized their domestic life by incorporating the American way of life haphazardly, just as Shinohara played with differences from the original art in "Imitation Art." Thus, *Imitation Box* effects its own lighthearted and yet unsettling critique of the hegemony of American art and culture, which had a drastic, bulldozing impact on Japan throughout the post-World War II years. With Bhabha's insight, it is arguable that Shinohara's imitation was a critical strategy to destabilize the authority of the very thing he was imitating.

Shinohara's strategy of imitation may not seem as witty as Rauschenberg's own subversion of the authority of Abstract Expressionism, which he demonstrated by enshrining *Erased de Kooning Drawing* in a golden frame. However, that kind of sophistication was not an option for Shinohara within his historical and cultural conditions. As noted before, Shinohara at the time had not even seen in person the works by Rauschenberg and Johns that he imitated—he met the actual artists first before seeing their works Interestingly enough, this encounter had a demystifying effect on the Japanese artist. When the "cool Yankee" presented himself as a real human being to Shinohara, the Japanese artist started to look at American art differently. As a consequence, by 1966, when "Twenty Years of American Painting"—the first large-scale postwar American art exhibition that was organized and sent to Japan by the Museum of Modern Art, New York—opened at the National Museum of Modern Art in Tokyo, Shinohara was no longer as enthusiastic about American art. Indeed, he was already disillusioned. Shinohara described his disappointment with the show in his autobiography under the subtitle "American art that lost its glory":

> American art—this vivid monster appeared before our eyes only through journals until a couple of years ago. It seemed as if American art had been marching toward the glorious prairie of the rainbow and oasis of the future, carrying all the world's expectations of modern painting.

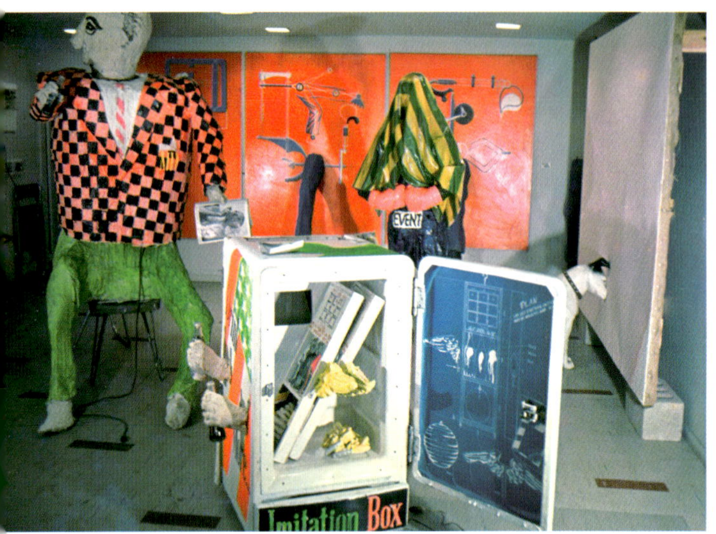

Figure 4.20
"Left Hook," installation view at the Tsubaki Kindai Gallery, December 1964. Courtesy Kazutada Tsubouchi.

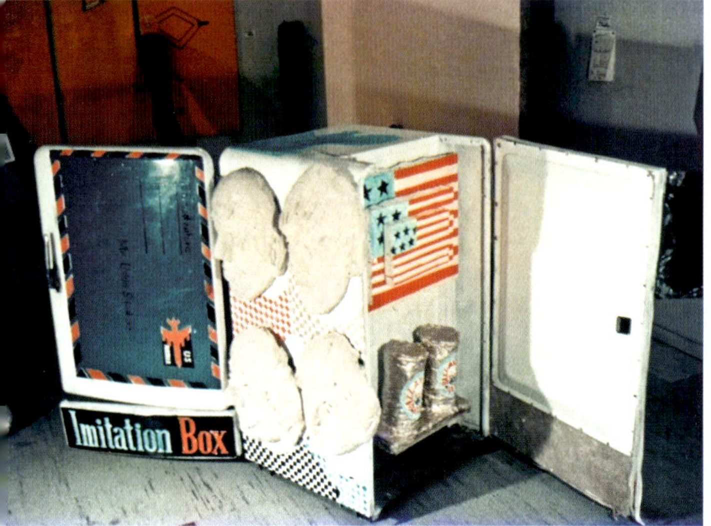

Figure 4.21
Ushio Shinohara, *Imitation Box*, view from back, 1964. Destroyed. Courtesy Kazutada Tsubouchi.

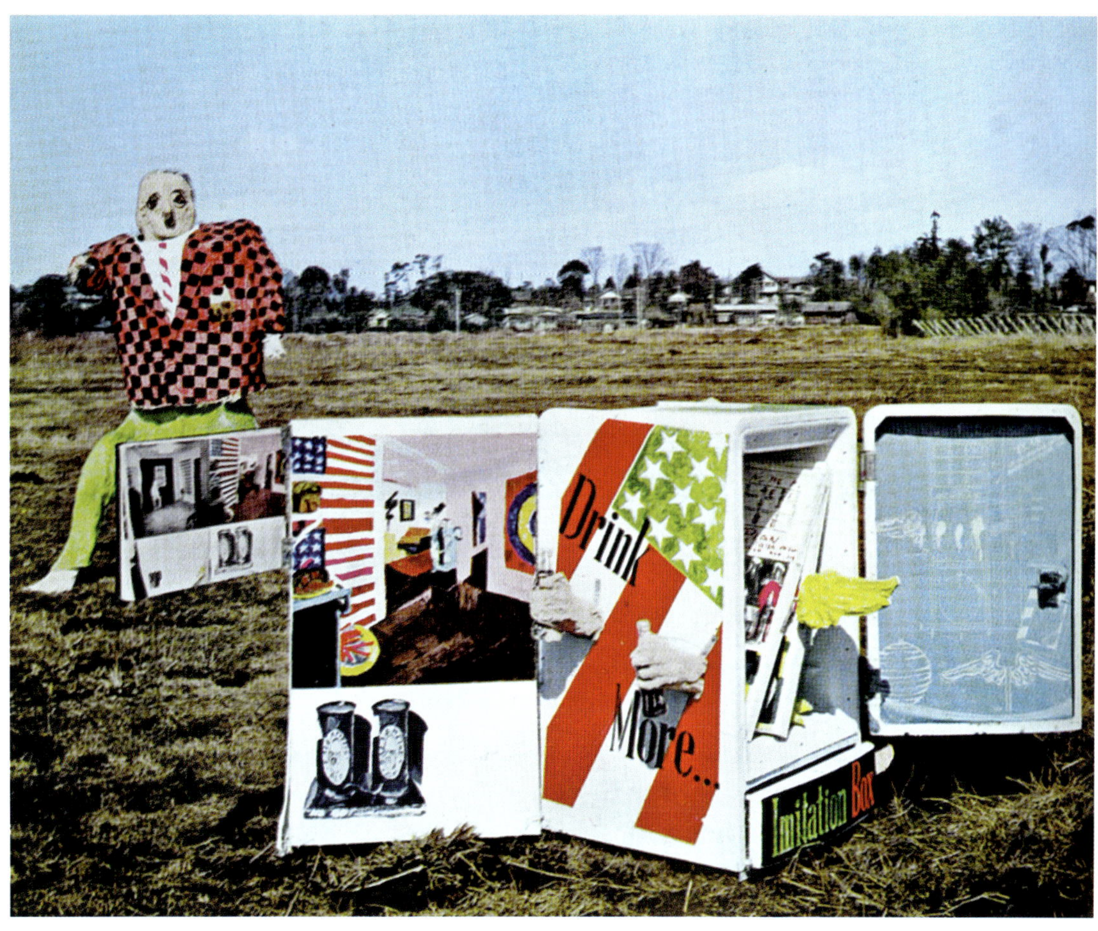

Figure 4.22
Imitation Box and *Marcel Duchamp in Thought*, left in an open field. Reproduced from Yūsuke Nakahara, “Essay on Shinohara Ushio,” *Gendai bijutsu* (Contemporary Art), no. 3 (March 1965): 27.

> However, what an old sight this digest of twenty years offers us!... Jasper Johns's *Target* or *Flag* was not our glorious saviour. The closer I got to Americans who came to Japan (Jasper, Jim [Rosenquist], and George [Montgomery]), the further their glory receded into the distance.[82]

Rauschenberg, who had come to Japan two years earlier, was not an exception; Shinohara no longer idolized the American artist as his hero. Therefore, *Imitation Box* should be understood as marking the end of Shinohara's "imitation era," a declaration that American art no longer represented such an immediate, irresistible appeal for him.

This independence of mind did not change the artist's situation immediately. Shinohara, thirty-two years old at the time of Rauschenberg's visit, had still never left Japan; he only dreamed of participating in the international art scene. His dream almost came true when William Lieberman, a curator at the Museum of Modern Art, New York, visited the "Left Hook" show and took an interest in Shinohara's work. The American curator had come to Japan to prepare for the traveling exhibition "The New Japanese Painting and Sculpture," which would be the first large Japanese contemporary art show to be held in the United States, as a counterpart of "Twenty Years of American Painting" in Japan. Lieberman suggested including Shinohara's *Marcel Duchamp in Thought* and Kojima's *Standing Figure* in the show of Japanese art. While Kojima's work was indeed included in the show, however, *Marcel Duchamp in Thought* did not find its way to America due to its fragility, to Shinohara's great disappointment.

Similarly, Kojima's work has survived, ensconced in the storage rooms of the Museum of Modern Art,[83] but Shinohara's *Imitation Box* and *Marcel Duchamp in Thought* sadly did not survive. Left in an open field by the artist, they eventually disintegrated under the force of the elements (figure 4.22). The photograph of Shinohara's works in the field epitomizes the financial situation of the Tokyo avant-garde in the 1960s. Without much support from art collectors or gallery owners, artists in Tokyo often had to destroy their works for lack of storage space or money to rent space. There were few art collectors or gallery owners in the first place, and these were not sympathetic to Japanese avant-garde art, which they often regarded as unprincipled youth culture.[84] The artists themselves maintained the pretension that the act of creation was more important than the resulting work. Accordingly, we can no longer see Shinohara's *Imitation Box* or *Marcel Duchamp in Thought*; and only a few examples of Shinohara's *Coca-Cola Plan* survive today.[85] After all, the idea of being a global artist was more a fantasy than a reality for Japanese artists, whereas American artists, such as Rauschenberg, more often had the means and the opportunity to travel around the world. Just as Shinohara spent a chapter of his autobiography describing his fantasy of having all the star artists from France and America, dead or alive, gathered in Tokyo, so the idea of participating in the world art scene was still very much in the realm of fantasy in Japan.

This situation is perfectly symbolized by a series of works titled *Air Mail* that Shinohara created prior to Rauschenberg's visit to Tokyo in 1964. One of the imaginary letters was

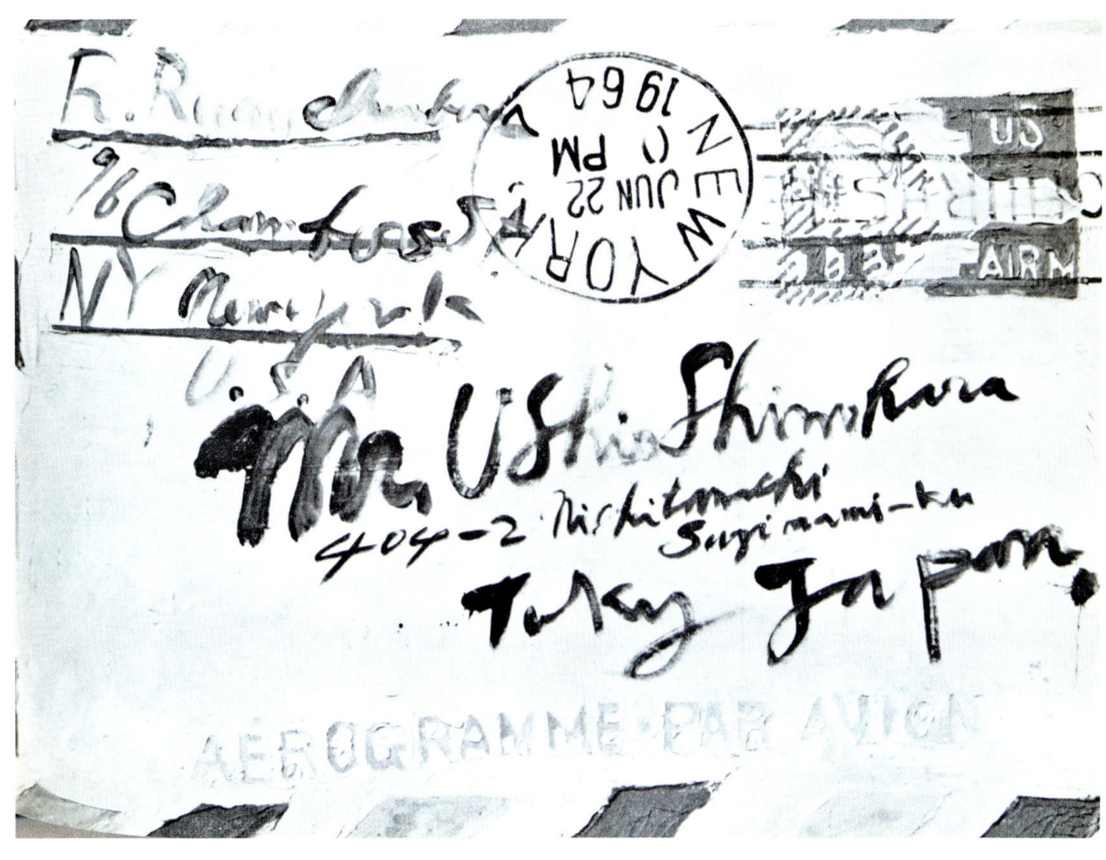

Figure 4.23
Shinohara Ushio, *Air Mail*, 1964. Destroyed. Reproduced from Yūsuke Nakahara, "Essay on Shinohara Ushio," *Gendai bijutsu* (Contemporary Art), no. 3 (March 1965): 32.

addressed from Rauschenberg in New York to Shinohara in Tokyo, dated June 22, 1964—right after his winning of the Grand Prize at the Venice Biennale (figure 4.23). This imagined correspondence with the internationally acclaimed American artist is another visual embodiment of the cross-cultural exchange, or nonexchange, between the American and Japanese avant-gardes at the time. While Rauschenberg moved from place to place as an agent of world art, Shinohara was only able to imagine participating in the field passively, as the recipient of the letter. In the era of nascent globalization, however, imagination concerns more than unrealistic fantasy. As Arjun Appadurai writes, imagination is "a staging ground for action, and not only for escape."[86] This statement rings true because it was none other than Marcel Duchamp who gave Shinohara a chance to move to New York. Although *Marcel Duchamp in Thought* did not travel to New York, its image did. Fascinated by the picture that Tōno showed him in New York, Duchamp recommended Shinohara for a two-thousand-dollar Copley Foundation grant. With this money, Shinohara made the *Oiran* (Courtesan) series, in which he stepped away from Anti-Art and "Imitation Art," returning to painting by combining a Pop Art vocabulary with a Japanese motif. With the critical success of this series, Shinohara received a grant from the JDR 3rd Fund and finally left for New York in 1969.

"Twenty Questions to Bob Rauschenberg" in Tokyo marked the last event of Rauschenberg's 1964 world trip. Unfortunately, the event marked the end of his involvement with Cunningham's company as well. When he learned that Cage and Cunningham had arrived late for his "Twenty Questions" performance and had left early—as did many in the audience—Rauschenberg made it known that he was no longer with the company. In his memoir of the 1964 world tour, Cunningham transcribed and annotated the messages they exchanged on the day following the Sōgetsu event:

> **dear john and merce**
> **i am not going to work with the company anymore. it was so nice of you to share last nite [*sic*] with me in such a friendly way.**
> **thanks bob**
>
> JC answered impolitely, I answered politely, and it was over.
>
> **I am sorry about last evening, and sad that our relationship will end this way. Thank you for many beautiful things—hours as well as objects. I am grateful to you for them. There were good times, too, you know. With affection, and regret.**
> **Merce**
>
> [later note from RR]

dear merce
my rudness [*sic*] last nite [*sic*] was brought on by over emotion, drink, exhaustion. please over look [*sic*] my manner. it has been an honer [*sic*] and pleasure to work for you. there is a basic difference in our attitudes that i think is responsible for our difficulties. i think your dances + dancing are great. i am grateful to have been able to see so much of it and be so close. i would very much like to be your friend and fan. i hope to look you in the eye with good conscince [*sic*] + love, if i haven't screwed that possibility up. thank you for this great tour.
bob
same Sunday[87]

As a consequence, the three artists did not work together again until 1977, when they collaborated on Cunningham's production *Travelogue*.

Rauschenberg's relationship with the Tokyo art community would also grow a little awkward. Originally, Kusuo Shimizu, the owner of the Minami Gallery, was going to plan a Rauschenberg exhibition during the artist's stay in Tokyo. At the time, the gallery was having an exhibition of works by Sam Francis, who (unlike Mathieu) was still respected and popular as an abstract painter in Japan. But when Shimizu saw Rauschenberg take a quick look at the Francis exhibition and leave the gallery with a disapproving look, he canceled the plan.[88] As a consequence, a Rauschenberg exhibition did not take place in Japan until 1986, when he held the "ROCI Japan" exhibition in Tokyo and showed the *Japanese Recreational Clayworks* series that he made in Shigaraki earlier in the decade. In contrast, Johns continued to show at the Minami Gallery as Tōno's favorite artist, eventually becoming more popular than Rauschenberg in Japan. This lengthy gap in Rauschenberg's interaction with the Japanese art world represents another level of discommunication brought about by his 1964 visit to Tokyo.

Finally, one further question needs to be addressed: What happened to *Gold Standard* after the performance event? Did Rauschenberg follow the supposed Japanese protocol and give it to the host, Sōfū Teshigahara, as his parting gift? In fact, *Gold Standard* turned out to be a serious case of cultural misunderstanding. While Rauschenberg assumed that Sōfū would purchase the work before he returned to New York, Sōfū expected that Rauschenberg would simply present it to him as a gift for sponsoring the Cunningham company. Unlike works by Japanese artists, Rauschenberg's *Gold Standard* was not abandoned in a field. After some negotiations, the work did enter Sōfū's art collection, later becoming one of the key works in the collection of the Sōgetsu Art Museum. The work remained there until the Sōgetsu Foundation had a financial crisis at the beginning of the twenty-first century, when it was forced to sell the work and close down the museum. Now *Gold Standard* is in a private collection in America, after having been resold from a commercial gallery in Tokyo to one in New York. In today's speculative art market, the name of Rauschenberg is an established brand, functioning as a "standard" that sets the high price of his work, which perhaps adds another layer of irony to the work's title.

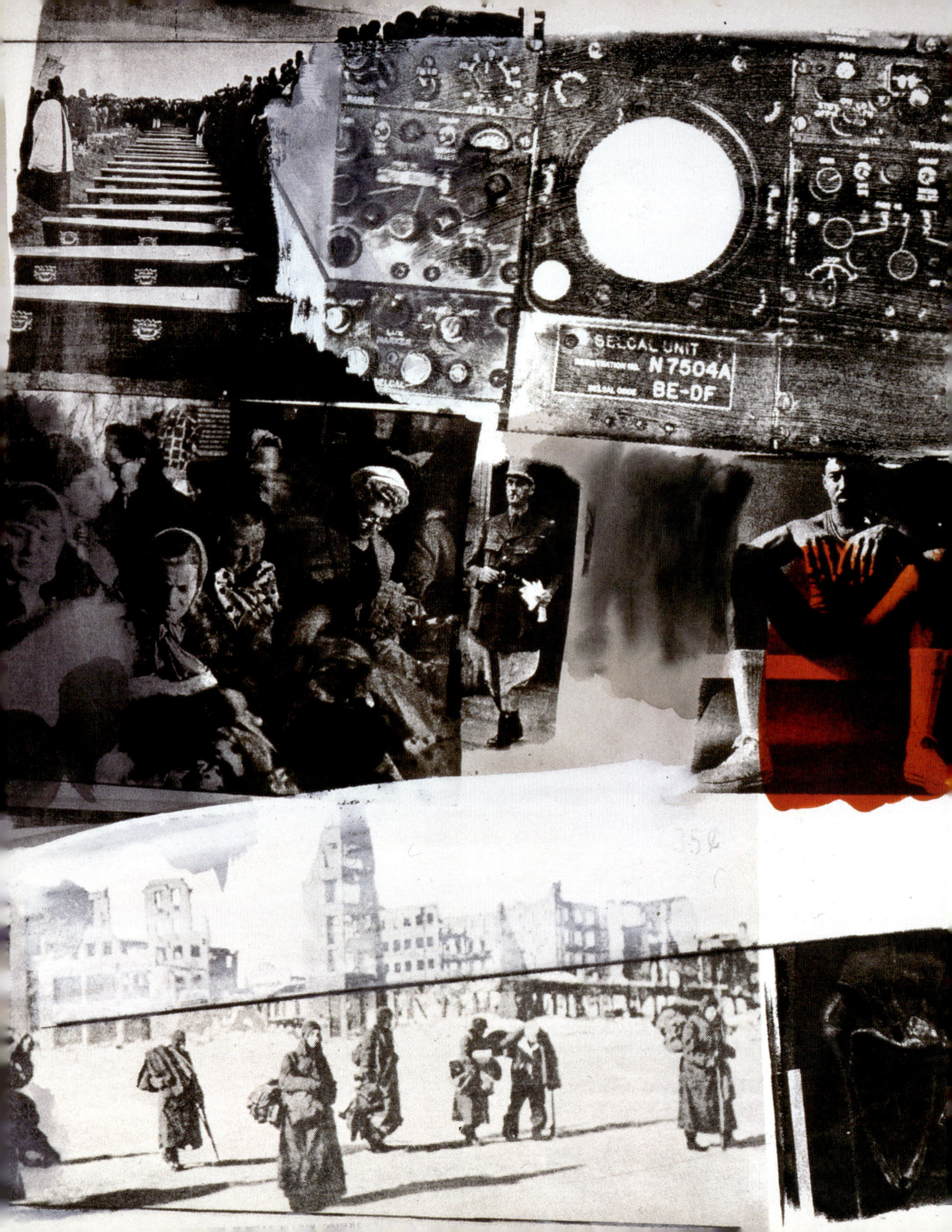
SELCAL UNIT
N7504A
BE-DF

CONCLUSION
BECOMING "THE" AMERICAN ARTIST

In following Robert Rauschenberg's world tour in 1964, this book has examined the global rise of American art as a subject of post-1945 world art history. As it has demonstrated, the four cities covered here were closely related to—or even instrumental to—the emergence of this phenomenon. This finding points to a need to reshape our understanding of American art in the context of international post–World War II art and to open up the U.S.-centered discourse of postwar art history to a global perspective.

The response in and around 1964 to the increasing international dominance of American art varied from one city to another. Paris was the first to acknowledge the virtue of American art, although Parisians resisted buying it; Venice needed the powerful presence of American art to rejuvenate its Biennale; similarly, Stockholm imported the New York avant-garde to transform the city into a new artistic center; and Tokyo, though succumbing to American cultural temptations, threatened the authority of American art by imitating and hybridizing American Pop. Thus, while each art community struggled to articulate its own cultural identity within the increasingly Americanizing art scene, each also tried to capitalize on the force of American art in order to become an active and unique participant in the world art scene. It was this multiply located, reciprocal, and yet always somewhat compromised and conflicted process that engendered the global rise of American art.

Against this background, as elucidated in this volume, we must also ask how Rauschenberg was affected by the phenomenon as an individual artist. Certainly, he emerged from the rise of American art as *the* global artist through his engagement with a number of local art communities in Europe and Asia. Paradoxically, however, he was yet to become *the* American artist. With the sad ending of the world tour, the "great migrator" returned to New York. The analogy of the migrating bird proves very fitting for Rauschenberg: he was not a nomad or exile but always had a home to which he could return. Still, his home base, the New York art community as well as the American public in general, saw him differently after his world trip. He was now a global celebrity, the first American Grand Prize winner of the Venice Biennale. This celebrity became a double-edged sword, as it made him vulnerable to scandal and criticism. In New York, there was no official event or exhibition to celebrate his "triumphal" homecoming or to commemorate his victory in Venice. In fact, Rauschenberg— who had telephoned a friend in New York from Venice and asked him to go to the Broadway loft and destroy all the silkscreen paintings the artist had produced earlier[1]—virtually stopped painting for a considerable period after the world tour. He devoted himself instead to organizing such events as "First New York Theater Rally" in 1965 and "Nine Evenings: Theater and Engineering" in 1966, the launching event of EAT.

It was thus not easy to reestablish Rauschenberg's status as the representative American artist. His winning of the gold medal at the 1965 Biennial Exhibition of Contemporary American Painting at the Corcoran Gallery of Art did not seem to significantly improve his standing in New York, either.[2] Things began to change at the end of 1965, when the Museum of Modern Art exhibited the Dante Drawings for the first time since their acquisition in 1963.[3] This show became, in effect, the much-belated celebration of the artist's "triumphal return," as the series had just finished its 1964–1965 European circulation, which included the period of the Venice Biennale. Organized by the International Council of the Museum of Modern Art and circulated by the USIA, the exhibition traveled to twenty venues in Europe.[4] It opened in February 1964 in London as part of the Rauschenberg retrospective at the Whitechapel Gallery, which attracted record audiences and established Rauschenberg's reputation in the United Kingdom as "the most important artist that America had produced since Pollock."[5] Reviews outside London were also favorable: a reviewer in Cambridge appreciated the subdued refinement of the drawings as opposed to the Combines,[6] while another in Newcastle-upon-Tyne called them "so satisfying."[7]

In Germany, the reception was even more positive. The drawings were first shown at the Krefeld Museum as part of a larger Rauschenberg exhibition. Although some critics regarded his recent works as less provocative than his earlier Combines exhibited at Documenta II in 1959,[8] the Dante Drawings were welcomed as a "completely different side"[9] of Rauschenberg after the sensation at the Venice Biennale. One critic specifically commented on this difference: "For those who knew only the work exhibited in Venice, Rauschenberg's interpretation of Dante was a real surprise.… Here one encounters a more analytic Rauschenberg, one who achieves a convincing degree of intensity and a remarkable mastery of content.… These 34 leaves demonstrate that Rauschenberg is a first-class artist!"[10] Calling the drawings a "silent joy"[11] possessing a sudden "lyrical glow,"[12] other critics praised how well the artist understood his own time and incorporated it into the drawings; one even wished that Rauschenberg "would return to the manner of his Dante illustrations in order to push ahead again from here."[13] Thus, the Dante Drawings confirmed Rauschenberg's artistic virtue after the controversy over his winning the Grand Prize in Venice.

It was again Italy that decided the favorable reception of the Dante Drawings. Although the exhibition did not travel to the country, its deluxe, real-size facsimile edition was issued in 1965 in American and Italian editions, the latter of which was exhibited in Milan and Rome as part of the celebration of the seven-hundredth anniversary of Dante's birth.[14] This in itself was a significant achievement, as it meant that Rauschenberg's drawings were recognized as worthy of belonging to the long tradition of illustrating the *Divine Comedy*, which includes such renowned artists as Sandro Botticelli, William Blake, and Gustave Doré. Moreover, Rauschenberg's facsimile edition was published in the country in which every single town seems to have a street named after Dante, and where high school students are still required to recite every line of the *Divine Comedy* from the edition with illustrations by Doré. In fact, it was precisely because of the Italian audience's full knowledge of the original text and its visual tradition that Rauschenberg's drawings received serious consideration there. In contrast to the negative reactions generated by the Biennale from the previous year, Italian reviewers were full of praise for the Dante Drawings. In *Opera Aperta*, a critic commented, "Although in the past we happened to speak critically of this current [i.e., Pop Art], we want to make clear that, in regard to Rauschenberg, we have dropped any reservation."[15] In *Domus*, Edgardo Macorini, the publisher of the drawings' Italian edition, wrote a long review and praised Rauschenberg's work as a "powerful challenge to our mental habits and to our visual stereotypes," referring to Doré's romanticized illustrations in the popular edition of the poem.[16] Impressed by Rauschenberg's contemporary version of Dante's *Inferno*, an editor of *Domus*, G.P. (most likely Gio Ponti, the magazine's founder) even dedicated a poem to the series, in which he called Rauschenberg the "American Virgil" who showed Italians a new way to better understand Dante's world.[17]

Renato Barilli, a professor at Bologna University, appraised the Dante Drawings in comparison to the earlier illustrations of the *Divine Comedy*. Unlike so many unsuccessful illustrations that deviated from the actual dynamics of the poetry in favor of the "empty décor of the background," he argued that Rauschenberg's work demonstrated "an exemplification of the same method developed by Dante" by turning to ready-made everyday images of people that appeared in the popular press.[18] He likened the asyntactic nature of Rauschenberg's cutout technique to film montage, another clever strategy that kept pace with the quick, disjunctive structure of Dante's narrative. Barilli also praised Rauschenberg's handling of a "particular 'atmospheric' component achieved through sensuous and chromatic effects" as effectively reabsorbing various episodes into a coherent atmosphere, which is "again in complete adherence to Dante's model."[19] Finally, Paolo Barozzi, who saw Rauschenberg's inferno as an allegory of America (see chapter 2), concluded his essay as follows:

> The question that he seems to raise is, What do American people want from life? And what is real in life? With these illustrations, Rauschenberg reflects on the confusion of American life. The images give form to the artist's fear of a success that he felt coming too soon, as if to ask whether a success too easy to achieve could come from a misunderstanding of his art. These are, therefore, images of his personal inferno, which express the artist's fear that the world could entrap and pin him down in a role that he would inevitably have to accept.[20]

This interpretation reflects Barozzi's own post-Biennale observations on the artist, since Rauschenberg had yet to attain such fame when he created the drawings. The critic's view is nonetheless insightful, as Rauschenberg would certainly have to come to terms with his fame in years to come.

After their return from Europe, the Dante Drawings toured the United States, starting at the Museum of Modern Art, New York. As if to mark his triumph and his first solo exhibition at this museum, the drawings were kept on view for no less than four months, from December 1965 to March 1966, then traveled to eight more venues until April 1967.[21] As a matter of fact, this was not the first showing of the Dante Drawings in the United States; Rauschenberg had exhibited them at the Leo Castelli Gallery in December 1960–January 1961, soon after their completion. At that point he was still an enfant terrible of the New York art community, whose fame had suddenly been eclipsed by the critical and commercial success of his younger partner, Jasper Johns. At the time, the Dante Drawings had contributed to raising his reputation as a serious artist. Most significantly, the series had helped to create Rauschenberg's image as a "painter," an indication of a serious artist in those days; critic Lawrence Campbell had written, "Rauschenberg is essentially a painter no matter what he does," praising his capacity to seek out in his environment what interested him and integrate it into his pictures.[22]

In 1965, before the return of the Dante Drawings to New York, Rauschenberg's status was still oddly shaky in that city. His victory in Venice had paradoxically undermined his reputation at home, a situation confounded by a backlash against his dealer, Leo Castelli, who was perceived as the impresario behind the scandal about the Grand Prize. With its aura of a successful tour in Europe, however, the series markedly turned critics' attitudes around, as the long visual tradition and rich literary content of Dante's *Inferno* helped remind the art audience that Rauschenberg was a seriously committed artist. Critics were full of praise in general, and even Emily Genauer, who was so bitter about the American presentation in Venice, called the show "a must" and praised the drawings as "profoundly moving."[23] Mel Bochner, a younger conceptual artist who admired Rauschenberg, also praised them as "a high point in the already considerable achievements of Rauschenberg."[24] Thus, the Dante Drawings served to boost Rauschenberg's reputation in America once again—and this time on a grander scale—and reestablished him as *the* representative American artist.

Just before the exhibition opened at the Museum of Modern Art, *Life* magazine published "A Modern Inferno," a special issue to commemorate the seven-hundredth anniversary of Dante's birth, prominently illustrated with a new set of work by Rauschenberg on the *Inferno* (figure 5.1). To execute the work for *Life*, Rauschenberg did not go back to the painstaking and demanding transfer technique that he had used for the Dante Drawings. Instead, he chose to work with silkscreen, using overtly political and disquieting images related to such events as the Holocaust, the civil rights movement, and the atomic bomb. Unlike the subdued anxiety manifested in the Dante Drawings, these works for *Life* were bombastic and large (three pages pieced together as a double-sided foldout), leaving behind the intimacy of the artist's endeavor from five years earlier. Rauschenberg's relationship with *Life* magazine can, in fact, be seen as paralleling the arc of his career: from 1958 to 1960, he had used *Life* as his source of images; in 1964, the magazine featured him as the Grand

Prize winner of the Venice Biennale; and in 1965, he was publishing his own work in the same nationally circulating journal, which signals the fact that Rauschenberg now was "the" American artist. This is perhaps what the Italian critic Barozzi feared: that the artist would eventually have to accept the stereotyped image of himself as the contemporary history painter of America.

As if to move beyond that fixated image, Rauschenberg began traveling abroad again after his period of intense engagement with theater and technology, such as his work with EAT. In fact, EAT itself was an international organization, for its projects often took place outside the United States: the Anan Project in India in 1969, the Pepsi Pavilion at Expo '70 in Osaka, and the Central America Project in El Salvador and Guatemala in 1973.[25] As if to follow this trend, Rauschenberg expanded his artistic collaboration into the unfamiliar realm of the cultural other, embarking on a series of international projects in the 1970s and 1980s. Besides creating works in Israel and in India in the 1970s, he worked with craftsmen at the world's oldest paper mill in China and with Japanese ceramic chemists in the early 1980s. The artist then founded Rauschenberg Overseas Culture Interchange (ROCI) in 1984 and spent the rest of the decade visiting ten different places, where he created works and held exhibitions with help from both American and local assistants. For his itinerary, Rauschenberg consciously chose countries that were "either developing nations or controlled by totalitarian governments, or that [had] little contact with the United States," which included the following in chronological order; Mexico, Chile, Venezuela, China, Tibet, Japan, Cuba, the Soviet Union, East Germany, and Malaysia.[26] The whole project was finally completed in 1991 with the ROCI exhibition at the National Gallery of Art in Washington, D.C.[27]

Rauschenberg believed in the power of cross-cultural communication through art with quixotic optimism. As he explained the ROCI project to the Japanese critic Yoshiaki Tōno: "The work I make in each specific country can be nothing else than a mixture of my American energy and each country's reality. I want to use my energy to translate those countries' special cultures and things internal to that reality so that I can see them with my own eyes. The people of those countries should be able to grasp a new method of seeing the world around them."[28] To Tōno's skeptical question, "Do you really believe that you will be able to create communication there?" the artist answered enthusiastically, "Of course." Nearly two decades had created a significant change in the artist who had questioned the concept of communication during "Twenty Questions to Bob Rauschenberg" in Tokyo. Now feeling quite at ease representing his country, he took on the self-appointed role of American cultural ambassador in the ROCI project. The historical account of the entire project has yet to be written,[29] but it will certainly have to address the project's ambivalent legacy:[30] while Rauschenberg's undertaking displayed—and was criticized for—cultural appropriation and a lack of critical distance, it also created a channel of communication between cultures and set an operational model for the subsequent generation of contemporary artists with international ambitions.[31]

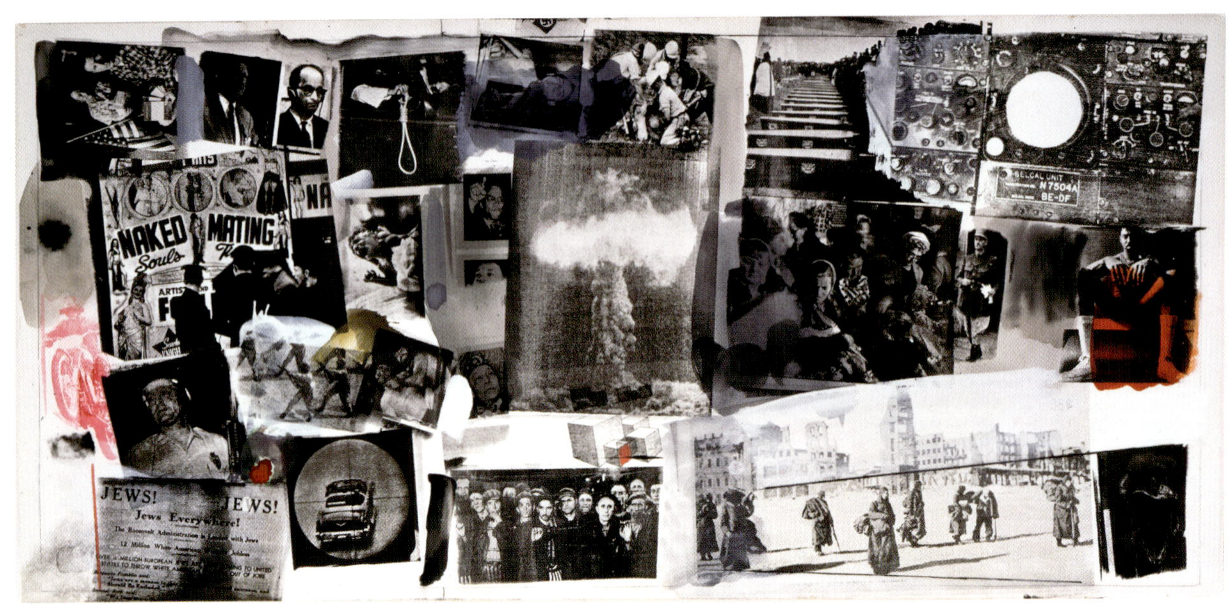
NAKED
Souls
MATING
JEWS! JEWS!
Jews Everywhere!
The Roosevelt Administration in League with Jews
12 Million White
BELCAL UNIT
N7504A
BE-DF

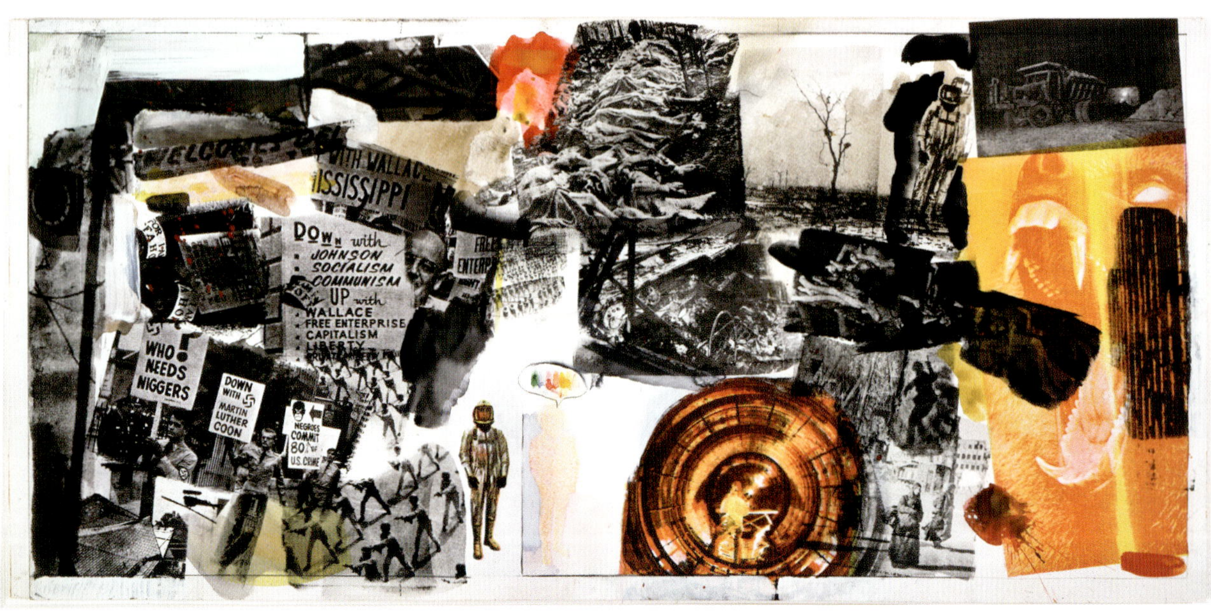
WITH WALLACE
ISSISSIPPI
DOWN with
JOHNSON
SOCIALISM
COMMUNISM
UP with
WALLACE
FREE ENTERPRISE
CAPITALISM
LIBERTY
WHO NEEDS NIGGERS
DOWN WITH MARTIN LUTHER COON
NEGROES COMMIT 80% OF U.S. CRIME

Figure 5.1
Robert Rauschenberg, *Drawings for Dante's 700th Birthday*, 1965. Collage with colored crayon, graphite, acrylic, gouache and colored inks, silkscreened on composition board, in two parts, approx. 36 × 36 inches (91.4 × 91.4 cm).

Indeed, it is a common or even imperative practice today for any successful artists to create works of art in a location other than their home, whether through participation in a residency program, via commissions from local art institutions, or as a result of outsourcing cheaper labor or materials. While one origin of site specificity in contemporary art has been located in Minimalism and Conceptual Art,[32] I hope that this study has shown that another precursor to today's globalized art practice was Rauschenberg's role as a centerpiece of the transnational avant-garde network during the 1960s. By traveling to one place after another and having contact with local art communities, he revealed both the possibilities and the conflicts of the globalizing art scene, which continue to be present in the art world of the twenty-first century. In this sense, the first half of the 1960s, the period of Rauschenberg's first "great migration," offers invaluable insight into the nature of the current globalization of art, wherein successful artists follow in his footsteps and beyond, traversing a vast geopolitical map of art while capitalizing on the ideal of cultural diversity.

APPENDIX: ROBERT RAUSCHENBERG'S EXHIBITION HISTORY OUTSIDE THE UNITED STATES, 1953–1968

1953

"Bob Rauschenberg: Scatole e feticci personali," Galleria dell'Obelisco, Rome, opened March 3. Traveled to Galleria d'Arte Contemporanea, Florence, as "Scatole e costruzioni contemplative di Bob Rauschenberg," opened March 14.

1959

"Rauschenberg," Galleria la Tartaruga, Rome, opened May 30.

Documenta II: Kunst nach 1945, Museum Fridericianum, Kassel, July 11–October 11.

V Bienal de São Paulo, Museu de Arte Moderna, São Paulo, September 21–December 2.

Première Biennale de Paris, Musée d'Art Moderne de la Ville de Paris, Paris, October 2–25.

"Exposition inteRnatiOnale du Surréalisme: 1959–1960" (EROS), Galerie Daniel Cordier, Paris, December 15, 1959–January 9, 1960.

1960

"Rauschenberg, Twombly: Zwei amerikanische Maler," Galerie 22, Düsseldorf, April 22–May 30.

1961

"Abstract Drawings and Watercolors: USA," Museo de Bellas Artes, Caracas, January 14, 1961–February 14, 1962. Organized under the auspices of the International Council, the Museum of Modern Art, New York. Traveled to Rio de Janeiro, São Paulo, Buenos Aires, Montevidéo, Santiago, Lima, Quito, Guayaquil, Bogotá, Panama City, and Mexico City, March 1962–May 1963.

"Bewogen Beweging," Stedelijk Museum, Amsterdam, March 10–April 17. Traveled to Moderna Museet, Stockholm, as "Rörelse i konsten," May 17–September 3; and to Louisiana Museum of Modern Art, Humlebaek, Denmark, as "Bevaegelse i kunsten," September–October.

"Vanguard American Painting," organized by the United States Information Agency. Traveled to Vienna, Belgrade, Skopje, Zagreb, Maubon, Ljubljana, Rijeka, London, Darmstadt, and Salzburg, in June 1961–1962.

"Robert Rauschenberg," Galerie Daniel Cordier, Paris, April 27–May.

"Rauschenberg," Galleria dell'Ariete, Milan, October 24 –November.

1962

"4 amerikanare: Jasper Johns, Alfred Leslie, Robert Rauschenberg, Richard Stankiewicz," Moderna Museet, Stockholm, March 17–May 6. Traveled to Stedelijk Museum, Amsterdam, May–June; and Kunsthalle Bern, July–August.

XVIII Salon de Mai, Musée d'Art Moderne de la Ville de Paris, Paris, May 6–27.

"Dylaby (Dynamisch Labyrint)," Stedelijk Museum, Amsterdam, August 30–September 30.

"The Third International Biennial Exhibition of Prints in Tokyo 1962," National Museum of Modern Art, Tokyo, October 6–November 11. Organized by Yomiuri Newspaper Company. Traveled to Municipal Museum of Art, Osaka, January 6–February 1963.

1963

"Robert Rauschenberg: Première exposition (œuvres 1954–1961)," Galerie Ileana Sonnabend, Paris, February 1–16.

"Robert Rauschenberg: Seconde exposition (œuvres 1962–1963)," Galerie Ileana Sonnabend, Paris, February 20–March 9.

"Schrift en beeld," Stedelijk Museum, Amsterdam, May 3–June 10. Traveled to Staatliche Kunsthalle, Baden-Baden, June 14–August 4.

"V. mednarodna graficna razstavna/Ve. Exposition internationale de gravure," Moderna Galerija Ljubljana, June 9–September 15.

"Art USA Now," originally organized and exhibited by Milwaukee Art Center in 1962. Traveled through Europe, 1963–1965.

1964

"Robert Rauschenberg: Paintings, Drawings and Combines, 1949–1964," Whitechapel Art Gallery, London, February 4–March 8.

"Rauschenberg: Illustrations for Dante's *Inferno*." Organized under the auspices of the International Council of the Museum of Modern Art, New York. Traveled through Europe, 1964–1965.

"54–64: Painting and Sculpture of a Decade," Tate Gallery, London, April 22–June 28.

"Robert Rauschenberg," Galerie Ileana Sonnabend, Paris, May 14–30.

XXXII Esposizione Biennale Internazionale d'Arte Venezia, Venice, June 20–October 18.

"Nieuwe Realisten," Haags Gemeentemuseum, The Hague, June 24–August 31. Traveled to Akademie der Künste, Berlin, as "Neue Realisten & Pop Art," and to Palais des Beaux-Arts, Brussels, as "Pop Art, Nouveau Réalisme, Etc.," February 5–March 1, 1965.

Documenta III, Museum Fridericianum, Kassel, June 27–October 5.

"Robert Rauschenberg," Museum Haus Lange, Krefeld, September 12–October 18.

"Robert Rauschenberg: *Untitled* 1953–1954 and Thirty-four Dante Drawings," Galerie Ileana Sonnabend, Paris, December 1964–January 13, 1965.

1965

"Robert Rauschenberg: Bilder, Zeichnungen, Lithos," Amerika Haus, Berlin, January 8–February 4.

"Rauschenberg: 34 illustrazioni per l'Inferno di Dante," Galleria Apollinaire, Milan, and Galleria dell'Obelisco, March. Facsimile edition was shown.

"VI. mednarodna graficna razstavna/VIe. Exposition internationale de gravure," Moderna Galerija Ljubljana, May.

"Den inre och den yttre rymden: En utställning rörande en universell konst," Moderna Museet, Stockholm, December 26, 1965–February 13, 1966.

1966

"Two Decades of American Painting," National Museum of Modern Art, Tokyo, October 15–November 27. Organized by the National Museum of Modern Art and the International Council of the Museum of Modern Art, New York. Traveled to Kyoto, New Delhi, Melbourne, and Sydney, December 1966–August 1967.

1967

"American Painting Now," U.S. Pavilion, Expo '67, Montreal, April 28–October 27.

"VII. mednarodna graficna razstavna/VIe. Exposition internationale de gravure," Moderna Galerija Ljubljana, May.

"Environment USA: 1957–1967," IX Bienal de São Paulo, Museu de Arte Moderna, São Paulo, September 22–January 8, 1968.

"Kompass 3: Paintings after 1945 in New York," Stedelijk van Abbemuseum, Eindhoven, November 9–December 17. Traveled to Frankfurter Kunstverein, December 30–February 11, 1968.

1968

"Robert Rauschenberg," Stedelijk Museum, Amsterdam, February 23–April 7. Traveled to Kölnischer Kunstverein, Cologne, April 19–May 26; and to Musée d'Art Moderne de la Ville de Paris, Paris, October 10–November 10.

"L'Art vivant 1965–68," Fondation Maeght, Saint Paul-de-Vence, April 13–June 30.

Documenta IV, Museum Fridericianum, Kassel, June 27–October 6.

"Robert Rauschenberg: XXXIV Drawings for Dante's *Inferno*," Galerie Gérald Cramer, Geneva, June 5–October 19. Facsimile edition was shown.

"Rauschenberg: Drawings," Galerie Ileana Sonnabend, Paris, mid-October–mid-November.

NOTES

INTRODUCTION

1. John O'Reilly, "The Great Migrator," *Sports Illustrated* 8, no. 18 (April 21, 1958): 60–61.

2. The word in fact served as a title for one of Rauschenberg's Combine paintings, *Migration* (1959), now in the collection of the Herbert F. Johnson Museum of Art, Cornell University. In addition, a few scholars have discussed the structural theme of movement and migration in his work. In the early 1980s, Roger Cranshaw and Adrian Lewis discussed significations of "circularity and motion" in relation to the recurrent motif of the tire in Rauschenberg's work, while Robert Hughes observed a theme of "flight" in *Rebus* (1955). More recently, Branden W. Joseph examined the artist's performance in terms of "moving images," and Thomas E. Crow discussed the theme of "rise and fall" in Combines from the 1950s. See Roger Cranshaw and Adrian Lewis, "Re-reading Rauschenberg," *Artscribe*, no. 29 (June 1981): 45; Robert Hughes, *Shock of the New* (1981; reprinted, New York: Alfred A.Knopf, 1998), p. 334; Branden W. Joseph, *Random Order: Robert Rauschenberg and the Neo-Avant-Garde* (Cambridge, Mass.: MIT Press, 2003), especially chapter 5, "Moving Images," pp. 208–279; and Thomas E. Crow, "Rise and Fall: Theme and Idea in the Combines of Robert Rauschenberg," in Paul Schimmel, ed., *Robert Rauschenberg: Combines*, exh. cat. (Los Angeles: Museum of Contemporary Art, 2005), pp. 213–255.

3. O'Reilly, "The Great Migrator," p. 62.

4. "Triumphs and Tribulations," *Sports Illustrated* 8, no. 19 (May 12, 1958): 20.

5. For Cunningham's memoir of this world tour, see Merce Cunningham, "Story: Tale of a Dance and Tour," parts 1–3, *Dance Ink* 6, no. 1 (Spring 1995): 14–21; no. 2 (Summer 1995): 18–22; no. 3 (Fall 1995): 32–36. For a memoir of the trip by an *étoile* of the company, see Carolyn Brown, *Chance and Circumstance: Twenty Years with Cage and Cunningham* (New York: Alfred A. Knopf, 2007), pp. 375–446.

6. Quoted in David Vaughan, *Merce Cunningham: Fifty Years* (New York: Aperture, 1997), p. 130. With an indeterminate and flexible structure that involved a variable number of dancers and a changing duration, *Story* could be enacted in any given circumstance and was performed twenty-nine times during the entire tour. Toshi Ichiyanagi, a Japanese composer who studied with John Cage in the 1950s, composed its music.

7. Although Sweden was not part of NATO and therefore technically not part of the Western Bloc, the country shared much with the Western Bloc in terms of politics, economics, and culture. Japan, geographically located in East, was in alliance with the United States and thus part of the West in the Cold War context.

8. Despite its geographical limitations, the global rise of American art in the 1960s can be seen as part of a nascent stage of cultural globalization, which assumed full force from the 1980s on. For the impact of globalization on culture, see Arjun Appadurai, *Modernity*

at Large: Cultural Dimensions of Globalization (Minneapolis: University of Minnesota Press, 1996), and also Fredric Jameson and Masao Miyoshi, eds., *The Cultures of Globalization* (Durham: Duke University Press, 1998).

9. For representative revisionist accounts of the international dominance of American art, see Max Kozloff, "American Painting during the Cold War," *Artforum* 11, no. 9 (May 1973): 43–54; Eva Cockcroft, "Abstract Expressionism, Weapon of the Cold War," *Artforum* 12, no. 10 (June 1974): 39–41; and David and Cecile Shapiro, "Abstract Expressionism: The Politics of Apolitical Painting," *Prospects* 3 (1977): 175–214. For accounts from the eighties, see Annette Cox, *Art-as-Politics: The Abstract Expressionist Avant-Garde and Society* (Ann Arbor: UMI Research Press, 1982); and Serge Guilbaut, *How New York Stole the Idea of Modern Art: Abstract Expressionism, Freedom, and the Cold War* (Chicago: University of Chicago Press, 1983).

10. Frédéric Martel, *De la culture en Amérique* (Paris: Éditions Gallimard, 2006). Although Martel himself accepts some of the revisionists' argument, the dynamic of American culture described in his book is far more complicated than that assumed by revisionist critics of the 1970s and 1980s.

11. Ibid., p. 15.

12. Naima Prevots, *Dance for Export: Cultural Diplomacy and the Cold War* (Middletown, Conn.: Wesleyan University Press, 1998), p. 53. See also pp. 56–57.

13. David Vaughan, "Adventures on a World Tour," *New York Times*, January 3, 1965, section 2, p. 13.

14. In 1963, supporters of Cunningham created the Foundation for Contemporary Performance Arts and raised about twenty thousand dollars for his forthcoming Broadway season. When the season was eventually canceled, the funds were applied to the cost of the world tour. The company also received a travel grant to Asia from the JDR 3rd Fund. However, as performance fees covered only about a third of the tour's expense, these grants were not nearly enough to cover the rest. See Vaughan, *Merce Cunningham*, pp. 129, 134, 145.

15. The most recent and vehement example is Irving Sandler's "Abstract Expressionism and the Cold War," *Art in America* 96, no. 6 (June–July 2008): 65–74, included as chapter 5 in his *Abstract Expressionism and the American Experience: A Reevaluation* (Lenox, Mass.: Hard Press Editions, 2009). See also Michael Kimmelman, "Revisiting the Revisionists: The Modern, Its Critics, and the Cold War," and Helen M. Franc, "The Early Years of the International Program and Council," both in John Elderfield, ed., *The Museum of Modern Art at Mid-Century: At Home and Abroad*, Studies in Modern Art, no. 4 (New York: Museum of Modern Art, 1994), respectively pp. 38–55 and pp. 108–149.

16. For a representative revisionist study on the 1964 Venice Biennale, see Laurie J. Monahan, "Cultural Cartography: American Designs at the 1964 Venice Biennale," in Serge Guilbaut, ed., *Reconstructing Modernism: Art in New York, Paris, and Montreal 1945–64* (Cambridge, Mass.: MIT Press, 1990), pp. 369–416.

17. For instance, this shift was clerly marked in the 32nd International Congress of the History of Art (Comité internationale d'histoire de l'art, CIHA) held in Melbourne in 2008. Entitled "Crossing Cultures: Conflict, Migration and Convergence," the conference focused on issues around globalism and art, while Thomas Da Costa Kaufmann and Peter

J. Schneeman chaired a session on "The Idea of World Art History." For this conference, see Jaynie Anderson, ed., *Crossing Cultures: Conflict, Migration and Convergence*, Proceedings of the 32nd International Congress of the History of Art (Melbourne: Miegunyah Press, 2009). For the topic of global art history, see also discussions in James Elkins, ed., *Is Art History Global?* (New York: Routledge, 2006), and James Elkins, Alice Kim, and Zhivka Valiavicharska, eds., *Art and Globalization* (University Park: Pennsylvania State University Press, forthcoming).

18. An important work done under this rubric is David Summers, *Real Spaces: World Art History and the Rise of Western Modernism* (London: Phaidon, 2003). See also James Elkins's review of Summers's book, in which he calls the issue of world art history "the most pressing problem facing the discipline of art history," in *Art Bulletin* 86, no. 2 (June 2004): 373–381. Another polemicist in the field is John Onians, who played a major role in founding the School of World Art Studies at the University of East Anglia in 1992 and edited *Atlas of World Art* (Oxford: Oxford University Press, 2004). Leiden University also has a center for World Art Studies, where Wilfried van Damme and Kitty Zijlmans edited *World Art Studies: Exploring Concepts and Approaches* (Amsterdam: Valiz, 2008). However, these scholars' approaches are each different and do not cohere as a unified voice.

19. Thomas DaCosta Kaufmann, *Toward a Geography of Art* (Chicago: University of Chicago Press, 2004), p. 13.

20. Partha Mitter, "Interventions: Decentering Modernism: Art History and Avant-Garde from the Periphery," *Art Bulletin* 90, no. 4 (December 2008): 544.

21. Among important examples are Partha Mitter, *The Triumph of Modernism: India's Artists and the Avant-Garde, 1922–1947* (London: Reaktion Books, 2007); Andrea Giunta, *Avant-Garde, Internationalism, and Politics: Argentine Art in the Sixties* (Durham: Duke University Press, 2007); Sylvester Okwunodu Ogbechie, *Ben Enwonwu: The Making of an African Modernist* (Rochester, N.Y.: University of Rochester Press, 2008); and Ming Tiampo, *Gutai: Decentering Modernism* (Chicago: University of Chicago Press, 2010).

22. For instance, in "Abstract Expressionism, Weapon of the Cold War," Cockcroft repeatedly asserts a connection between CIA officials and the Museum of Modern Art's executives without providing a specific example of their actual collaboration. This view is challenged by Louis Menand in "Unpopular Front: American Art and the Cold War," *New Yorker* 81, no. 32 (October 17, 2005): 174–179.

23. In this regard, it is no coincidence that a significant number of recent postrevisionist voices have come from outside the United States. For instance, see Robert Burstow, "The Limits of Modernist Art as a Weapon of the Cold War: Reassessing the Unknown Patron of the Monument to the Unknown Political Prisoner," *Oxford Art Journal* 20, no. 1 (1997): 68–80; Sigrid Ruby, "The Give and Take of American Painting in Postwar Western Europe," *Cahiers Charles V*, no. 28, special issue "Transmission des valeurs nationales: Théories, individus, institutions (domaine anglo-américain)," ed. Marie-Jeanne Rossignol and Barbara Karsky (2000): 171–196; and Kenji Kajiya, "Malfunctioning Weapon: Clement Greenberg, the Cultural Cold War, and Globalization," *American Review*, no. 37 (March 2003): 83–105 [J]. In his article, Burstow makes an important observation that the leftist intellectual historians wrote their revisionist critique "in the climate of political disaffection that followed the Vietnam War and Watergate Affair" (p. 68). Their work should thus be understood within their own historical and political conditions.

24. For this topic, see the now classic text by Benedict Anderson, *Imagined Communities: Reflections on the Origin and Spread of Nationalism*, revised and extended edition (London: Verso, 1991). The first edition was published in 1983. It is important to note that in recent years Anderson revised his idea of nations and examined the transnational network of nationalists and anarchists in the late nineteenth century as the early stage of globalization in intellectual history. See *Under Three Flags: Anarchism and the Anti-colonial Imagination* (London: Verso, 2005). It is also interesting that he sees a positive quality in nationalism as well, despite his awareness of its obvious problems. See "Benedict Anderson: 'I Like Nationalism's Utopian Elements,'" interview with Benedict Anderson, conducted by Lorenz Khazaleh for the research program CULCOM (Cultural Complexity in the New Norway) at the University of Oslo, http://www.culcom.uio.no/english/news/2005/anderson.html (accessed February 13, 2010).

25. Gerhard Richter gives the most notable testimony in this regard: seeing works by Jackson Pollock and Lucio Fontana at Documenta II in 1959 affected him so strongly that he decided to migrate from East to West Germany a couple of years later. See Gerhard Richter, "Interview with Benjamin H. D. Buchloh, 1986," in Richter, *The Daily Practice of Painting: Writings and Interviews 1962–1993*, ed. Hans-Ulrich Obrist (Cambridge, Mass.: MIT Press, 1995), p. 132.

26. Alan Solomon, interview with Leo Castelli conducted for National Education Television, April 12, 1966, Alan R. Solomon Papers, 1930–1972, reel 3922, no. 1155, Archives of American Art, Smithsonian Institution, Washington, D.C. (hereafter Alan R. Solomon Papers, followed by reel and frame numbers).

27. Calvin Tomkins, *Off the Wall: Robert Rauschenberg and the Art World of Our Time* (New York: Penguin Books, 1980). Although an updated edition of this book in new page layout is now available as *Off the Wall: A Portrait of Robert Rauschenberg* (New York: Picador, 2005), I will cite from the original edition. For Tomkins's earliest substantial writing on Rauschenberg, see "Moving Out," *New Yorker* 40, no. 2 (February 29, 1964): 39–105.

28. Thomas E. Crow, "Southern Boys Go to Europe," in Stephanie Barron and Lynn Zelevansky, eds., *Jasper Johns to Jeff Koons: Four Decades of Art from the Broad Collections*, exh. cat. (Los Angeles: Los Angeles County Museum of Art, 2001), pp. 45–61; and Crow, "Rise and Fall."

29. Jean-Paul Ameline, "Comment les *Combines* de Rauschenberg ont conquis l'Europe: Essai d'histoire culturelle (1958–1964)," in Jean-Paul Ameline, ed., *Robert Rauschenberg: Combines*, French edition, exh. cat. (Paris: Centre Georges Pompidou, 2006), pp. 287–306.

30. For representative postmodernist writings, see Leo Steinberg, "Reflections on the Status of Criticism," *Artforum* 10, no. 7 (March 1972): 37–49; Rosalind Krauss, "Rauschenberg and the Materialized Image," *Artforum* 13, no. 4 (December 1974): 36–43; Douglas Crimp, "On the Museum's Ruins," *October*, no. 13 (Summer 1980): 41–57; Craig Owens, "The Allegorical Impulse: Toward a Theory of Postmodernism," part 2, *October*, no. 13 (Summer 1980): 59–80; and Branden Joseph's *Random Order*. See also Branden W. Joseph, ed., *Robert Rauschenberg*, October Files, no. 4 (Cambridge, Mass.: MIT Press, 2002).

31. For the representative literature in this vein, see Charles F. Stuckey, "Reading Rauschenberg," *Art in America* 65, no. 2 (March–April 1977): 74–84; Kenneth Bendiner, "Robert Rauschenberg's *Canyon*," *Arts Magazine* 56, no. 10 (June 1982): 57–59; Jonathan

Katz, "The Art of Code: Jasper Johns and Robert Rauschenberg," in Whitney Chadwick and Isabelle de Courtivron, eds., *Significant Others: Creativity and Intimate Partnership* (London: Thames and Hudson, 1993), pp. 188–207; and Laura Auricchio, "Lifting the Veil: Robert Rauschenberg's *Thirty-Four Drawings for Dante's Inferno* and the Commercial Homoerotic Imagery of 1950s America," *Genders*, no. 26 (Fall 1997): 119–154.

32. For instance, see Brian O'Doherty, "Rauschenberg and the Vernacular Glance," *Art in America* 61, no. 5 (September–October 1973): 82–87, expanded and reprinted as "Robert Rauschenberg: The Sixties," in his *American Masters: The Voice and the Myth* (New York: Random House, 1973); Roni Feinstein, *Robert Rauschenberg: The Silkscreen Paintings, 1962–64*, exh. cat. (New York: Whitney Museum of American Art, 1990); and Christin J. Mamiya, "We the People: The Art of Robert Rauschenberg and the Construction of American National Identity," *American Art* 7, no. 3 (Summer 1993): 41–63.

33. Joshua Shannon recently made an important attempt to go beyond the controversy by discussing Rauschenberg's "materialist" Combines from 1960 to 1961 as the artist's historically and geographically specific engagement with the concerted demolition of lower Manhattan, which was then undergoing the first stage of postmodernization. See chapter 3 in Shannon, *Disappearance of Objects: New York Art and the Rise of the Postmodern City* (New Haven: Yale University Press, 2009), pp. 93–148.

34. Barr did not buy any works from Rauschenberg's 1958 exhibition at the Leo Castelli Gallery, whereas he had chosen three works from Johns's exhibition held a couple of months before. Calvin Tomkins notes Barr's reservation about Rauschenberg's work as follows: "Barr tried hard to like Rauschenberg, told Leo he knew he was important but that he couldn't see it. Finally he asked Philip Johnson to buy something for the museum, and they got *First Landing Jump*." Notes from interview with Leo Castelli by Calvin Tomkins, January 8, 1976, Calvin Tomkins Papers, II.B.29, Museum of Modern Art Archives, New York (hereafter Calvin Tomkins Papers, followed by a folder number).

35. For Greenberg's derogatory view of Rauschenberg, see his "Recentness of Sculpture," in Clement Greenberg, *The Collected Essays and Criticism*, ed. John O'Brian, vol. 4 (Chicago: University of Chicago Press, 1993), p. 251.

36. Donald Judd, statement in Bruce Glazer, "Questions to Stella and Judd," *ARTnews* 65, no. 5 (September 1966): 57.

CHAPTER 1

1. Merce Cunningham, "Story: Tale of a Dance and Tour," part 1, *Dance Ink* 6, no. 1 (Spring 1995): 16.

2. P.C. [Pierre Cabanne], "Les plus grands artistes revelés depuis 20 ans: 100 personnalités les ont choisis pour *Arts*," *Arts*, no. 1011 (June 23–July 6, 1965): 1–3.

3. Calvin Tomkins, "A Good Eye and a Good Ear," *New Yorker* 56, no. 14 (May 26, 1980): 52.

4. Calvin Tomkins, "An Eye for the New," *New Yorker* 75, no. 42 (January 17, 2000): 56.

5. The Académie Julian was one of the French art schools that Americans could attend under the G.I. Bill. Disappointed by the apathy of both teachers and students at the school, however, Rauschenberg went back to the United States in order to attend Black Mountain College with Susan Weil, whom he met in Paris and later married.

6. Eric de Chassey, "Paris–New York: Rivalry and Denial," in *Paris: Capital of the Arts, 1900–1968*, exh. cat. (London: Royal Academy of Arts, 2002), p. 344.

7. Ibid., p. 345.

8. Oral history interview with Leo Castelli, conducted by Paul Cummings, May 14, 1969–June 8, 1973, Archives of American Art, Smithsonian Institution (hereafter Castelli, AAA interview).

9. The exhibition showed twenty American artists, including representative Abstract Expressionists such as Jackson Pollock, Arshile Gorky, Willem de Kooning, and Franz Kline.

10. Castelli, AAA interview. After Janis dropped the project, Castelli discussed the possibility with Alfred Barr Jr. at the Museum of Modern Art. Barr was interested but unable to provide any practical help.

11. Oral history interview with Darthea Speyer, conducted by Paul Cummings, June 28, 1976, Archives of American Art, Smithsonian Institution (hereafter Speyer, AAA interview). For the Museum of Modern Art's International Program, see also Oral History Interview with Porter A. McCray, conducted by Paul Cummings, September 17–October 4, 1977, Archives of American Art, Smithsonian Institution.

12. See Helen M. Franc, "The Early Years of the International Program and Council," in John Elderfield, ed., *The Museum of Modern Art at Mid-Century: At Home and Abroad*, Studies in Modern Art, no. 4 (New York: Museum of Modern Art, 1994), p. 125. Portions of the show subsequently toured European cities as "Modern Art in the United States: A Selection from the Collections of the Museum of Modern Art, New York."

13. See Michael Kimmelman, "Revisiting the Revisionists: The Modern, Its Critics, and the Cold War," in Elderfield, *The Museum of Modern Art at Mid-Century*, p. 49. See also Sigrid Ruby, "The Give and Take of American Painting in Postwar Western Europe," *Cahiers Charles V*, no. 28, special issue,"Transmission des valeurs nationales: Théories, individus, institutions (domaine anglo-américain), ed. Marie-Jeanne Rossignol and Barbara Karsky (2000): 185–186.

14. Pierre Restany, "U.S. Go Home and Come Back Later," *Cimaise* 6, no. 3 (January–March 1959): 37. *Cimaise* was published in French, English, German, and Spanish until its July–October issue of 1963, when it became a French-English journal. Here I have paraphrased the English section of the article for clarity. I have done the same for other citations from *Cimaise* in this chapter.

15. Speyer, AAA interview.

16. See *Cimaise* 4, no. 2 (November–December 1956), and *Cimaise* 6, no. 3 (January–March 1959).

17. For Mathieu's biography, see Lydia Harambourg, *Georges Mathieu* (Neuchâtel: Éditions Ides et Calendes, 2001).

18. For Tapié's concept of Informel, see his treatise in Michel Tapié, *Un art autre, où il s'agit de nouveaux dévidages du réel* (Paris: Gabriel-Giraud et Fils, 1952).

19. De Chassey, "Paris–New York: Rivalry and Denial," p. 346.

20. Harambourg, *Georges Mathieu*, p. 70.

21. There were of course some exceptions: While Kootz showed Soulages, Martha Jackson showed Informel-related artists such as Hisao Dōmoto and Gutai from Japan.

22. On this topic, see Deirdre Robson, "The Market for Abstract Expressionism: The Time Lag between Critical and Commercial Acceptance," *Archives of American Art Journal* 25, no. 5 (1985): 19–23.

23. For a complete listing of exhibitions at the Leo Castelli Gallery from 1957 to 1967, see David Whitney, ed., *Leo Castelli: Ten Years* (New York: Leo Castelli, 1967).

24. Leo Castelli, "The Reminiscences of Leo Castelli" (May 1977), pp. 25–26, in the Oral History Collection of Columbia University.

25. Leo Castelli to Giuseppe Panza, April 10, 1959, Giuseppe Panza Papers, Special Collection at the Getty Research Institute, Los Angeles. Panza became interested in Rauschenberg and Johns after talking to John Cage in Milan in 1959. Because of Castelli's hesitation, however, it was only in 1960 that he was able to start purchasing Rauschenberg's works.

26. Leo Steinberg, "Jasper Johns," *Metro,* nos. 4–5 (May 1962): 87–109, and "Reflections on the State of Criticism," *Artforum* 10, no. 7 (March 1972): 37–49. The latter article was originally given as a lecture at the Museum of Modern Art, New York, in 1968. Both essays were revised and reprinted in Steinberg's *Other Criteria: Confrontations with Twentieth-Century Art* (London: Oxford University Press, 1972).

27. Leo Steinberg, conversation with author, February 27, 2008, New York.

28. See Robert Jensen, *Marketing Modernism in Fin-de-Siècle Europe* (Princeton: Princeton University Press, 1994).

29. On this issue, see Robert Jensen, "Velocity: Cubism, Nationalism, and Transnationalism," trans. Yūsuke Isotani, *Studies in Western Art*, no. 14 (2008): 82–105 [J].

30. Harambourg, *Georges Mathieu*, p. 43.

31. To reevaluate Informel, it is necessary to stop discussing the movement solely in connection to Tapié and Mathieu and to expand the discussion to a larger transnational phenomenon of gestural abstraction in the postwar years, which included Abstract Expressionism, CoBrA, and the Gutai Art Association, among others. The process should also involve a reevaluation of Informel painters who were not French: Sam Francis from America, Antoni Tàpies from Spain, Zao Wou-ki from China, and Hisao Dōmoto from Japan.

32. Lilian Tone, "Chronology" in Kirk Varnedoe, *Jasper Johns: A Retrospective*, exh. cat. (New York: Museum of Modern Art, 1996), p. 164.

33. Michel Ragon, "L'art actuel aux États-Unis," *Cimaise* 6, no. 3 (January–March 1959): 28–29.

34. Calvin Tomkins Papers, IV.C.23.

35. Leo Castelli, interview by Alan Solomon, April 12, 1966, conducted for National Education Television, Alan R. Solomon Papers, reel 3922, nos. 1154–1155.

36. Before 1959, Rauschenberg had two solo shows in Italy in 1953 during his trip with Cy Twombly. For more on these shows, see Thomas E. Crow, "Rise and Fall: Theme and Idea in the Combines of Robert Rauschenberg," in Paul Schimmel, ed., *Robert Rauschenberg: Combines*, exh. cat. (Los Angeles: Museum of Contemporary Art, 2005).

37. As a conscious attempt to rejuvenate the city as an artistic capital, the Paris Biennale set the maximum age of participating artists at thirty-five.

38. See Jean-Paul Ameline, "Comment les *Combines* de Rauschenberg ont conquis l'Europe: Essai d'histoire culturelle (1958–1964)," in Jean-Paul Ameline, ed., *Robert Rauschenberg: Combines*, French edition, exh. cat. (Paris: Centre Georges Pompidou, 2006), p. 289.

39. Calvin Tomkins Papers, IV.C.23.

40. "Le première exposition Rauschenberg à Paris, Galerie Daniel Cordier," in Pontus Hultén, ed., *Paris–New York: 1908–1968*, exh. cat. (Paris: Centre Georges Pompidou, 1977), p. 580.

41. Ileana Sonnabend, interview by William L. Weiss, conducted March 2, 1995, transcribed by the author from sound cassettes held at the Archives of American Art, Smithsonian Institution.

42. See Calvin Tomkins, *The Bride and the Bachelors: Five Masters of the Avant-Garde* (New York: Penguin Books, 1976), p. 227.

43. André Parinaud, "Un 'misfit' de la peinture new-yorkaise se confesse," *Arts*, no. 821 (May 10, 1961): 18.

44. Ibid.

45. Calvin Tomkins, *Off the Wall: Robert Rauschenberg and the Art World of Our Time* (New York: Penguin Books, 1980), p. 190.

46. Michel Ragon, "Expositions: L'avant-garde," *Arts*, no. 821 (May 10, 1961). See also Françoise Choay, "Dada, Néo-dada, et Rauschenberg," *Art International* 5, no. 8 (October 20, 1961): 82–84, 88.

47. Tomkins, *Off the Wall*, p. 190.

48. Calvin Tomkins Papers, IV.C.23.

49. For the most comprehensive discussion of Johns's early work and its reception in New York, see Fred Orton, *Figuring Jasper Johns* (London: Reaktion Books, 1994).

50. On this topic, see Joachim Pissarro, *Cézanne/Pissarro, Johns/Rauschenberg: Comparative Studies on Intersubjectivity in Modern Art* (New York: Cambridge University Press, 2006). See also Jonathan Katz, *The Silent Camp: Jasper Johns, Robert Rauschenberg, and the Cold War* (Chicago: University of Chicago Press, forthcoming).

51. Tomkins, *Off the Wall*, p. 145.

52. See Pierre Restany, "Jasper Johns et la métaphysique du lieu commun," *Cimaise* 9, no. 55 (September–October 1961): 90–97.

53. Robert Pincus-Witten, interview by author, August 31, 2006, New York.

54. José Pierre, "Où va l'art abstrait?," *Combat*, no. 79 (June 5, 1961): 2.

55. Parinaud, "Un 'misfit' de la peinture new-yorkaise se confesse," p. 18.

56. Ibid.

57. Pontus Hultén, "Afterword," in Schimmel, *Robert Rauschenberg: Combines*, p. 285.

58. Ibid.

59. Alain Jouffroy, "Rauschenberg," *L'Oeil*, no. 113 (May 1964): 34.

60. Quoted in Tomkins, *Off the Wall*, p. 190.

61. On Restany's technological optimism and his involvement with fantastic realism in the post–World War II French intellectual scene, see Kaira Cabañas, "Toward a Performative Realism: Art in France, 1957–1962" (Ph. D. diss., Princeton University, 2007).

62. Quoted in Michèle C. Cone, "Pierre Restany and the Nouveaux Réalistes," *Yale French Studies*, no. 98 (2000): 57.

63. Ibid., p. 54.

64. Pierre Restany, "La réalité dépasse la fiction," in Restany, *Avec le nouveau réalisme sur l'autre face de l'art* (Nîmes: Éditions Jacqueline Chambon, 2000), pp. 49–50.

65. Tomkins, *Off the Wall*, pp. 192–193.

66. Darthea Speyer, interview by author, March 17, 2004, Paris.

67. Pierre Restany, "Chelsea 1960," in Hultén, *Paris–New York: 1908–1968*, p. 148. A more concise version of this essay is reprinted as "Modern Nature" in *Breakthroughs: Avant-Garde Artists in Europe and America, 1950–1990*, exh. cat. (Columbus, Ohio: Wexner Center for the Arts, 1991).

68. William C. Seitz, *The Art of Assemblage*, exh. cat. (New York: Museum of Modern Art, 1961), p. 74.

69. Rebecca Solnit, *The Secret Exhibition: Six California Artists of the Cold War Era* (San Francisco: City Light Books, 1990), p. 88.

70. See, for instance, Öyvind Fahlström, "The Art of Assemblage," *Konstrevy*, nos. 5–6 (1961): 227 [S]; and Thomas B. Hess, "Collage as an Historical Method," *ARTnews* 60, no. 7 (October 1961): 31–33, 69–71.

71. Despite the importance of his presence, Rauschenberg had difficulty in making his points understood by the other panelists. See Branden W. Joseph, *Random Order: Robert Rauschenberg and the Neo-Avant-Garde* (Cambridge, Mass.: MIT Press, 2003), pp. 4–8.

72. Restany, "Chelsea 1960," p. 152.

73. Ibid.

74. Pierre Restany, "A Metamorphosis in Nature," in *The New Realists*, exh. cat. (New York: Sidney Janis Gallery, 1962), n.p. For the complete version of the essay, see "Un nouveau sens de la nature" in Restany, *Avec le nouveau réalisme*, p. 52.

75. Kaira Cabañas, "'Maigres et poussiéreux': Les nouveaux réalistes à New York," in *Le nouveau réalisme*, exh. cat. (Paris: Galeries nationales du Grand Palais, 2007), p. 125.

76. Pierre Restany, "Le nouveau réalisme à la conquête de New York," *Art International* 7, no. 1 (January 1963): 36.

77. Restany, "Chelsea 1960," p. 152.

78. Tomkins, *Off the Wall*, p. 225.

79. Quoted in Patrik Andersson, "Euro-Pop: The Mechanical Bride Stripped Bare in Stockholm, Even" (Ph.D. diss., University of British Columbia, 2001), p. 114, note 210.

80. Robert Pincus-Witten, interview by author, August 31, 2006, New York.

81. Annette Michelson, interview by author, September 7, 2006, New York.

82. For Rubin's career in Paris, see Laura de Coppet and Alan Jones, eds., *The Art Dealers* (New York: Cooper Square Press, 2002).

83. Antonio Homem, telephone interview by author, September 7, 2006, New York.

84. Ileana Sonnabend, interview conducted by Calvin Tomkins, February 11, 1976. Calvin Tomkins Papers, II.B.29.

85. Alfred Pacquement, "Leo Castelli, Daniel Cordier, Ileana Sonnabend: Le rôle des galeries," in Hultén, *Paris–New York: 1908–1968*, p. 176.

86. Tomkins, "A Good Eye and a Good Ear," p. 71.

87. Castelli, AAA interview.

88. Tomkins, "An Eye for the New," p. 56.

89. Ileana Sonnabend to Leo Castelli, November 18, 1962; quoted in Tone, "Chronology" in Varnedoe, *Jasper Johns: A Retrospective*, p. 198.

90. Antonio Homem, e-mail to author, September 9, 2006.

91. Tomkins, "A Good Eye and a Good Ear," p. 71.

92. Sonnabend, interview by Calvin Tomkins, February 11, 1976. Calvin Tomkins Papers, II.B.29.

93. It is to be noted, though, that a number of Nouveaux Réalistes such as Arman and Tinguely showed at the Virginia Dwan Gallery in Los Angeles in the early 1960s and interacted with the West Coast artists. But a market for avant-garde art had yet to emerge in the city because of its cultural conservatism. Oral history interview with Virginia Dwan, conducted by Charles F. Stuckey, March 21, 1984, Archives of American Art, Smithsonian Institution.

94. Quoted in Jan van der Marck, "Le nouveau réalisme et sa reception outre-Atlantique," in *Le nouveau réalisme* (Paris: Édition du Jeu de Paume, 1999), p. 23.

95. For reviews, see J.M., "À travers les galeries," *Le Monde*, February 8, 1963, p. 9; P.D., "Rauschenberg et son mouton," *Tribune de Lausanne*, February 10, 1963, p. 8; and Simone Frigerio, "Rauschenberg," *Aujourd'hui*, no. 41 (May 1963): 38.

96. Sonnabend, interview by William L. Weiss, 1995.

97. Sonnabend told Tomkins that she wanted to sell *Charlene* to the Museum of Modern Art but that the museum did not want it, which was a major disappointment to Rauschenberg. Sonnabend, interview by Tomkins, November 6, 1998. Calvin Tomkins Papers, II.B.52. As for *Monogram*, in 1959 Alfred Barr Jr. declined Robert Scull's offer to purchase the work and donate it to the museum. See chapter 3 on the acquisition of *Monogram* by the Moderna Museet, Stockholm.

98. Ibid.

99. Otto Hahn, "Pop Art and Happenings," *Les Temps Modernes*, no. 212 (January 1964): 1331.

100. Ileana Sonnabend to Alan Solomon, January 9, 1964, Alan R. Solomon Papers, reel 3921, no. 406.

101. Alain Jouffroy, "Rauschenberg," *L'Oeil*, no. 113 (May 1964): 28–35, 68–69; "Barge," *Quadrum*, no. 15 (second issue, 1963): 99–106, 182.

102. Michel Ragon, "Rauschenberg: La vedette de l'École de New York," *Arts*, no. 1011 (June 23–July 6, 1965): 4.

103. As a result, Bissière was given an honorary mention at the award ceremony. See Jean-François Revel, "XXIIe Biennale de Venise: 'Triomphe de réalisme nationaliste,'" *L'Oeil*, nos. 115–116 (July–August 1964): 3.

104. D.C., "Pop'Art & Dollars ou la semaine de Venise," *La Côte des Peintres* 2, no. 18 (July–August 1964): 25.

105. Pierre Cabanne, "À Venise, l'Amérique proclame la fin de l'École de Paris et lance le Pop'Art pour coloniser l'Europe," *Arts*, no. 968 (June 24–June 30, 1964): n.p.

106. Quoted in Tomkins, *Off the Wall*, p. 7.

107. Sonnabend, interview by William L. Weiss, 1995.

108. Revel, "XXIIe Biennale de Venise," p. 7.

109. Alain Bosquet, "Désarroi à Venise," *La Côte des Peintres* 2, no. 18 (July–August 1964): 29.

110. Pierre Restany, "La XXXII Biennale di Venezia, Biennale della irregolarità," *Domus*, no. 417 (August 1964): 37.

111. Jean-Robert Arnaud, "Mise à mort dans Venise La Rouge?," *Cimaise* 11, nos. 69–70 (July–October 1964): 105.

112. Pierrre Cabanne, "Comment la France a perdu la première place sur le marché de l'art international," *Arts*, no. 986 (December 23, 1964–January 5, 1965): 5. Cabanne criticized André Malraux's policy of trying to stop the drain of artworks from France by taxing art sales, which actually caused further stagnation of the Parisian art market.

113. Quoted in John Ashbery, "Art News from Paris," *ARTnews* 63, no. 5 (September 1964): 50.

114. Michel Ragon, "L'École de Paris va-t-elle démissionner?," *Arts*, no. 969 (July 1–6, 1964): n.p.

115. John Ashbery, "Venice Biennale: Center of Controversy," *New York Herald Tribune*, Paris edition, June 23, 1964, p. 5.

116. Ashbery, "Art News from Paris," p. 50.

117. Sonnabend to Solomon, July 1, 1964, Alan R. Solomon Papers, reel 3921, no. 553.

118. Marc Albert-Levin, "Art U.S.A. Now," *Cimaise* 11, nos. 69–70 (July–October 1964): 123. Organized by the Milwaukee Art Center, the exhibition traveled through Europe from 1963 to 1965.

119. Ragon, "L'École de Paris va-t-elle démissionner?," n.p.

120. Otto Hahn, "Otto Hahn: Le terrorisme américain a secoué Paris," interview by Jean-Jacques Lévêque, *Arts*, no. 985 (December 16–22, 1964): n.p.

121. Pierre Restany, "Les Biennales contre l'École de Paris," *Galerie des Arts*, no. 18 (July–September 1964): 20.

122. For this debate, see Julien Alvard, "Paris sans école," *Cimaise* 3, no. 1 (October–November 1955): 10–11; Michel Ragon, "L'École de Paris se porte bien," *Cimaise* 3, no. 2 (December 1955): 17; Herta Wescher, "À l'École de Paris," *Cimaise* 3, no. 3 (January–February 1956): 16; and R. V. Gindertael, "Le complexe de l'École de Paris," *Cimaise* 3, no. 4 (March 1956): 9.

123. Ragon, "Rauschenberg: La vedette de l'École de New York," p. 4.

124. P.C. [Pierre Cabanne], "Les plus grands artistes revelés depuis 20 ans," pp. 1–3. The other nine artists, in descending order, were Jean Tinguely, Pierre Soulages, Georges Mathieu, Yves Klein, Hundertwasser, Bernard Buffet, Paul Guiramand, François Arnal, and César.

125. Castelli, AAA interview.

126. See Dieter Honisch and Jens Christian Jensen, eds., *Amerikanische Kunst von 1945 bis heute: Kunst der USA in europäischen Sammlungen* (Cologne: Dumont Buchverlag, 1976). It is in fact doubtful that any works by the Nouveaux Réalistes had entered public collections in Paris by 1965. For the formation of American art collections in Germany, see Phyllis Tuchman, "American Art in Germany: The History of a Phenomenon," *Artforum* 9, no. 3 (November 1970): 58–69.

CHAPTER 2

1. Calvin Tomkins, handwritten notes taken in Venice, June 18, 1964, Calvin Tomkins Papers, IV.C.1.

2. Calvin Tomkins, "The Big Show in Venice," *Harper's Magazine*, no. 230 (April 1965): 104.

3. Calvin Tomkins, *Off the Wall: Robert Rauschenberg and the Art World of Our Time* (New York: Penguin Books, 1980), p. 10.

4. Carolyn Brown, *Chance and Circumstance: Twenty Years with Cage and Cunningham* (New York: Alfred A. Knopf, 2007), p. 385.

5. Laurie J. Monahan, "Cultural Cartography: American Designs at the 1964 Venice Biennale," in Serge Guilbaut, ed., *Reconstructing Modernism: Art in New York, Paris, and Montreal 1945–64* (Cambridge, Mass.: MIT Press, 1990), p. 402.

6. Tomkins, "The Big Show in Venice," p. 104.

7. For example, see Monahan's "Cultural Cartography."

8. Tomkins, *Off the Wall*, pp. 206–207.

9. Calvin Tomkins Papers, IV.C.26.

10. Leo Castelli, AAA interview.

11. Alan R. Solomon, "The New Art," *Art International* 7, no.7 (September 25, 1963): 39.

12. Ibid., p. 40.

13. Alan R. Solomon, "Robert Rauschenberg," in Solomon, *Robert Rauschenberg*, exh. cat. (New York: Jewish Museum, 1963), n.p.

14. Donald M. Wilson (Acting Director at the USIA) to Alan R. Solomon, November 7, 1963, Alan R. Solomon Papers, reel 3921, no. 320.

15. Tomkins, handwritten notes, June 21, 1964, in Calvin Tomkins Papers, IV.C.1. Tomkins introduced this statement from the show's preparation period in his article "The Big Show in Venice."

16. Alan R. Solomon, interview by Tomkins in May 1964, Calvin Tomkins Papers, IV.C.1.

17. Tomkins, handwritten notes, June 21, 1964, Calvin Tomkins Papers, IV.C.1.

18. Tomkins, "The Big Show in Venice," p. 100.

19. Castelli, AAA interview.

20. Quoted in Rosa Martinez and Maria de Corral, *Always a Little Further: 51st International Art Exhibition*, exh. cat. (Venice: Biennale di Venezia, 2005), p. 41.

21. Leonard Bernstein composed the song for the 1957 Broadway musical *West Side Story*, with lyrics written by Stephen Sondheim.

22. Cited lyrics are from the movie version of *West Side Story*. For the full lyrics of "America," see www.westsidestory.com/site/level2/lyrics/america.html (accessed November 20, 2009).

23. Calvin Tomkins, "Letter from the Biennale," in Calvin Tomkins Papers, IV.C.1. This is probably the manuscript Tomkins prepared for the *New Yorker*, which was somehow turned down.

24. Alan R. Solomon, "Americans in Venice at the Biennale," *Art Gallery* 7, no. 9 (June 1964): 15. Also printed in Italian in *Catalogo della XXXII Esposizione Biennale Internazionale d'Arte Venezia*, exh. cat. (Venice: Biennale di Venezia, 1964), p. 275.

25. Alan R. Solomon, *XXXII International Biennial Exhibition of Art Venice 1964, United States of America, The New American Art: Four Germinal Painters, Four Younger Artists*, exh. cat. (New York: Jewish Museum, 1964), n.p. (hereafter *The New American Art*).

26. Thomas E. Crow, "Rise and Fall: Theme and Idea in the Combines of Robert Rauschenberg," in Paul Schimmel, ed., *Robert Rauschenberg: Combines*, exh. cat. (Los Angeles: Museum of Contemporary Art, 2005), pp. 240–241.

27. Paul Schimmel, "Autobiography and Self-Portraiture in Rauschenberg's Combines," in Schimmel, *Robert Rauschenberg: Combines*, p. 218.

28. "'It's What We Volunteered For,'" *Life* 44, no. 3 (May 5, 1958): 22–23.

29. Ibid., p. 21.

30. Solomon, *The New American Art*, n.p.

31. Schimmel, "Autobiography and Self-Portraiture in Rauschenberg's Combines," p. 221.

32. Clement Greenberg, "Collage" (1959), reprinted in Greenberg, *Art and Culture* (Boston: Beacon Press, 1961), p. 78.

33. Clement Greenberg, "Abstract and Representational," originally presented as a lecture at Yale University, 1954; published in Greenberg, *The Collected Essays and Criticism*, vol. 3, ed. John O'Brian (Chicago: University of Chicago Press, 1993), p. 192.

34. For Kozloff's critique of Greenberg's art criticism, see Max Kozloff, letter to the editor, *Art International* 7, no. 6 (June 25, 1963): 88–92.

35. Leo Steinberg, "Reflections on the State of Criticism," *Artforum* 10, no. 7 (March 1972): 49.

36. Craig Owens, "The Allegorical Impulse: Toward a Theory of Postmodernism," parts 1–2, *October*, no. 12 (Spring 1980): 67–86; and no. 13 (Summer 1980): 59–80; hereafter cited from Owens, *Beyond Recognition: Representation, Power and Culture*, ed. Scott Bryson et al. (Berkeley: University of California Press, 1992).

37. Owens, *Beyond Recognition*, p. 76.

38. Crow, "Rise and Fall," p. 253.

39. Laura Auricchio, "Lifting the Veil: Robert Rauschenberg's *Thirty-Four Drawings for Dante's Inferno* and the Commercial Homoerotic Imagery of 1950s America," *Genders*, no. 26 (Fall 1997): 119.

40. Rosalind Krauss, "Perpetual Inventory," in Walter Hopps and Susan Davidson, eds., *Robert Rauschenberg: A Retrospective*, exh. cat. (New York: Solomon R. Guggenheim Museum, 1997), p. 223.

41. Crow, "Rise and Fall," p. 254.

42. For early studies on the series, see Dore Ashton, "Rauschenberg's Thirty-Four Drawings Illustrating Dante's Inferno," *Metro*, no. 2 (May 1961): 52–61; "The Collaboration Wheel: A Comment on Robert Rauschenberg's Comment on Dante," *Arts and Architecture* 80, no. 12 (December 1963): 10–11, 37. Also, on the relationship between transfer drawings and television, see Branden W. Joseph, *Random Order: Robert Rauschenberg and the Neo-Avant-Garde* (Cambridge, Mass.: MIT Press, 2003), pp. 175–180.

43. Paolo Barozzi, "L'Inferno di Rauschenberg," *Tempo Presente* (July 1965): 66.

44. He discovered the technique during a trip he took to Cuba with Cy Twombly in 1952.

45. In this sense, it is arguable that the creation of the Dante Drawings was actually Rauschenberg's own allegorical attempt to search for and recreate his artistic identity, just as the *Inferno* has often been read as Dante's introspective journey through the self. But this will be a topic for another paper.

46. Tomkins, *Off the Wall*, p. 157. It is also reported that Theresa Egan, the wife of Charles Egan, suggested the project to Rauschenberg, Johns, and Knox Martin. See Joan Young with Susan Davidson, "Chronology," in Hopps and Davidson, *Robert Rauschenberg: A Retrospective*, p. 556.

47. Tomkins, *Off the Wall*, p. 158.

48. See Roni Feinstein, "Random Order: The First Fifteen Years of Robert Rauschenberg's Art, 1949–1964" (Ph.D. diss., New York University, 1990), p. 350.

49. "The Endless Fascination of Water," *Sports Illustrated* 9, no. 9 (September 1, 1958): 37.

50. For the corresponding scene in the *Inferno*, see the edition consulted by Rauschenberg: Dante Alighieri, *The Inferno*, trans. John Ciardi (New York: Penguin Books, 1954), p. 162. Michael Sonnabend, an amateur Dante scholar, helped Rauschenberg read the poem.

51. Owens, *Beyond Recognition*, p. 54.

52. For another strong thesis on allegorical practices in contemporary art, see Benjamin H. D. Buchloh, "Allegorical Procedures: Appropriation and Montage in Contemporary Art," *Artforum* 21, no. 1 (September 1982): 43–56.

53. Monahan, "Cultural Cartography," p. 385.

54. Alan R. Solomon to Marietta Stern, January 31, 1964, Alan R. Solomon Papers, reel 3921, nos. 410–411.

55. Tomkins, "The Big Show in Venice," p. 101.

56. All the commissioners were requested to make their own nominations for the jury, from which Marcazzan made the final selection. See Gian Alberto Dell'Acqua (the head of the Biennale officials), letter to Alan R. Solomon, April 16, 1964, Alan R. Solomon Papers, reel 3921, no. 490.

57. Yasuo Kamon, that year's commissioner for the Japanese Pavilion, guessed that the Americans' lobbying to include Hunter in the jury delayed the selection process. See Yasuo Kamon, "Venice Diary," *Geijutsu seikatsu* [Art Life], no. 198 (September 1964): 82–83 [J].

58. Tomkins, "The Big Show in Venice," p. 102.

59. Tomkins, handwritten notes, June 19, 1964, in Calvin Tomkins Papers, IV.C.1.

60. David Vaughan, interview by author, June 13, 2003, New York.

61. According to Solomon, "The proposal was received with great enthusiasm not only by Dell'Acqua and Apollonio of the Biennale, but also by Labroca, the Artistic Director of the Theatre, and Soncin, of the Venice Tourist Office. We were made to feel that their enthusiasm was real rather than polite." Alan R. Solomon to Marietta Stern, February 19, 1964, Alan R. Solomon Papers, reel 3921, no. 433.

62. Marietta Stern to Alan R. Solomon, March 28, 1964, Alan R. Solomon Papers, reel 3921, no. 467.

63. Alan R. Solomon to Ben Heller, May 19, 1964, Venice Biennale Files, The Jewish Museum Archives, New York. It remains unclear who ended up paying the performance fee to the company.

64. Alan R. Solomon to Lois Bingham, undated, Alan R. Solomon Papers, reel 3921, no. 87.

65. Ibid.

66. Alan R. Solomon, interview by Calvin Tomkins, May 1964, in Calvin Tomkins Papers, IV.C.1.

67. Solomon to Bingham, undated, Alan R. Solomon Papers, reel 3921, no. 87.

68. Ibid.

69. Calvin Tomkins, handwritten notes, June 21, 1964, in Calvin Tomkins Papers, IV.C.1 (emphasis in original). Hunter seems to have at least partly fulfilled his duty: he persuaded the other jurors to take a look at the Consulate exhibition, and Meyer, the Swiss juror, remembers that Hunter convinced him of the virtue of Rauschenberg's work after the first vote. See Monahan, "Cultural Cartography," p. 402.

70. Calvin Tomkins, interview by author, June 28, 2005, New York.

71. The only exception was 1958, when the prize was given to the Italian painter Osvaldo Licini.

72. Monahan, "Cultural Cartography," p. 382.

73. Alan R. Solomon, "Report on the American Participation in the XXXII Venice Biennale 1964," Alan R. Solomon Papers, reel 3921, no. 959. This report was printed in U.S. Senate *Congressional Record,* 89th Congress, 1st sess. (August 31–September 13, 1965) vol. 3, part 17 pp. 22563–22564.

74. Lawrence Alloway, *The Venice Biennale 1895–1968: From Salon to Goldfish Bowl* (Greenwich, Conn.: New York Graphic Society, 1968), p. 151.

75. Giulio Carlo Argan, *Oltre l'informale,* exh. cat. (San Marino: San Marino Biennale, 1963), p. 12.

76. For instance, artists to be included in the 1964 American Pavilion, such as Noland, Louis, Dine, and Chamberlain, had already been shown in San Marino in 1963.

77. See John Ashbery, “Venice Biennale: Center of Controversy,” *New York Herald Tribune*, Paris edition, June 23, 1964, p.5, where he listed names such as Gastone Novelli, Titina Maselli, and Franco Angeli.

78. Giorgio De Marchis, “The Significance of the 1964 Venice Biennale,” *Art International* 8, no. 9 (November 25, 1964): 21. Originally published in Italian in *La Fiera Letteraria*.

79. Milton Gendel, “Hugger-Mugger in the Giardini,” *ARTnews* 63, no. 5 (September 1964): 34.

80. Pierre Restany, “La XXXII Biennale di Venezia, Biennale della irregolarità,” *Domus*, no. 417 (August 1964): 37.

81. Giulio Carlo Argan, “Arte d'oggi nei musei,” in *Catalogo della XXXII Esposizione Biennale Internazionale d'Arte Venezia*, p. 9. Invited museums, listed in the Biennale catalog in alphabetical order by city, are as follows: Nationalgalerie in Berlin, Musées Royaux des Beaux-Arts in Brussels, Hamburger Kunsthalle in Hamburg, Wallraf-Richartz-Museum in Cologne, Kaiser Wilhelm Museum in Krefeld, Tate Gallery in London, Neue Staatsgalerie in Munich, Solomon R. Guggenheim Museum in New York, Nasjonalgalleriet in Oslo, Musée National d'Art Moderne in Paris, Museu de Arte Moderna in Rio de Janeiro, Galleria Nazionale d'Arte Moderna in Rome, Moderna Museet in Stockholm, Galleria Civica d'Arte Moderna in Turin, Galleria Internazionale d'Arte Moderna in Venice, Museum des 20 Jahrhunderts in Vienna, Galerija Suvremene Umjetnosti in Zagreb, and Kunsthaus in Zurich.

82. Ibid., p. 12.

83. Leo Castelli, interview by Alan R. Solomon for National Educational Television, Alan R. Solomon Papers, reel 3922, no. 1163.

84. For instance, see “Pop Goes the Biennale,” *Time* 84, no. 1 (July 3, 1964): 54; and Rosalind Constable, “Art Pops In: Europe Explodes as American Takes Prize,” *Life* 57, no. 2 (July 10, 1964): 65–66, 68.

85. “Carnival in Venice,” *Newsweek* 64, no. 1 (July 6, 1964): 74–75.

86. Gendel, “Hugger-Mugger in the Giardini,” pp. 34–35.

87. Gene Baro, “The Canal Goes Pop,” *International Herald Tribune*, June 28, 1964.

88. Gene Baro, “The Venice Biennale,” *Arts Magazine* 38, no. 10 (September 1964): 32, 37.

89. Tomkins wrote to Solomon, “*The New Yorker* decided not to run my Biennale piece, for reasons too Byzantine to go into,” in Calvin Tomkins to Alan R. Solomon, September 11, 1964, Alan R. Solomon Papers, reel 3921, no. 830.

90. Emily Genauer, “The Merchandise of Venice,” *New York Herald Tribune*, July 12, 1964, Sunday Magazine section, p. 21.

91. Robert Rauschenberg, interview by Alan R. Solomon for National Educational Television, February 1966, Alan R. Solomon Papers, reel 3923, no. 258.

92. Castelli, interview by Solomon for National Educational Television.

93. Leo Castelli, interview by Calvin Tomkins, undated, in Calvin Tomkins Papers, II.B.29.

94. Alan R. Solomon to Leo Castelli, August 3, 1964, Alan R. Solomon Papers, reel 3921, no. 623.

95. Greenberg's advice is acknowledged in the preface of the catalog to the American Pavilion.

96. Annette Michelson, "The 1964 Biennale," *Art International* 8, no. 7 (September 25, 1964): 38.

97. Ibid. Michelson herself saw the Pop movement as "an art of satiety" produced in "the extraordinary prosperous and permissive climate of the 1950's and 1960's in urban America."

98. Ibid., p. 39.

99. Annette Michelson, interview by author, September 7, 2006, New York.

100. Virgilio Guzzi, "Troppe americanate," *Il Tempo*, June 20, 1964.

101. Renata Pisu, "Tutto è perduto, anche il pudore," ABC, June 28, 1964, p. 8.

102. "Noi paghiamo per queste buffonate," *Epoca*, no. 718 (June 28, 1964): 26.

103. Reported in USIS Rome, Venice Biennale report to USIA Washington, July 6, 1964, Venice Biennale Files, Smithsonian Institution Archives (hereafter Venice Biennale Files).

104. Franco Passoni, "Non ci piace perché contiene i germi di un nuovo fascismo," *Avanti*, August 2, 1964.

105. USIS Rome, Venice Biennale report to USIA Washington, August 3, 1964, Venice Biennale Files.

106. Da. Mi., "Venezia: Oggi si apre la Biennale," *L'Unità*, June 20, 1964, p. 6.

107. Renzo Guasco, "La XXXII Biennale d'Arte di Venezia," *Radio Corriere*, June 28, 1964, p. 14.

108. Pisu, "Tutto è perduto, anche il pudore," p. 10.

109. Guido Piovene, "Astrattismo e 'pop-art' hanno un valido significato," *La Stampa*, July 21, 1964.

110. De Marchis, "The Significance of the 1964 Venice Biennale," p. 21.

111. USIS Stockholm, press report to USIA Washington, July 28, 1964, Venice Biennale Files.

112. Folke Edwards, "A New Generation," *Stockholms-Tidningen*, June 28, 1964, quoted in USIS Stockholm, press report to USIA Washington, July 28, 1964, Venice Biennale Files.

113. Unidentified article in *Die Welt*, June 29, 1964, quoted in USIS Bonn, press report to USIA Washington, August 7, 1964, Venice Biennale Files.

114. Unidentified article in *Der Tagesspiegel*, July 24, 1964, quoted in USIS Bonn, press report to USIA Washington, August 7, 1964, Venice Biennale Files.

115. Torsten Bergmark, "Afterthoughts on Venice," *Dagens Nyheter*, July 9, 1964, quoted in USIS Stockholm, press report to USIA Washington, July 28, 1964, Venice Biennale Files.

116. Unidentified article in *Echo der Zeit*, August 2, 1964, quoted in USIS Bonn, press report to USIA Washington, August 19, 1964, Venice Biennale Files.

117. Yasuo Kamon, "Venice Diary," p. 82.

118. Jun Ebara, Kusuo Shimizu, and Toshinbu Onosato, "American Art Is the Victor, Japanese Artists Are above Standard," *Yomiuri shinbun*, July 6, 1964, evening edition, p. 9 [J].

This roundtable discussion is also reported in USIS Tokyo, operations memorandum to USIA Washington, July 13, 1964, Venice Biennale Files.

119. Shūji Takashina, "Robert Rauschenberg," unidentified journal (September 1964): 33 [J], Robert Rauschenberg Archives.

120. For a discussion of this controversy, see Avram Kampf, "The Jewish Museum: An Institution Adrift," *Judaism* 17, no. 3 (Summer 1968): 282–298.

121. For his obituary, see "Dr. Solomon Dies at 49: Ex-Director of Jewish Museum," *New York Times*, February 19, 1970, p. 47; and Sam Hunter, "Alan Solomon: 1920–1970," *New York Times*, March 1, 1970, section II, p. 26.

122. Solomon to Bingham, undated, Alan R. Solomon Papers, reel 3921, no. 87.

CHAPTER 3

1. There was originally no booking for the month of August. Seeing the improving ticket sales at Sadler's Wells, the London producer, Michael White, arranged for the company to perform for another two and a half weeks at the Phoenix Theater in Charing Cross. See David Vaughan, *Merce Cunningham: Fifty Years* (New York: Aperture, 1997), pp. 140–142.

2. Convinced of the need for a modern art museum in Sweden earlier in the 1950s, Hultén persuaded Otte Sköld, the director of the Nationalmuseum, to secure the government's agreement to separate the museum's modern art collection as the foundation for the Moderna Museet.

3. For a discussion of Hultén's entire curatorial career, from the 1950s to the 1990s, see Lutz Jahre, ed., *Das gedruckte Museum von Pontus Hultén: Kunstausstellungen und ihre Bücher* (Bonn: Kunst- und Ausstellungshalle der Bundesrepublik Deutschland, 1996).

4. Rauschenberg's long and intense involvement with the Stockholm art scene was memorialized in 2007 by a Swedish art history journal, *Konsthistorisk tidskrift* (Journal of Art History), which dedicated a special issue to this topic: "Rauschenberg and Sweden: Essays, Documents, Comments," vol. 76, nos. 1–2 (2007).

5. Billy Klüver to Pontus Hultén, June 3, 1964, "5 New York Evenings" Files, Moderna Museet Archives, Stockholm.

6. After resigning from the Stedelijk Museum in December 1962, Sandberg became the chairman of the Executive Committee of the Israel Museum, which opened in 1965. He spent most of his time in Jerusalem from 1964 to 1968.

7. Patrik Andersson, "Euro-Pop: The Mechanical Bride Stripped Bare in Stockholm, Even" (Ph.D. diss., University of British Columbia, 2001), p. 2.

8. Hultén was appointed the director of the Moderna Museet when Otte Sköld, who had concurrently held its directorship with that of the Nationalmuseum, died in the fall of 1958. Since Sköld had occupied the position part-time and for only about half a year, Hultén was practically the "first" director of the Moderna Museet.

9. Pontus Hultén, "Five Fragments from Moderna Museet's History," in Olle Granath and Monica Nieckels, eds., *Moderna Museet 1958–83* (Stockholm: Moderna Museet Press, 1983), p. 54 [S].

10. Pontus Hultén, interview by author, March 16, 2004, La Motte, France.

11. Hultén, "Five Fragments from Moderna Museet's History," p. 35.

12. Ibid., p. 36.

13. Ibid.

14. Billy Klüver and Robert Rauschenberg, "Art en mouvement: Souvenirs conjugués," in Olle Granath and Monica Nieckels, eds., *Le Moderna Museet de Stockholm à Bruxelles* (Brussels: Palais des Beaux-Arts, 1981), pp. 38–40. The article is reprinted in Swedish in Granath and Nieckels, *Moderna Museet 1958–1983*, and in English in *Konsthistorisk tidskrift* 76, nos. 1–2 (2007), as "Art in Motion—A Combined Memory."

15. Branden Joseph discussed the piece in terms of hybridity of media and Jacques Derrida's concept of writing in "Rauschenberg's Refusal," in Paul Schimmel, ed., *Robert Rauschenberg: Combines*, exh. cat. (Los Angeles: Museum of Contemporary Art, 2005), p. 267. More recently, Joshua Shannon conducted a close analysis of the piece in relation to the rapidly changing cityscape of Manhattan in the early 1960s. See Shannon, *Disappearance of Objects: New York Art and the Rise of the Postmodern City* (New Haven: Yale University Press, 2009), esp. pp. 134–148.

16. Klüver and Rauschenberg, "Art en mouvement: Souvenirs conjugués," pp. 35–36.

17. See George Rickey, "The Kinetic International," *Arts Magazine* 35, no. 10 (September 1961): 16.

18. See Andersson, "Euro-Pop," p. 77.

19. The Moderna Museet Archives holds many letters from overseas requesting copies of the catalog in its file on "Art in Motion." The Japanese art critic Yoshiaki Tōno also wrote to Hultén to thank him for having sent the catalog to him.

20. Pontus Hultén, foreword to *4 Americans: Alfred Leslie, Jasper Johns, Robert Rauschenberg, Richard Stankiewicz*, exh. cat. (Stockholm: Moderna Museet, 1962), p. 5 [S]. The English translation of this text is available in *Konsthistorisk tidskrift* 76, nos. 1–2 (2007), although I have used a translation by Eva Pankenier here.

21. Rauschenberg's solo show at Galerie Daniel Cordier, held in April–May 1961, traveled to Milan.

22. Ileana Sonnabend to Pontus Hultén, January 26, January 31, and February 2, 1962, "4 Americans" Files, Moderna Museet Archives, Stockholm.

23. Among these events was a presentation of contemporary experimental film, entitled "The New American Cinema—New York Film." Also, John Cage, who happened to be in the city with David Tudor through an invitation from Fylkingen, gave an opening lecture for a program entitled "New American Music and Poetry."

24. Pontus Hultén to Calvin Tomkins, August 2, 1963, in Calvin Tomkins Papers, IV.C.23.

25. Ulf Linde, interview by author, March 12, 2004, Stockholm.

26. Kathryn Boyer et al., "From the Editorial Board," *Konsthistorisk tidskrift* 76, nos. 1–2 (2007): 3.

27. Per-Olov Zennström, "Americans in Motion," *Dagens Nyheter*, April 6, 1962 [S].

28. Tord Bæckström, "Four Americans at the Moderna Museet," *Göteborgs Posten*, March 29, 1962 [S].

29. Harry Osbornson, "Art on Dangerous Roads," *Smålandsposten*, April 12, 1962, p. 5 [S].

30. See Hultén, "Five Fragments from Moderna Museet's History," p. 40.

31. Lars Erik Åström, "Image and Life in the U.S.A.," *Svenska Dagbladet*, March 17, 1962 [S].

32. Anna Lundström, "Comments on *4 Americans*," *Konsthistorisk tidskrift* 76, nos. 1–2 (2007): 113. According to Lundström, the most precise Swedish words for "4 Americans" would be "4 amerikaner" rather than "4 amerikanare."

33. See Zennström, "Americans in Motion."

34. Ulf Linde, quoted in Lars Widding, "The Moderna Museet Has Become Art's Gröna Lund," *Expressen*, March 25, 1962 [S]. Gröna Lund is an amusement park in Stockholm.

35. An unidentified Swedish newspaper, May 15, 1962. It is also reported that a man rode on the goat for a snapshot at Sonnabend's gallery in Paris in 1963, causing one of its legs to collapse. See Calvin Tomkins, *Off the Wall: Robert Rauschenberg and the Art World of Our Time* (New York: Penguin Books, 1980), p. 20.

36. Ulf Linde, interview by author, October 18, 2004, Stockholm.

37. Thomas E. Crow, "Rise and Fall: Theme and Idea in the Combines of Robert Rauschenberg," in Schimmel, *Robert Rauschenberg: Combines*, p. 253.

38. Alan R. Solomon, *Robert Rauschenberg*, exh. cat. (New York: Jewish Museum, 1963), n.p.

39. For an iconographic study that discusses *Monogram* as the artist's self-portrait, see Lisa Wainwright, "Reading Junk: Thematic Imagery in the Art of Robert Rauschenberg from 1952 to 1964" (Ph.D. diss., University of Illinois at Urbana-Champaign, 1993).

40. Roger Cranshaw and Adrian Lewis, "Re-reading Rauschenberg," *Artscribe*, no. 29 (June 1981): 47.

41. Robert Hughes, *Shock of the New* (1981; reprinted, New York: Alfred A. Knopf, 1998), p. 335.

42. Leo Steinberg, *Encounters with Rauschenberg* (Houston: Menil Foundation, 2000), pp. 59–60.

43. Ibid., p. 54.

44. See Robert Rauschenberg, interview by Barbro Schultz Lundestam and Marianne Hultman for the Swedish film program *Amerikanarna och Pontus Hultén* (Americans and Pontus Hultén), 1997; transcribed by the author from the videotape held at Robert Rauschenberg Archives in New York.

45. Tomkins also interviewed Rauschenberg about the making of *Monogram*. See Calvin Tomkins, *The Bride and the Bachelors: Five Masters of the Avant-Garde* (New York: Penguin Books, 1976), pp. 218–219.

46. Rauschenberg, interview for *Amerikanarna och Pontus Hultén*.

47. *Rhyme* is now in the collection of the Museum of Modern Art, New York.

48. Rauschenberg, interview for *Amerikanarna och Pontus Hultén*. It is also reported that it was Johns who suggested that the goat be placed on the square panel. See Joan Young with Susan Davidson, "Chronology," in Walter Hopps and Susan Davidson, eds., *Robert Rauschenberg: A Retrospective*, exh. cat. (New York: Solomon R. Guggenheim Museum, 1997), p. 557.

49. David White, curator at the Estate of Robert Rauschenberg, suggests that this study could have been made after *Monogram* was completed.

50. Rauschenberg, interview for *Amerikanarna och Pontus Hultén.*

51. Steinberg, *Encounters with Rauschenberg*, p. 61.

52. Pontus Hultén and Julia Brown Turrell, "A Conversation about the Sculpture of Robert Rauschenberg," in Julia Brown Turrell, ed., *Rauschenberg: Sculpture*, exh. cat. (Fort Worth: Modern Art Museum of Fort Worth, 1995), p. 34.

53. Ibid.

54. Ileana Sonnabend, interview by Calvin Tomkins, undated, in Calvin Tomkins Papers, IV.C.15.

55. For the English version of the catalog essay, see Alan R. Solomon, "The New American Art," *Art International* 8, no. 2 (March 20, 1964): 50–55.

56. Ileana Sonnabend to Pontus Hultén, August 2, 1963, "American Pop Art" Files, Moderna Museet Archives.

57. Sonnabend to Hultén, January 29, 1964, "American Pop Art" Files.

58. Sonnabend to Hultén, March 19, 1964, "American Pop Art" Files.

59. The museum received a special grant of five million Swedish crowns from the government in 1964, and used the money to acquire works by modern European masters such as Picasso, Kandinsky, and Mondrian.

60. For Ultvedt's involvement with *Pelican*, see Annika Öhrner, "Recalling Pelican: On P. O. Ultvedt, Robert Rauschenberg and Two 'Ballets,'" *Konsthistorisk tidskrift* 76, nos. 1–2 (2007): 27–39.

61. Oral History Interview with Alice Denny, May 13, 1976, Archives of American Art, Smithsonian Institution. Steve Paxton tells a slightly different version of the story: Denny accidentally listed Rauschenberg as a choreographer rather than as technical crew in the festival's publicity, which prompted the artist to create the piece. See Steve Paxton, "Rauschenberg for Cunningham and Three of His Own," in Hopps and Davidson, *Robert Rauschenberg: A Retrospective*, p. 263. For a discussion of Rauschenberg's performances in general, see also Nina Sundell, *Rauschenberg/Performance: 1954–1984*, exh. cat. (Cleveland: Cleveland Center for Contemporary Art, 1983).

62. Erica Abeel, "Daedalus at the Rollerdrome," *Saturday Review*, August 28, 1965, p. 53.

63. Paxton, "Rauschenberg for Cunningham and Three of His Own," p. 264.

64. Branden W. Joseph, *Random Order: Robert Rauschenberg and the Neo-Avant-Garde* (Cambridge, Mass.: MIT Press, 2003), p. 219.

65. See Teddy Hultberg, ed., *Fylkingen: New Music and Intermedia Art, 1933–1993* (Stockholm: Fylkingen, 1994), p. 180 [S]. I would like to thank Annika Öhrner for translating these titles into English for me, as well as for informing me of Fahlström's sound piece.

66. For Rauschenberg's artistic relationship with Fahlström, see Branden W. Joseph, "BL(U)BROB TRRRCRRAATCHURBUP: Bob Rauschenberg in Swedish Bird Call," *Konsthistorisk tidskrift* 76, nos. 1–2 (2007): 6–26.

67. Quoted in Nancy Spector, "Rauschenberg and Performance," in Hopps and Davidson, *Robert Rauschenberg: A Retrospective*, p. 237.

68. Quoted in Rosalind E. Krauss, *The Optical Unconscious* (Cambridge, Mass.: MIT Press, 1993), p. 302.

69. For this topic see William St. Clair, *Lord Elgin and the Marbles* (Oxford: Oxford University Press, 1998)

70. Pontus Hultén, interview by author, March 16, 2004, La Motte, France.

71. Although Tomkins wrote in *Off the Wall* that the tasks also included such activities as "changing into a new pair of socks" and "eating a sandwich" (p. 231), photographic documentation of the performance does not record them.

72. Rauschenberg, interview for *Amerikanarna och Pontus Hultén*.

73. Quoted in Tomkins, *Off the Wall*, p. 230.

74. Ibid.

75. Ibid., p. 231.

76. See Joseph, *Random Order*, p. 225.

77. Hultén and Turrell, "A Conversation about the Sculpture of Robert Rauschenberg," p. 28.

78. See Young with Davidson, "Chronology," in Hopps and Davidson, *Robert Rauschenberg: A Retrospective*, p. 557.

79. See Calvin Tomkins, "A Good Eye and a Good Ear," *New Yorker* 56, no. 14 (May 26, 1980): 61. In 1963, Barr did accept an offer for the Dante Drawings, which he exceptionally liked, as an anonymous gift for the museum.

80. I found a copy of the invoice at the Robert Rauschenberg Archives, New York.

81. Ulf Linde, interview by author, March 12, 2004, Stockholm. Linde further observed that *Elgin Tie* lacked the symbolic unity of *Monogram*, as the diverse elements in the performance piece were too lively to be integrated into a unified work of art.

82. Hultén, "Five Fragments from Moderna Museet's History," p. 56.

83. Hultén to David Vaughan, April 27, 1964, "5 New York Evenings" Files.

84. Quoted in Andersson, "Euro-Pop," p. 126. Ultvedt provided Andersson with the translation of these coded letters in 1992. Letters were sent to Ultvedt from 1963 to 1966.

85. See Fredrik Logevall, "The Swedish-American Conflict over Vietnam," *Diplomatic History* 17, no. 3 (Summer 1993): 421–445.

86. Ulf Linde, quoted in Andersson, "Euro-Pop," p. 129.

87. Ulf Linde and Olof Lagercrantz, "An American in Hell," *Dagens Nyheter*, March 23, 1965 [S].

88. See Ulf Linde, "The Open Art: The Inheritance from Munich," *Dagens Nyheter*, March 26, 1965, p.4 [S]; "The Open Art: The Myth Surrounding the Ahistorical Man," *Dagens Nyheter*, March 30, 1965, p.4 [S]; "The Open Art: The Picture 'One/Man' Has," *Dagens Nyheter*, April 1965, p.4 [S]; "The Open Art: A Dialogue without an End," *Dagens Nyheter*, May 13, 1965, p.4 [S]. For a detailed analysis of these articles, see Andersson, "Euro-Pop," pp. 152–169.

89. Alan R. Solomon, "Jim Dine and Psychology of the New Art," *Art International* 8, no. 8 (October 1964): 52.

90. Andersson, "Euro-Pop," p. 158.

91. Logevall, "The Swedish-American Conflict over Vietnam," pp. 426–427.

92. Rauschenberg gave Hultén instructions to fabricate a new set of *White Paintings* for the show, but only a two-panel version was made and exhibited.

93. Franklin Königsberg to Knut Wiggen (representative of Fylkingen), May 11, 1966, David Tudor Papers, Box 16, Folder 1, Special Collections at the Getty Research Institute.

94. Fylkingen to the American artists, undated, David Tudor Papers, Box 16, Folder 1.

95. Franklin Königsberg to Knut Wiggen, August 4, 1966, David Tudor Papers, Box 16, Folder 1.

96. Billy Klüver to Pontus Hultén, November 13, 1971, "New York Collection for Stockholm" Files, Moderna Museet Archives.

97. Logevall, "The Swedish-American Conflict over Vietnam," pp. 440–441.

98. To enhance the fundraising, each artist also later donated one print to a portfolio, but the prints did not sell very well.

99. Karl Olov Björk et al., "There Is Also a World beyond the Paris–New York Axis," *Dagens Nyheter*, June 27, 1972 [S]. Quoted in Marianne Hultman, "The New York Collection for Stockholm," in Marianne Hultman, ed., *Technology for Life: On Experiments in Art and Technology*, exh. cat. (Norrköpings: Norrköpings Konstmuseum, 2004), p. 161 [S].

100. Ibid.

101. Marianne Hultman, "Mud Muse 1968–1971: Work behind an Artwork," in Hultman, *Technology for Life*, p. 153 [S].

102. Tomkins, *Off the Wall*, p. 287. The source of this information is Brice Marden, who was then working as Rauschenberg's assistant. See the transcript of Tomkins's interview with Marden conducted on February 10, 1978, in Calvin Tomkins Papers, IV.C.38.

103. Susan Hartnett (an assistant for Rauschenberg from 1965 to 1969), interview by Tomkins, January 7, 1978, in Calvin Tomkins Papers, IV.C.38.

104. Bo Ahlsén et al., "Debate on New York Collection: 'Left-over Stock at Moderna Museet,'" *Dagens Nyheter*, November 18, 1973 [S]. Quoted in Hultman, "The New York Collection for Stockholm," p. 164.

105. Philip von Schantz, quoted in "Moderna Museet—Forty Years," in David Elliott et al., *Moderna Museet—Modern Museum* (London: Scala Books, 1998), p. 20.

106. Ludvig Rasmusson, "The Decadence of American Art and Its Ripple Effect on Swedish Art," *Paletten*, no. 209 (February 1992): 27 [S].

107. For more on *Monogram*'s reception in Stockholm, see Cecilia Widenheim, "A Goat's-Eye View: *Monogram* at the Moderna Museet," and Emma Stenström, "Another Kind of Combine: *Monogram* and the Moderna Museet," both in *Konsthistorisk tidskrift* 76, nos. 1–2 (2007): 40–47 and 48–59.

108. Björn Springfeldt to Rauschenberg, May 15, 1991, Moderna Museet Registrar Files on Robert Rauschenberg. As the billboard project was executed in collaboration with *Dagens*

Nyheter, there was a logotype of "DN" beside the image. Springfeldt wrote, "We all loved to see this image on large billboards, knowing the '*Monogram*' and the reference to Moderna Museet, to be seen all over Sweden," in his letter to Bradley Jeffries (staff at Rauschenberg Studio in Captiva, Florida), November 11, 1991.

109. Björn Springfeldt to Rauschenberg, June 8, 1994, Moderna Museet Registrar Files on Robert Rauschenberg.

110. Rauschenberg, interview for *Amerikanarna och Pontus Hultén*.

111. Lovisa Lönnebo, interview by author, October 12, 2004. According to Lönnebo, who served as the head of communication at the museum at the time of the interview, the design firm Stockholm Design Lab was commissioned for the "New Identity Programme" for the Moderna Museet. When the firm came up with several designs for the new museum logo, the one based on Rauschenberg's handwriting was unanimously chosen to be the new logotype.

CHAPTER 4

1. Merce Cunningham, "Story: Tale of a Dance and Tour," part 2, *Dance Ink* 6, no. 2 (Summer 1995): 20–21.

2. Ushio Shinohara, *Avant-Garde Road* (Tokyo: Bijutsu Shuppan-sha, 1968), p. 142 [J].

3. Carolyn Brown notes that the tensions were mounting already in Stockholm, which led to a practical falling-out between Cage and Rauschenberg in Ahmedabad. See Carolyn Brown, *Chance and Circumstance: Twenty Years with Cage and Cunningham* (New York: Alfred A. Knopf, 2007), pp. 407, 431.

4. Kuniharu Akiyama, "Sōgetsu Art Center: Ground Zero of the Sixties' Avant-Garde," in Yoshimi Nara et al., eds., *The Glory of the Sixties: The Complete Records of the Sōgetsu Art Center* (Tokyo: Film Art, 2002), pp. 53–54 [J].

5. This workshop took place at the Sōgetsu Art Center on November 20, 1964. American participants were Rauschenberg, Paxton, Lloyd, and Hays, while Japanese participants included celebrated dancers and performers such as Tatsumi Hijikata, Takehisa Kosugi, and Mariko Sanjō.

6. Yoshiaki Tōno, "Madness and Scandal: Fantastic New Faces of the World," *Geijutsu shinchō* (New Trends in Art) 10, no. 11 (November 1959): 104–112 [J].

7. For postwar Japanese art in general, see Alexandra Munroe, *Japanese Art after 1945: Scream against the Sky*, exh. cat. (New York: Solomon R. Guggenheim Museum, 1994); and Charles Merewether with Rika Iezumi Hiro, eds., *Art, Anti-Art, Non-Art: Experimentations in the Public Sphere in Postwar Japan, 1950–1970*, exh. cat. (Los Angeles: Getty Research Institute, 2007).

8. See the chronology compiled by Masatoshi Nakajima in *Hisao Dōmoto: A Retrospective*, exh. cat. (Kyoto: National Museum of Modern Art, 2005), p. 146 [J].

9. For the most vivid memoir of this legendary exhibition, see Genpei Akasegawa, *Anti-Art Independent* (Tokyo: Chikuma Shobō, 1994), pocketbook edition [J].

10. Jirō Yoshihara, "Beauty of Abstract Painting," *Asahi shinbun*, April 17, 1951. Quoted in Shin'ichirō Osaki, "Realism and Avant-Garde: A Postwar Restart," in *Encyclopedia of Modern Japanese Art* (Tokyo: Tokyo Shoseki, 2007), p. 92 [J].

11. The show was titled "Sekai: Konnichi no bijutsu" in Japanese and subtitled "Exposition internationale de l'art actuel" in French. Segi recollected in detail how he organized the exhibition in Oral History Interview with Shin'ichi Segi, August 6, 2009, conducted by Tetsuya Miyata and Gen Adachi, Oral History Archives of Japanese Art, www.oralarthistory.org.

12. Shinohara, *Avant-Garde Road*, p. 28.

13. In accordance with the Japanese convention of calling an artist after his or her "art name" (*gagō*).

14. For Tapié's collaboration with Yoshihara, see chapter 5 of Ming Tiampo, *Gutai: Decentering Modernism* (Chicago: University of Chicago Press, 2010).

15. For more on this topic, see Mizuho Katō, "The Reception of Informel in Japan," in *Sōgetsu and Its Era, 1945–1970* (Ashiya: Ashiya City Museum of Art & History, 1998), pp. 88–98 [J]. This essay provides a detailed analysis of Tapié's concept of Informel and its reception in Japan.

16. A Gutai member, Shōzō Shimamoto, discussed how Tapié's influence led Yoshihara to value paintings, sometimes at the cost of the performance aspect of Gutai's activities. Oral History Interview with Shōzō Shimamoto, August 21, 2009, conducted by Mizuho Katō and Hiroko Ikegami, Oral History Archives of Japanese Art, www.oralarthistory.org.

17. Shin'ichi Segi, "A Scandal about Informel," *Geijutsu shinchō* 9, no. 2 (February 1958): 54–66 [J].

18. Shūzō Takiguchi, "Crisis of Expression: The 9th Yomiuri Independent," *Yomiuri shinbun*, March 1, 1957. See Osaki, "Realism and Avant-Garde," p. 96.

19. Tōno, "Madness and Scandal," p. 106.

20. Yoshiaki Tōno, "The Adventures of the Younger Generation," *Mizue*, no. 659 (March 1960): 23–32 [J]; "Notes for a Discussion of American Avant-Garde Art," *Ongaku geijutsu* (Musical Art) 18, no. 7 (July 1960): 7–12 [J]; and "Robert Rauschenberg, or the New York Inferno," *Mizue* (Watercolor), no. 683 (February 1962): 42–56 [J].

21. The earliest serious writings on the artist were published by John Cage and Dore Ashton in 1961, not in American outlets but in an Italian journal, *Metro*.

22. Through Hultén's friendship with Tōno, the Moderna Museet hosted an exhibition of work by Sengai, the Japanese premodern Zen calligrapher, in 1963.

23. For the Japanese avant-garde art of the day, see Reiko Tomii, ed., "1960s Japan: Art Outside the Box," *Review of Japanese Culture and Society* (Jōsai University) 17, special issue (December 2005).

24. The Japanese Neo Dada group is normally notated without a hyphen between the two words. See translator's note in ibid., p. 53.

25. Although Hi Red Center was officially founded in 1963, its major members had been active as a group since October 1962. For the activities of this group, see Akasegawa's memoir *Tokyo Mixer Plans: Documents of Hi Red Center's Direct Actions* (Tokyo: Chikuma Shobō, 1994), pocketbook edition [J].

26. For the concept of Anti-Art, see Reiko Tomii, "*Geijutsu* on Their Minds: Memorable Words on Anti-Art," in Merewether, *Art, Anti-Art, Non-Art*, pp. 35–62.

27. Among the four artists, Johns and Klein had been to Japan before: Johns was stationed in Sendai as a soldier in the U.S. Army during the Korean War, and Klein lived in Tokyo from 1952 to 1953, where he studied judo to gain a black belt and also claimed to have created his first monochrome paintings.

28. The other two were the Tokyo Gallery and the Nantenshi Gallery.

29. See Akasegawa, *Anti-Art Independent*, chapter 5.

30. "Oh, Say Can You See?," *Time* 87, no. 2 (January 14, 1966): 70–71. See also Shinohara, *Avant-Garde Road*, p. 135. In addition, Shinohara recounts this story in Oral History Interview with Ushio Shinohara, February 13, 2009, conducted by Hiroko Ikegami and Reiko Tomii, Oral History Archives of Japanese Art, www.oralarthistory.org.

31. Akira Suga, "Artists Migrating to America," in *Neo-Dada* JAPAN *1958–1998: Arata Isozaki and the Artists of "White House,"* exh. cat. (Ōita: Ōita City Museum of Art, 1998), pp. 84–89 [J].

32. Shinohara, *Avant-Garde Road*, p. 177.

33. The Japanese "bullet train" between Tokyo and Osaka also started that year before the opening of the Olympic Games.

34. For Cage's activities and reception in Japan, see Masaaki Ueno, "Cage and Japan" (Ph.D. diss., Osaka University, 1998) [J].

35. Today, this piece is usually designated as *o′ oo″ (4′33″ No. 2)*. For a discussion of it, see James Pritchett, *The Music of John Cage* (Cambridge: Cambridge University Press, 1996), pp. 138–140.

36. For this phenomenon, see Akiyama, "Sōgetsu Art Center," pp. 49–50.

37. Yūsuke Nakahara, "Art Version of 'Passing Year, Coming Year,'" SAC *Journal*, no. 28 (December 25, 1962): n.p. [J].

38. John Cage, *Silence: Lectures and Writings* (Middletown, Conn.: Wesleyan University Press, 1961), p. xi.

39. Fujiko Nakaya, interview by author, July 31, 2003, Tokyo.

40. Yoshiaki Tōno, "Pop Art and Myself: An Interview with Rauschenberg," *Geijutsu shinchō*, no. 182 (February 1965): 58 [J].

41. The person in charge was most likely Hideo Kaidō, a legendary chief editor of Yomiuri's cultural news department in post–World War II years. Convinced of the need to demolish the conservative salon-based art groups (known as *dontai*) in Japan, he was one of the central figures who launched the Yomiuri Independent Exhibition.

42. Tōno, "Pop Art and Myself" p.58.

43. Ibid.

44. Marshall McLuhan, *The Mechanical Bride: Folklore of Industrial Man* (1951; reprinted, Corte Madera, Calif.: Gingko Press, 2002), p. 3.

45. Oral History Interview with Ushio Shinohara, February 13, 2009.

46. Tōno, "Robert Rauschenberg, or the New York Inferno," p. 46.

47. Ushio Shinohara, interview by author, July 3, 2003, Brooklyn.

48. This autobiography was originally titled *The Road to the Avant-Garde*, but retitled *Avant-Garde Road* when published as a book in 1968.

49. For these articles, see Barbara Rose, "Dada Then and Now," Sonya Rudikoff, "New Realists in New York," and Ellen H. Johnson, "The Living Object," in *Art International* 7, no. 1 (January 25, 1963): respectively 22–28, 38–41, and 42–45.

50. Shinohara, *Avant-Garde Road*, p. 118.

51. Ibid., p. 131.

52. Ushio Shinohara, "*Coca-Cola Plan* Episode," an unpublished statement prepared for the exhibition "Shūzo Takiguchi: Drifting Objects on Dream" held at Toyama Prefectural Hall Museum in 2001.

53. Shinohara, interview by author.

54. Quoted in Atsushi Miyakawa, "Anti-Art: Its Descent to the Everyday," *Bijutshu techō*, (Art Notebooks), no. 234 (April 1964): 49 [J].

55. [Sumio] Kuwabara, "American Artists, No. 4: Rauschenberg—Elegant Culprit of Pop Art," *Tokyo shinbun*, July 29, 1963 [J].

56. Shinohara, *Avant-Garde Road*, pp. 142–143.

57. Shinohara, interview by author.

58. Ibid. For Rauschenberg's response to Shinohara, see Oral History Interview with Ushio Shinohara, February 13, 2009.

59. Yoshiaki Tōno, "Call for Questions for Rauschenberg's Public Interview," *Bijutsu techō*, no. 244 (November 1964): 103 [J].

60. Nakaya, interview by author.

61. Robert Rauschenberg, statement, in Dorothy Miller, ed., *Sixteen Americans*, exh. cat. (New York: Museum of Modern Art, 1959), p. 58.

62. Tōno, "Pop Art and Myself," p. 58.

63. Shinohara made the figure of Marcel Duchamp after he saw the August 1963 issue of *Mizue*, which was dedicated to Duchamp.

64. For the text of Shinohara's original questions, see *Avant-Garde Road*, p. 144.

65. Shūji Takashina, interview by author, August 8, 2003, Kurashiki.

66. Tōno, "Pop Art and Myself," p. 59.

67. Yoshiaki Tōno, "This Work by Rauschenberg—*Gold Standard*," *Bijutsu techō*, no. 294 (February 1968): 66 [J].

68. Ibid., p. 65.

69. According to Tōno, this mini television was a Sony product, but the Sony museum was unable to identify the model.

70. Nakaya, interview by author.

71. Tōno, "Pop Art and Myself," p. 59.

72. Nobuaki Kojima, interview by author, December 19, 2003, Tokyo. See also Hisanori Gogota, "Introduction: 'Nobuaki Kojima,'" in *Nobuaki Kojima*, vol. 1 of *Aspects of Fukui Contemporary Art*, exh. cat. (Fukui: Fukui Fine Arts Museum, 1990), p. 5 [J].

73. Homi K. Bhabha, *The Location of Culture* (London: Routledge, 1994), p. 86.

74. Quoted in Tōno, "Pop Art and Myself," p. 59.

75. For de Gaulle's critique of the gold standard system, see chapter 7 of Richard Kuisel, *Seducing the French: The Dilemma of Americanization* (Berkeley: University of California Press, 1993), esp. pp. 171–176.

76. Milton Gilbert, "The Gold-Dollar System: Conditions of Equilibrium and the Price of Gold," reprinted in Barry Eichengreen and Marc Flandreau, eds., *The Gold Standard in Theory and History* (London: Routledge, 1997), pp. 291–312.

77. Nakaya, interview by author.

78. Also in this exhibition, artist Kazutada Tsubouchi showed a pink monochrome painting with a Victor dog, which he had made prior to Rauschenberg's visit to Tokyo.

79. For a review of Shinohara's work from the early to mid-sixties, see Yūsuke Nakahara, "Essay on Shinohara Ushio," *Gendai bijutsu* (Contemporary Art), no. 3 (March 1965): 24–34.

80. The name of the magazine has not been identified, but Shinohara recalls it was not an art journal but a home décor magazine.

81. Bhabha, *Location of Culture*, p. 86.

82. Shinohara, *Avant-Garde Road*, p. 185.

83. One of Kojima's figures was purchased by Lieberman, who later donated it to the Museum of Modern Art, New York.

84. For instance, the activities of the Japanese avant-garde were often covered not in art journals but in weekly magazines. This was partly because of the artists' efforts to win public attention through their peculiar actions and fashions, most representative of which was Shinohara's Mohawk haircut.

85. One of Shinohara's imitations of *Coca-Cola Plan* survived because the artist gave it to the critic Shūzo Takiguchi. It is now in the collection of Toyama Prefectural Museum of Modern Art.

86. Arjun Appadurai, *Modernity at Large: Cultural Dimensions of Globalization* (Minneapolis: University of Minnesota Press, 1996), p. 7.

87. Merce Cunningham, "Story: Tale of a Dance and Tour," part 3, *Dance Ink* 6, no. 3 (Fall 1995): 36.

88. Nakaya, interview by author.

CONCLUSION

1. Calvin Tomkins, *Off the Wall: Robert Rauschenberg and the Art World of Our Time* (New York: Penguin Books, 1980), p. 235.

2. Rauschenberg exhibited *Axle* (1964) at this exhibition and received the William A. Clarke gold medal with a two-thousand-dollar prize.

3. For the story of the Museum of Modern Art's acquisition of the Dante Drawings, see Tomkins, *Off the Wall*, pp. 160–161.

4. The itinerary included the following venues: Whitechapel Gallery, London; USIS Gallery, American Embassy, London; Hatton Gallery at the University of Newcastle-upon-Tyne,

Newcastle-upon-Tyne; Ashmolean Museum at Oxford University, Oxford; Arts Council Gallery, Cambridge; International Künstlerklub, Vienna; Neue Galerie am Landesmuseum Joanneum, Graz; Kaiser Wilhelm Museum, Krefeld; Museum am Ostwall, Dortmund; Amerika Haus, Hamburg; Kunstverein, Stuttgart; Amerika Haus, Berlin; Kunsternes Hus, Oslo; Moderna Museet, Stockholm; Galerie Hörhammer, Helsinki; Stedelijk Museum, Amsterdam; Belgrade Cultural Center, Belgrade; unidentified location, Ljubljana; Umetnostna Galerija, Maribor; and Palais des Beaux-Arts, Brussels. See the itinerary in International Council/International Program Exhibition Records, *Thirty-four Drawings for Dante's Inferno*: V.ICE-F-97-64.1, Museum of Modern Art Archives, New York (hereafter Dante Drawings Files, followed by a folder number).

5. Edwin Mullins, "Not Just a Joker," *Sunday Telegraph* (London), February 9, 1964, p. 11.

6. A.D., "Strong View of Originality in This Excursion in Dadaism," *Cambridge News*, May 21, 1964, Dante Drawing Files, V.ICE-F-97-64.3.

7. Scott Dobson, "These Dante Drawings Are So Satisfying," unidentified newspaper clipping from Newcastle-upon-Tyne, Dante Drawings Files,V.ICE-F-97-64.3.

8. Anna Klapheck, "Pop Art, die nicht provoziert," *Rheinische Post Allgemeiner Teil,* September 17, 1964, Dante Drawings Files,V.ICE-F-97-64.3.

9. D.W., "Kein Kinderschreck, auch keine Offenbarung," *Westdeutsche Zeitung*, October 7, 1964, Dante Drawings Files,V.ICE-F-97-64.3. Translation by MOMA's Press Department.

10. Walter Fedler, "Lettera dalla Germania," *D'Ars Agency* (April 20, 1965), Dante Drawings Files,V.ICE-F-97-64.3.

11. "Es wird ein Rauschen um Rauschenberg geben," *Neue Rhein-Zeitung*, September 14, 1964, Dante Drawings Files,V.ICE-F-97-4.3. Translation by MOMA's Press Department.

12. Albert Schulze Vellinghausen, "Auf dem Weg zur Sublimierung," *Frankfurter Allgemeine Zeitung*, October 9, 1964, Dante Drawings Files, V.ICE-F-97-4.3. Translation by MOMA's Press Department.

13. "Es wird ein Rauschen um Rauschenberg geben."

14. The Italian edition was shown at the Galleria Domus Antiqua and the Galleria Apollinaire in Milan and at the Galleria dell'Obelisco in Rome. The American edition was published by Harry N. Abrams.

15. Vittorio Del Gaizo, "Rauschenberg illustratore di Dante," *Opera Aperta* 1, no. 2 (March–April 1965): 146.

16. E[dgardo] Macorini, "Le illustrazioni di Rauschenberg per l'Inferno di Dante," *Domus*, no. 431 (October 1965): 41.

17. G.P., untitled poem dedicated to Rauschenberg's Dante Drawings, published as epigraph in *Domus*, no. 431 (October 1965).

18. Renato Barilli, "L'Inferno di R. Rauschenberg," *Linea Struttura*, no. 1 (1966): 77.

19. Ibid., pp. 77–78.

20. Paolo Barozzi, "L'Inferno di Rauschenberg," *Tempo Presente* (July 1965): 66.

21. The domestic itinerary consisted of shows at the Arts Club of Chicago; Fresno State College; Southwest Texas State College; Memphis State University; Baltimore Museum of

Art; Columbia Museum of Art; J. B. Speed Art Museum, Louisville; and Museum of Art, University of Michigan.

22. Lawrence Campbell, "Robert Rauschenberg," *ARTnews* 59, no. 9 (January 1961): 13–14.

23. E[mily] G[enauer], "Rauschenberg's Drawings for Dante's *Inferno*," *New York Herald Tribune*, December 25, 1965, p. 7.

24. Mel Bochner, "Robert Rauschenberg," *Arts Magazine* 40, no. 5 (March 1966): 50.

25. For a chronology of EAT, see Hiroko Tasaka with InterCommunication Center, "Brief Chronology of EAT," in *EAT: The Story of Experiments in Art and Technology*, exh. cat. (Tokyo: NTT InterCommunication Center, 2003), pp. 89–97 [J]. Although Rauschenberg was not directly involved with the projects listed here, he contributed the basic concept of "invisible environment" for the Pepsi Pavilion at Expo '70 in Osaka.

26. Joan Young with Susan Davidson, "Chronology," in Walter Hopps and Susan Davidson, eds., *Robert Rauschenberg: A Retrospective*, exh. cat. (New York: Solomon R. Guggenheim Museum, 1997), p. 580.

27. See Mary Yakush, ed., *ROCI: Rauschenberg Overseas Culture Interchange*, exh. cat. (Washington, D.C.: National Gallery of Art, 1991).

28. Robert Rauschenberg and Yoshiaki Tōno, "Tying a Work of Art to an Elephant: About the ROCI Project," in *Rauschenberg Overseas Culture Interchange*, exh. cat. (Tokyo: Setagaya Museum of Art, 1986), p. 10 [J]. The interview took place in Tokyo in May 1983.

29. For a detailed account of ROCI Chile, see Robert S. Mattison, *Robert Rauschenberg: Breaking Boundaries* (New Haven: Yale University Press, 2003), pp. 220–259. For ROCI USSR, see Pamela Kachurin, "The ROCI Road to Peace: Robert Rauschenberg, Perestroika, and the End of the Cold War," *Journal of Cold War Studies* 4, no. 1 (Winter 2002): 27–43.

30. For an ambivalent legacy of the ROCI project, especially in China, see Hiroko Ikegami, "ROCI East: Considering Rauschenberg's Agency in China," in Cynthia Millis, ed., *East-West Interchanges in American Art: "A Long and Tumultuous Relationship"* (Washington, D.C.: Smithsonian Institution Scholarly Press, forthcoming).

31. Branden Joseph makes a similar observation on ROCI as a precedence for today's multinational art practice in his tribute to Rauschenberg in "Media Player," *Artforum* 47, no. 1 (September 2008): 441.

32. See Miwon Kwon, "Genealogy of Site Specificity," chapter 1 of Kwon, *One Place after Another: Site-Specific Art and Locational Identity* (Cambridge, Mass.: MIT Press, 2002).

BIBLIOGRAPHY

UNPUBLISHED SOURCES

1. Archival Material

Archives of American Art, Smithsonian Institution, Washington, D.C.
Leo Castelli Papers
Alan R. Solomon Papers

Getty Research Institute, Special Collections, Los Angeles
Giuseppe Panza Papers
David Tudor Papers

The Jewish Museum Archives, New York
Venice Biennale Files
Papers related to Alan Solomon

Moderna Museet Archives, Stockholm
"Americansk pop-konst: 106 former av kärlek och förtvivlan" [American Pop Art: 106 Forms of Love and Despair] Files
"5 New York kväller" [5 New York Evenings] Files
"4 amerikanare" [4 Americans] Files
"The New York Collection for Stockholm" Files
"Rörelse i konsten" [Art in Motion] Files
Registrar Files on Robert Rauschenberg

The Museum of Modern Art Archives, New York
Calvin Tomkins Papers
International Council/International Program Exhibition Records, *Thirty-Four Drawings for Dante's Inferno*

Robert Rauschenberg Archives, New York
Robert Rauschenberg Papers

Smithsonian Institution Archives, Washington, D.C.
Venice Biennale Files

Sōgetsu Foundation Archives, Tokyo
Papers related to the Merce Cunningham Dance Company
Papers related to "Twenty Questions to Bob Rauschenberg"

2. Interviews in Research Collections

Archives of American Art, Smithsonian Institution, Washington, D.C.
Ileana Sonnabend, March 2, 1995, conducted by William L. Weiss, sound cassettes of interview held at the Archives

Archives of American Art, Oral History Interviews, Smithsonian Institution, Washington, D.C.
Leo Castelli, May 14, 1969–June 8, 1973, conducted by Paul Cummings
Alice Denny, May 13, 1976, conducted by Walter Hopps
Virginia Dwan, March 21, 1984, conducted by Charles F. Stuckey
Porter A. McCray, September 17–October 4, 1977, conducted by Paul Cummings
Darthea Speyer, June 28, 1976, conducted by Paul Cummings

Columbia University, Oral History Collection, New York
Leo Castelli, "The Reminiscences of Leo Castelli," May 1977, conducted by Barbaralee Diamonstein

Oral History Archives of Japanese Art, http://www.oralarthistory.org
Shin'ichi Segi, August 6, 2009, conducted by Tetsuya Miyata and Gen Adachi
Shōzō Shimamoto, August 21 and 30, 2008, conducted by Mizuho Katō and Hiroko Ikegami
Ushio Shinohara, September 17, 2008, and February 13 and 20, 2009, conducted by Hiroko Ikegami and Reiko Tomii

Robert Rauschenberg Archives, New York
Robert Rauschenberg, 1997, conducted by Barbro Schultz Lundestam and Marianne Hultman for the film program *Amerikanarna och Pontus Hultén* [Americans and Pountus Hultén]

3. Interviews Conducted by the Author

Antonio Homem, telephone interview, September 7, 2006, New York
Pontus Hultén, March 16, 2004, La Motte, France
Nobuaki Kojima, December 19, 2003, Tokyo
Ulf Linde, March 12 and October 18, 2004, Stockholm
Lovisa Lönnebo, October 12, 2004, Stockholm
Annette Michelson, September 7, 2006, New York
Fujiko Nakaya, July 31 and August 22, 2003, Tokyo
Robert Pincus-Witten, August 31, 2006, New York
Ushio Shinohara, July 3 and December 7, 2003, Brooklyn
Darthea Speyer, March 17, 2004, Paris
Shūji Takashina, August 8, 2003, Kurashiki
Calvin Tomkins, June 28, 2005, New York
David Vaughan, June 13, 2003, New York

PUBLISHED SOURCES

1. Selected Literature on Robert Rauschenberg

Ameline, Jean-Paul. "Comment les Combines de Rauschenberg ont conquis l'Europe: Essai d'histoire culturelle (1958–1964)." In Jean-Paul Ameline, ed., *Robert Rauschenberg: Combines*, pp. 287–306. Exh. cat., French edition. Paris: Centre Georges Pompidou, 2006.

Ashton, Dore. "The Collaboration Wheel: A Comment on Robert Rauschenberg's Comment on Dante." *Arts and Architecture* 80, no. 12 (December 1963): 10–11, 37.

Ashton, Dore. "Thirty-four Illustrations for Dante's Inferno." *Metro*, no. 2 (May 1961): 52–61.

Auricchio, Laura. "Lifting the Veil: Robert Rauschenberg's *Thirty-Four Drawings for Dante's Inferno* and the Commercial Homoerotic Imagery of 1950s America." *Genders*, no. 26 (Fall 1997): 119–154.

Bendiner, Kenneth. "Robert Rauschenberg's *Canyon*." *Arts Magazine* 56, no. 10 (June 1982): 57–59.

Boyer, Kathryn, Hans Heyden, Anna Tellgren, and Annika Öhrner, eds. "Rauschenberg and Sweden: Essays, Documents, Comments." Special issue of *Konsthistorisk tidskrift/Journal of Art History* 76, nos. 1–2 (2007).

Clark, Carroll S., and Kathleen A. Preciado, eds. *Robert Rauschenberg*. Exh. cat. Washington, D.C.: National Collection of Fine Arts, Smithsonian Institution, 1976.

Cranshaw, Roger, and Adrian Lewis. "Re-reading Rauschenberg." *Artscribe*, no. 29 (June 1981): 44–51.

Crow, Thomas E. "Rise and Fall: Theme and Idea in the Combines of Robert Rauschenberg." In Schimmel, *Robert Rauschenberg: Combines*, pp. 213–255.

Crow, Thomas E. "Southern Boys Go to Europe." In Stephanie Barron and Lynn Zelevansky, eds., *Jasper Johns to Jeff Koons: Four Decades of Art from the Broad Collections*, pp. 44–61. Exh. cat. Los Angeles: Los Angeles County Museum of Art, 2001.

Feinstein, Roni. "Random Order: The First Fifteen Years of Robert Rauschenberg's Art, 1949–1964." Ph.D. diss., New York University, 1990.

Feinstein, Roni. *Robert Rauschenberg: The Silkscreen Paintings, 1962–64. Exh. cat.* New York: Whitney Museum of American Art, 1990.

Hopps, Walter, and Susan Davidson, eds. *Robert Rauschenberg: A Retrospective. Exh. cat.* New York: Solomon R. Guggenheim Museum, 1997.

Hultén, Pontus. "Afterword." In Schimmel, *Robert Rauschenberg: Combines*, pp. 284–285.

Ikegami, Hiroko. "ROCI East: Considering Rauschenberg's Agency in China." In Cynthia Millis, ed., *East-West Interchanges in American Art: "A Long and Tumultuous Relationship."* Washington, D.C.: Smithsonian Institution Scholarly Press, forthcoming.

Joseph, Branden W. "BL(U)BROB TRRRCRRAATCHURBUP: Bob Rauschenberg in Swedish Bird Call." *Konsthistorisk tidskrift* 76, nos. 1–2 (2007): 6–26.

Joseph, Branden W. "Media Player." *Artforum* 47, no. 1 (September 2008): 438–441, 492.

Joseph, Branden W. *Random Order: Robert Rauschenberg and the Neo-Avant-Garde*. Cambridge, Mass.: MIT Press, 2003.

Joseph, Branden W. "Rauschenberg's Refusal." In Schimmel, *Robert Rauschenberg: Combines*, pp. 257–283.

Joseph, Branden W., ed. *Robert Rauschenberg*. October Files 4. Cambridge, Mass.: MIT Press, 2002.

Kachurin, Pamela. "The ROCI Road to Peace: Robert Rauschenberg, Perestroika, and the End of the Cold War." *Journal of Cold War Studies* 4, no. 1 (Winter 2002): 27–43.

Katz, Jonathan. "The Art of Code: Jasper Johns and Robert Rauschenberg." In Whitney Chadwick and Isabelle de Courtivron, eds., *Significant Others: Creativity and Intimate Partnership*, pp. 189–207. London: Thames and Hudson, 1993.

Katz, Jonathan. *The Silent Camp: Jasper Johns, Robert Rauschenberg, and the Cold War*. Chicago: University of Chicago Press, forthcoming.

Krauss, Rosalind. "Perpetual Inventory." In Hopps and Davidson, *Robert Rauschenberg: A Retrospective*, pp. 206–223.

Krauss, Rosalind. "Rauschenberg and the Materialized Image." *Artforum* 13, no. 4 (December 1974): 36–43.

Mamiya, Christin J. "We the People: The Art of Robert Rauschenberg and the Construction of American National Identity." *American Art* 7, no. 3 (Summer 1993): 41–63.

Mattison, Robert S. *Robert Rauschenberg: Breaking Boundaries*. New Haven: Yale University Press, 2003.

Monahan, Laurie J. "Cultural Cartography: American Designs at the 1964 Venice Biennale." In Serge Guilbaut, ed., *Reconstructing Modernism: Art in New York, Paris, Montreal, 1945–1964*, pp. 369–416. Cambridge, Mass.: MIT Press, 1990.

O'Doherty, Brian. "Rauschenberg and the Vernacular Glance." *Art in America* 61, no. 5 (September–October 1973): 82–87.

Öhrner, Annika. "Recalling Pelican: On P. O. Ultvedt, Robert Rauschenberg and Two 'Ballets.'" *Konsthistorisk tidskrift* 76, nos. 1–2 (2007): 27–39.

Paxton, Steve. "Rauschenberg for Cunningham and Three of His Own." In Hopps and Davidson, *Robert Rauschenberg: A Retrospective*, pp. 260–267.

Pissarro, Joachim. *Cézanne/Pissarro, Johns/Rauschenberg: Comparative Studies on Intersubjectivity in Modern Art*. New York: Cambridge University Press, 2006.

Rauschenberg, Robert. Artist statement. In Dorothy Miller, ed., *Sixteen Americans*, p. 58. Exh. cat. New York: Museum of Modern Art, 1959.

Schimmel, Paul. "Autobiography and Self-Portraiture in Rauschenberg's Combines." In Schimmel, *Robert Rauschenberg: Combines*, pp. 211–228.

Schimmel, Paul, ed. *Robert Rauschenberg: Combines*. Exh. cat. Los Angeles: Museum of Contemporary Art, 2005.

Solomon, Alan R. *Robert Rauschenberg*. Exh. cat. New York: Jewish Museum, 1963.

Spector, Nancy. "Rauschenberg and Performance." In Hopps and Davidson, *Robert Rauschenberg: A Retrospective*, pp. 226–245.

Steinberg, Leo. *Encounters with Rauschenberg: A Lavishly Illustrated Lecture*. Houston: Menil Foundation, 2000.

Stenström, Emma. "Another Kind of Combine: Monogram and the Moderna Museet." *Konsthistorisk tidskrift* 76, nos. 1–2 (2007): 48–59.

Stuckey, Charles F. "Reading Rauschenberg." *Art in America* 65, no. 2 (March–April 1977): 74–84.

Sundell, Nina. *Rauschenberg/Performance: 1954–1984*. Exh. cat. Cleveland: Cleveland Center for Contemporary Art, 1983.

Tomkins, Calvin. "The Big Show in Venice." *Harper's Magazine* 230, no. 1379 (April 1965): 98–104.

Tomkins, Calvin. "Moving Out." *New Yorker* 40, no. 2 (February 29, 1964): 39–105.

Tomkins, Calvin. *Off the Wall: Robert Rauschenberg and the Art World of Our Time*. New York: Penguin Books, 1980.

Turrell, Julia Brown, ed. *Rauschenberg: Sculpture*. Exh. cat. Fort Worth: Modern Art Museum of Fort Worth, 1995.

Wainwright, Lisa. "Reading Junk: Thematic Imagery in the Art of Robert Rauschenberg from 1952 to 1964." Ph. D. diss., University of Illinois at Urbana-Champaign, 1993.

Widenheim, Cecilia. "A Goat's-Eye View: Monogram at the Moderna Museet." *Konsthistorisk tidskrift* 76, nos. 1–2 (2007): 40–47.

Yakush, Mary, ed. *ROCI: Rauschenberg Overseas Culture Interchange. Exh. cat.* Washington, D.C.: National Gallery of Art, 1991.

Young, Joan, with Susan Davidson. "Chronology." In Hopps and Davidson, *Robert Rauschenberg: A Retrospective*, pp. 550–587.

2. Other English-Language Sources

Abeel, Erica. "Daedalus at the Rollerdrome." *Saturday Review,* August 28, 1965, 51–53.

Alighieri, Dante. *The Inferno.* Translated by John Ciardi. New York: Penguin Books, 1954.

Alloway, Lawrence. *The Venice Biennale 1895–1968: From Salon to Goldfish Bowl*. Greenwich, Conn.: New York Graphic Society, 1968.

Anderson, Benedict. *Imagined Communities: Reflections on the Origin and Spread of Nationalism*. Rev. ed. London: Verso, 1991.

Anderson, Benedict. *Under Three Flags: Anarchism and the Anti-colonial Imagination*. London: Verso, 2005.

Anderson, Jaynie, ed. *Crossing Cultures: Conflict, Migration and Convergence.* Proceedings of the 32nd International Congress of the History of Art. Melbourne: Miegunyah Press, 2009.

Andersson, Patrik. "Euro-Pop: The Mechanical Bride Stripped Bare in Stockholm, Even." Ph.D. diss., University of British Columbia, 2001.

Appadurai, Arjun. *Modernity at Large: Cultural Dimensions of Globalization*. Minneapolis: University of Minnesota Press, 1996.

Ashbery, John. "Art News from Paris." *ARTnews* 63, no. 5 (September 1964): 50–51.

Ashbery, John. "Venice Biennale: Center of Controversy." *New York Herald Tribune*, Paris edition, June 23, 1964, p. 5.

Baro, Gene. "The Canal Goes Pop." *International Herald Tribune*, June 28, 1964.

Baro, Gene. "The Venice Biennale." *Arts Magazine* 38, no. 10 (September 1964): 32–37.

Bhabha, Homi K. *The Location of Culture*. London: Routledge, 1994.

Bochner, Mel. "Robert Rauschenberg." *Arts Magazine* 40, no. 5 (March 1966): 50.

Brown, Carolyn. *Chance and Circumstance: Twenty Years with Cage and Cunningham*. New York: Alfred A. Knopf, 2007.

Buchloh, Benjamin H.D. "Allegorical Procedures: Appropriation and Montage in Contemporary Art." *Artforum* 21, no. 1 (September 1982):43–56.

Burstow, Robert. "The Limits of Modernist Art as a Weapon of the Cold War: Reassessing the Unknown Patron of the Monument to the Unknown Political Prisoner." *Oxford Art Journal* 20, no. 1 (1997): 68–80.

Cabañas, Kaira. "Toward a Performative Realism: Art in France, 1957–1962." Ph. D. diss., Princeton University, 2007.

Cage, John. *Silence*. Middletown, Conn.: Wesleyan University Press, 1961.

Campbell, Lawrence. "Robert Rauschenberg." *ARTnews* 59, no. 9 (January 1961): 13–14.

"Carnival in Venice." *Newsweek*, 64, no. 1 (July 6, 1964): 74–75.

Cockcroft, Eva. "Abstract Expressionism, Weapon of the Cold War." *Artforum* 12, no. 10 (June 1974): 39–41.

Cone, Michéle C. "Pierre Restany and the Nouveaux Réalistes." *Yale French Studies*, no. 98 (2000): 50–65.

Constable, Rosalind. "Art Pops In: Europe Explodes as American Takes Prize." *Life* 57, no. 2 (July 10, 1964): 65–66, 68.

Cox, Annette. *Art-as-Politics: The Abstract Expressionist Avant-Garde and Society*. Ann Arbor, Mich.: UMI Research Press, 1982.

Crimp, Douglas. "On the Museum's Ruins." *October* 13 (Summer 1980): 41–57.

Cunningham, Merce. "Story: Tale of a Dance and Tour." Parts 1–3. *Dance Ink* 6, no. 1 (Spring 1995): 14–21; no. 2 (Summer 1995): 18–22; and no. 3 (Fall 1995): 32–36.

De Chassey, Eric. "Paris–New York: Rivalry and Denial." In *Paris: Capital of the Arts, 1900–1968*, pp. 344–351. Exh. cat. London: Royal Academy of Arts, 2002.

De Coppet, Laura, and Alan Jones, eds. *The Art Dealers*. New York: Cooper Square Press, 2002.

De Marchis, Giorgio. "The Significance of the 1964 Venice Biennale." *Art International* 8, no. 9 (November 25, 1964): 21–23.

"Dr. Solomon Dies at 49: Ex-Director of Jewish Museum." *New York Times*, February 19, 1970, p. 47.

Elderfield, John, ed. *The Museum of Modern Art at Mid-Century: At Home and Abroad*. Studies in Modern Art, no. 4. New York: Museum of Modern Art, 1994.

Elkins, James, ed. *Is Art History Global?* New York: Routledge, 2007.

Elkins, James. Review of *Real Spaces: World Art History and the Rise of Western Modernism* by David Summers. *Art Bulletin* 86, no. 2 (June 2004): 373–381.

Elkins, James, Alice Kim, and Zhivka Valiavicharska, eds. *Art and Globalization*. University Park: Penn State University Press, forthcoming.

Elliot, David, Theresa Hahr, Carl-Fredrik Hårleman, Henrik Orrje, Left Wigh, and Nina Öhman. *Moderna Museet–Modern Museum*. London: Scala Books, 1998.

"The Endless Fascination of Water." *Sports Illustrated* 9, no. 9 (September 1, 1958): 34–37.

Franc, Helen M. "The Early Years of the International Program and Council." In Elderfield, *The Museum of Modern Art at Mid-Century*, pp. 108–149.

Genauer, Emily. "The Merchandise of Venice." *New York Herald Tribune*, July 12, 1964, Sunday Magazine section, p. 21.

Genauer, Emily. "Rauschenberg's Drawings for Dante's *Inferno*." *New York Herald Tribune*, December 25, 1965, p. 7.

Gendel, Milton. "Hugger-Mugger in the Giardini." *ARTnews* 63, no. 5 (September 1964): 32–35, 53.

Gilbert, Milton. "The Gold-Dollar System: Conditions of Equilibrium and the Price of Gold." In Barry Eichengreen and Marc Flandreau, eds., *The Gold Standard in Theory and History*, pp. 291–326. London: Routledge, 1997.

Giunta, Andrea. *Avant-Garde, Internationalism, and Politics: Argentine Art in the Sixties*. Durham: Duke University Press, 2007.

Glazer, Bruce. "Questions to Stella and Judd." *ARTnews* 65, no. 5 (September 1966): 55–61.

Greenberg, Clement. *Art and Culture*. Boston: Beacon Press, 1961.

Greenberg, Clement. *The Collected Essays and Criticism*. Vols. 2–3. Ed. John O'Brian. Chicago: University of Chicago Press, 1986 and 1993.

Guilbaut, Serge. *How New York Stole the Idea of Modern Art: Abstract Expressionism, Freedom, and the Cold War*. Chicago: University of Chicago Press, 1983.

Guilbaut, Serge, ed. *Reconstructing Modernism: Art in New York, Paris, Montreal, 1945–1964*. Cambridge, Mass.: MIT Press, 1990.

Hess, Thomas B. "Collage as an Historical Method." *ARTnews* 60, no. 7 (October 1961): 31–33, 69–71.

Hughes, Robert. *The Shock of the New*. 1981; reprinted, New York: Alfred A. Knopf, 1998.

Hunter, Sam. "Alan Solomon: 1920–1970." *New York Times*, March 1, 1970, section II, p. 26.

"It's What We Volunteered For." *Life* 44, no. 3 (May 5, 1958): 21–25.

Jameson, Frederic, and Masao Miyoshi, eds. *The Cultures of Globalization*. Durham: Duke University Press, 1998.

Janis, Sidney, ed. *The New Realists*. New York: Sidney Janis Gallery, 1962.

Jensen, Robert. *Marketing Modernism in Fin-de-Siècle Europe*. Princeton: Princeton University Press, 1994.

Johnson, Ellen H. "The Living Object." *Art International* 7, no. 1 (January 25, 1963): 42–45.

Kampf, Avram. "The Jewish Museum: An Institution Adrift." *Judaism* 17, no. 3 (Summer 1968): 282–298.

Kaufmann, Thomas DaCosta. *Toward a Geography of Art*. Chicago: University of Chicago Press, 2004.

Kimmelman, Michael. "Revisiting the Revisionists: The Modern, Its Critics and the Cold War." In Elderfield, *The Museum of Modern Art at Mid-Century*, pp. 38–55.

Kozloff, Max. "American Painting during the Cold War." *Artforum* 11, no. 9 (May 1973): 43–54.

Kozloff, Max. Letter to the editor. *Art Interna*tional 7, no. 6 (June 25, 1963): 88–92.

Krauss, Rosalind. *The Optical Unconscious*. Cambridge, Mass.: MIT Press, 1993.

Kuisel, Richard. *Seducing the French: The Dilemma of Americanization*. Berkeley: University of California Press, 1993.

Kwon, Miwon. *One Place after Another: Site-Specific Art and Locational Identity*. Cambridge, Mass.: MIT Press, 2002.

Logevall, Fredrik. "The Swedish-American Conflict over Vietnam." *Diplomatic History* 17, no. 3 (Summer 1993): 421–445.

Lundström, Anna. "Comments on 4 Americans." *Konsthistorisk tidskrift* 76, nos. 1–2 (2007): 112–113.

Martinez, Rosa, and Maria de Corral. *Always a Little Further: 51st International Art Exhibition. Exh. cat.* Venice: Biennale di Venezia, 2005.

McLuhan, Marshall. *The Mechanical Bride: Folklore of Industrial Man.* 1951; reprinted, Corte Madera, Calif.: Gingko Press, 2002.

Menand, Louis. "Unpopular Front: American Art and the Cold War." *New Yorker* 81, no. 32 (October 17, 2005): 174–179.

Merewether, Charles, with Rika Iezumi Hiro, eds. *Art, Anti-Art, Non-Art: Experimentations in the Public Sphere in Postwar Japan, 1950–1970.* Exh. cat. Los Angeles: Getty Research Institute, 2007.

Michelson, Annette. "The 1964 Biennale." *Art International* 8, no. 7 (September 25, 1964): 38–40.

Miller, Dorothy, ed. *Sixteen Americans.* Exh. cat. New York: Museum of Modern Art, 1959.

Mitter, Partha. "Interventions: Decentering Modernism: Art History and Avant-Garde from the Periphery." *Art Bulletin* 90, no. 4 (December 2008): 531–548.

Mitter, Partha. *The Triumph of Modernism: India's Artists and the Avant-Garde, 1922–1947.* London: Reaktion Books, 2007.

Mullins, Edwin. "Not Just a Joker." *Sunday Telegraph* (London), February 9, 1964, p. 11.

Munroe, Alexandra. *Japanese Art after 1945: Scream against the Sky. Exh. cat.* New York: Solomon R. Guggenheim Museum, 1994.

O'Doherty, Brian. *American Masters: The Voice and the Myth.* New York: Random House, 1973.

Ogbechie, Sylvester Okwunodu. *Ben Enwonwu: The Making of an African Modernist.* Rochester, N.Y.: University of Rochester Press, 2008.

"Oh, Say Can You See?" *Time* 87, no. 2 (January 14, 1966): 70–71.

Onians, John, ed. *Atlas of World Art.* Oxford: Oxford University Press, 2004.

O'Reilly, John. "The Great Migrator." *Sports Illustrated* 8, no. 18 (April 21, 1958): 60–63.

Orton, Fred. *Figuring Jasper Johns.* London: Reaktion Books, 1994.

Owens, Craig. "The Allegorical Impulse: Toward a Theory of Postmodernism." Parts 1–2. *October*, no. 12 (Spring 1980): 67–86; and no. 13 (Summer 1980): 59–80.

Owens, Craig. *Beyond Recognition: Representation, Power and Culture.* Berkeley: University of California Press, 1992.

"Pop Goes the Biennale." *Time* 84, no. 1 (July 3, 1964): 54.

Prevots, Naima. *Dance for Export: Cultural Diplomacy and the Cold War.* Middletown, Conn.: Wesleyan University Press, 1998.

Pritchett, James. *The Music of John Cage.* Cambridge: Cambridge University Press, 1996.

Restany, Pierre. "A Metamorphosis in Nature." In Janis, *The New Realists*, not paginated.

Restany, Pierre. "Modern Nature." Translated by Joachim Neugroschel. In *Breakthroughs: Avant-Garde Artists in Europe and America, 1950–1990*, pp. 33–47. Exh. cat. Columbus, Ohio: Wexner Center for the Arts, 1991.

Richter, Gerhard. *The Daily Practice of Painting: Writings and Interviews 1962–1993*. Ed. Hans-Ulrich Obrist. Cambridge, Mass.: MIT Press, 1995.

Rickey, George. "The Kinetic International." *Arts Magazine* 35, no. 10 (September 1961): 16–19.

Robson, Deirdre. "The Market for Abstract Expressionism: The Time Lag between Critical and Commercial Acceptance." *Archives of American Art Journal* 25, no. 5 (1985): 19–23.

Rose, Barbara. "Dada Then and Now." *Art International* 7, no. 1 (January 25, 1963): 22–28.

Ruby, Sigrid. "The Give and Take of American Painting in Postwar Western Europe." In *Cahiers Charles V*, no. 28, special issue, "Transmission des valeurs nationales: Théories, individus, institutions (domaine anglo-américan)," ed. Marie-Jeanne Rossignol and Barbara Karsky (2000): 171–196.

Rudikoff, Sonya. "New Realists in New York." *Art International* 7, no. 1 (January 25, 1963): 38–41.

Sandler, Irving. *Abstract Expressionism and the American Experience: A Reevaluation*. Lenox, Mass.: Hard Press Editions, 2009.

Sandler, Irving. "Abstract Expressionism and the Cold War." *Art in America* 96, no. 6 (June/July 2008): 65–74.

Seitz, William C., ed. *The Art of Assemblage*. Exh. cat. New York: Museum of Modern Art, 1961.

Shannon, Joshua. *Disappearance of Objects: New York Art and the Rise of the Postmodern City*. New Haven: Yale University Press, 2009.

Shapiro, David, and Cecile Shapiro. "Abstract Expressionism: The Politics of Apolitical Painting." *Prospects* 3 (1977): 175–214.

Solnit, Rebecca. *The Secret Exhibition: Six California Artists of the Cold War Era*. San Francisco: City Light Books, 1990.

Solomon, Alan R. "Americans in Venice at the Biennale." *Art Gallery* 7, no. 9 (June 1964): 14–21.

Solomon, Alan R. "Jim Dine and the New Psychology of the New Art." *Art International* 8, no. 8 (October 20, 1964): 52–56.

Solomon, Alan R. "The New American Art." *Art International* 8, no. 2 (March 20, 1964): 50–55.

Solomon, Alan R. "The New Art." *Art International* 7, no. 7 (September 25, 1963): 37–41.

Solomon, Alan R. "Report on the American Participation in the XXXII Venice Biennale 1964." In U.S. Senate, *Congressional Record*, 89th Cong., 1st sess. (August 31–September 13, 1965), vol. 3, part 17, pp. 22563–22564.

Solomon, Alan R. *XXXII International Biennial Exhibition of Art Venice 1964, United States of America, The New American Art: Four Germinal Painters, Four Younger Artists. Exh. cat.* New York: Jewish Museum, 1964.

St. Clair, William. *Lord Elgin and the Marbles*. Oxford: Oxford University Press, 1998.

Steinberg, Leo. "Jasper Johns." *Metro,* nos. 4–5 (May 1962): 87–109.

Steinberg, Leo. *Other Criteria: Confrontations with Twentieth-Century Art*. London: Oxford University Press, 1972.

Steinberg, Leo. "Reflections on the State of Criticism." *Artforum* 10, no. 7 (March 1972): 37–49.

Summers, David. *Real Spaces: World Art History and the Rise of Western Modernism*. London: Phaidon, 2003.

Tiampo, Ming. *Gutai: Decentering Modernism*. Chicago: University of Chicago Press, 2010.

Tomii, Reiko. "Geijutsu on Their Minds: Memorable Words on Anti-Art." In Merewether, *Art, Anti-Art, Non-Art*, pp. 35–62.

Tomii, Reiko, ed. "1960s Japan: Art Outside the Box." Special issue of *Review of Japanese Culture and Society* (Jōsai University) 17 (December 2005).

Tomkins, Calvin. *The Bride and the Bachelors: Five Masters of the Avant-Garde*. New York: Penguin Books, 1976.

Tomkins, Calvin. "An Eye for the New." *New Yorker* 75, no. 42 (January 17, 2000): 54–64.

Tomkins, Calvin. "A Good Eye and a Good Ear." *New Yorker* 56, no. 14 (May 26, 1980): 40–72.

Tone, Lilian. "Chronology: 1961–1963." In Varnedoe, *Jasper Johns: A Retrospective*, pp. 191–201.

"Triumphs and Tribulations." *Sports Illustrated* 8, no. 19 (May 12, 1958): 20–21.

Tuchman, Phyllis. "American Art in Germany: The History of a Phenomenon." *Artforum* 9, no. 3 (November 1970): 58–69.

Van Damme, Wilfried, and Kitty Zijlmans, eds. *World Art Studies: Exploring Concepts and Approaches*. Amsterdam: Valiz, 2008.

Varnedoe, Kirk. *Jasper Johns: A Retrospective*. Exh. cat. New York: Museum of Modern Art, 1996.

Vaughan, David. "Adventures on a World Tour." *New York Times*, January 3, 1965, section 2, p. 13.

Vaughan, David. *Merce Cunningham: Fifty Years*. New York: Aperture, 1997.

Whitney, David, ed. *Leo Castelli: Ten Years*. New York: Leo Castelli Gallery, 1967.

3. French-Language Sources

Albert-Levin, Marc. "Art U.S.A. Now." *Cimaise* 11, nos. 69–70 (July–October 1964): 123.

Alvard, Julien. "Paris sans école." *Cimaise* 3, no. 1 (October–November 1955): 10–11.

Arnaud, Jean-Robert. "Mise à mort dans Venise La Rouge?" *Cimaise* 11, nos. 69–70 (July–October 1964): 104–105.

Bosquet, Alain. "Désarroi à Venise." *La Côte des Peintres* 2, no. 18 (July–August 1964): 29.

C., D. "Pop'Art & Dollars ou la semaine de Venise." *La Côte des Peintres* 2, no. 18 (July–August 1964): 24–27.

Cabañas, Kaira. "'Maigres et poussiéreux': Les nouveaux réalistes à New York." In *Le nouveau réalisme*, pp. 126–129. Exh. cat. Paris: Galeries nationales du Grand Palais, 2007.

Cabanne, Pierre. "À Venise, l'Amérique proclame la fin de l'École de Paris et lance le Pop'Art pour coloniser l'Europe." *Arts*, no. 968 (June 24–June 30, 1964).

Cabanne, Pierre. "Comment la France a perdu la première place sur le marché de l'art international." *Arts*, no. 986 (December 23, 1964–January 5, 1965): 5.

Cabanne, Pierre. "Les plus grands artistes revelés depuis 20 ans: 100 personnalités les ont choisis pour *Arts*." *Arts*, no. 1011 (June 23–July 6, 1965): 1–3.

Choay, Françoise. "Dada, Néo-dada, et Rauschenberg." *Art International* 5, no. 8 (October 20, 1961): 82–84, 88.

D., P. "Rauschenberg et son mouton." *Tribune de Lausanne*, February 10, 1963, p. 8.

Frigerio, Simone. "Rauschenberg." *Aujourd'hui*, no. 41 (May 1963): 38.

Gindertael, R. V. "Le complexe de l'École de Paris." *Cimaise* 3 no. 4 (March 1956): 9.

Hahn, Otto. "Pop Art and Happenings." *Les Temps Moderne*, no. 212 (January 1964): 1318–1331.

Harambourg, Lydia. *Georges Mathieu*. Neuchâtel: Editions Ides et Calendes, 2001.

Hultén, Pontus, ed. *Paris–New York: 1908–1968. Exh. cat.* Paris: Centre Georges Pompidou, 1977.

Jouffroy, Alain. "Barge." *Quadrum*, no. 15 (second issue, 1963): 99–106, 182.

Jouffroy, Alain. "Rauschenberg." *L'Oeil*, no. 113 (May 1964): 28–35, 68, 69.

Klüver, Billy, and Robert Rauschenberg. "Art en mouvement: Souvenir conjugués." In Olle Granath and Monica Nieckels, eds., *Le Moderna Museet de Stockholm à Bruxelles*, pp. 35–40. Brussels: Palais des Beaux-Arts, 1981.

Lévêque, Jean-Jacques. "Otto Hahn: Le terrorisme américain a secoué Paris." *Arts*, no. 985 (December 16–22, 1964).

M., J. "À travers les galeries." *Le Monde*, February 8, 1963, p. 9.

Martel, Frédéric. *De la culture en Amérique*. Paris: Éditions Gallimard, 2006.

Pacquement, Alfred. "Leo Castelli, Daniel Cordier, Ileana Sonnabend: Le rôle des galeries." In Hultén, *Paris–New York: 1908–1968*, pp. 173–178.

Parinaud, André. "Un 'misfit' de la peinture new-yorkaise se confesse." *Arts*, no. 821 (May 10, 1961): 18.

Pierre, José. "Où va l'art abstrait?" *Combat*, no. 79 (June 5, 1961): 2.

"Le première exposition Rauschenberg à Paris, Galerie Daniel Cordier." In Hultén, *Paris–New York: 1908–1968*, p. 580.

Ragon, Michel. "L'art actuel aux États-Unis." *Cimaise* 6, no. 3 (January–March 1959): 6–35.

Ragon, Michel. "L'École de Paris se porte bien." *Cimaise* 3, no. 2 (December 1955): 17.

Ragon, Michel. "L'École de Paris va-t-elle démissionner?" *Arts*, no. 969 (July 1–July 6, 1964).

Ragon, Michel. "Expositions: L'avant-garde." *Arts*, no. 821 (May 10, 1961).

Ragon, Michel. "Rauschenberg: La vedette de l'École de New York." *Arts*, no. 1011 (June 23–July 6, 1965): 4.

Restany, Pierre. *Avec le nouveau réalisme sur l'autre face de l'art*. Nîmes: Éditions Jacqueline Chambon, 2000.

Restany, Pierre. "Les Biennale contre l'École de Paris." *Galerie des Arts*, no. 18 (July–September 1964): 12–21.

Restany, Pierre. "Chelsea 1960." In Hultén, *Paris–New York: 1908–1968*, pp. 142–157.

Restany, Pierre. "Jasper Johns et la métaphysique du lieu commun." *Cimaise* 9, no. 55 (September–October 1961): 90–97.

Restany, Pierre. "Le nouveau réalisme à la conquête de New York." *Art International* 7, no. 1 (January 1963): 29–36.

Restany, Pierre. "U.S. Go Home and Come Back Later." *Cimaise* 6, no. 3 (January–March 1959): 36–37.

Revel, Jean-François. "XXIIe Biennale de Venise: 'Triomphe de réalisme nationaliste.'" *L'Oeil*, nos. 115–116 (July–August 1964): 2–11.

Robert Rauschenberg. Exh. cat. Paris: Galerie Daniel Cordier, 1961.

Robert Rauschenberg. Exh. cat. Paris: Galerie Ileana Sonnabend, 1963.

Tapié, Michel. *Un art autre, où il s'agit de nouveaux dévidages du réel*. Paris: Gabriel-Giraud et Fils, 1952.

Van der Marck, Jan. "Le nouveau réalisme et sa reception outre-Atlantique." In *Le nouveau réalisme*, pp. 15–24. Paris: Édition du Jeu de Paume, 1999.

Wescher, Herta. "À l'École de Paris." *Cimaise* 3, no. 3 (January–February 1956): 16.

4. German-Language Sources

"Es wird ein Rauschen um Rauschenberg geben." *Neue Rhein-Zeitung*, September 14, 1964.

Honisch, Dieter, and Jens Christian Jensen, eds. *Amerikanische Kunst von 1945 bis heute: Kunst der USA in europäischen Sammlungen*. Cologne: Dumont Buchverlag, 1976.

Jahre, Lutz, ed. *Das gedruckte Museum von Pontus Hultén: Kunstausstellungen und ihre Bücher*. Bonn: Kunst- und Ausstellungshalle der Bundesrepublik Deutschland, 1995.

Klapheck, Anna. "Pop Art, die nicht provoziert." *Rheinische Post Allgemeiner Teil*, September 17, 1964.

Lämmel, Josef Otto. "Bilder der vorbeiflutenden Welt." *Volksblatt*, July 25, 1964.

Vellinghausen, Albert Schulze. "Auf dem Weg zur Sublimierung." *Frankfurter Allgemeine Zeitung*, October 9, 1964.

W., D. "Kein Kinderschreck, auch keine Offenbarung." *Westdeutsche Zeitung*, October 7, 1964.

5. Italian-Language Sources

Argan, Giulio Carlo. "Arte d'oggi nei musei." In *Catalogo della XXXII Esposizione Biennale Internazionale d'Arte Venezia*, pp. 9–13. Exh. cat. Venice: Biennale di Venezia, 1964.

Argan, Giulio Carlo. *Oltre l'informale. Exh. cat.* San Marino: San Marino Biennale., 1963.

Barilli, Renato. "L'Inferno di R. Rauschenberg." *Linea Struttura*, no. 1 (1966): 77–79.

Barozzi, Paolo. "L'Inferno di Rauschenberg." *Tempo Presente*, July 1965, 63–66.

Del Gaizo, Vittorio. "Rauschenberg illustratore di Dante." *Opera Aperta* 1, no. 2 (March 1965): 144–146.

Fedler, Walter. "Lettere dalla Germania." *D'Ars Agency* 6, no. 1 (January 20, 1965): 91.

Guasco, Renzo. "La XXXII Biennale d'Arte Venezia." *Radio Corriere*, June 28, 1964, 14–15.

Guzzi, Virgilio. "Troppe americanate." *Il Tempo,* June 20, 1964.

Macorini, Edgardo. "Le illustrazioni di Rauschenberg per l'Inferno di Dante." *Domus*, no. 431 (October 1965): 41–47.

Mi., Da. "Venezia: Oggi si apre la Biennale." *L'Unità*, June 20, 1964, p. 6.

"Noi paghiamo per queste buffonate." *Epoca*, no. 718 (June 28, 1964): 26–29.

Passoni, Franco. "Non ci piace perché contiene i germi di un nuovo fascismo." *Avanti,* August 2, 1964.

Piovene, Guido. "Astrattismo e 'pop-art' hanno un valido significato." *La Stampa*, July 21, 1964.

Pisu, Renata. "Tutto è perduto, anche il pudore." *ABC*, June 28, 1964, pp. 8–11.

Restany, Pierre. "La XXXII Biennale di Venezia, Biennale della irregolarità." *Domus*, no. 417 (August 1964): 27–40, 42.

Solomon, Alan R. Commissioner Statement. In *Catalogo della XXXII Esposizione Biennale Internationale d'Arte Venezia*, pp. 275–276. Exh. cat. Venice: Biennale di Venezia, 1964.

6. Swedish-Language Sources

Ahlsén, Bo, Karl Olof Björck, Margareta Carlstedt, Sten Dunér, Pär Stolpe, and Per Olof Ultvedt. "Debatten om New York Collection: 'Restlager på Moderna Museet'" [Debate on the New York Collection: "Left-over Stock at the Moderna Museet"]. *Dagens Nyheter*, November 18, 1973.

Åström, Lars Erik. "Bild och Liv i USA" [Image and Life in the U.S.A.]. *Svenska Dagbladet*, March 17, 1962.

Bæckström, Tord. "Fyre amerikaner på Moderna Museet" [Four Americans at the Moderna Museet]. *Göteborgs Posten*, March 29, 1962.

Björk, Karl Olov, Margareta Carlstedt, Sten Dunér, Bror Marklund, and Per Olof Ultvedt. "Det finns en värld utanför axeln Paris–New York" [There Is Also a World beyond the Paris–New York Axis]. *Dagens Nyheter*, June 27, 1972.

Fahlström, Öyvind. "The Art of Assemblage." *Konstrevy*, nos. 5–6 (1961): 227.

Granath, Olle, and Monica Nieckels, eds. *Moderna Museet 1958–83. Exh. cat.* Stockholm: Moderna Museet Press, 1983.

Hultberg, Teddy, ed. *Fylkingen: Ny musik & intermediakonst, 1933–1993* [*Fylkingen: New Music and Intermedia Art, 1933–1993*]. Stockholm: Fylkingen, 1994.

Hultén, Pontus. "Fem fragment ur Moderna Museet's historia" [Five Fragments from Moderna Museet's History]. In Granath and Nieckels, *Moderna Museet 1958–83*, pp. 30–57.

Hultén, Pontus, ed. *4 amerikanare: Alfred Leslie, Jasper Johns, Robert Rauschenberg, Richard Stankiewicz* [4 Americans: Alfred Leslie, Jasper Johns, Robert Rauschenberg, Richard Stankiewicz]. Exh. cat. Stockholm: Moderna Museet, 1962.

Hultman, Marianne, ed. *Teknologi för livet: Om Experiments in Art and Technology* [Technology for Life: On Experiments in Art and Technology]. Exh. cat. Norrköping: Norrköpings Konstmuseum, 2004.

Linde, Ulf. "Den Öppna konsten: Arvet från Munchen" [The Open Art: The Inheritance from Munich]. *Dagens Nyheter*, March 26, 1965, p. 4.

Linde, Ulf. "Den Öppna konsten: Den bild 'man' har" [The Open Art: The Picture "One/Man" Has]. *Dagens Nyheter*, April 4, 1965, p. 4.

Linde, Ulf. "Den Öppna konsten: Dialogue utan slut" [The Open Art: A Dialogue without an End]. *Dagens Nyheter*, May 13, 1965, p. 4.

Linde, Ulf. "Den Öppna konsten: Myten om den historielösa formen" [The Open Art: The Myth Surrounding the Ahistorical Man]. *Dagens Nyheter*, March 30, 1965, p. 4.

Linde, Ulf, and Olof Lagercrantz. "En Amerikan i hel vetet" [An American in Hell]. *Dagens Nyheter*, March 23, 1965.

Osbornson, Harry. "Konst på farliga vägar" [Art on Dangerous Roads]. *Smålandsposten*, April 12, 1962, p. 5.

Rasmusson, Ludvig. "Den Amerikanska konstens dekadens och den svenska konstens följdekter" [The Decadence of American Art and Its Ripple Effect on Swedish Art]. *Paletten*, no. 209 (February 1992): 24–27.

Widding, Lars. "Moderna Museet har blivit ett konstens Gröna Lund" [The Moderna Museet Has Become Art's Gröna Lund]. *Expressen*, March 25, 1962.

Zennström, Per-Olov. "Amerikanare i farten" [Americans in Motion]. *Dagens Nyheter*, April 6, 1962.

7. Japanese-Language Sources

Akasegawa, Genpei 赤瀬川原平. *Hangeijutsu anpan* 反芸術アンパン [Anti-Art Independent]. Tokyo: Chikuma Shobō, 1994, pocketbook edition.

Akasegawa, Genpei 赤瀬川原平. *Tokyo mikisā keikaku: Hai Reddo Sentā chokusetsu kōdō no kiroku* [Tokyo Mixer Plans: Documents of Hi Red Center's Direct Actions]. Tokyo: Chikuma Shobō, 1994, pocketbook edition.

Akiyama, Kuniharu 秋山邦晴. "Soko wa 60-nendai zen'ei geijutsu no shingenchi datta" そこは60年代前衛芸術の震源地だった [Sōgetsu Art Center: Ground Zero of the Sixties' Avant-garde]. In Nara et al., *Kagayake 60-nendai: Sōgestu āto sentā no zen kiroku*, pp. 33–66.

Ebara, Jun 江原順, Kusuo Shimizu 志水楠男, and Toshinobu Onosato オノサトトシノブ. "Amerika bijutsu no shōri: Nihon sakka mo suijun o nuku" アメリカ美術の勝利：日本作家も水準を抜く [American Art Is the Victor, Japanese Artists Are above Standard]. *Yomiuri shinbun*, July 6, 1964, evening edition, p. 9.

Gogota, Hisanori 後々田寿徳. "Kojima Nobuaki no sakuhin" 小島信明の作品 [Introduction: "Nobuaki Kojima"]. In *Fukui no bijutsu, gendai*, vol. 1: *Kojima Nobuaki* 福井の美術・現代 vol. 1: 小島信明 [Aspects of Fukui Contemporary Art, vol. 1: Nobuaki Kojima]. Exh. cat. Fukui: Fukui Fine Arts Museum, 1990.

Jensen, Robert ロバート・ジェンセン. "Denpa no sokudo: Kyubisumu, nashonarizumu, toransunashonarizumu" 伝播の速度: キュビスム、ナショナリズム、トランスナショナリズム [Velocity: Cubism, Nationalism, and Transnationalism, translated by Yūsuke Isotani]. *Seiyō bijutsu kenkyū* 西洋美術研究 [Studies in Western Art], no. 14 (2008): 82–105.

Kajiya, Kenji 加治屋健司. "Gosadō suru buki: Kuremento Gurīnbāgu, bunka reisen, gurōbarizēshon" 誤作動する武器: クレメント・グリーンバーグ、文化冷戦、グローバリゼーション [Malfunctioning Weapon: Clement Greenberg, the Cultural Cold War, and Globalization]. *Amerika kenkyū* アメリカ研究 [American Review], no. 37 (March 2003): 83–105.

Kamon, Yasuo 嘉門安雄. "Venisu nikki" ヴェニス日記 [Venice Diary]. *Geijutsu seikatsu* 芸術生活 [Art Life], no. 198 (September 1964): 80–84.

Katō, Mizuho 加藤瑞穂. "Nihon ni okeru Anforumeru no juyō" 日本におけるアンフォルメルの受容 [The Reception of Informel in Japan]. In *Sōgetsu to sono jidai 1945–1970* 草月とその時代 1945–1970 [Sōgetsu and Its Era, 1945–1970], pp. 88–98. Exh. cat. Ashiya: Ashiya City Museum of Art & History, 1998.

Kuwabara, [Sumio] 桑原[住雄]. "Amerika no bijutsuka 4: Poppu āto no yūbi na genkyō—Raushenbāgu" アメリカの美術家4: ポップ・アートの優美な元凶—ラウシェンバーグ [American Artists, no. 4: Rauschenberg—Elegant Culprit of Pop Art]. *Tokyo shinbun* 東京新聞, July 29, 1963.

Miyakawa, Atsushi 宮川淳. "Hangeijutsu: Nichijōsei e no kakō" 反芸術:日常性への下降 [Anti-Art: Its Descent to the Everyday]. *Bijutsu techō* 美術手帖 [Art Notebook], no. 234 (April 1964): 48–57.

Nakahara, Yūsuke 中原佑介. "Geijutsu ban 'yuku toshi kuru toshi'" 芸術版〈ゆく年くる年〉 [Art Version of "Passing Year, Coming Year"]. *SAC Jānaru* SACジャーナル [SAC Journal], no. 28 (December 25, 1962), not paginated.

Nakahara, Yūsuke 中原佑介. "Shinohara Ushio ron" 篠原有司男論 [Essay on Shinohara Ushio]. *Gendai bijutsu* 現代美術 [Contemporary Art], no. 3 (March 1965): 24–34.

Nakajima, Masatoshi 中嶋理壽. "Dōmoto Hisao: Nenpu" 堂本尚郎年譜 [Dōmoto Hisao: Chronology]. In *Dōmoto Hisao ten* 堂本尚郎展 [Hisao Dōmoto: Retrospective], pp. 146–158. Exh. cat. Kyoto: National Museum of Modern Art, Kyoto, 2005.

Nara, Yoshimi 奈良義巳, Noriko Nomura 野村紀子, Kaoruko Ōtani 大谷薫子, and Haruo Fukuzumi 福住治夫, eds. *Kagayake 60-nendai: Sōgestu āto sentā no zen kiroku* 輝け60年代：草月アートセンターの全記録 [The Glory of the Sixties: The Complete Records of the Sōgetsu Art Center]. Tokyo: Film Art, 2002.

Osaki, Shin'ichirō 尾崎信一郎. "Riarizumu to avangyarudo: Sengo no sai shuppatsu" リアリズムとアヴァンギャルド: 戦後の再出発 [Realism and Avant-garde: A Postwar Restart]. In *Nihon kingendai bijutsushi jiten* 日本近現代美術史事典 [Encyclopedia of Modern Japanese Art], supervised by Kōji Taki 多木浩二 and Teruo Fujieda 藤枝晃雄, pp. 86–99. Tokyo: Tokyo Shoseki, 2007.

Rauschenberg, Robert, and Yoshiaki Tōno ラウシェンバーグ、ロバート、東野芳明. "Zō ni sakuhin o kukuri tsuketari: Rokkī purojekuto o megutte" 象に作品をくくりつけたり: ロッキー・プロジェクトを巡って [Tying a Work of Art to an Elephant: About the ROCI Project]. In *Raushenbāg: Rokkī Nihon ten* ラウシェンバーグ: ROCI日本展 [Rauschenberg Overseas Culture Interchange], pp. 7–11. Exh. cat. Tokyo: Setagaya Museum of Art, 1986.

Segi, Shin'ichi 瀬木慎一. "Anforumeru o meguru sukyandaru" アンフォルメルをめぐるスキャンダル [A Scandal about Informel]. *Geijutsu shinchō* [New Trends in Art] 9, no. 2 (February 1958): 54–66.

Shinohara, Ushio 篠原有司男. *Zen'ei no michi* 前衛の道 [Avant-garde Road]. Tokyo: Bijutsu Shuppan-sha, 1968.

Shinohara, Ushio 篠原有司男. "Koka kōra puran episōdo" コカコーラプラン・エピソード ["Coca-Cola Plan" Episode]. Unpublished statement prepared for the exhibition "Takiguchi

Shūzo: Yume no hyōryū butsu" 瀧口修造: 夢の漂流物 [Shūzo Takiguchi: Drifting Objects on Dream], Toyama Prefectural Hall Museum, 2001.

Suga, Akira 菅章. "Tobei suru ātisuto tachi" 渡米するアーティストたち [Artists Migrating to America]. In *Neo-Dada JAPAN 1958–1998: Isozaki Arata to howaito hausu no menmen* ネオ・ダダJAPAN 1958–1998: 磯崎新とホワイトハウスの面々 [Neo-Dada JAPAN 1958–1998: Arata Isozaki and the Artists of "White House"], pp. 84–89. Exh. cat. Ōita: Ōita City Board of Education, 1998.

Tasaka, Hiroko, with ICC 田坂博子+ ICC. "E.A.T. katsudō nenpyō" E.A.T. 活動年表 [Brief Chronology of EAT]. In *E.A.T.: Geijutsu to gijutsu no jikken* E.A.T.: 芸術と技術の実験 [EAT: The Story of Experiments in Art and Technology], pp. 89–97. Exh. cat. Tokyo: NTT InterCommunication Center, 2003.

Tōno, Yoshiaki 東野芳明. "Yangā jenerēshon no bōken" ヤンガー・ジェネレーションの冒険 [The Adventures of the Younger Generation]. *Mizue* みづゑ [Watercolor], no. 659 (March 1960): 23–32.

Tōno, Yoshiaki 東野芳明. "Rōshenbāgu e no kōkai shitsumon kai: Shitsumon boshū ローシェンバーグへの公開質問会: 質問募集 [Call for Questions for Rauschenberg's Public Interview]. *Bijutsu techō*, no. 244 (November 1964): 103.

Tōno, Yoshiaki 東野芳明. "Kyōki to sukyandaru: Katayaburi no sekai no shinjin tachi" 狂気とスキャンダル: 型破りの世界の新人たち [Madness and Scandal: Fantastic New Faces of the World]. *Geijutsu shinchō* 10, no. 11 (November 1959): 104–112.

Tōno, Yoshiaki 東野芳明. "Amerika zen'ei geijutsu ron no tame no nōto" アメリカ前衛芸術論のためのノート [Notes for a Discussion of American Avant-garde Art]. *Ongaku geijutsu* 音楽芸術 [*Musical Art]* 18, no.7 (July 1960): 7–12.

Tōno, Yoshiaki 東野芳明. "Poppu āto to watashi: Raushenbāgu" ポップ・アートと私—ラウシェンバーグ [Pop Art and Myself: An Interview with Rauschenberg]. *Geijutsu shinchō*, no. 182 (February 1965): 58–61.

Tōno, Yoshiaki 東野芳明. "Robāto Raushenbāgu arui wa Nyūyōku no 'Jigoku hen'" ロバート・ラウシェンバーグあるいはニューヨークの"地獄篇" [Robert Rauschenberg, or the New York Inferno]. *Mizue*, no. 683 (February 1962): 42–56.

Tōno, Yoshiaki 東野芳明. "Raushenbāgu, kono itten: *Gōrudo sutandādo*" ラウシェンバーグ=この一点《ゴールド・スタンダード》 [This Work by Rauschenberg: *Gold Standard*]. *Bijutsu techō*, no. 294 (February 1968): 58–67.

Ueno, Masaaki 上野正章. "Kēji to Nihon: Sengo gendai ongaku no fuchi" ケージと日本: 戦後現代音楽の布置 [Cage and Japan: Mapping Postwar Contemporary Music]. Ph.D. diss., Osaka University, 1998.

INDEX

Note: Exhibitions are listed under venue. Page numbers in **boldface** indicate illustrations.

Abeel, Erica, 132
Abstract Expressionism, 7, 12, 21, 29, 34, 62, 79, 180, 197
  and Art Informel, 23–24, 223n31
  and assemblage art, 37
  and Combines by Rauschenberg, 29, 37, 46
  and Japanese art scene, 160, 163
  marketing of, 24, 40
Ahlsén, Bo
  "Debate on New York Collection," 144–146, **147**
Akasegawa, Genpei, 163
Akiyama, Kuniharu, 155, 181
Alloway, Lawrence, 37, 44
Ameline, Jean-Paul, 14
Anderson, David K., 40
Andersson, Patrik, 105
Anti-Art, 163, 202
Appadurai, Arjun, 202
Appel, Karl, 160
Argan, Giulio Carlo, 93, 94
Arman, 31, 34, 38, 44, 94, 226n93
Arnaud, Robert, 53
Art Informel, 23, 33, 34, 93–94
  and Abstract Expressionism, 23–24, 223n31
  decline of, and Pop Art, 98
  in Japan, 24, 99, 160–162
  marketing of, 24, 27, 223n21
  and Nouveau Réalisme, 34, 223n31
Ashbery, John, 53
Ashton, Dore, 96, 241n21
Auricchio, Laura, 79

Bangkok, Thailand
  Merce Cunningham Dance Company in, 7, 153
Barilli, Renato, 207
Baro, Gene, 95
Barozzi, Paolo, 80, 207, 209
Barr, Alfred, Jr., 14, 96, 138, 221n34, 222n10, 226n97, 238n79
Benjamin, Walter, 88
Bhabha, Homi K., 189, 197
Bhumibol, king of Thailand, 153
Bingham, Lois, 63, 92, 93, 101
Bissière, Roger, 51, 227n103
Björck, Karl Olof
  "Debate on New York Collection," 144–146, **147**
Bochner, Mel, 208
Bombay (Mumbai), India
  Merce Cunningham Dance Company in, 7, 153
Bontecou, Lee
  Untitled, **42**
Bosquet, Alain, 51
Braque, Georges, 93
Breton, André, 29
Brown, Carolyn, 58, 132, 240n3
  performing *Pelican* for First New York Theater Rally, **134**
Bryen, Camille, 23
Burri, Alberto, 94
Bykert Gallery, New York, 142

Cabanne, Pierre, 53
  "À Venise, L'Amérique proclame la fin de l'Ecole de Paris et lance le Pop'Art pour coloniser l'Europe," *Arts*, 51, **52**
Cage, John, 11, 44, 92, 129, 140–141, 153, 155, 185, 188, 202, 217n6, 223n25, 235n23
  collaborations with Rauschenberg, 10, 124

For John Cage (Rauschenberg), 168–169, **170–171**
and Japan, 162, 163, 168–169
0′00″ dedicated to toshi ichiyanagi and yoko ono, 168
Theater Piece, 168
Variations II, 35
Campbell, Lawrence, 208
Carlstedt, Margareta
"Debate on New York Collection," 144–146, **147**
Castelli, Leo, 21, 24–25, 43, 59, 129, 208. *See also* Leo Castelli Gallery
and international art market, 21, 25, 55
and Johns, 27, 40, 114
promotion of American artists, 27, 40–41, 114
and Rauschenberg, 19, 25, 40, 57, 138, 208
on Rauschenberg, 29
and Solomon, 25, 89, 92, 96
and Ileana Sonnabend, 19, 39, 40–41
on 1964 Venice Biennale, 69, 95, 96
César, 94, 228n124
Chamberlain, John, 34, 38
Butternut, **42**
exhibition, Galerie Ileana Sonnabend, 43
and 1964 Venice Biennale, 63, 69, 89, 231n76
Choay, Françoise, 44
Color Field painting, 40, 59, 62
"Construction of Boston, The" (Saint-Phalle, Rauschenberg, Tinguely), 35
Cordier, Daniel, 29–31, 53. *See also* Galerie Daniel Cordier; Cordier-Warren Gallery
Cordier-Warren Gallery, New York, 44, 53
Cranshaw, Roger, 116
Crow, Thomas, 14, 74, 79, 116, 117
Cunningham, Merce, 7, 10, 17, 185, 188, 202–203, 218n14. *See also* Merce Cunningham Dance Company
Story, 7, **8**, **9**, 58, 217n6
Summerscape, 58
Travelogue, 203
Dada, 29, 34, 35, 37, 62, 71
Rauschenberg on, 31
Dante Alighieri, 1, 39, 80, 81, 88, 206–208
Divine Comedy, illustrations of, 206–207 (*see also* Rauschenberg, Robert, works by: Dante Drawings; Rauschenberg, Robert, works by: *Drawings for Dante's 700th Birthday*)
de Kooning, Willem, 37, 97, 111
in exhibitions, 21, 23, 160, 222n9
De Marchis, Giorgio, 94, 98
Denny, Alice, 132, 237n61
Dine, Jim, 38, 43, 128, 129
exhibition, Galerie Ileana Sonnabend, 41
and 1964 Venice Biennale, 63, 69, 89, 231n76
Dōmoto, Hisao, 94, 223n21, 223n31
Dorfles, Gillo, 44
Drouin, René, 21
Dubuffet, Jean, 21, 162
Duchamp, Marcel, 29, 35, 38, 202
and assemblage art, 35–37, 111
and Kinetic Art, 109
Large Glass, replica by Linde, 109
Rotoreliefs, replicas by Linde and Ultvedt, 109
Dufy, Raoul, 93
Dunér, Sten
"Debate on New York Collection," 144–146, **147**
"Dynamisch Labyrint" (Dylaby) (Rauschenberg, Raysse, Saint-Phalle, Spoerri, Tinguely, Ultvedt), 39, 139

EAT. *See* Experiments in Art and Technology
Ebara, Jun, 98–99
Ernst, Max, 93
Experiments in Art and Technology (EAT), 142, 146, 209

Fahlström, Öyvind, 38, 129, 132, 237n66
and "Dylaby II," 139
Fautrier, Jean, 93, 161

"5 New York kväller" (Five New York Evenings), 103–105, 128, 129–140, 142
Poster for "Five New York Evenings" (Rauschenberg), 129, **130**
Rauschenberg performing *Elgin Tie* at, 133, **136–137**
Flagg, James Montgomery, 129
Fontana, Lucio, 94, 220n25
Francis, Sam, 160, 163, 181, 203, 223n31
exhibition, Moderna Museet, Stockholm, 114
Fried, Michael, 14, 96
Friedman, Martin, 92
Fylkingen, 105, 115, 163, 235n23
and Stockholm Festival, 142

Galerie Anderson-Mayer, Paris, 40
Galerie Daniel Cordier, Paris, 40, 53, 96
exhibition of Rauschenberg, 1, 19, 29–33, 40, 44, 109
"L'Exposition inteRnatiOnale du Surréalisme," 29
installation view with *Bed* by Rauschenberg, **16**, **28**
Galerie Ileana Sonnabend, Paris, 19, 39–50
advertisement for, in *L'Oeil*, 47, **50**
advertisements for, in *Art International*, 47, **48–49**
commercial aspects of, 41–44
"Dessins pop," 43
exhibition list, 41–43
"Pop art américain," 41, **42**
"Rauschenberg: Première exposition (oeuvres 1954–61)," 40, 41, 44, **45**, 46
"Rauschenberg: Seconde exposition (oeuvres 1962–63)," 41, 44, **46**
"Robert Rauschenberg: *Untitled* 1953–1954 and Thirty-four Dante Drawings," 43, 47, 80
Galerie Neufville, Paris, 40
Galerie Paul Facchetti, Paris exhibition of Pollock, 23, 40
Galerie Rive Droite
exhibitions of Johns, 27, 31
"Nouveau Réalisme à Paris et à New York," 34
Galleria dell'Ariete, Milan
exhibition of Rauschenberg, 114
Gaulle, Charles de, 29, 193
Geldzahler, Henry, 129
Genauer, Emily, 95, 208
Gendel, Milton, 95
Gilbert, Milton, 193
Gorky, Arshile, 23, 222n9
Grand Prize, Venice Biennale. *See* Venice Biennale (1964): International Grand Prize in Painting
Greenberg, Clement, 14, 62, 75, 96
Green Gallery, New York, 43
Gustav VI Adolf, king of Sweden, 142
Gutai Art Association, 160, 223n31
"The 6th Gutai Art Exhibition," Martha Jackson Gallery, 162, 223n21

Hahn, Otto, 54
"Pop Art and Happenings," 47
Hains, Raymond, 34, 38
Hammacher, Arno, 89
Hartung, Hans, 23, 93
Hay, Alex, 155, 184, 196, 240n5
Colorado Plateau, 132
performing *Pelican* for First New York Theater Rally, **134**
Hay, Deborah, 155, 184
Heller, Ben, 92
Hess, Thomas, 39
Hi Red Center, 163
Cleaning Event, 193, **194**
Homem, Antonio, 40
"Hommage à David Tudor" (Johns, Rauschenberg, Saint-Phalle, Tinguely), 35, **36**
Huelsenbeck, Richard, 37
Hughes, Robert, 116
Hultén, Pontus, 10, 43, **104**, 105, 109, 111, 157, 163
art collection of, 129
as director of Moderna Museet, 98, 105, 150, 234n2, 234n8
and *Elgin Tie*, 133, 138
and Klüver, 105, **108**, 109, 111, 138
and *Monogram*, 46, 105–107, 124

and “The New York Collection for Stockholm,” 142–146
promotion of American art, 111–114
on Rauschenberg, 33, 138
and Ileana Sonnabend, 105–107, 114, 128–129
Hunter, Sam, 89, 92, 93, 96, 231n57, 231n69

Ichiyanagi, Toshi, 168, 217n6
Indiana, Robert, 38
Informel. *See* Art Informel

Jackson, Martha, 40. *See also* Martha Jackson Gallery
Janis, Sidney, 21, 38, 41, 59. *See also* Sidney Janis Gallery
Japanese art scene, 157–168, 174, 175, 179, 200
and Abstract Expressionism, 160, 163
and European modernism, 157, 179
and “Informel whirlwind,” 24, 160–162
and New York art scene, 168, 175, 197
and originality versus imitation, 10, 174, 179–181, 189, 197
and Pop Art, 175, 180, 205
Yomiuri Independent Exhibition, 160, 163, 166–168, 242n41
Jewish Museum, New York
Johns retrospective, 25, 59, 114
Rauschenberg retrospective, 25, 44, 59, 114, 116
Solomon as director of, 25, 59, 99
“Toward a New Abstraction,” 59
Johansson, Ingmar, 109
Johns, Jasper, 25, 27, 29, 34, 37, 38, 47, 75, 107, 157, 162, 175, 236n48, 242n27
exhibition, Galerie Ileana Sonnabend, 40–41
exhibition, Leo Castelli Gallery, 24, 80
Flag, **26**, 27, 162, 166, 200
Flags, 40–41
Flags (1965), 166
“4 amerikanare” (4 Americans), Moderna Museet, **102**, 105, 111, **112–113**, 114–116, 128
“Hommage à David Tudor” (with Rauschenberg, Saint-Phalle, Tinguely), 35, **36**
and Japanese art scene, 162, 166, 175, 203
Painted Bronze, 196
and Pop Art, 37, 47, 62
posing with Kojima’s *Standing Figures*, 166, **167**, 189
reception in Paris, 27, 31, 40
retrospective, Jewish Museum, 59
and Shinohara, 166, 175, 197–200
Slow Fields, 129
Souvenir, 166
success of, 24, 27, 29, 80, 208
Target, 200
Target (made of real flowers), 35, **36**
Target with Plaster Casts, 29
Three Flags, 71, 166, 196
Two Flags, 69
and 1958 Venice Biennale, 27
and 1964 Venice Biennale, 63, 69, 71, 89, 93, 94
Watchman, 166
Joseph, Branden W., 132
Jouffroy, Alain, 33, 43, 44, 47
Judd, Donald, 14, 141
Untitled, 144

Kaidō, Hideo, 242n41
Kamon, Yasuo, 98–99, 231n57
Kandinsky, Vassily, 141, 237n59
Kaprow, Allan, 107, 109
Karp, Ivan, 41
Kassel, Germany
Documenta, 29, 206, 220n25
Kaufmann, Thomas DaCosta, 12
Kennedy, John F., 13, 63, 93, 97
and *Buffalo II*, 13, 69, 71, 93
and Dante Drawings, 80–81
Kertess, Klaus, 142
Kinetic Art, 35, 107–109
Kitaj, R. J., 94

Klein, Yves, 37, 38, 94, 157, 162, 163, 228n124
exhibition, Leo Castelli Gallery, 44
in Japan, 242n27
monochrome paintings, 34, 44, 141
Kline, Franz, 21, 111, 160, 222n9
Klüver, Billy, 105, 107, 109, 111, 114, 129, 132, 142, 146
and "The New York Collection for Stockholm," 142, 146
note to Hultén, 105, **108**, 138
Oracle (with Rauschenberg), 141
Kojima, Nobuaki
Standing Figure, 166, 184, **186**, 189, **192**, 196, **198**, 200, 244n83
Johns posing with, 166, **167**, 189
and "Twenty Questions for Bob Rauschenberg," 184, 189
Königsberg, Franklin, 142
Kootz, Samuel, 24
Kootz Gallery, New York, 24, 223n21
Kozloff, Max, 75
Krauss, Rosalind E., 79
Krefeld Museum, Germany, 94
exhibition of Rauschenberg, 206
Kunsthalle, Bern
"4 Americans," 114

Leo Castelli Gallery, New York, 21, 24–25, 43, 44, 138, 162
exhibition of Dante Drawings, 1, 208
exhibition of Johns, 24, 221n34
exhibition of Rauschenberg, 24, 59, 162, 221n34
Leslie, Alfred, 94
"4 amerikanare" (4 Americans), Moderna Museet, **102**, 105, 111, **112–113**, 114–116, 128
Lewis, Adrian, 116
Lichtenstein, Roy, 38, 40, 128, 129, 146, 175
exhibition, Galerie Ileana Sonnabend, 41
Foot Medication, 129
poster, "American Pop Art," 129
Lieberman, William, 200, 244n83
Life magazine, 69, 80, 208
"'It's What We Volunteered For,'" 74–75, **76–78**, 80, 117
"A Modern Inferno," **204**, 208, **210**
Linde, Ulf, 109, 115, 116, 138
criticism of open art, 140–141
Large Glass (Duchamp), replica of, 109
Rotoreliefs (Duchamp), replicas of (with Ultvedt), 109
Lloyd, Barbara, 155, 240n5
London, England, 53, 55, 128, 133, 206
Merce Cunningham Dance Company in, 7, 103, 105, 234n1
Louis, Morris, 40
and 1964 Venice Biennale, 63, 69, 96, 231n76
Louisiana Museum, Denmark, 105
"American Pop Art," 114, 128
"Art in Motion," 111
Ludwig, Peter, 43
Lundquist, Evert, 146

Macorini, Edgardo, 207
Malraux, André, 227n112
Manessier, Alfred, 93
Marcazzan, Mario, 88–89, 230n56
Marchiori, Giuseppe, 89, 93
Martel, Frédéric, 11, 218n10
Martha Jackson Gallery, New York, 223n21
"The 6th Gutai Art Exhibition," Martha Jackson Gallery, 162, 223n21
Mathieu, Georges, 23–24, 188, 228n124
and Art Informel, 27, 223n31
in Japan, 24, 160, 162, 174, 181, 203
Toyotomi Hideyoshi, creation of, 160, **161**
Matisse, Henri, 93, 157, 179
McCray, Porter, 21
McLuhan, Marshall, 174
Mendes, Murillo, 89
Merce Cunningham Dance Company, 11, 103, 201
conflict in, 155, 202–203
Rauschenberg as designer and stage manager, 7, 58, 89, 155
world tour of (1964), 6, 7–10, 11–12, 17, 51, 99, 153

in London, 7, 103, 234n1
in Paris, 7, 17
in Stockholm, 7, 103, 105, 128, 129, 139 (*see also* "5 New York kväller")
in Tokyo, 7, **8**, **9**, 10, 153–155, 181
in Venice, 7, 57–58, 89–92
Meyer, Franz, 89, 231n69
Michelson, Annette, 39–40, 96–97
Mili, Gjon
photographs of Picasso's *Space Drawing*, 133
Minami Gallery, Tokyo, 99, 163, 203
exhibition of Francis, 203
exhibitions of Johns, 166, 203
exhibition of Tinguely, 163
Mitter, Partha, 12
Moderna Museet, Stockholm, 10, 33, 43, 94, 98, 105, 107, 114, 129, 142, 146, 150, 163, 234n2. *See also* "5 New York kväller"; "New York Collection for Stockholm"
"American Pop Art," 114, 128–129
exhibition of Dante Drawings and *Monogram*, 140
exhibition of Oldenburg, 114, 141
exhibitions of American art, 111–115
exhibitions of Swedish artists, 146
"4 amerikanare" (4 Americans), **102**, 105, 111, **112–113**, 114–116, 128
Hon (She), 139, 141
logo of, 151, **151**
and *Monogram*, 115–116, 129, 138–139, 147
acquisition of, 10, 46, 105, 138
as symbol of Moderna Museet, **148**, 150–151
"Rörelse i konsten" (Art in Motion), 35, 107–111, 114, 129, 141
Black Market in, 109–111, **110**
Monk, Thelonious, 109
Morita, Shiryū, 160
Morris, Robert, 129, 142
Musée d'Art Moderne de la Ville de Paris
"Art USA Now," 53
Musée National d'Art Moderne, Paris, 53, 94
"Twelve Modern American Painters and Sculptors," 21, **22**
Museum of American Art (group), 69–70
Alan R. Solomon Gallery: "USA 64," installation view at 2005 Venice Biennale, 69, **70**
Museum of Modern Art, New York, 14, 21–23, 35, 92, 151, 200
acquisition of works by Rauschenberg, 46, 138, 206, 221n34, 226n97
"The Art of Assemblage," 35–37, 38, 111
exhibition of Dante Drawings, 206, 208
exhibitions abroad, 21–23, 111, 197, 206
"The Family of Man," 111
"The New Japanese Painting and Sculpture," 200
"Twelve Modern American Painters and Sculptors," 21
"Twenty Years of American Painting," 197, 200

Nakahara, Yūsuke, 168–169
Nakanishi, Natsuyuki, 163, 166
Nakaya, Fujiko, 169, 181, 188
National Gallery of Art, Washington
ROCI exhibition, 209
National Museum of Modern Art, Tokyo
"Twenty Years of American Painting," 197
Neo-Dada, 7, 34, 37, 62, 162, 179
marketing of, 24, 43
and Nouveau Réalisme, 34–35, 39
Neo Dada (group), 163, 168
Newman, Barnett, 141
New York City
art market in, 14, 24–25
avant-garde, promoted by Hultén, 10, 105–107, 114
European art shown in, 24
as new center of world art, 7, 14, 35, 37, 51–55, 71, 98, 105, 111, 162, 168, 175
Rauschenberg's reputation in, 29, 31, 59, 205–206, 208
rivalry with Paris, 19, 23, 24, 44, 51, 54
"New York Collection for Stockholm," 142–147
"Debate on New York Collection," 144–146, **147**
Mud Muse, installed, **145**, 146

Rauschenberg poster for, **143**, 144
Nilsson, Torsten, 140–141
Noland, Kenneth, 40, 141
and 1964 Venice Biennale, 63, 69, 89, 93, 96, 231n76
Nouveau Réalisme, 29, 31, 33, 34–39, 162, 175, 228n126
exhibitions of, 34, 35, 44, 128, 226n93
Novelli, Gastone, 93, 94

Oldenburg, Claes, 38, 43, 128, 129, 175
Cheese Slice, 129
and "Dylaby II," 139
exhibition, Galerie Ileana Sonnabend, 43
exhibition, Moderna Museet, 114, 128, 129, 141
Geometric Mouse, Scale A5/5, Aluminum, 3.6m High, 146
Hamburger and *Ice Cream Cone*, **42**
Ping Pong Table, 129
and 1964 Venice Biennale, 63, 69, 89
Ono, Yoko, 168
Onosato, Toshinobu, 99
O'Reilly, John
"The Great Migrator," *Sports Illustrated*, 1, **2**, 79–80, 81
Owens, Craig, 79, 88

Palme, Olof, 141, 144
Panza, Giuseppe, 25, 43, 114, 223n25
Paolozzi, Eduardo, 94
Parinaud, André, 33
interview of Rauschenberg, **30**, 31
Paris, France, 7, 10
American art in public collections, 54–55
art market in, 19–21, 25–27, 44, 53
art scene in, 19–21, 23, 29, 54, 160
Biennale, 29
exhibitions of American art in, 21–23, 27, 40, 41–47
and Grand Prize controversy, 10, 51–55, 95
Merce Cunningham Dance Company in, 7, 17
Rauschenberg in, 1, 19–21, 29–33, 51
Rauschenberg's reputation in, 19, 27–29, 31–34, 44, 47, 51, 54
reception of American art, 23, 27, 40, 47, 51, 205
rivalry with New York, 19, 23, 24, 44, 51, 54
Salon de Mai, 96, 99, 157
as world art center, 19–21, 37, 51–54, 93, 162
Pasadena Museum of Art, California
"Painting in New York: 1944–1969," 101
Paxton, Steve, 132, 155, 184, 237n61, 240n5
Jag vill gärna telefonera, 132
Picabia, Francis, 23
Picasso, Pablo, 37, 157, 179
Space Drawing, 133
Pierre, José, 33
Pincus-Witten, Robert, 33, 39
Pistoletto, Michelangelo
exhibition, Galerie Ileana Sonnabend, 43
Pollock, Jackson, 14, 23, 24, 31, 79, 111, 133, 160, 162, 206, 220n25, 222n9
exhibition, Galerie Paul Facchetti, 23, 40
"Jackson Pollock," Moderna Museet, 114
"Jackson Pollock: 1912–1956," 23
and Japan, 160, 162
reputation in Paris, 19, 23
"second Pollock," Rauschenberg as, 23, 27, 29
The Wooden Horse, 144
Ponti, Gio, 207
Pop Art, 7, 37–38, 47, 51, 62, 96, 128–129, 132, 157, 175, 207
"American Pop Art," Moderna Museet, 114, 128–129
and Japan, 157, 175, 180, 202
marketing of, 24, 43
"The New Realists," Sidney Janis Gallery, 37–39, **38**, 44, 59, 175
and "Nuova Figurazione," 94
"Pop art américain," Galerie Ileana Sonnabend, 41, **42**
and Rauschenberg, 47, 128, 139
at 1964 Venice Biennale, 63, 71, 94, 97–99
Prevots, Naima, 11

Ragon, Michel, 27–29, 31, 43, 44, 51, 53–54
Rainer, Yvonne, 129, 142
Rauschenberg, Robert
at Académie Julian, 19–21, 221n5
and Castelli, 19, 25, 29, 40, 57, 138, 208
as choreographer, 132
collaborations with Cage, 10, 124
conflict in Merce Cunningham Dance Company, 155, 202–203
as designer and stage manager, 7, **8**, 58, 89, 155 (*see also* Merce Cunningham Dance Company: world tour of)
and Hultén, 33, 46, 105–107, 138
international projects of (1970s–1980s), 209
in Paris, 1, 19–21, 29–33, 44–46, 51
as "second Pollock," 23, 27, 29
and Shinohara, 155, 174–181, 184, 189, 196–197, 200 (*see also* Shinohara, Ushio: "Imitation Art"; "Twenty Questions to Bob Rauschenberg")
and Solomon, 7, 10, 13, 71–74, 75, 116, 128 (*see also* Solomon, Alan R.: and Grand Prize for Rauschenberg)
postcard to Solomon, **100**, 101
and Ileana Sonnabend, 10, 19, 31, 44–46, 47, 92, 105, 128
and Steinberg, 25, 75, 96, 116–117, 124
in Stockholm, 7, 103, 105, 109, 129, 139 (*see also* "5 New York kväller")
and Tinguely, 35, 39, 109, 139
in Tokyo, 99, 155, **156**, 157, 166–174, 203 (*see also* "Twenty Questions to Bob Rauschenberg")
and Tōno, 155, 157, 162, 163, 173, 180, 181–185, 209
in Venice, 57–58, 89, 93 (*see also* Venice Biennale (1964): American Pavilion; Venice Biennale (1964): International Grand Prize in Painting)
Rauschenberg, Robert, works by. *See also* "Construction of Boston, The"; "Dynamisch Labyrint"; "5 New York kväller"; "Hommage à David Tudor"; "Twenty Questions to Bob Rauschenberg"
Allegory, 128
Automobile Tire Print (with Cage), 124
Axle, 244n2
Barge, 47
Bed, 29, 114, 115
installation at "L'Exposition inteRnatiOnale du Surréalisme," **16**, **28**
Black Market, 109–111, **110**
Buffalo II, 13, **68**, 69, 71, 74, 93
Canyon, 59
Charlene, 43, 44, 114, 128
acquired by Stedelijk Museum, 46, 105, 226n97
Coca-Cola Plan, 13, 163, 166, 174–175, **176**, 179–181
Course, 1, **3**, 81
Dante Drawings, 1, 13, 79–88, 140, 206–208. *See also* Rauschenberg, Robert, works by: *Drawings for Dante's 700th Birthday*
Canto II: The Descent, 1, **56**, 81, **83**
Canto XIV: Circle Seven, Round 3, The Violent against God, Nature, and Art, 81, **84**
Canto XVIII: Circle Eight, Malebolge, the Evil Ditches, the Fraudulent and Malicious; Bolgia 1, the Panderers and Seducers; Bolgia 2, the Flatterers, 81, **86**, 88
Canto XXXI: The Central Pit of Malebolge, the Giants, 1, 81, **85**
exhibitions of, 1, 43, 80, 114, 140, 206, 208
facsimile edition, 206–207
sources for, 80–88
Door, 109
Drawing for the New York Collection for Stockholm Poster, **143**, 144
Drawings for Dante's 700th Birthday, **204**, 208–209, **210**
Elgin Tie, 132–139
and *Monogram*, 138–139
Rauschenberg performing at Moderna Museet, 133, **136–137**
Erased De Kooning Drawing, 180, 181, 197

Factum I and *Factum II*, 180
First Landing Jump, 221n34
First Time Painting at "Hommage à David Tudor," 35, **36**
For John Cage, 168–169, **170–171**
Gift for Apollo, 114, 128
Gold Standard, **152**, 155, **159**, 181–196, **187**, **195**, 203
Rauschenberg creating, **182–183**, **190–191**
Hawk, 114
Johanson's Painting, 109
Migration, 217n2
Money Thrower for Tinguely's H.T.N.Y., 35, 129
Monogram, 10, 19, 43, 44, 59, 80, **106**, 107, 114, 115–128, 162
elements of, 74, 117, **118–120**, 124
and *Elgin Tie*, 138–139
first state, 117, **122**
homosexual interpretations of, 116, 138–139
and Moderna Museet, 10, 46, 105, 129, 138, 140, **148**, 150–151
and movement, 116–117, 124
postmodern interpretations of, 116, 138–139
Preliminary Study I, 117, **121**
Preliminary Study II, **123**, 124
reception in Stockholm, 107, 115–116, 146, 150–151
rejection by Museum of Modern Art, 46, 138, 226n97
second state, 124, **125**
Sketch for, 124, **126**
stages in creation of, 117–124
as symbol of American cultural invasion, 10, 146
Monogram: Preliminary Study I, 117, **121**
Monogram: Preliminary Study II, **123**, 124
Mud Muse, 146
installed in "The New York Collection for Stockholm," Moderna Museet, **145**
Odalisk, 80, 114
Oracle (with Klüver), 141
Pelican, 132
Rauschenberg, Hay, and Brown performing for First New York Theater Rally, **134**
Pilgrim, **32**, 33, 114
Poster for "5 New York Evenings," 129, **130**
Rebus, 114, 217n2
Rhyme, 117, 236n47
Short Circuit, 196
Shot Put, 132–133
Rauschenberg performing at Surplus Dance Theater, **135**
Sketch for Monogram, 124, **126**
Story, 103
Summer Storm, 124
Tokyo, 169, **172**, 173–174
Untitled ("Man with White Shoes"), 69, 71, **72–73**, 74–78, 79, 80
dating of, 74
sources of images, 74–78, 117
Untitled works, 43
White Paintings, 141
Winterpool, 114
Rauschenberg Overseas Culture Interchange (ROCI), 203, 209
Raysse, Martial, 31, 38
"Dynamisch Labyrint" (Dylaby) (with Rauschenberg, Saint-Phalle, Spoerri, Tinguely, Ultvedt), 39, 139
Renqvist, Torsten, 146
Restany, Paul, 23, 34–35, 37–39, 44, 94, 140, 175
on exhibitions of American art in Paris, 23, 111
on Grand Prize controversy, 51–54
and Johns, 27
Reuben Gallery, New York, 43
Rosenberg, Harold, 39, 62
Rosenquist, James, 38, 43, 128, 129, 200
exhibition, Galerie Ileana Sonnabend, 43
F111, 141
I Love You with My Ford, 129
Vestigial Appendage, **42**
Rothko, Mark, 21, 55, 141, 160
Rubin, Lawrence, 40

Saint-Phalle, Niki de, 34, 35, 109
"The Construction of Boston" (with Rauschenberg, Tinguely), 35
and "Dylaby II," 139
"Dynamisch Labyrint" (Dylaby) (with Rauschenberg, Raysse, Spoerri, Tinguely, Ultvedt), 39, 139
"Hommage à David Tudor" (with Johns, Rauschenberg, Tinguely), 35, **36**
Hon (She) (with Saint-Phalle, Ultvedt), 139, 141
Shooting Paintings, 34
Tir, 35, **36**
Sandberg, Willem, 39, 43, 105, 107, 234n6
São Paulo, Brazil
V Bienal de São Paulo, 29, 107
Sartre, Jean-Paul, 47
Schantz, Philip von, 146–150
Schifano, Mario, 38, 94
exhibition, Galerie Ileana Sonnabend, 41
Schimmel, Paul, 74
Scull, Ethel, 25
Scull, Robert, 25, 138, 226n97
Segal, George, 38, 128, 129, 175
exhibition, Galerie Ileana Sonnabend, 41
Segi, Shin'ichi, 160, 162
Seitz, William, 35–37, 92, 96
Shahn, Ben
exhibition, Moderna Museet, 114
Shattuck, Roger, 37
Shimizu, Kusuo, 99, 203
Shinohara, Ushio, 155, 160, 162, 163, 166, 168, 189, 197–202
Air Mail, 180, 196, 200, **201**
Avant-Garde Road, 175
The Beatles, 180, 196
Boxing Painting, 162, **164–165**, 174, 175
Coca-Cola Plan, 163, 166, 174–175, **177**, 179–181, 184, 196, 200, 244n85
Don Shorander with Four Gold Medals, 180
Drink More, 166, 175, **178**, 196
"Imitation Art," 163, 166, 174–181, 196–197, 202
Imitation Box, 196–197, **198**, **199**, 200
and Johns, 166
Lovely Lovely America, 180
Marcel Duchamp in Thought, 184, 196, **199**, 200–202
Oiran (Courtesan) series, 202
and Rauschenberg, 155, 174–181, 184, 189, 196–197, 200
Three Flags, 166
and "Twenty Questions to Bob Rauschenberg," 155, 184, **186**, 189
Sidney Janis Gallery, New York, 21
"American Vanguard for Paris," 21
"The New Realists," 37–38, **38**, 44, 59, 175
"Young Painters in the U.S. and France," **20**, 21
Sirikit, queen of Thailand, 153
Sköld, Otte, 234n2, 234n8
Smith, W. Eugene
"The Endless Fascination of Water," *Sports Illustrated*, 81, **87**, 88
Sōfū. *See* Teshigahara, Sōfū
Sōgetsu Art Center, Tokyo, 155, 163
and "Twenty Questions for Bob Rauschenberg," 168, 181
U.S.-Japan dance exchange workshop, 155, 240n5
Sōgetsu Art Museum, Tokyo, 203
Sōgetsu Hall, Tokyo, 163
murals for (Mathieu and Francis), 160, 181
Solnit, Rebecca, 37
Solomon, Alan R., 7, 59–71, 129, 132, 140, 157
and Castelli, 25, 69, 96
as commissioner of American Pavilion, Venice Biennale, 7, 10, 25, 47, 59, 62–71
commissioner's statement, 51–54, 71, 98, 111
and Grand Prize for Rauschenberg, 10, 51, 58, **60**, 63, 71, 88–94, 95, 96, 101
as Jewish Museum director, 25, 59, 99
later life, 99–101
and "The New American Art," 59–62, 75
postcard from Rauschenberg, **100**, 101
on Rauschenberg, 13, 62, 71–74, 75, 116, 128
Sonnabend, Ileana, **18**, 29, 33, 39, 97, 157. *See also* Galerie Ileana Sonnabend
and Castelli, 19, 39, 40–41
and Grand Prize controversy, 51, 96

and Hultén, 105–107, 114, 128–129
promotion of American art, 10, 19, 47, 55, 107, 114, 128–129
promotion of European art, 55
promotion of Rauschenberg, 10, 19, 47, 92, 105
on Rauschenberg, 31, 34, 46, 128
and Solomon, 47, 53
Sonnabend, Michael, 31, 39, 51
Soulages, Pierre, 21, 223n21, 228n124
Speyer, Darthea, 21–23, 35, 44
Spoerri, Daniel, 38, 43, 107
"Dynamisch Labyrint" (Dylaby) (with Rauschenberg, Raysse, Saint-Phalle, Tinguely, Ultvedt), 39, 139
Sports Illustrated, 1, 80
advertisement for golf clubs, 80, **82**
"The Endless Fascination of Water," 81, **87**, 88
"The Great Migrator," 1, **2**, 79–80, 81
"Triumphs and Tribulations," 1, **4**, 81
Springfeldt, Björn, 150, 151
Stäel, Nicolas de, 21
Stankiewicz, Richard, 34, 38, 94, 107
"4 amerikanare" (4 Americans), Moderna Museet, **102**, 105, 111, **112–113**, 114–116, 128
Starzyński, Juliusz, 89
Stedelijk Museum, Amsterdam, 43, 46, 105
"American Pop Art," 114, 128
"Bewogen Beweging" (Art in Motion), 107–111
"Dynamisch Labyrint" (Dylaby), 39, 139
Steichen, Edward, 111
Steinberg, Leo, 25, 75, 96
and Rauschenberg, 25, 75, 96, 116–117, 124
Stella, Frank
Claroquesi, 144
and 1964 Venice Biennale, 63, 69, 89
Stern, Marietta, 92
Stevenson, Adlai, 80–81
Stockholm, Sweden, 7–10. *See also* Moderna Museet
art world of, relationship with New York, 139–140, 144–150
and conflict over Vietnam, 140, 144, 146
Merce Cunningham Dance Company in, 7, 103, 105, 129, 139
Monogram, reception in, 107, 115–116, 146, 150–151
Rauschenberg in, 7, 103, 105, 109, 129, 139
Rauschenberg's reputation in, 10, 98, 114–115, 129
reception of American art, 98, 107, 111–116, 139, 205
Stockholm Festival, 142
Stolpe, Pär
"Debate on New York Collection," 144–146, **147**
Strasbourg, France
Merce Cunningham Dance Company in, 7, 17
Surrealism, 29, 35
Suzuki, D. T., 169

Takamatsu, Jirō, 163, 166
Takashina, Shūji, 99, 184
Takiguchi, Shūzō, 162, 244n85
Tapié, Michel, 23, 34
and Art Informel, 27, 160–162, 223n31
and Japan, 160–162
Tàpies, Antoni, 223n31
Tate Gallery, London
and "Arte d'oggi nei musei," 94
exhibition with American Pop artists, 128
technology and art, 141, 142–146
Teshigahara, Hiroshi, 163
Teshigahara, Sōfū, 160, 162, 163, 181, 188, 203
Théâtre de l'Ambassade des États-Unis, Paris
"Hommage à David Tudor" (Johns, Rauschenberg, Saint-Phalle, Tinguely), 35, **36**
Tinguely, Jean, 34, 35, 37, 38, 94, 107, 109, 162, 226n93, 228n124
and "Art in Motion," 109
"The Construction of Boston" (with Saint-Phalle, Rauschenberg), 35
and "Dylaby II," 139
"Dynamisch Labyrint" (Dylaby) (with Rauschenberg, Raysse, Saint-Phalle, Spoerri, Ultvedt), 39, 139
exhibitions of, 35, 162, 163, 226n93

Homage to New York, 35
"Hommage à David Tudor" (with Johns, Rauschenberg, Saint-Phalle), 35, **36**
Hon (She) (with Saint-Phalle, Ultvedt), 139, 141
and Japan, 157, 162, 163–166
Méta-Matics, 34, 109, 166
and Rauschenberg, 35, 39, 109, 139
Tobey, Mark, 23
Tokyo, Japan, 7–10, 168, 205. *See also* Japanese art scene
Art Informel in, 24, 99, 160–162
Merce Cunningham Dance Company in, 7, 10, 153–155
Olympic Games, 168, 193, 242n33
Rauschenberg in, 99, 155, **156**, 157, 166–174, 203
Tomkins, Calvin, 14, 29, 40, 58, 89, 115
and 1964 Venice Biennale, 58, 63–70, 93, 95
Tōno, Yoshiaki, 10, 27, **154**, 155, 162, 202
and Johns, 27, 157, 166, 203
"Madness and Scandal: Fantastic New Faces of the World," 157, 162
and Rauschenberg, 155, 157, 169, 173, 180, 209
on Rauschenberg, 155, 162, 163, 175
"Robert Rauschenberg, or the New York Inferno," 163, 175
and "Twenty Questions to Bob Rauschenberg," 155, 181–185, 188
Tremaine, Burton, 25
Tremaine, Emily, 25
"Triumphs and Tribulations," *Sports Illustrated*, 1, **4**, 81
Tsubaki Kindai Gallery, Tokyo, 166
"Left Hook," 196, **198**, 200
"Off Museum," 166
Tsubouchi, Kazutada, 244n78
Tudor, David, 35, 129, 132, 235n23
"Hommage à David Tudor" (Johns, Rauschenberg, Saint-Phalle, Tinguely), 35, **36**
in Japan, 163, 168
"Twenty Questions to Bob Rauschenberg," 10, 99, 155, 166, 168, 181–185, 188–196, 201, 209
Rauschenberg creating *Gold Standard* during, 155, **182–183**, **190–191**
Shinohara asking Rauschenberg questions onstage, 155, **186**
Twombly, Cy, 94, 223n36, 230n44

Ultvedt, Per Olof, 35, 38, 132, 139, 140, 146
and "Art in Motion," 109
and "Dylaby II," 139
"Dynamisch Labyrint" (Dylaby) (with Rauschenberg, Raysse, Saint-Phalle, Spoerri, Tinguely), 39, 139
Hon (She) (with Saint-Phalle, Tinguely), 139, 141
and "The New York Collection," 144–146, **147**
Rotoreliefs (Duchamp), replicas of (with Linde), 109
United States Information Agency (USIA), 11, 21, 23, 92
Dante Drawings exhibition, 206
and 1964 Venice Biennale, 62–63, 71, 75, 92, 94, 96, 97

Valsecchi, Marco, 89
Vaughan, David, 89, 139
Venice, Italy, 7–10, 205
art community of, 93
Merce Cunningham Dance Company in, 7, 57–58, 89–92
Rauschenberg in, 57–58, 89, 93
Venice Biennale (1958), 27, 162
Venice Biennale (1962), 39
Venice Biennale (1964), 54–55, 57, 93
American Pavilion, 25, 58, 62–71, 88–89
annex of, American Consulate, 63, 71, 88
commissioner's statement, 51–54, 71, 98, 111
installation in, 63–70, **67**, 89, **91**
"The Pop artist's artworks being transported in the Laguna," 89, **90**
Solomon as commissioner of, 7, 10, 25, 47, 59,62–71

United States Air Force unloading art from plane for, 63, **64–65**
International Grand Prize in Painting, 57, 71, 89, 93, 230n56
American response to, 94–97, 101, 205, 208
awarded to Rauschenberg, 7, 10, 12, 14, 46, 51, 58, 88–95, 129, 155, 205, 206
awards ceremony, 58, **60**, 63
controversy over, 10, 19, 51–55, 94–101, 208
international response to, 97–99, 101
Solomon and, 10, 51, 59, 63, 71, 88–94, 95, 96, 101
Italian Pavilion, 94
Venice Biennale (1970), 146
Venice Biennale (2005)
Museum of American Art, *Alan R. Solomon Gallery: "USA 64,"* installation, 69, **70**
Villeglé, Jacques, 34
Villon, Jacques, 93
Virginia Dwan Gallery, Los Angeles, 226n93
Rauschenberg exhibition, 40

Warhol, Andy, 38, 40, 43, 128, 129, 140, 146
Black and White Marilyns, **42**
Brillo Box, 129
exhibition, Galerie Ileana Sonnabend, 43
exhibition, Moderna Museet, Stockholm, 114
Marilyn in Black and White, 129
Washington Gallery of Modern Art, Washington
"Popular Image Exhibition," 132
Weil, Susan, 196, 221n5
Wesselmann, Tom, 128, 129
Whitechapel Gallery, London
Rauschenberg retrospective, 103, 128, 206
Wilde, Edy de, 43, 105

Yoshihara, Jirō, 160–162

Zao, Wou-ki, 223n31